P9-BAW-861

Principles and Practices of

Principles and Practices of

TEACHING READING

ARTHUR W. HEILMAN
Pennsylvania State University

CHARLES E. MERRILL BOOKS, INC.
Columbus, Ohio

Library of Congress Catalog Number: 61-7948

First printing .... February, 1961
Second printing .... July, 1961
Third printing .... May, 1962
Fourth printing .... November, 1962
Fifth printing .... June, 1963
Sixth printing .... January, 1964

PRINTED IN THE UNITED STATES OF AMERICA

PREFACE

This book is addressed to the teachers who are or will be trusted with the responsibility of teaching children to read. It is designed to assist the teacher in developing:

1. An understanding of child growth and behavior and the ability to relate this knowledge to the developmental process called reading.
2. An understanding of how children learn and an understanding of the factors which interfere with learning the complicated symbolic process of reading.
3. A wide array of techniques for teaching specific, immediate short-term goals in reading.
4. A set of principles to follow in teaching which will serve as a test for any method or technique employed.

The major objective of this book is to present a balanced combination of theory and suggested practices. Several portions of the book break new ground or at least extend discussion of particular problems beyond what is usually found in a book on teaching reading. For example:

1. The first chapter presents principles which, it is advocated, should be followed in all teaching of reading. The point is stressed that violating sound principles of teaching leads to the production of reading problems, pupil problems, and teaching problems.
2. Emphasis is placed on the necessity of understanding the learner as a prerequisite for teaching him the complicated process called reading. Chapter 3 is devoted to children as beginning readers and Chapter 10 deals with the relationship between emotional problems and reading problems.

3. A chapter on sex differences in learning to read invites educators to see this as an educational problem and not just as a statistic.

4. The problem of teaching children who have experienced failure in learning to read is dealt with at some length. Although labeled *remedial reading*, the discussion in this book applies to any classroom in which such children are found. Concrete illustrations of procedures for dealing with specific reading problems are included.

The importance of a good start in beginning reading is stressed, but it is also emphasized that reading is a developmental process and that barriers to progress are found at all levels of instruction.

ARTHUR W. HEILMAN

ACKNOWLEDGMENTS

For their help in providing photographic subjects for most of the illustrations used in this book, acknowledgment is made to the students and administration of Bexley Schools, Bexley, Ohio. Gratefully acknowledged is the co-operation of Dr. E. D. Jarvis, Superintendent, Susan Scatterday, Floyd Stolzenburg, and Z. W. Wulber, principals, and Janet Buessem, Peggy Johnson, Thelma Kellar, Dorothy McCoy, Janice Minton, Sara Neidig, Harriet Offenberg, Shirley Priest, Martha Randall, Arlene Robinson, Becky Tschetter, and Lucille Zimpfer, all teachers in the Bexley Schools.

The following schools have been very helpful in supplying some of the photographs used in this book: Eastern Illinois University, University of Florida, the Saint Paul Public Schools, and the San Diego City Schools.

The writer is indebted to a great number of persons who, through their research, writing, or discussion, have contributed much to this book. Special thanks are due to Ruth Elder, Myron Lieberman, Omer Rupiper, Nelson Peach, Ken Macrorie, and Dorothy Heilman for reading portions of the manuscript and making valuable suggestions. The author is especially grateful to Dr. James B. Stroud who has given of his sage guidance both as teacher and as friend.

The author also wishes to acknowledge the contribution of Tom Abrams, Niels Buessem, and Bob Craven for their valuable help in the editing and illustrating of this book. Finally, the writer wishes to thank the many students and teachers whose insights and knowledge are inevitably reflected in the book.

ARTHUR W. HEILMAN

CONTENTS

OK

chapter 7 PHONICS INSTRUCTION 210

chapter 8 THE INTERMEDIATE GRADES 248

chapter 12 REMEDIAL READING (cont.)

chapter 13 WORKING WITH REMEDIAL READERS 394

chapter 14 IMPROVING TEACHING 428

chapter 1

PRINCIPLES OF TEACHING READING

When teachers read books, attend workshops, or enroll in courses in order to improve their teaching of reading, they are apt to become impatient with materials on "the theory of reading." They want instead concrete techniques to help Johnny, who is having difficulty in learning to read. Johnny is ten years old, is in the fifth grade, and has adequate intelligence, but he reads at first grade level. Lately he has become a behavior problem. The teacher wants to know: "What can I do with Johnny? I've tried everything. What would you do?" Johnny comes in all sizes, ages, grade levels, and degrees of impairment.

Frequently the college teacher who works with teachers of reading is frustrated with the repetition of "What would you do with Johnny?" If he evades the question, he invites the suspicion of gross ignorance. On the other hand, attempting to give an answer to the question in the context in which it is asked does not come to grips with the real problem of improving the teaching of reading. The instructor in teacher-training courses wants to go back step by step along the trail of reading failure, searching for all clues to the cause of Johnny's present difficulties. The classroom teacher pleads: "What do I do now?"

This difference in approach is the outgrowth of three factors. First, the classroom teacher's role is defined by society and the educational institution in which she functions. Her task is to teach all children assigned to her classroom. If the number of children is large, she has less time to concern herself with institutional practices which produce maladjusted learners. Furthermore, she is likely to regard the analysis of these institutional practices as beyond the scope of her authority. As the number of reading casualties mounts, she often turns to "newer practices" in the vain search for a solution.

Second, the university professor enjoys the luxury of being able to remain aloof from the immediate problems of the individual classroom. Although not unsympathetic with Johnny's problem or the teacher's problem, he knows that the "Johnnies" are legion and their number is growing. Hence he prefers that the teacher phrase her question in such a way as to lead to a long-range solution for the whole problem. As he tries to come to grips with the larger problem, he inevitably deals with theory, or "principles."

Third, most teachers feel that there is a vast body of "newer" practices available on college campuses, in the latest books on reading, or just across the border in the next state. These teachers might be happily surprised to learn that what they have known for years about teaching reading is substantially the same as the practices recommended in the more recent books on techniques of reading. The truth is that improvements in teaching the mechanics of reading evolve slowly. One premise of this book is that reading problems in American schools are due less to the teachers' lack of knowledge than to their disinclination or inability to follow the sound principles of teaching which they already know.

As the term is used here, "principles" of teaching reading are those basic rules which constitute the theoretical framework out of which all practices are evolved. The principles do not spell out the best procedures or practices for particular situations. However, when one accepts a set of principles, he will be inconsistent if he uses practices which violate the principles.

Principles are necessarily stated in broad and general terms, but if we are to understand their meaning they should never be vague or nebulous. The principles of teaching reading evolve from the best knowledge available in the fields of psychology, educational psychology, and curriculum planning, from studies in child growth and development, and from child-guidance and psychological clinics. In formulating these principles, it is necessary to consider all facets of human growth and development, including the intellectual, physiological, and emotional.

Most teachers are familiar with the principles discussed in the following pages. Like scientific laws, the principles of teaching reading are subject to modification or repeal as new data are discovered and new theories erected on the basis of this data. Some readers will undoubtedly feel that one (or more) of the following principles is not absolutely valid. Such questioning is healthy, especially if it stimulates the formulation of rational alternatives. If the following principles are a sound basis for teaching reading at all levels of instruction, there are many practices in our schools which need to be re-examined.

PRINCIPLES

1. *Learning to read is a complicated process and is sensitive to a variety of pressures. Too much pressure or the wrong kind of pressure may result in non-learning.*

A fact that attests to the complexity of the reading process is that authorities have never agreed on *a* definition of reading. There are, however, many statements about the complexity of reading on which experts would agree. One such statement is that reading involves more than the mechanical process of correctly pronouncing words, that it involves the recognition of meaning. On the other hand, reading cannot be defined as getting the only correct meaning from written symbols. This definition cannot be reconciled with the variety of interpretations that good readers have given to the Constitution of the United States, laws on negligence, the Bible, or passages from Shakespeare. It is evident that such readers have brought something of themselves to the reading materials. Although reading cannot be defined as "what the reader brings to the reading situation," it is apparent that there must be interaction between the reader and the printed symbols. At the moment, "reading is thinking" has become a popular phrase, but the reading and thinking are not always synonymous. To modify this phrase to "critical reading is thinking while reading" will help to satisfy some readers and to frustrate others. Reading is not the simple sum of its parts because in every case the reader must be considered in the process and each reader is unique. Reading always involves the simultaneous application of a great number of mechanical skills and comprehension skills, all of which are influenced by the reader's attitudes, knowledge, and past experience. Reading is a complicated process.

Reading is a language function. It is the manipulation of symbolic materials. Psychologists and other observers of human behavior tell us that the symbolic process is sensitive to pressures of any kind. It is axiomatic that language is the most sensitive indicator of personal or emotional maladjustment. Yet in no area of learning in our schools is greater pressure brought to bear on the pupil than in the area of reading. This is partly due to the high value which our society places on education and to the recognition that education is based on reading skill.

Often the school and the home present a united front in exerting overt and subtle pressures on the child. Reading is the first school task in which the child is deliberately or inadvertently compared with others in his peer group. It is the first task in which he must compete. How he fares in this competition has a tremendous impact on his ego, his concept of himself, and the attitudes of his peers toward him. But, most important, this is the first school activity in which his performance has a direct impact on his parents' egos. Parents may sense that their anxiety is not an intelligent or mature response. Insofar as the average parents can be coldly analytical of their motivation and involvement in their child's non-success in reading, they know their feelings are never far below the surface. These feelings of disappointment are perceived by the child as a judgment that he does not measure up to parents' expectations.

Teachers are familiar with the sources of many of the pressures which converge on the child in a reading situation and which often become acute when a child experiences failure. Table 1 outlines some of these pressures along with possible psychological consequences.

A detailed discussion of the relationship between emotional problems and reading is found in Chapter 11. The examples cited here are intended to be illustrative rather than exhaustive.

TABLE 1

SOURCES OF PRESSURES ON CHILDREN EXPERIENCING DIFFICULTY IN READING

Pressure from home and parents	Parents are ego-involved in their child's success. They set "high goals" for him. They cannot hide their disappointment in their child's non-success.
Pressure from the child himself (stems from ego-needs and concept of self)	The child senses that he is not living up to parents' expectations. He feels that he is a failure. He has guilt feelings, since he has let his parents down. He may develop a conscious or unconscious feeling that his parents have withdrawn affection. This becomes a further threat to the child's ego and security.
Pressure from school	Children's attitudes result from the competitive atmosphere fostered by adults (parents, school, teacher) and from the conformity pattern imposed by society. The child has a need to conform or measure up to norms set by the school or teacher and fears non-promotion. Non-readers are a threat to the teacher because they frustrate her ego need for success. Fortunately this is not true of all teachers.
Pressure from basal reading materials	Many basal reader series may pose a threat to some children since the home life of Dick, Jane, Sally, Billy, and Baby, etc., may not be at all like the environment of the child with home problems. Some children find it impossible to identify with these characters. Since they are rejected, they may unconsciously reject that which infringes on the "traumatic area." This idea is hypothetical. At present there are little experimental data to support it.

2. *Learning to read is an individual process.*

Although group activities associated with reading enhance the learning process and even though it is true that learning is partly a social process, each child in a group who learns how to read learns as an individual. The complicated stimuli confronting the child are mastered by an individual nervous system. Dividing a class into three or more smaller groups on the basis of reading ability may be a wise procedure, but this in itself will not teach the children how to read. Even though all children in the lowest group have the common characteristic that they are poor readers, grouping them physically in the classroom and psychologically in the teacher's mind is of negligible value unless the teacher adjusts learning situations to each child's need for instruction.

3. *Proper reading instruction depends on the diagnosis of each child's weaknesses and needs.*

This principle is applicable to ordinary classroom teaching as well as to remedial reading. Individual diagnosis in reading has somehow become associated more with "retarded" readers and pupils with a clinical history of non-learning than with ordinary classroom procedure. Diagnosis has become associated too often with cure or remedy rather than with preventing the development of poor reading. In many cases, proper diagnosis will warn a teacher before bad habits or unhealthy emotional reactions cripple a potentially capable reader.

A survey test used as the basis for grouping children into poorest, average, and best categories is not in itself a diagnosis. To know that children A, B, and C are among the poorest in the class and that they are reading at least a year below their grade level tells us nothing about what it is that inhibits their reading progress. Nor does such a test tell us what aspect of reading should be attacked first in order to improve the child's reading. To establish the fact that a child is reading below what might be expected is not diagnosis. It is an invitation to diagnosis.

4. *The best diagnosis is useless unless it is used as a blueprint for instruction.*

Diagnosis itself has no salutary effect on the performance of the child tested. If diagnosis alone had salutary effects, it would be possible to raise a child's level of performance indefinitely by more and more diagnosis. In this connection it may be noted that extensive testing and metal filing cabinets full of individual folders do not necessarily make a better school. Testing in many American schools has become an end in itself. When test results are not used for instructional purposes, the educational objectives of the testing program are defeated.

There is no area of the curriculum in American schools more ideally suited to constant diagnosis than reading in the elementary and intermediate grades. The good teacher knows this and proceeds with continuous diagnosis of the children in her room. She knows that numerous factors inhibit progress in reading during this period. Any skill not mastered or only partially mastered may be instrumental in producing other reading problems. A teacher's manual or curriculum guide can point out a logical sequence for introducing skills and tasks, but it offers no help in determining what in the sequence has been learned. The manual or guide is like an artist's conception of the total edifice before it is constructed. Intelligent instruction must be based on accurate information regarding children's present accomplishments and weaknesses. In this sense, a thorough diagnosis is a blueprint for instruction.

5. *No child should be expected or forced to read material which at the moment he is incapable of reading.*

Although applied here specifically to reading, this principle has a much wider application in our schools. All curriculum study and the placing of learning tasks at different points on the educational continuum are related to this principle. The principle should be followed in all areas of child growth and development—physical, social, emotional, intellectual. The principle amounts to a rejection of the myth that "the child is a miniature adult." We know that he is not. Today, informed teachers and parents expect the average child of six years to have developed social and emotional responses only to a level of maturity commensurate with his experience.

This principle is also related to the fact that different children develop at different rates and that the growth pattern of an individual child is not uniform. The data from which we derive norms or averages of physical, emotional, social, and intellectual growth warn us that there are differences in rates of development. The principle does not imply that children should avoid difficult tasks or that a child should be able to read a passage perfectly before he attempts to read it. It does imply that we cannot expect a child to perform up to a given standard when at the moment he is incapable of such performance. To do this is to expect the impossible.

The following episode, although it illustrates the point under discussion, is not advanced as being representative of teacher practice. Arrangements were made in an elementary school for thorough testing of a number of pupils who were not making expected academic progress. One fourth grade boy could read successfully no higher than primer level. The counselor inquired of the boy's teacher what reading program the boy was following. The teacher explained that for a while she had the boy attempt to read third grade materials. Failing in these, he was given second grade materials with no better success. Since the boy read these materials no better than he read the fourth grade texts, the teacher concluded that he might as well read the fourth grade books. Teachers who would not endorse this solution may occasionally expect a child to do what he cannot do at the moment. Untold numbers of pupils face such a situation, and probably more instances occur because of lack of reading ability than for all other reasons combined.

A given child may have average or superior ability but may be below grade norm today in his reading. With proper guidance, he may later master the reading process commensurate with his over-all ability. Each child is entitled to the best guidance available. It is not conducive to social, emotional, or educational growth to subject a child to failure experiences because he is physically present in a classroom where arbitrary achievement goals have been set.

6. *Reading is a process of getting meaning from printed word symbols. It is not merely a process of making conventionalized noises associated with these symbols.*

This principle means that reading is more than a mechanical process, even though mechanics are an essential part of the process. Mechanical word-calling is not reading any more than a parakeet making the noises "pretty-bird-sing-sing" can properly be said to be using language. Because of the limitations of children just beginning to read and the necessity for repetition of a relatively small number of words in beginning instruction, one might easily confuse beginning reading with the mechanics of reading.

The principle stated above has been phrased with a view to avoiding certain semantic quicksands. By not using the phrase "reading is the process of getting *the* meaning," an attempt has been made to avoid the implication that there is one and only one meaning which every reader gets from reading the same passage. This could not be achieved if it were a goal of teaching reading. McKee avoids the implication of *the* meaning or one meaning when he refers to reading as the process of "making meaning."[1]

7. *Any given technique, practice, or procedure is likely to work better with some children than with others. Hence, the teacher of reading must have a variety of approaches.*

Virtually every method and procedure described in the vast literature on reading is reported to have been successful with some children and unsuccessful with others. Creativity and versatility are basic requirements for successful teaching. If a teacher begins to take sides in methodological squabbles or if she begins to crystalize her ideas on an either/or basis, she is likely to be less receptive to other points of view and approaches which may be helpful to her in teaching some of the children in her class.

Authorities in the field of reading are in general agreement that "There is no one best method of teaching." The evidence indicates that one method is not necessarily superior to another. Regardless of the efficiency of a given method of teaching reading, it will produce its share of problem cases and impaired readers if used exclusively. If there are significant individual differences in the way children learn to read, it follows that different approaches are advisable. Unfortunately, children do not have identifiable characteristics which make it possible to know at a glance which approach will yield the highest return in learning. It is for this reason that flexibility, ingenuity, and creativity are essential to successful teaching, and particularly for teaching reading.

When a teacher becomes enamored of one method to the exclusion of others, she shuts out the possibility of adjusting method to individual pupil needs. Although such a teacher may be highly successful in teaching some of her pupils, she will inevitably produce a number

[1] Paul McKee, *The Teaching of Reading* (Boston: Houghton Mifflin Co., 1948), 194.

of frustrated, unhappy misfits in the educational arena. If she is authoritarian and presses hard, some of her pupils will develop behaviors which result in such labels as "bad," "dull," "dreamers," "lazy," and "anti-social." These behaviors, instead of being interpreted as the logical psychological outcome of failure, frustration, and tension evolving from the reading situation, become in turn the explanations of why the child failed in reading.

8. *The concept of readiness should be extended upward to all grades.*

Few teachers maintain that readiness applies more to one level of education than to another. Nevertheless, in the area of reading, there seems to be a predilection for associating readiness with beginning reading or first grade reading. This is the level at which we have "readiness tests," and much of the literature on readiness is concerned with the beginning reader. Even though readiness has been achieved at one level of experience, it does not necessarily follow that readiness is retained at a higher level of experience. There should be as much concern with readiness at the third, fourth, or sixth grade levels as there is at the first grade level.

A good start is an important factor in the learning process. But a good start is not always half the race, because reading is a developmental process. What is learned today is the foundation for what is learned tomorrow. A smooth, unfaltering first step is not a guarantee that succeeding steps will be equally smooth. For example, some children display no complications in the learning process until they are asked to sound out a number of words not known at sight. At this point they encounter difficulties, the degree of which could not have been predicted on the basis of readiness tests administered in the first grade. Even so, some of these failures stem from non-readiness for the experience.

9. *Early in the learning process the child must acquire ways of gaining independence in identifying words whose meanings are known to him but which are unknown to him as sight words.*

Pronouncing words is not reading, but sounding out words not known as sight words is essential in independent reading. The more widely a child reads the less likely it is that he will know every word he meets as a sight word. Hence, developing independence in reading depends on acquiring methods of unlocking the pronunciation of words. The clues used in identifying words are discussed in later chapters. These clues are unique configuration of words, structural analysis (prefixes, suffixes), context clues, and phonic analysis. The phonetic method is probably the most important of the word analysis skills.[2] In accordance with principle seven, no particular phonics method is specified in later chapters nor is any rejected.

This principle is not in conflict with number six above, which states that reading is getting meaning.

10. *Children should not be in the classroom if they have emotional problems sufficiently serious to make them uneducable at the moment or if they interfere with or disrupt the learning process.*

Physical disturbances such as a slight temperature, an inflamed throat, an abscessed tooth, or a skin blemish are cause for removing a child from the classroom. Many schools require that children not come to school until inoculated against certain diseases; other schools strongly urge these precautions. These measures seem natural and logical today. The suggestion that children with serious emotional problems get their maladies corrected as a condition for attending school will probably be scoffed at—today. Tomorrow the concept of emotional health will be as readily accepted as the concept of physical health. Just as the practice of beating the devil out of the obsessed came to an end, so we will stop trying to beat learning into a child who is at the moment uneducable.

The reason for emphasizing emotional health in a book on reading is that our entire educational structure is based on the ability to read. One of the principles stated earlier was that a child should not be expected to do something he cannot do. When a child is uneducable because of serious emotional involvements and we persist in drilling him on sight words when he cannot learn at the moment, we are violating this earlier principle. Unless the classroom teacher can overcome the barrier to learning, the uneducable child should be removed for treatment and returned when he is educable. The vast majority of youngsters with emotional problems can be salvaged with personal and environmental therapy. If the emotional problem is not severe, it is possible for some children to continue in school while receiving outside treatment; in some cases the treatment can

---

[2] See Chapter 7.

take place in the classroom, concurrently with the regular learning situation. In the latter type of case, the teacher is a key factor.

11. *Emphasis should be on prevention rather than cure. Reading problems should be detected early and corrected before they deteriorate into failure-frustration-reaction cases.*

However excellent the instruction in our schools, some children will not profit as much as others. The early detection of impairments and immediate attention to them are cornerstones of effective reading instruction. Although this is obvious, the emphasis in our schools is still on cure, not on prevention. The following discussion of school practices explains in part how this came about.

SCHOOL PRACTICES WHICH INTERFERE WITH TEACHERS' FOLLOWING SOUND PRINCIPLES

It is logical that a book on teaching reading should open with a statement of the principles upon which good teaching is based. For principles should evolve ahead of practices so that teacher and school practices can be evaluated in light of these principles. The view accepted here is that the principles formulated above are sound and that teachers who find them so should follow them in teaching reading. Some of the techniques used by teachers in their daily practice of the art of teaching may inadvertently or unconsciously inhibit teachers from the application of principles which they have accepted as sound and desirable.

With a particular principle in mind, a teacher may use practices which violate another principle because she fails to recognize that both impinge on the case at hand. According to one principle, proper instruction depends on individual diagnosis of each child's weaknesses and needs. According to another, diagnosis is useless unless used as a blueprint for instruction. It has been pointed out that the act of administering a diagnostic instrument has no salutary effect on poor readers. A series of standardized tests which discloses a number of weaknesses in the mechanics of reading may lead to instruction aimed at specific weaknesses and still be ineffective because some other principle has been overlooked.

For example, assume an impaired reader is given a series of standardized reading tests and an intelligence test. Frank W., age

9 years, 6 months; I.Q. 112; reading level 2-0. Specific weaknesses include inadequate sight vocabulary, inability to sound unknown words, mispronouncing small service words, omitting words, and substitutions. The boy appears cooperative, but his attention span is short. He states that he wishes to learn to read. With these data in hand the teacher may feel that the logical procedure is to launch into work aimed at mastering sight words and phonic analysis. A factor not taken into consideration was Frank's attitude toward reading and his attitude toward his ability to learn to read. These were such that, even though Frank seemed passive, cooperative, and compliant, he was so emotionally upset by being confronted with reading tasks that no amount of individual help that embraced help only in reading would have the desired results. The lack of overt behavior symptoms may have been a factor in the teacher's failure to perceive Frank's serious emotional involvement in relation to reading. At the moment he was incapable of harnessing energy for the task of learning to read. What the teacher interpreted as individual help was to Frank undue pressure. Reading materials threatened him, as did his teacher's knowledge of his weaknesses. He adjusted better while lost in the class than he did to individual work in reading. Thus principles three and four above, though sound in themselves, were not an adequate basis for procedure until other principles were made a part of the total picture.

As a matter of habit a teacher may follow sound principles even though she does not verbalize them. She grades carefully all lessons in the reading workbook and works individually with children as they correct errors. She explains and re-explains the basic idea of the lesson. She works with different children on different aspects of the reading process. When asked what she is doing, she may reply: "I am providing drill for the children who need it. John needs drill on hearing the long sound of vowels. Mike is confused by figurative language. He always tries to get a concrete meaning from these sentences. 'The man pulled the horses to the side of the road.' Mike said that the man got down from the seat and dragged the horses off the road. He was confused also by 'the bird ate on the wing.' I have had some materials dittoed that are not found in the workbook he is using. He is working on these now. On the other hand, Mary breezes through the pages of examples on figurative language, so I had her write five other examples. She came up with some pretty high-level examples. She certainly doesn't need any more drill on this phase of reading."

While this activity might be construed as drill, it happens that it follows logically from some of the principles of reading we have just reviewed, namely:

1. Proper instruction is dependent on individual diagnosis.
2. Diagnosis is useless unless used as a blueprint for instruction.
3. Reading is a process of getting meaning.
4. Any given practice is likely to work better with some children than with others. (Mike could not have done what Mary did because he missed the point of the exercise. Therefore, to ask him to write new illustrations of figurative language would have violated other principles we have discussed.)

SCHOOL PRACTICES AFFECTING INSTRUCTION

Most defections from sound principles of teaching reading probably stem from undesirable classroom conditions. For the most part, these conditions are institutionalized practices that have become part of American education. The practices have often evolved from economic pressures or community pressures, sometimes advocated as emergency measures. It is doubtful if any of these practices have been accepted because someone thought that they would enhance the quality of American education.

Schools do not deliberately produce non-readers or impaired readers, but educators often sacrifice sound principles and practices in the face of pressure. Emergencies produce compromises which tend to become permanent. These compromises often become standard procedure to such an extent that after a while they are defended on the basis that "we've been doing this for years." Some of the more obvious school practices which prevent teachers from doing as well as they know how are listed below.

Class Size. Classes containing thirty-five to forty students are, unfortunately, numerous.[3] Teachers of reading in these classrooms

---

[3] Some data relative to class size are misleading. Some school systems may report class size or pupil-teacher ratio as somewhat smaller than is actually the case. This can occur when supervising personnel, school counselors, nurses, psychologists, speech therapists, etc., are included as instructional staff. Class size, as used in this discussion, refers to the actual mean number of children present in one teacher's classroom during the school year.

complain that they cannot do the job. They mean that they cannot find time for thorough, ongoing diagnosis and individual programs for the children who need individual help. If this is true, large classes prevent teachers from following some of the principles we have discussed.

When conditions force one sound principle to be ignored, it is likely that other principles will also be violated. Some children will be expected to read materials which are too difficult. When a teacher lacks an accurate picture of a child's ability and specific reading weaknesses, she will have a tendency to expect him to read at grade level. When this happens, another danger is that pressures both overt and subtle will be brought to bear on the child experiencing failure. These pressures are not conducive to reading facility, at least not for all children.

Too often teachers are not aware that they work under conditions which prevent them from applying sound reading principles. But if teaching is a profession, the violation of sound principles of teaching is unprofessional. There is a tendency to absolve teachers of responsibility for teaching practices resulting from over-crowded classrooms with the statement that the community desires large classes or that teachers have no recourse since class size is an administrative decision. Teachers who feel responsible for making professional decisions will perceive that these arguments are rationalizations.[4]

Promotion Versus Concept of Mastery of Skills. The problems arising from large classes are compounded by the widespread school practice of universal or almost universal promotion. We are not concerned here with the merits of promotion versus retention, but rather to point up the inevitable results of our present-day practices.

Our schools are set up on a grade-level basis on which the curricula of the various grades are progressively more difficult. Everyone agrees that the learning tasks in the second grade are more difficult than those in the first. This is inherent in the grade-level system. This arrangement is obviously logical, but the logic implies that children in the second grade have mastered the skills taught in the first grade, because the second grade curriculum is based on the assumption of mastery of first grade skills. In similar manner, the third grade curriculum is based on skills presumably mastered in the second grade.

---

[4] See Myron Lieberman, *Education as a Profession* (Englewood Cliffs, N. J.: Prentice-Hall, Inc., 1956).

As school systems adopted the practice of social promotion one might expect that the grade-level concept would be abandoned or drastically revised. In the majority of our schools neither of these things happened. The result is that today we find children moving from grade to grade mainly because they have been physically present in a particular grade for an academic year. True, many children master the skills required for the next year's curriculum, but many do not. And when many do not, the grade-level concept is unsound because it was not designed to function under these conditions. The higher the grade level under consideration, the more apparent becomes the inadequacy of our efforts to impose automatic promotion on a graded system. When we attempt to justify automatic promotion on the grounds that it is psychologically sound because promotion prevents failure, we are being unrealistic in our concept of failure. Children who progress through the grades without adequate skills to deal with the tasks expected of them experience failure every day they attend school.

The foregoing is not intended to imply that non-promotion is desirable. Such data as we have on retaining students in the same grade for another year indicate that this is also an ineffective practice. A truly ungraded primary school will accept various levels of competency. As students master certain skills, they move on to the next level of tasks. The emphasis on promotion abates and each child moves at his own pace.[5]

Non-Teaching Activities in and out of the Classroom. In addition to the increase in class size, there have been many encroachments on the teacher's time and energy which leave less time for teaching. It is disturbing, especially during a time of acknowledged teacher shortages and increased class size, that teachers are compelled to fill out complicated daily attendance forms, collect lunch money, supervise playgrounds before school and during recess periods, supervise the cafeteria, collect tickets at athletic events, sponsor and advise student organizations, attend frequent staff meetings on their own time, and serve as members of school committees and P.T.A. These activities are closely related to children's failure to learn. A tired, harassed teacher can hardly be expected to be an

[5] See Chapter 4 for a discussion of the ungraded primary plan.

effective teacher. A teacher responsible for a host of administrative duties will have less time and energy for creative teaching activities. It is unfortunate when teachers accept these encroachments which reduce teacher effectiveness and contribute to the failure and maladjustment of students.

Teacher morale and effectiveness of instruction would be greatly increased if teachers could have short periods of time, morning and afternoon, when they are completely free of all school activities and pressures—free from children, grading workbooks, preparing records, and filling out forms. Teachers now enjoying such free periods may be surprised to learn that many teachers do not.

Disinclination to Wait for Readiness. Reading readiness is one of the most talked about and most written about aspects of teaching reading. But in the practice of teaching reading, it is surprising that readiness—or more precisely, the lack of readiness—is so often ignored. As noted earlier, reading readiness is a factor in reading at all levels. At the moment, however, let us concern ourselves with beginning reading. According to prevailing theory, reading readiness activities blend almost imperceptibly into formal instruction. In practice, most first grade teachers follow a schedule of a given number of weeks of readiness activities, including tests of readiness, followed by instruction in basal reading materials. Some teachers are quick to point out that all students do not start on the same day with the latter materials. Others point out that, while they start their pupils together, they do not insist that all progress at the same rate. They point out that these practices are followed because of differing degrees of readiness among pupils.

Rarely does the teacher withhold basal reading materials from the least ready for more than a few weeks after the rest of the class has started to use them. As a rule, teachers readily admit that some of their pupils are not ready for formal instruction, but the instruction is begun. Ironically, teachers frequently rationalize these practices on the grounds that "parents insist that their child start reading" or that "the school administration expects it." This is another example of teacher knowledge being far ahead of practice. If teachers are professionally qualified, it is essential that they work toward achieving conditions in which it will not be necessary for them to sacrifice their professional integrity and their pupils' psychological well-being because of pressures from the community.

School Entrance Based on Chronological Age. Another school practice that tends to produce problems in the teaching of reading is the use of chronological age as the criterion for admitting children to school. Educators generally agree that instruction should be based on readiness for attempting the tasks to be performed. Once the school and community accept the chronological-age criterion for entering school, however, it is a simple step for parents and communities to reason: "Johnny is six years old. Therefore, he is ready for school."

Systematic Reading Instruction Not Found in Upper Grades. Reading is taught systematically in the elementary grades. Reading instruction is part of the curriculum. As we go upward in the grades more reading is required, but instruction in reading is not as systematic as in the lower grades. In practice, reading seems to be regarded as a skill to be acquired in the elementary and intermediate grades and used in all areas of the curriculum from that point on. Although most schools and teachers know that many children need thorough, planned, deliberate instruction above the sixth grade, they are also aware that systematic instruction at these levels is lacking.

At the junior high and high school levels we tend to rely more on slogans than planned instruction. "Every teacher is a teacher of reading" is such a slogan. The slogan does not fit the facts because some teachers are not qualified to teach reading. The job calls for specific training, knowledge, and skills, just as it does at lower grade levels. It is wrong to assume that poor readers will outgrow poor reading habits when they reach these grades, and it is wrong to assume that poor readers will read widely and better because they have more reading assigned in these grades. If children entering seventh and eighth grades had mastered the fundamental reading skills required for the reading tasks in these grades, present practices in our schools would be justified. Research data for these upper grades tell a different story. It has been found that in these grades about one in four students functions at a level one grade below actual placement; more than 10 per cent function at a level two grades below, and 5 per cent at three grades below placement.[6]

---

[6] J. B. Stroud, *Psychology in Education* (Rev. ed.; New York: Longmans, Green & Co., Inc., 1956), 375-77.

More and more we hear criticism that students are not proficient readers and that they cannot meet the demands of the curriculum. There is a growing consensus that one of the major ills of our educational system is that the systematic teaching of reading is terminated too early.

These are a few of the school practices which have led observant teachers to the conclusion that we do not live in the best of all educational worlds. In our schools we have the ready and the non-ready; we have increased class size to the point that the teacher finds it impossible to deal adequately with the problems of the individual child; we have adopted the practice of almost universal promotion while clinging to a grade-level concept based on mastery of skills taught in preceding grades. There are few schools which teach reading systematically beyond the sixth grade. If one examines these practices separately, he might conclude that they are exclusively administrative in nature. But when one looks at the effect of the whole group of practices on what happens in the classroom, he cannot escape the conclusion that they have a considerable impact on instruction.

Although this book has been designed as a guide for teaching reading, *how to teach* cannot be divorced from the environment in which teaching must take place. Specific methods for dealing with some of these problems are discussed later, but it is beyond the scope of this book to attempt a prescription for bringing about needed changes in the structure of American education. Certainly the school practices just discussed cannot be modified by individual teachers. Thus, the teacher who is a trained professional in the classroom finds that she has little control over a number of school practices which determine the degree to which she can apply what she knows about teaching reading. These practices, which have prevented or militated against teachers' assuming the role of competent professionals, have also been contributing factors in the production of reading problems as well as teaching problems.

YOUR POINT OF VIEW?

The problems following each chapter are not intended primarily to test recall of material presented. The problems may serve as a basis for class discussion or, in some instances, library research papers.

1. Chronological age is the most practical and most justifiable criterion for having children enter school.

2. Parents' ego-involvement in their child's learning to read is a causal factor in many reading failures and is a major problem for the schools and first grade teachers.

3. *"Individual differences in achievement increase as we move upward through the grades."*

Which one of the following factors would you prefer to defend as being most important in effecting these differences in achievement? Why?

A. Pupil ability
B. School promotion policies
C. Competency of instruction
D. Factors outside the school

4. Assume that the use of standardized reading tests in the elementary grades was prohibited for the next five years. Suggest logical hypotheses as to what would happen in reading instruction if this unlikely event occurred.

5. Assume that you are assigned the task of improving the teaching of reading in your state and that you can eliminate or modify *one* school practice which is now prevalent. What would be your recommendation? Why?

BIBLIOGRAPHY

(Chapter bibliographies contain some references cited in the text and other selected references.)

Dewey, John. "The Primary Education Fetish," *Forum*, XXV (May, 1898), 315-28.

Dodson, Dan W. "Factors Influencing Curriculum Development," *Review of Educational Research*, XXVII (June, 1957), 262-69.

Gray, William S., and Larrick, Nancy (eds.). *Better Readers for Our Times*, International Reading Association Conference Proceedings, I (1956). New York: Scholastic Magazines, Part 4.

Greene, Harry A., and Petty, Walter T. *Developing Language Skills in the Elementary School.* Boston: Allyn and Bacon, Inc., 1959, Chap. 1.

Haskew, Lawrence D. *This Is Teaching*. Chicago: Scott, Foresman & Co., 1956.

King, Edmund J. *Other Schools and Ours.* New York: Holt, Rinehart & Winston, Inc., 1958, Chap. 1 and Chap. 5.

Lieberman, Myron. *Teaching as a Profession.* Englewood Cliffs, N. J.: Prentice-Hall, Inc., 1956.

McKee, Paul. *The Teaching of Reading.* Boston: Houghton Mifflin Co., 1948.

McKim, Margaret G., and Hansen, Carl W., and Carter, William L. *Learning to Teach in the Elementary School.* New York: The Macmillan Co., 1959, Chap. 2.

Oliver, W. A. "Teachers' Educational Beliefs versus Their Classroom Practices," *Journal of Educational Research,* XLVII (September, 1953), 47-55.

Rowland, Thomas D., and Nelson, Calvin C. "Off to School—At What Age?" *Elementary School Journal,* LX (October, 1959).

Slagle, Allen T. "What Is the Tack of Our Schools?" *Elementary School Journal,* LX (December, 1959), 140-45.

Smith, Henry P. *Psychology in Teaching.* Englewood Cliffs, N. J.: Prentice-Hall, Inc., 1954, Chap. 1.

Stroud, J. B. *Psychology in Education* (Rev. ed.). New York: Longmans, Green and Co., 375-77.

Thorndike, Edward L. "Reading as Reasoning: A Study of Mistakes in Paragraph Reading," *Journal of Educational Psychology,* VIII (June, 1917), 323-32.

Traxler, Arthur. "Current Organization and Procedures in Remedial Teaching," *Journal of Experimental Education,* XX (March, 1952), 305-12.

Ward, Douglas S. "Should Teachers Specialize in Teaching?" *Elementary School Journal,* LX (November, 1959), 64-69.

chapter 2

PREPARING FOR READING

THE TASK OF THE SCHOOL

Every generation has questioned its educational system, its school's curriculum, and the school's current methodology in teaching basic subjects. Questions such as education for whom and education for what have apparently never been answered satisfactorily, because these questions continue to be asked again and again. At the present time, debate on the question of what courses of study will sharpen the mind and prepare children for living in tomorrow's world is particularly intense. Past technological advances may have caused each generation to believe that the educational problems facing it were greater than at any other time in the nation's history. Nevertheless, it is doubtful whether we have ever been further away from understanding our environment and our major problems than we are today. This dilemma raises the question of how a people who do not understand the world in which they now live can devise a curriculum that will prepare their children for *tomorrow*—a tomorrow which will undoubtedly make today's science fiction appear workaday and unimaginative.

This "cultural lag" in education has made the job of the school so complicated and involved that frustration is inevitable. Yet there is one element in yesterday's curriculum which is equally germane to today's world and also the best hope for preparing today's children for tomorrow. This is the mastery of communication skills. Without knowing what will be important and worthwhile tomorrow, we know that what will be essential and worthwhile in science, the arts, and the humanities will belong to those who can read. Keeping its eye on the future, the school cannot be content with teaching a number of interesting facts about the remarkable world in which the pupils live. It must teach skills as rapidly as possible so that these pupils can mine the vast mountain of knowledge available to them.

The first step in teaching the developmental process called reading is to provide guidance aimed at getting the learner ready for the various tasks involved in the process.

CONCEPT OF READING READINESS

The differences in the past experiences of first graders is one of the reasons why the reading readiness period is so important. Briefly, the purpose of this period is to lay the foundation upon which later maximum success in reading can be built. The readiness period is not a waiting period but a highly structured, deliberately teacher-planned program. It is not aimed at removing individual differences among pupils, but at seeing that each child has experiences which will remove blocks to learning. It can be thought of as a filling in and smoothing out process. There must be no gaps in the foundation upon which reading skill is to be built.[1]

The readiness period attempts to synthesize new experiences with the previous experiences that children have had. These previous experiences, or the lack of them, are extremely important, since they determine to a large degree the kind and the amount of experience that is still needed and which the school must provide prior to formal

---

[1] Lillian Gray and Dora Reese, *Teaching Children to Read* (2nd ed.; New York: The Ronald Press Co., 1957).

instruction in reading. How accurately the teacher discerns what is still needed and how successful she is in filling these needs may well be the most important factor in determining each child's later success or failure in reading.

Reading readiness has received considerable attention from experimenters and theorists.[2] Investigations have attempted to determine the relationship between a great number of factors and success in reading. It is very difficult to measure such a relationship because no factor is ever found operating in isolation. On the other hand, it is not easy to rule out a given factor completely as having no relationship to reading, except on an *a priori* basis. Thus, the term reading readiness is often thought of as being much more concrete than is actually the case.

Everyone who has taught beginning reading knows that there is validity to the readiness concept. This belief is often strengthened by the widespread use of reading readiness tests. When we use such tests we automatically subscribe to the theory that "we know what we are measuring since we have tests that measure it." Readiness tests, like all tests, have both value and limitation.

READING READINESS TESTS

These tests are standardized instruments designed to assess the child's ability to profit from formal instruction in reading. They fulfill their purpose insofar as they predict success in learning to read. That is, the score made on the test itself must be indicative of what can be expected in achievement in reading during the first year or two of formal reading instruction.

The term *readiness* applies to all facets of development as well as to subject-matter achievement at all grade levels. Nevertheless, the term *reading readiness test* applied for many years exclusively to the first grade, and to a large extent still refers to instruments devised to measure skills related to success in *beginning* reading. The discus-

---

[2] A study of W. S. Gray's "Summaries of Research in Reading," found annually in the *Journal of Educational Research,* would disclose no abatement of interest in various facets of readiness during the past twenty-five years.

sion here is concerned with the general topic of reading readiness tests and not with an attempt to compare the values of different tests.[3]

Readiness tests are, as a rule, administered as group tests. Some tests are primarily group tests but may contain one or more subtests which must be given individually. Examples of such subtests include appraisal of the child's ability to recognize letters of the alphabet or tell whether words rhyme. In general, readiness tests contain items which attempt to measure physiological maturity, information, comprehension of spoken language, ability to perceive similarities and differences, ability to follow directions, and ability to draw simple figures. Representative test items include:

1. *Associating pictured objects with the spoken word for that object.* The child has before him a series of four or five pictures in a line running across the page. The pictures might be of a frog, a boat, a shoe, and a turkey. He is asked to "underline (or circle) the shoe."
2. *Visual discrimination.* Four or five similar objects are shown. One is already circled or checked. One other picture in the row is exactly like this one. The child is to mark the identical picture. Variations of this test include the recognition of one or more digits or letters which are identical to the stimulus at the beginning of the line.
3. *Sentence comprehension.* The child must grasp the meaning of an entire sentence. Before him are pictures of a calendar, clock, lawnmower, and thermometer. "Mark the one which tells us the time."
4. *Drawing a human figure.* In a space provided on the test booklet, the child is asked to draw a man or a woman.
5. *Ability to count and to write numbers.* A series of identical objects are shown, and the child is told to mark the second, fourth, or fifth object from the left.

---

[3] See for example:

O. K. Buros (Ed.), *Mental Measurement Yearbook* (New Jersey: The Gryphon Press).

Arthur I. Gates, *The Improvement of Reading* (3rd ed.; New York: The Macmillan Co., 1947), 140-77.

Kathleen B. Hester, *Teaching Every Child to Read* (New York: Harper & Brothers, 1955), Chap. 7.

Lucile M. Harrison, *Reading Readiness* (Boston: Houghton Mifflin Co., 1939).

Gerald A. Yoakam, *Basal Reading Instruction* (New York: McGraw-Hill Book Co., Inc., 1955), 103-19.

To test his ability to recognize digits he is told to underline or put an "X" on one digit in a series.

6. *Word recognition.* A common object (doll, house, barn, cow, man, etc.) is pictured. Three or four words, including the symbol for the picture, are shown, and the child is to mark the word represented by the picture.

7. *Copying a model.* A series of geometric figures and capital letters serve as models. The child is to duplicate the stimulus.

8. *Auditory discrimination.* On a group test this might consist of a series of pictures placed horizontally across the page. At the left of each series is a stimulus picture. The child marks each object in the series whose name begins with the same initial sound as the name of the stimulus. If the first picture is that of a dog, for example, it might be followed by illustrations of a doll, a cow, a door, and a ball. Another test situation would be marking each picture whose name rhymes with the name of the stimulus picture.

Readiness tests vary as to the types of skills tested. Some of the earlier tests lack provision for measuring auditory discrimination, but most of the more recently published tests include such a subtest.[4] In general, norms are based on total scores which determine pupil placement in categories such as superior, above average, average, or poor. Since the chief objective of readiness tests is prediction of success in learning to read, it is hoped that the test will separate the ready from the non-ready and that when first grade pupils are thus identified the school will adjust the curriculum accordingly. This brings us to the question of how accurately reading readiness tests predict success in beginning reading.

PREDICTIVE VALUE OF READINESS TESTS

In general, the experimental data indicate that the relationship between scores on readiness tests and success in beginning reading is not high. Bremer tested over 2,000 first graders with a reading readiness test and later with a test of reading achievement. He reported only a slight relationship between the scores on the two tests.[5] Studies

---

[4] M. Lucile Harrison and J. B. Stroud, *Reading Readiness Profiles* (Boston: Houghton Mifflin Co.).

[5] Neville Bremer, "Do Readiness Tests Predict Success in Reading?" *Elementary School Journal,* LIX (1959), 222-24.

also report that teacher estimates of pupil success in reading, made without a knowledge of readiness test scores, correlate as high with achievement as do the actual test scores.[6] Karlin studied over one hundred first grade children, all of whom had an I.Q. of 90 or above, had attended kindergarten, and had no serious visual, hearing, or emotional problem. He found a correlation of .36 between scores on the Metropolitan Reading Readiness Test administered in September and achievement on the Gates Primary Reading Test (paragraph) administered at the end of the school year. In this study, prediction of reading achievement based on readiness test scores was only about 4 per cent superior to teacher prediction made in the absence of the readiness data. Karlin concluded, "The confidence which teachers place in the concept of reading-readiness is well merited, but the desirability of using existing reading-readiness tests almost exclusively to measure extent of readiness should be re-examined."[7]

Lee and others[8] testing 164 first grade children, found a correlation of .49 between scores on the Lee-Clark Readiness Test and the Lee-Clark Primary Reading Test and a correlation of .54 between the former and the Gates Silent Reading Test. In the same study a group of teachers predicted the reading achievement of the pupils in their respective classes. The correlation between individual teachers' predictions and actual achievement ranged from .10 to .88. About half of the teachers were as effective in predicting pupil achievement as was the readiness test.

In an early study by Deputy, first grade children were pre-tested with an intelligence test and various measures of reading readiness. The correlations between these tests and later reading achievement were as follows: the Pintner-Cunningham primary mental test .70; visual readiness .52; word recognition .49; visual-auditory association .39, and comprehension and recall .37.[9]

---

[6] Max S. Henig, "Predictive Value of a Reading Readiness Test and of Teacher Forecasts," *Elementary School Journal*, L (1949), 41-46.

[7] Robert Karlin, "The Prediction of Reading Success and Reading Readiness Tests," *Elementary English,* XXXV (1957), 320-22.

[8] J. M. Lee, W. W. Clark, and D. M. Lee, "Measuring Reading Readiness," *Elementary School Journal,* XXXIV (1934), 656-66.

[9] E. C. Deputy, *Predicting First Grade Reading Achievement,* Columbia University Contributions to Education, No. 426 (New York: Bureau of Publications, Teachers College, Columbia University, 1930).

Long-term prediction of reading achievement, based on readiness tests administered in first grade, is also hazardous. Moreau reports a correlation of .46 between readiness scores made in first grade and reading achievement in sixth grade.[10] Baker reports data for over 200 children in grades four, five, and six who read below grade norm, many of them showing severe retardation. Readiness scores achieved on tests administered during first grade showed that an extremely high percentage of these reading failures had exceeded the national norm on the readiness tests (63 per cent of the fourth grade pupils, 71 per cent of fifth, and 83 per cent of sixth grade). Baker hypothesized that these findings stem from two factors: standardized readiness tests rate children too high; and the elementary classrooms from which these pupils came were characterized by drab, stereotyped instruction with emphasis on workbooks, intensive reading of a few books, and oral reading.[11]

Thus, experimental data suggest that readiness tests, intelligence tests, and teacher evaluations appear to be about equally effective in predicting success in beginning reading. This does not imply that readiness tests have little value to teachers. It does suggest that educators should not project into these tests a degree of predictive infallibility which they do not possess. It appears that some readiness tests "over-rate" children in regard to their readiness to deal with reading. It is possible that some of the tasks on the test are more closely related to the child's previous experiences than to what he will actually encounter in beginning reading.

It must be kept in mind that readiness tests measure only selected factors which are believed to be related to reading. There are many other factors which affect learning to read, such as the instruction the child receives, his attitude toward his teacher and toward reading, his reaction to varying degrees of success and failure, his home stability, and the like. This points up the need for intelligent use of readiness test results. The purpose of administering such tests is not

---

[10] Margaret Moreau, "Long Term Prediction of Reading Success," *California Journal of Educational Research* (September, 1950), 173-76.

[11] Emily V. Baker, "Reading Readiness Is Still Important," *Elementary English*, XXXII (1955), 17-23.

to get a score for each child or to rank or compare children in the group, but rather to secure data for planning experiences.

In fact, unless the teacher is alert, actual scores may divert attention from child behavior which merits close scrutiny. This tendency is particularly marked where the administration of tests has become an end in itself. When this occurs, the inevitable result is that many trees become obscured by the forest. If teachers would analyze readiness test results and if they could adjust their teaching to each child's needs, numerous reading problems might be averted.

RELATIONSHIP BETWEEN MENTAL AGE AND SUCCESS IN BEGINNING READING

Of all the factors assumed to be related to success in beginning reading, mental age has received the lion's share of attention in the literature on reading. Research data appear to be in agreement that mental age is more closely related to success in reading than is chronological age or I.Q. Wilson and Fleming[12] compiled over 300 correlations comparing the relationships between C.A., I.Q., and M.A. with approximately 100 other abilities which were conceivably related to learning to read. A few of the correlations relevant to this discussion follow:

TABLE 2

Test	Correlation found with		
	C.A.	*I.Q.*	*M.A.*
Gates Primary Reading Test (Para.) Administered at end of first grade.	.18	.43	.54
Metropolitan Readiness Test	.29	.59	.79
Tests of letter abilities	.14	.39	.47

[12] Frank T. Wilson and Cecil W. Fleming, "Correlations of Chronological Age, Mental Age and Intelligence Quotient with Other Abilities and Traits in Grade I," *Journal of Genetic Psychology*, L (1937), 323-37.

Authorities do not agree as to the minimum mental age which should be attained before beginning reading. The most often repeated figure is six years and six months. In fact, this figure is so often quoted in the literature that one would assume that a vast array of evidence must be available to substantiate this position. However, very little experimental data is to be found. A great deal of generalization from one or a few studies is apparent in the literature on reading. The study which initiated most of the discussion was published by Morphett and Washburne in 1931.[13] They report data for 141 first grade children who were given an intelligence test at the beginning of the school year and tested on reading achievement in February. The subjects were then divided into nine groups on the basis of mental age. The lowest range was 4-5 to 4-11, the highest 8-6 to 9-0 (these figures represent years and months of mental age). Of approximately 100 children who had attained an M.A. of 6-6 or higher, 78 per cent made satisfactory progress in general reading and 87 per cent made satisfactory progress in sight words. Of a group of twenty children whose M.A. ranged from 6-0 to 6-5, 52 per cent made satisfactory progress in reading and 41 per cent in sight words. Children below this range in M.A. showed little success in reading achievement.

In a follow-up study Washburne reports on a group of twenty-five pupils who were delayed in beginning reading instruction until the middle of second grade.[14] Their reading achievement was compared with a number of control pupils who began reading at the usual time in first grade. By the end of the third grade the experimental group had caught up with the controls; by the end of fourth grade they had surpassed them; and at the end of seventh grade they were approximately one year ahead of the controls in reading. Unfortunately, the original experimental group of twenty-five had been reduced to approximately half that number by the end of the experiment and drawing conclusions on such a small sample is precarious. In addition there were, according to the author, important variables which could not be controlled.

---

[13] Mabel V. Morphett and Carleton Washburne, "When Should Children Begin to Read?" *Elementary School Journal,* XXXI (1931), 496-503.

[14] Carleton Washburne, "Individualized Plan of Instruction in Winnetka," *Adjusting Reading Programs to Individuals,* W. S. Gray (Ed.), (Chicago: University of Chicago Press, 1941), 90-95.

Gates unequivocally challenges the contention that research data have established a "critical point" on the M.A. continuum below which reading cannot be mastered. He states: "The fact remains . . . that it has by no means been proved as yet that a mental age of six and a half years is a proper minimum to prescribe for learning to read by all school methods or organizations or *all* types of teaching skills and procedures."[15] In a study of four different first grade classes, Gates reports the correlation between M.A. and reading achievement as .62, .55, .44, and .34. He postulated that much of the discrepancy between these figures was actually accounted for by the instructional procedures found in the classrooms and that good instruction results in a higher correlation between pupil M.A. and success in reading.[16]

The aim of the preceding discussion is not to minimize the importance of mental capacity in learning to read, but rather to see it in its proper perspective. The data available attest to the importance of M.A. but at the same time do not establish a particular point on the mental-age continuum as the point below which children will not achieve success in reading. To posit that 6-6 mental age is such a point implies that all children with this M.A. are alike and ignores the fact that teachers, teaching methods, and programs are not everywhere comparable.

Other investigations attest to the importance of factors such as pre-reading activities, methodology, and readiness programs in determining how well children learn to read. One such study, carried on in first grade, reports that some children with an M.A. of 5-6 who had had no specific readiness program did not achieve up to grade norms in reading, while a group with M.A.'s of 5-0 who had had an extensive twelve week readiness program did achieve up to national norms. Furthermore, a number of children who did poorly on readiness tests, and for whom prognosis in reading achievement was poor, achieved up to grade norm following specific readiness instruction.[17]

---

[15] A. I. Gates, "The Necessary Mental Age for Beginning Reading," *Elementary School Journal,* XXXVII (1937), 497-508.

[16] *Ibid.,* p. 507.

[17] R. W. Edmiston and Bessie Peyton, "Improving First Grade Achievement by Readiness Instruction." *School and Society,* LXXI (1950), 230-32.

PRE-SCHOOL EXPERIENCE AND INFORMATIONAL BACKGROUND

Pre-school experience and informational background have been studied to determine their relationship to reading readiness. In one study, scores made by first grade children on a readiness test correlated .49 with later achievement in reading. However, when only the scores of those children who had attended kindergarten were treated separately the correlation between the two measures was .68.[18] After studying a group of children who had kindergarten experience and a group which had no such experience, Pratt questioned the validity of using the same reading readiness tests and applying the same assumptions to both groups.[19]

In a study designed to show the relationship between children's informational background and progress in reading, first grade children were tested on vocabulary, picture completion, and previous experience. On the basis of data secured, children were divided into "rich background" and "meager background" groups. Reading readiness tests were administered to all children at the beginning of first grade. Reading achievement tests were administered to first graders in January and again in December of their second year. The rich background group was superior on both readiness tests and later reading achievement although there was no significant difference between the groups in mental age.[20] Another study revealed that the knowledge or information which first grade children possess and readiness scores showed almost identical correlations with reading achievement in first grade.[21]

---

[18] J. M. Lee, W. W. Clark, and D. M. Lee, "Measuring Reading Readiness," *Elementary School Journal,* XXXIV (1934), 656-66.

[19] Willis E. Pratt, "A Study of the Differences in the Prediction of Reading Success of Kindergarten and Non-Kindergarten Children," *Journal of Educational Research,* XLII (March, 1949), 525-33.

[20] G. H. Hilliard and Eleanor Troxell, "Informational Background As a Factor in the Reading Readiness Program," *Elementary School Journal,* XXXVIII (1937), 255-63.

[21] Leigh Peck and Lillian E. McGlothlin, "Children's Information and Success in First Grade Reading," *Journal of Educational Psychology,* XXXI (1940), 653-64.

Learning to read is probably one of the most important accomplishments that the child will achieve during his formal schooling. This is not to imply that learning to read will be his most difficult or dramatic academic achievement, for if he gets off to a good start the whole process may be so uneventful that he will not recall how this particular learning took place. On the other hand, if he fails in reading, the frustrations and defeats which can beset him in the future are so numerous and varied that they have never been tabulated in one source. Thus, the experiences which the school arranges for children prior to launching into the formal teaching of reading are extremely important.

LANGUAGE DEVELOPMENT AND THE CURRICULUM

Reading readiness is not confined specifically to experiences found on readiness tests. As a child grows and matures in all phases of human growth—intellectual, social, emotional, and physiological—he is growing into reading. Children can "grow" without a professionally planned curriculum. However, the school's function is to provide guidance and direction, to structure learning situations so that certain experiences are likely to result. A program aimed at preparing children for beginning reading is limited only by the facilities and resources of the school and the understanding and creativeness of the teacher. A great majority of pre-reading activities can be encompassed under the heading *language.*

The role of the school in preparing children for reading begins the first day of school and continues for varying lengths of time for different children. Whatever the school does in the reading readiness period will be done in order to guide each child into being a "good risk" as a beginning reader. The school attempts to structure the situation so that each child will acquire the right combination of abilities, skills, and attitudes. The study of how children acquire language is both interesting and rewarding. The understanding of this process is a prerequisite to planning a curriculum for children or putting it into practice.

The child first develops oral language, acquiring the ability to make sounds in isolation and then in combination. As sounds are combined into words they become associated with meanings. The range of meaningful language one uses is referred to as his *speaking vocabulary*. The child beginning school has a speaking vocabulary of several thousand words. He can say, and has concepts for, a great variety of speech sounds, such as *horse, train, jet, farm, elephant, river*. In addition he will have some concept of the relationship of *up* to *down, over* to *under, high* to *low, hot* to *cold, dry* to *wet, large* to *small, dark* to *light*. Speech sounds, coupled with the mysteries of meaning, fascinate the child. Some first graders will tend to "talk over their heads," to use speech sounds for which they have not learned meanings. Every child at this age has been exposed to more language than he has absorbed.[22]

It is inevitable that the child will harbor many misconceptions. He will probably be vague about *good* and *bad, right* and *wrong, justice, government, God, Heaven,* and *death*. Children come to school with varying degrees of insight into concepts such as these. Many decades later, even if he has earned the title of Philosopher, one may still be attempting to develop, extend, and clarify some of these concepts.

Language cuts across every goal and function of the school. Everything that is taught in the school must pass through a communication process before it is learned by a pupil. Excellent books have been written about the school curriculum. These books discuss objectives, the impact of the school's curriculum on our culture, and the factors in our culture which in turn shape the school curriculum. The merits of various curricular philosophies such as the "traditional," "progressive," "integrated," and "core" are often debated. In these debates the point is sometimes overlooked that the real function of the school is to provide children with guidance in developing concepts. Our schools at all levels rely heavily on reading as the means of building and extending concepts in all subject areas.

No matter how one organizes the curriculum or the debate on the curriculum, the school can do no more than guide and direct the development of concepts. Therefore, the debate must center on *what* concepts, *when* to teach them, and *how* best to teach them. As Ragan points out: "The curriculum does not exist in the content to be

---

[22] Arnold Gesell and Frances L. Ilg, *Child Development* (New York: Harper & Brothers, 1949).

learned. The selection of useful, accurate content is a very important responsibility of the teacher, *but content does not constitute the curriculum until it becomes a part of the experience of the child.*"[23] (Italics added.) The effectiveness of any curriculum cannot be judged by the statements in the curriculum guide, but rather by the learning which takes place in the classroom.

Individuals learn and use language skills in social and cultural and emotional settings. The teacher is expected, and to some degree is trained, to become cognizant of and concerned with all facets of human growth and development—physical, social, emotional, and intellectual. The one reason why the school *must* be concerned is that these factors influence learning.

LANGUAGE AND SOCIALIZATION

The school is very much involved in guiding the social growth of its pupils. In the case of normal children, socialization is almost exclusively built around communication. Up to the time children reach school age, spoken language is the chief means of communication. There is no better tool than language facility for gauging the social needs or social maturity of children. Among the first experiences provided in the modern school's curriculum are those which have to do with social growth. The logic of this is apparent. Many children have had little or no experience in a group as large as that in which they will find themselves upon beginning school. There will be many learning situations which will call for group coherence. Each member of the group will have to follow certain social patterns in order not to disrupt the learning situation for the others in the group.

Gradually, step by step, the teacher moves in the direction of establishing social control within the class so that learning can take place. Whether the teacher structures this control on an authoritarian basis or has the group control evolve out of the group itself, the medium for establishing control will be language. Many group activities in the classroom, if they are to end successfully, will call for

[23] William B. Ragan, *Modern Elementary Curriculum* (New York: Holt, Rinehart & Winston, Inc., 1953), 4.

co-operation and sharing among pupils. Language is the most important basis for co-operation. Co-operation and sharing help the child grow and develop from a very self-centered organism into a social being. If the process breaks down and the individual, for any reason, does not learn the social rules, or does not within certain limits follow them, his behavior sets him apart from the group. When this behavior is reacted to by those in the peer group, he and the group are out of adjustment.

These maladjustments among children beginning school are almost inevitable because some children have further to go in order to live up to the group standards, some learn slowly, and some have learned to use anti-social responses when attempting to satisfy their needs. A teacher who does not perceive the symptoms of maladjustment fairly early may soon have cases of non-affiliation in her class. These can develop very rapidly into isolates, or children rejected by the group. The teacher may be the best teacher of reading in the district, but if she lets the security of some children become seriously threatened in the school situation the odds are that she will not teach them reading. In their unskilled efforts to strike back at threats they do not understand, these pupils may disrupt the learning for others in the group.

LANGUAGE AND EMOTIONAL ADJUSTMENT

Language usage is a most important factor in the study of emotional maladjustment and the revelation of psychological needs. Clinicians state that language is the most sensitive indicator of maladjustment. The classroom, the playground, in fact the total environment, is one never-ending projective technique if one but heeds the language of children. Both as adults and as teachers, we sometimes learn very little about children from children. This happens when we consciously or unconsciously feel that what children say is not important. The truth of the matter is that their language mirrors their needs, feelings, aspirations, and fears, and if one's job is to help children grow, knowledge of these is essential.

A child's need for ego satisfaction seems to increase by a geometric ratio in the face of frustration. That is, a little denial of love, attention, and acceptance, or a little threat to self worth and integrity, is reacted to by an increased drive for these goals. If rebuffed again, the child seems to redouble his efforts to maintain his prestige and self worth. It is apparent that when children are trying to fulfill ego needs, they invariably use behavior which by adult logic seems ill conceived and not likely to achieve the child's goal. The child who wants and needs friendship and is rebuffed may resort to the use of aggressive, hostile, or abusive language, perhaps feeling that he can force acceptance or that his language will reduce the stature of those persons to whom it is addressed. Another child, after each failure, may withdraw more and more and make very few language overtures to others in his peer group. This non-use of language is itself a clue which should have diagnostic value for the teacher. Here is a child who has elected to withdraw from the arena, but the fight to salvage his ego will go on within himself. This child, at the moment, poses no problem to the teacher or society, but his response is potentially more dangerous than overt aggression.

LANGUAGE AND MENTAL GROWTH

Psychologists agree that the most valuable insights into the child's mental growth are gained from a study of the development of language facility. A brief though acceptable definition of intelligence is that it is "the ability to do abstract thinking." Stated another way, it is the ability to manipulate in a meaningful manner symbolic materials of which language is our best example. Intelligence itself cannot be measured but is inferred from behavior which can be measured. We measure certain behavior which by agreement is said to be representative of intelligence.[24] The one kind of behavior most universally measured on intelligence tests is language behavior. Our society puts a high value on the ability to use and understand language. The degree of the child's mastery of communication skills determines to a large extent his readiness to do school tasks and to profit from instruction. Although he cannot read, spell, or write when he starts school, he has had years of experience with language. His language proficiency is used as an index of his mental growth, just

---

[24] E. T. Prothro and P. T. Teska, *Psychology: A Biosocial Study of Behavior* (Boston: Ginn & Co., 1950), 468.

as it provides data for appraisal of social and emotional growth and adjustment.

Furthermore, when we wish to assess what the student has learned at any grade level, we rely on language usage. In other words, a change in language behavior is often the sole criterion of learning. Language reveals the number and breadth of concepts acquired. All concepts exist within the framework of some symbolic process and all are arrived at and refined through thought processes which in turn depend on the manipulation of language symbols.

It is a truism that a society such as we have today could not have evolved without language. It is equally obvious that education would not have developed along the lines it has without language. Language provides a bridge which permits ideas, information, and data to pass between parent and child, teacher and pupil, and child and peer. As an individual masters new forms of language usage, he is developing "mind tools" which he can use from that time forward in the pursuit of knowledge. Reading is our best example of such a tool.

LANGUAGE DEVELOPMENT AND READING

Over and above what the child's language usage can tell the teacher about intellectual, social, and emotional development is the relationship of previous language experiences to the specific learning task called *reading*. Skillful, effective teaching of beginning reading is based on the teacher's understanding:

1. That reading is related to all language functions found in the curriculum.

2. That learning to read is related to, and built upon, past language experiences.

3. That learning to read should be a natural outgrowth of these past language experiences.

4. That learning to read is a developmental process that involves years of guided study.

5. That different methods of teaching reading may be justified but the one criterion a method should meet is that it builds logically and systematically.

It is important for teachers who are preparing children for reading to be aware of the experiences and growth which have taken place during the pre-school years. Some children will have had many pleasant experiences with books, parents having read to them frequently. They will be able to recognize and point out the duck, the owl, the moose, the pony, the baby bear, or the tug boat and tell what each is doing in the picture, having learned to find meaning in pictures. Some children will be able to recite almost word for word certain of their favorite stories. Others will have a surprisingly large stock of concepts derived from viewing television, from travel, or from contact with adults. On the other hand, some children will have been read to rarely if at all. A depressing home environment will undoubtedly be reflected in a child's language usage and stock of concepts. The range of previous experiences among first grade children is tremendous.

The curriculum of the first grade cannot be unrelated to the child's previous development since what is done in the classroom must of necessity be built on previous experience. Even before the child begins to read, the numerous activities included in the curriculum are related to reading. This relationship is easy to see in such activities as hikes, visits, excursions, field trips, bulletin boards, stories read by teachers, and the like. But other activities, such as drawing, painting, rhythm, sharing periods, planning periods, play, and problem-solving, are also related. All are bound together with language and communication; all involve developing and extending concepts. Each of these in turn is fixed by word symbols. Reading is an extension of the communicative process which involves learning the printed equivalent for the known spoken symbols.

There are certain differences between the language experiences which children have before coming to school and those they encounter early in the school situation. The first new adjustment will be using speech in groups larger than those in which the child has thus far participated. More speech responses will have to be inhibited, since the child will have to share talking time with so many others. His pre-school language was probably more ego-involved than will be acceptable in the school situation. Here the speaker must consider his listeners or lose them. The pre-schooler can flit from topic to topic; his response need not dovetail with what has just been said by another. However, in the group discussion in the classroom there is usually a central topic, and children must gradually learn to follow a discussion and to build logically on what has been said previously.[25]

RECOMMENDED LANGUAGE EXPERIENCES

There are many types of experiences which the school arranges so that skill in language and communication will be developed as rapidly as possible. Some of these tasks may at first seem unrelated to teaching reading. However, they involve skills used in reading, such as perception in noting details and making comparisons, extending the span of attention, learning to see relationships between events, and drawing inferences. What follows is a representative but not exhaustive list of such experiences:

1. Coloring, cutting, pasting
2. Working a jigsaw puzzle
3. An excursion to observe animals:
   a) at a farm
   b) at a zoo
4. Listening to musical records—"Do what the music tells you."
5. Listening to the teacher read a story
6. Celebrating birthdays
7. Bringing pets to the classroom—parakeet, puppy, duck, rabbit
8. Gathering leaves
9. Discussing the seasons
10. Growing a sweet potato in a glass of water
11. Using a medicine dropper—How can it pick up water?
12. Imitating sounds of animals—rooster, horse, dog, cat, frog
13. Learning what objects float—wide-mouthed gallon jar and numerous objects
14. Discussing the eating habits of different animals—cow, chicken, fish, frog
15. Taking an excursion to observe different occupations—to a bakery, a dairy, a farm
16. Planning a party (experience chart)
17. Flying a kite—Why does it fly?

[25] Louis V. Johnson, "Group Discussion and the Development of Oral Language," *Elementary English*, XXXIII (1956), 496-99.

Numerous activities can be integrated with beginning instruction in reading. Developing sensory skills stressing fine muscle co-ordination, noting details, expressing ideas symbolically—these activities are related to reading and, like reading, are developmental in nature. *(Courtesy of Bexley Schools, Bexley, Ohio; photographer: Arthur Burt, Inc.)*

18. Using a balance (scale)
19. Observing animals that can swim—fish, frog, duck
20. Using an electric fan with a home-made weather vane
21. Going on a nature hike. Turn over a fair-sized rock—Why is it damp underneath? Why do we find worms here?
22. Pouring water from quart jar into funnel—Why does the funnel run over?
23. Watching plants grow (outside garden or inside window box)
24. Planning an excursion and making an experience chart
25. Using clay, fingerpaints, colored paper, pictures, objects to express ideas

All of these experiences involve sensory experiences. It should be remembered that as the child matures, sensory impressions are automatically translated into language equivalents and are the basis for all learning. When the child feels the turtle's shell, he translates the sensation into language symbols. A duck is how a duck looks, how it swims, how it quacks, how it waddles, and how it eats. A concept of the wind grows out of sensory perceptions of paper blowing across a yard, sand or grit against one's face, a hat blown off, and trees and bushes bending. This process, like reading, is developmental in nature and illustrates how concepts evolve and develop.

"Show and Tell." A technique used frequently to help children develop language facility and extend concepts is "show and tell," or sharing periods. The child brings something to school or makes something in school which he thinks may be of interest to the group. Since he is familiar with the object, even the shy child can tell something about it. Attention is focused on the object rather than the child and his speaking. This has psychological value for those children who fear speaking to the group. It is a situation that can be kept concrete. "I brought a box full of my rocks. I want to show you some of the ones I like. I collect these when we go on trips. This one is quartz. This one has iron in it. It's heavy. You can see the iron in it. These rocks are very smooth. They came from Lake Michigan. The waves rub the rocks with sand. They get smooth and round."

Precise descriptions with full explanations of processes and smooth transitions may be lacking, but communication has taken place, self-confidence has been strengthened, status has been enhanced. The speaker is asked some questions and he answers with considerable poise. The teacher compliments him on his fine talk. He senses that when he has something interesting to tell, others will listen. "Show and tell" can be a very ego-satisfying experience for children.

Not all children will be successful. Some will have a difficult time even stating what they are showing the group. The teacher is the only hope of salvaging something from such a situation. A question at the right moment may possibly evoke a response. The tone of voice in which the question is asked will condition the group's reaction to the speaker. A child who cannot speak successfully to the entire class may be able to speak to a smaller group, but this can

Telling about some interesting object permits a child to function in a real audience situation. He sees that language is the vehicle for his thoughts as well as the bridge between him and his listeners. Showing the object while telling about it helps the inexperienced public speaker to be more facile in his language usage. *(Courtesy of Bexley Schools, Bexley, Ohio; photographer: Arthur Burt, Inc.)*

come about only if the teacher perceives the child's problem and structures the situation so that he participates.

"Show and tell" experiences can contribute much to the child's social and language development, but there are some pitfalls which must be avoided if this practice is to contribute its maximum to children's growth. Some teachers use the "show and tell" period as a means of obtaining a little time for their daily administrative chores. They call on youngsters and try to give the impression that they are avidly interested, but they actually are filling out attendance reports, checking lunch money, tabulating returns from a P.T.A. questionnaire which the children brought from home, setting up schedules for parents' conferences, and so forth.

Another factor which can detract from the effectiveness of this practice is the unequal distribution of experiences. Unless the teacher keeps some record, certain children will monopolize the "show and tell" periods while others will rarely have an opportunity to contribute. This may result in a neglect of those who need the experience most. The shy, unsure child is not likely to volunteer, although he may have come to class with some object in his pocket about which he had hoped to talk.

An illustration of this tendency is provided by an experienced teacher who checked back on the past week's activity in the sharing period and found that she had inadvertently been calling on the most persistent volunteers and more or less ignoring some of the other children. Figure 1 sets down her data for the most-called-on five children and the least-called-on in the "show and tell" period. Even if we assume some inaccuracy due to faulty memory, the data are suggestive of how easy it is to let some children develop habits of non-participation.

FIGURE 1

A TEACHER'S RETROSPECTIVE RECORD OF THE FIVE STUDENTS WHO PARTICIPATED MOST AND THE FIVE WHO PARTICIPATED LEAST IN ONE WEEK'S "SHOW AND TELL" ACTIVITIES. THE SYMBOL *P* INDICATES PARTICIPATION.

Pupil	1	2	3	4	5	26	27	28	29	30
Mon.	P		P	P						
Tues.	P	P		P	P		P			
Wed.	P	P	P			P				
Thurs.	P	P		P	P			P		
Fri.	P	P	P		P					

Conversation Groups. Dividing the class into conversation groups is another method of helping children acquire facility in using language. The advantage in this device is that more children can participate in a given period of time and the teacher can spend more time with the group that most needs her guidance. However, the children must have developed the ability to co-operate with and respect others.

Other means of practicing language usage that are more or less self-explanatory include:

Telling a story (not about self)
"My pet . . . ."
"We took a trip to . . . ." (Either a group experience or an individual child's experience)
"I have a riddle"
"My three wishes are . . . ."
"Who am I describing?" (A child in class or a well-known person)

Discussing Trips and Excursions. Discussion of class trips or excursions to a farm, the zoo, a dairy, or the airport will result in some learning for all of the children who participate. Children differ in the amount they learn and in the degree of thoroughness with which they form certain concepts. This occurs because children differ in previous experience and sensory perceptions. They cannot all have the same experiences when they are visiting the same farm, zoo, market, or TV station. Therefore, visiting these interesting places is not the only important phase of the total experience. Equally important is the planning which tells the child what to look for and the discussion which follows the excursion. This discussion can extend partial concepts or clear up hazy concepts. Here again, the teacher can structure these sharing experiences so that all children become involved. The shy child or the one who will have only a limited contribution can often be called on early in the discussion. This precaution assures that their ideas will not have been advanced before they have an opportunity to speak.

DEVELOPING LISTENING SKILL

Listening and reading are the receptive language processes through which a large part of the school curriculum must pass on its way to becoming learning. Listening is closely related to many facets of reading, such as auditory discrimination, expansion of concepts, developing independent work habits, reading with expression, getting meaning from listening to others read, and the development of usage vocabulary. Children differ appreciably in listening ability. Some children come to school with poor listening habits, and others develop inadequate habits early in their school career. This naturally has an impact on classroom activities.

If we judge educators' interest in and respect for listening by their statements about its importance, we might conclude that there is a high degree of respect for listening as a means of learning. However, until very recently the research on listening has been meagre, despite the fact that during the past decade there has been more research on listening and more writing about listening than in the previous half century. Much of this work is at the college level and has little relationship to children beginning school. Hackett raises the question whether enough is known about the process of listening for teachers to be able to "teach listening."[26]

Teacher training programs and actual classroom practices suggest that listening ability is taken for granted. Children come to school with the ability to listen and it is sometimes assumed that they are listening whenever they are not involved in some overt ego-involved behavior. Studies indicate that the school does relatively little to help improve the listening abilities of pupils.[27] A recent review of a number of curriculum guides or bulletins used at the elementary level indicates a high degree of respect for listening. However, the amount of space devoted to this topic was extremely limited, and suggestions to teachers were very general. Listening situations found in the school were cited, but there were practically no concrete suggestions on how to *teach* children to become better listeners.[28]

Listening involves more than being physically present and immobile while the teacher is speaking. "It is just as important to provide experience-listening if we want learning to take place as it is to pro-

---

[26] Herbert Hackett, "A Null Hypothesis: There Is Not Enough Evidence," *Education,* LXXV (1955), 349-51. This entire issue of *Education* is devoted to the problem of listening and includes extensive bibliographical materials.

[27] Miriam E. Wilt, "A Study of Teacher Awareness of Listening as a Factor in Elementary Education," *Journal of Educational Research,* XLIII (1950), 626-36.

[28] Arthur Heilman, "Listening and the Curriculum," *Education,* LXXV (1955), 283-87.

vide experience-*reading*."[29] It is inevitable that there will be a great number of learning activities in the school which depend on listening. These include listening to recordings of stories, poetry, and songs; listening to music and acting out what the music suggests; listening to the teacher read stories; participating in speaking-listener situations; and many other experiences which need little explanation. A few exercises which can be used in pre-reading as well as at higher levels are briefly described below.

Critical listening from which to draw conclusions. Here the teacher reads short descriptive passages and the children are asked to identify or draw a picture of what is described. This technique can be tied in with motor co-ordination and imagination.

1. I grow outdoors.
   I grow tall.
   In summer I am full
   of leaves. Birds sit
   on my branches and sing.
   What am I?
   Draw a picture of me.
2. People live in me.
   I have windows and doors.
   I come in many different
   sizes and colors.
   Draw a picture of me.

The descriptions the teacher reads can vary in length and complexity, depending on the maturity or age level of the group. These exercises can help teachers discover many things about their pupils such as:

1. Which children can listen effectively and which cannot.
2. Which children are self-sufficient and able to work on their own initiative.
3. Which children are dependent and receive clues from others.
4. Information relative to the degree of maturity of each child.
5. Unusual responses which may suggest other problems needing attention.

---

[29] Clarence Wachner, "Listening in an Integrated Language Arts Program," *Elementary English*, XXXIII (1956), 491-96.

Children love to hear stories. They are better listeners during "story time" than during any other of the day's activities simply because they are *interested*. Reading to children emphasizes that the reading process should be *enjoyable* and *meaningful*. *(Courtesy of Bexley Schools, Bexley, Ohio; photographer: Arthur Burt, Inc.)*

Story periods. Practically all children can be held spellbound by a good story well told. When the teacher tells or reads stories, she plants the idea in the children's minds that good listening is the key to the enjoyment associated with the story. Equally important is the fact that she can stress a purpose for listening, whether for enjoyment, for information, for answers to specific questions, or for practice in social living.

Following directions can be used either as a class exercise, with small groups within a class, or with individual pupils. Several short commands are stated and the child, or the group, is to execute them in the order given. The performance will reveal ability to attend to oral directions and the ability to hold these in memory.

Finish the story provides practice in developing language skills such as training in listening, use of imagination, practice in using language, and expecting logic and meaning from reading. The teacher, while reading a story, interrupts it at a point of high interest and asks the children, "What happens next?"

"Once upon a time Jack went to visit his grandfather and grandmother. They lived on a farm. He went with his father and mother in their car. When they drove up to grandfather's house a big dog rushed out to the car and barked and barked. The boy and his parents had never seen this dog before. Father said '_______.'" (Child finishes story.)

"Jane and Henry were tired of running and playing. They sat down on the porch to rest and talk. Jane said, 'Henry, let's ask mother to make us some lemonade.'

"'Good,' said Henry, 'cold lemonade; I'm so thirsty I could drink three glasses.' They started into the house and Henry said: 'Jane, do you think your mother would make enough lemonade so we could have a lemonade stand and sell lemonade in paper cups?'

"Jane said, '_______.'"

Complete the sentence is a variation of the above in which the child supplies a word which has been omitted. "A big dog came up to the car and _______ at them." "Jim was tired of running. He sat down to _______." This exercise gives practice in listening and in getting meanings from context.

What word disagrees with the picture? While looking at a picture pupils listen to the teacher as she says a series of four words, one of which could not be logically associated with the picture. Children are then asked to identify the word which does not belong. This can be a challenging game, because children must observe closely, listen carefully, and remember the word while other stimuli are presented.

Retell a story. The teacher reads a story or passage to one group who then tell the story to children who have not heard it. This experience motivates children to be good listeners, since they must pay attention and comprehend if they are to retell the story successfully.

Emphasizing expression. The teacher reads a sentence or short passage word by word, without inflection, then reads it with good expression. Pupils are lead to see that how a passage is read affects its interpretation. McKee gives an excellent account of the technique and its values.[30]

DEVELOPING SENSORY SKILLS

VISUAL SKILLS

Here the teacher must be concerned with two developmental factors: the child's vision as it relates to reading and the task of developing skill in visual discrimination. Steps in acquiring visual discrimination include the visual readiness program, learning to recognize words, mastering a left-to-right sequence, and the like.

Vision. The bulk of all visual work in reading is at close range. The stimulus is about fourteen inches from the eyes. The retinas of both eyes reflect the image seen, in this case word symbols. For proper vision, the tiny images on both retinas must be perfectly synchronized or "fused." If fusion does not take place, the image will be blurred, or, in extreme cases, two distinct images will appear. When the stimulus is near the eyes, as in reading a book, the eyes must converge slightly. This convergence is accomplished by muscles in each eye. Any muscular imbalance between the eyes can result in the lack of fusion described above.

Other muscles operate to put pressure on the lens of the eye, which is capable of changing its shape (degree of convexity). This adjustment is essential in order to compensate for differences in the reflected light rays striking the two eyes. The muscular action determining the degree of convexity of the lens is called *accommodation.*[31]

Ruling out the more serious visual defects which prevent the child from seeing printed word symbols, it is difficult, on the basis of published research, to come to a conclusion regarding the precise relationship between visual problems and reading deficiency.[32] However,

---

[30] Paul McKee, *The Teaching of Reading* (Boston: Houghton Mifflin Co., 1948), 158-59.

[31] For further discussion and illustrations of the structure of the eye, see: William Kottmeyer, *Teachers Guide for Remedial Reading* (St. Louis: Webster Publishing Co., 1959), 49-64.

[32] Guy L. Bond and Miles A. Tinker, *Reading Difficulties: Their Diagnosis and Correction* (New York: Appleton-Century-Croft, Inc., 1957), 84-92.

many educators have warned that the school may be expecting too much physiologically of some children as they begin school and attempt to cope with the tasks the school has prescribed. Around 1898 John Dewey cautioned that children six years of age were physiologically immature "for more than incidental attention to visual and written language forms." Stone quotes a number of authorities who have suggested deferring the teaching of reading long past the age at which it is currently begun.[33] In discussing the relationship between poor vision and reading problems among children between six and eight, Broom and others conclude from research that the problem stems from a lack of maturation, or slow development, of good binocular vision, rather than from actual visual defects.[34] This point of view finds support among investigators in the area of child development who are not primarily concerned with reading behavior. "It is generally agreed that the sense of sight is probably the least perfect of the sensory reactions at birth and seems to be the slowest in reaching full maturity."[35]

However, even the tremendous emphasis on reading readiness which emerged during the 1930's and which continues today has had practically no effect either on the age at which children begin school or on the age at which they begin formal instruction in reading. When a child is expected to decipher word symbols before he is visually ready to do so, he is likely to fail. A visual problem may affect a six- or seven-year-old's reading adversely, but the visual problem may decrease with the maturation and development of eye muscles. Nevertheless, the reading deficiency may remain or even grow worse because of attitudes formed toward reading and the reaction to failure in this task.

One of the most common visual problems found among children beginning school is farsightedness (hyperopia). A child with this problem may see quite adequately and pass a far vision test such as the Snellen or be able to read an experience chart at the front of the

---

[33] Clarence R. Stone, *Progress in Primary Reading* (St. Louis: Webster Publishing Co., 1950), Chap. 7.

[34] M. E. Broom, M. A. Duncan, D. Emig, and J. Stueber, *Effective Reading Instruction* (2nd Ed.; New York: McGraw-Hill Book Co., Inc., 1951), 45.

[35] M. E. Breckenridge and E. L. Vincent, *Child Development* (3rd Ed.; Philadelphia: W. B. Saunders Co., 1955), 283.

room, and still be poorly equipped visually to deal with material in a book twelve to fourteen inches from his eyes. Any test of vision which purports to have a relationship to actual reading must include a test of near vision. The farsighted child may be able to compensate by straining eye muscles for short periods of time to correct some refractional problem, but he cannot do this for any great period of time without causing strain and fatigue. If the teacher can detect the visually immature child, she may be able to protect him from too much close work.

Teachers Are Not Optometrists. Since it is so obvious that adequate vision is important in reading, it is often suggested that teachers of reading should thoroughly understand the anatomy of the eye and the nature of problems such as myopia, hyperopia, astigmatism, fusion, and strabismus, as well as be proficient in administering tests such as the Snellen, Eames, and Keystone telebinocular.[36] It might be well for teachers to resist such responsibilities, or at least to question seriously whether they should take the time to become proficient in the use of eye charts, audiometers, or the telebinocular. If these devices are available in the school system, a trained person should use them. Elementary school teachers have more than enough to do in today's classrooms without getting involved in these procedures. Furthermore, if the teacher is not expert in the use of these instruments, she may create the illusion that her pupils have been adequately examined, an illusion which could be a serious matter for the child whose diagnosis is faulty. The less the classroom teacher gets involved in this type of diagnosis, the better. The less she gets involved in these matters the more time she will have for the teaching of reading. The issue here is not whether such a diagnosis should be made, but rather who should make it.

Developing Visual Discrimination. This is one of the major objectives of beginning instruction in reading. The child's need to make fine visual discriminations is self-evident since the symbols which must be read are visual stimuli. Even a cursory examination of words is sufficient to establish that many of them look very much alike. A

---

[36] *The Snellen Chart*, American Optical Co., Southbridge, Mass.; *The Eames Eye Test* (Tarrytown-On-Hudson, N. Y.: World Book Co.); *Keystone Visual Survey Test Telebinocular* (Meadville, Pa.: Keystone View Co.).

child who cannot differentiate between the various words in a passage cannot possibly get meaning from that passage. The widely accepted definition that "reading is getting meaning from printed symbols" does, to some degree, slight the sensory skills which are absolutely essential before reading can become "getting the meaning."

By the time he comes to school, a child has had thousands of experiences in seeing and noting likenesses and differences. He has developed the ability to make fairly high-order visual discriminations, in many cases based on relatively small clues. At the age of three years he was able to identify and claim his tricycle from a group of three-wheelers, even though he was not able to tell us the exact criteria he used in this identification. All we do know is that it was a visual discrimination. Later, two coins much the same size but bearing different symbols will not confuse him. The pictured head of a man or woman no larger than a postage stamp will contain enough visual clues for correct identification. Common trademarks are correctly identified on the basis of size, color, and configuration. A pack of playing cards can be sorted correctly as to suit on the basis of visual perception.

Goins reports a study of first grade children designed to determine (1) the relationship between visual perception and reading ability and (2) whether training in rapid recognition of digits and geometric and abstract figures would aid children in beginning reading achievement. A visual perception test consisting of fourteen subtests was designed. It included no verbal or reading content such as letters or words but did include numerous items of matching pictures and geometrical figures, completion of geometric designs which had a part missing, finding a reversed picture in a series otherwise identical, and a test of closure in which incomplete pictures were the stimulus and the child identified what was represented by the incomplete drawing.

The total scores of first grade pupils on the visual discrimination test showed a correlation of .49 with reading achievement at the end of grade one. Certain of the visual discrimination subtests showed considerable value in predicting first grade reading achievement. Further, certain of the subtests indicated that among first grade children poor and good readers appear to be "different types of perceivers." This was particularly true of the ability to achieve "closure" and to keep in mind a particular configuration. The hypothesis was advanced that children who are widely different in these skills possibly should be taught reading by different methods in grade one.

It was found that the training with the tachistoscope (flashing digits and figures on a screen for extremely brief exposures) was helpful with good readers in improving *their visual perception of such forms* but that this type training resulted in no appreciable improvement in reading achievement. (See Jean Turner Goins, *Visual Perceptual Abilities and Early Reading Progress.* Chicago, University of Chicago Press. Supplementary Educational Monographs, No. 87, 1958.)

Maturation cannot be hastened, but visual discrimination can be sharpened through experience and practice. The school must provide as much of this experience as is needed, and different children will need different amounts. Fortunately, there are many ready-made exercises which the teacher can use. Reading readiness books provide excellent practice in developing the ability to make finer and finer discriminations. Both reading readiness tests and workbooks can aid the teacher in evaluating the child's progress, provided they are used with diagnosis in mind. For the child who needs more practice than is provided in these activities, a number of teacher-made exercises can be developed. Such exercises take time to build; therefore, they should be duplicated in quantities and used from year to year. They never become outdated with one class use. One thorough preparation will provide for many pupils who need this particular type of experience.

A few examples of visual discrimination exercises follow. Each example could be developed by the teacher into a full page of work. In every case the child is to underline the object, figure, part of a word, or word which is identical to the stimulus in the box at the beginning of each row. See Figures 2-10. These exercises are designed to help develop the following skills:

1. Identification of similar geometric figures.
2. Identification of geometric figures with finer discriminations.
3. Identification of common objects with slight differences.
4. Recognition of similar digits.

5. Identification of letters and small words.
6. Finding a given letter in words of a sentence.
7. Finding identical elements at the beginning of words.
8. Finding identical elements at the end of words.
9. Recognizing "word families."

FIGURE 2

Underline the figure that is exactly like the sample at the left.

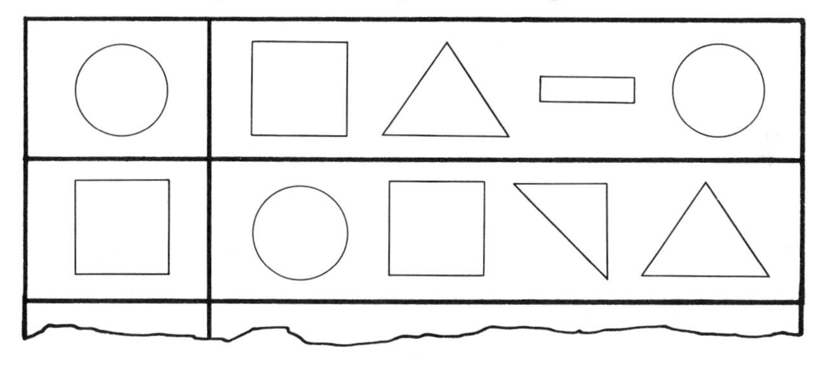

FIGURE 3

Underline the figure that is exactly like the sample at the left.

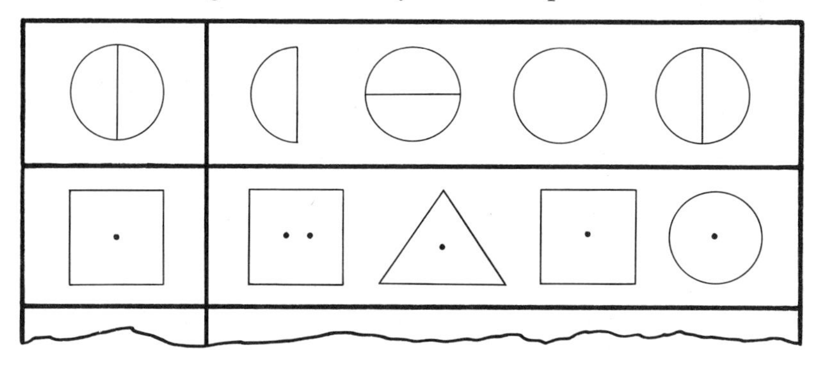

FIGURE 4

Underline the object that is exactly like the one at the left.

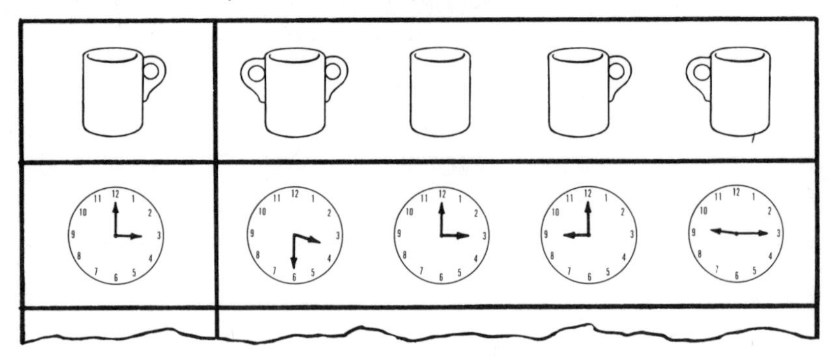

FIGURE 5

Underline the number that is exactly like the sample on the left.

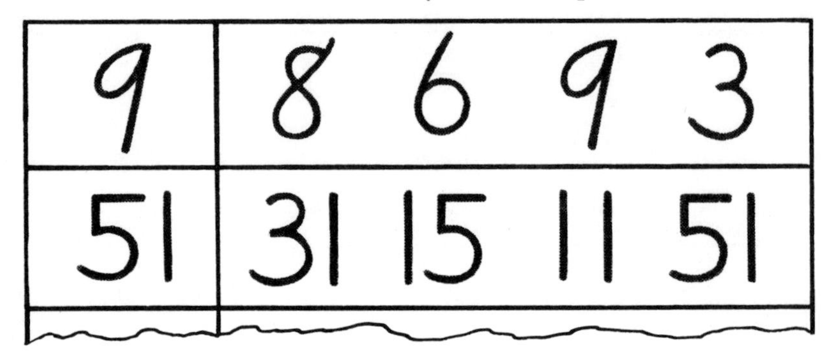

FIGURE 6

Underline the letter or word that is exactly like the one at the left.

M	N	W	M	Z	U
WHO	HOW	WON	WHO	WAH	

FIGURE 7

Underline each letter in the sentence which is like the sample at left.

a	a small black ant ate it all.
l	a small lady led the lads.

FIGURE 8

Underline the beginning of each word that is exactly like the sample.

shall	Sally	shot	hall	shut
from	frog	flap	fry	free

FIGURE 9

Underline the ending of words which are exactly like the sample.

hat	hit	hot	cat	has
home	come	cane	love	same

FIGURE 10

Underline the ending of words which are exactly like the sample.

hill	bell	mill	fill	call
ball	fall	pill	call	halt

Recognizing Words. The objective of the various experiences in the visual readiness program is to prepare the child for making very fine visual discriminations between words which look very much alike. It is as easy for a person who reads to see the difference between *cat* and *dog* as it is for the six-year-old to see the difference between *a* cat and *a* dog. Yet the child beginning to read must very rapidly develop the ability to distinguish between hundreds of written word symbols.

Prior to the use of pre-primers and long after their introduction, most teachers will provide classroom activities aimed at helping children to learn to recognize words. Teachers will employ different methods, but most prefer to teach words related to the child's actual experience. Discussion of the experience method and the use of experience charts is found in Chapter 4, "Beginning Reading." Examples of readiness experiences commonly used to help children in word recognition are briefly described here.

1. *Child's name.* Probably the easiest word to teach a child is his own name. He sees his name on his readiness book and on his pictures and drawings, which the teacher displays. In addition, there will be many occasions when the teacher will write pupils' names on the board for birthdays, committees, special assignments, and the like. The child will notice similarities between his own name and other pupils' names and will learn a few words in this manner.

2. *Color names.* To teach color names, large circles cut from solid-color construction paper can be placed on the blackboard or a table. Names of colors are printed on white cards. The pupil selects a card,

says the word, and places the color name on the proper colored circle.

3. *Matching words with pictures.* All children in the readiness group are capable of identifying a great number of objects and pictures of objects. Familiar pictures are found and word names are printed on separate cards: *car, swing, duck, cow, house.* Each child selects a word and places it beneath the proper picture.

4. *Objects in classroom.* A word card is made for familiar objects in the classroom such as door, table, window, book, chair. A child selects a word card, shows it to the group, and touches the object.

5. *Following directions.* Words previously studied can be used in "direction sentences" printed on heavy paper or oaktag. A child selects a sentence, reads it aloud, and does what it suggests: *walk to the door; clap your hands; ask John to stand.*

In any exercise that uses single words as stimuli, the teacher can ask that the word be used in a sentence. As she writes on the board, she pronounces each word and then the whole sentence. Emphasis can be placed on visual clues found in words, on the sentence as a meaning unit, and on left-to-right progression in reading.

Left-to-Right Sequence. It is important that during the readiness period and beginning reading stages children learn that the eyes move from left to right across the page while reading. There is apparently only one reason why teachers would neglect this skill: they might think that all children have mastered it. It is easy to project this ability onto children because, to adults who have learned to read, the technique appears to be one of the most simple of the procedures which make up reading. It is also true that the majority of children learn the proper sequence without trouble. A child may identify words without realizing that the conventional way to interpret words and sentences is left to right. However, embarking on the next steps in learning to read without having mastered this response can develop other serious and harmful reading habits including reversals, omissions, losing the place, and pointing with the finger. This skill should never be taken for granted by the teacher and "overlearning" it would certainly be justified.

There are a number of ways in which left-to-right sequence can be emphasized. Readiness workbooks contain training exercises calling for a line to be drawn from left to right over a series of dots. Sometimes the point of such an exercise is not grasped if the child fails to relate it to reading. A large square can be drawn on the blackboard with short horizontal lines representing words. The teacher states, "Let's play that this is a page from a book. The heavy little lines are words. Where should I start reading?" Children can draw a line through the "words" moving from left to right. In using experience charts the teacher can demonstrate left-to-right reading with hand or pointer.

Rearranging the Pictures. This exercise consists of two or more picture cards which tell a story when arranged properly from left to right. The cards are laid out in improper arrangement and after a child corrects the sequence he relates the story the cards tell. Telling the story forces him to progress from left to right, note details, see relationships, and organize the material in a logical manner. Figure 11 illustrates two teacher-made series. A pupil's story for each example is given here:

> Story A. "The tallest candle should be in the first picture—then it burns down a little and the third picture shows it real small."
>
> Story B. "Mother is baking pies. In the first picture she puts one on the table, then two on the table. In the third picture there are three pies."

Contact with Books, Stories, and Pictures. A child may come to school with an interest in learning to read, and this interest may grow or it may be inhibited by school experience. Practically all children can be held spellbound by a good story well told. After hearing the story, a picture of some dramatic incident in the story can be used to focus discussion and comment or to enhance understanding. When the teacher reads stories, she plants the idea in the children's minds that reading is the key to the enjoyment associated with the story. This is one important way to arouse interest in reading.

It is very important that the child have access to numerous books. The actual handling of books, turning pages, studying pictures, and the like, are an important part of readiness for reading. Most basal reader series contain good art work, are colorful, emphasize the story approach, and hold the student's interest until he moves on to the next higher level. However, in the case of a poor reader, the contin-

FIGURE 11

A. "The candle is burning."

B. "Mother is baking pies."

ued, uninterrupted diet of one or two books can color attitudes toward reading. The teacher and the school must assume responsibility for having available numerous good supplementary books at various reading levels.

Using Pictures. The use of pictures is an excellent method of drawing children to books. A picture illustrating a familiar story may give the child a sense of security. On the other hand, a picture illustrating a story new to the child may be so exciting that he will want to hear the story. If the teacher has made it clear that she will, on occasion, read stories selected by pupils, the child will have an added incentive to seek and find a "good story." If the class enjoys "his story," he will experience keen satisfaction that will be associated with the reading process; at the same time, he will reinforce the knowledge that he can get "meaning" from pictures. After selecting a picture illustrating an unknown story, the child can be invited to tell what he thinks the story will be. Using this technique, the teacher can get some measure of the child's creative ability and his language facility. The use of pictures can help develop various other needed skills such as visual discrimination, attention to detail, and extension of concepts.

AUDITORY DISCRIMINATION

There appears to be a lack of agreement in experimental data as to the relationship between learning to read and auditory discrimination. This is due in part to the fact that in the literature the term auditory discrimination is found to include such abilities as discrimination between the pitch of musical tones, discrimination between the intensity of sounds, and acuity in hearing different frequencies in the speech range. In general, such factors do not differentiate between good and poor readers.[37]

There are, however, studies which indicate that impaired readers lack skill in the discrimination of speech sounds. Robinson points out that this skill is linked to success in reading on two counts: its relation to language and speech, and its role in phonic analysis.[38] Durrell and Murphy state, "Although there are many factors which combine to determine the child's success in learning to read, it is apparent that his ability to notice the separate sounds in spoken words is a highly important one."[39] The authors indicate that most children who come to the Boston University Reading Clinic with reading ability below first grade level are unable to discriminate between speech sounds in words. Tests usually reveal that the problem of these children is not a hearing loss but an inability to discriminate between minute differences in speech sounds.

---

[37] Maynard C. Reynolds, "A Study of the Relationships Between Auditory Characteristics and Specific Silent Reading Abilities," *Journal of Educational Research,* XLVI (1953), 439-49; Lester R. Wheeler and Viola D. Wheeler, "A Study of the Relationship of Auditory Discrimination to Silent Reading Abilities," *Journal of Educational Research,* XLVIII (1954), 103-13.

[38] Helen M. Robinson, "Factors Which Affect Success In Reading," *Elementary School Journal,* LV (1955), 263-69.

[39] Donald D. Durrell and Helen A. Murphy, "The Auditory Discrimination Factor in Reading Readiness and Reading Disability," *Education,* LXXIII (1953), 556-60.

An illustration was recently provided by a third grade boy who read the word *wish* as *woush*. When asked, "What did you call this word?" he responded "woush." The teacher said, "You mean *wish* don't you?" He replied, "Sure, that's right, *woush*." The child who repeatedly says *tauk* for *talk*, *with* for *width*, *mus* for *must*, and *except* for *accept* is laying the foundations for trouble in later work in phonetic analysis as well as in spelling. After a child has said *artic* or *Febuary* fifty to a hundred times, he does not hear *arc tic* or *Feb ru ary* even if enunciated clearly by another person. When children approximate the sound of words, they reinforce these imprecise sounds each time they say them.

Hildreth asserts that the rapid noting of auditory clues results in more efficient reading.[40] Betts stresses a substantial relationship between a child's inability to name the letters and impaired reading. He adds that this does not imply that rote memorization of the alphabet is a desirable practice.[41] Barbe and others compiled the types of reading difficulties found among eighty remedial readers receiving help at a reading clinic. More than forty different problems were noted and tabulated. The weakness showing the highest incidence was sound of letters not known (found in 95 per cent of cases at the primary and 62 per cent at the intermediate age levels).

Other studies suggest the importance of the ability to synthesize or fuse phonetic elements of words.[42] Hester, reporting data gathered on approximately 200 children admitted to a reading laboratory, states that blending of consonant sounds was particularly difficult for these children.[43] Another study of over one hundred remedial readers (retarded two years or more on the basis of M.A.) indicated that these impaired readers were below average on auditory memory span as measured by specific subtests on the Stanford Binet.[44]

---

[40] Gertrude H. Hildreth, "The Role of Pronouncing and Sounding in Learning to Read," *Elementary School Journal*, LV (1954), 141-47.

[41] E. A. Betts, "Practical Considerations Based on Research," *Elementary English*, XXXIII (1956), 357-71.

[42] Robert L. Mulder and James Curtin, "Vocal Phonic Ability and Silent Reading Achievement: A First Report," *Elementary School Journal*, LVI (1955), 121-23.

[43] Kathleen B. Hester, "A Study of Phonetic Difficulties in Reading," *Elementary School Journal*, XLIII (1942), 171-73.

[44] Florence C. Rose, "The Occurrence of Short Auditory Memory Span Among School Children Referred for Diagnosis of Reading Difficulties," *Journal of Educational Research*, LI (1958), 459-64.

Sometimes a child can make progress in beginning reading by relying heavily on sight word recognition, but he can rarely become a facile, independent reader without the ability to sound out unknown words. The readiness and beginning reading program should provide sufficient experience and drill to assure that every child develops a good foundation in auditory discrimination. Some children will need much more instruction in this area than will others. A few suggestions follow.

Drill on Initial Letter Sounds. The teacher: "Listen carefully. I am going to say a word and I want you to think of any word that begins with the same sound." She then gives several examples such as *l*ady, *l*ake, *l*ine, *l*ook, emphasizing the sound of *l.* Next, other initial consonants are used—*m, c, p, b,* etc. The particular order of introducing initial sounds is not crucial and can vary with the individual teacher's preference. In all hearing-sounding exercises the teacher should make sure all children have an opportunity to participate. In this way, children who need further help in this skill can be identified.

Use children's names. "Listen to the sound that begins Mike's name—*M*ike. Can you think of any other children's first names which begin with this sound?" (Mary, Mark, Marcia) The beginning sound should be emphasized but not distorted.

Use pictures. Cut small pictures from magazines or catalogues and paste a number of them on a blank sheet of paper. Children select and name those which begin with the same letter sound (*b*icycle, *b*aby, *b*all; *c*ap, *c*ane, *c*ow; *t*iger, *t*elevision, *t*able).

Similar Sounds at the Ends of Words. The same procedure that is used with initial letter sounds is followed here, using words that rhyme. If the teacher selects the word *tall,* she stresses the likeness of the sound in words like *ball, call, tall, fall.* These words can be printed on the chalkboard to emphasize the visual likeness. It should be kept in mind that such workbook and teacher-made exercises can result in visual training only if they are done individually as seat work. To incorporate auditory training the children must say and hear the sounds being dealt with.

Hearing Differences at Beginnings or Ends of Words. Three or four words are clearly enunciated by the teacher, all but one of which begin or end like the first word pronounced (*p*en, *p*in, been, *p*each;

car, tall, tar, far). The child repeats the one that is different. Exercises such as this can help develop auditory discrimination and auditory memory.

Eye and Ear Training. Combination eye and ear training usually comes after children have learned to recognize letters and some words. A series of work sheets can be prepared using single letters, letter blends, or words.

A. *The teacher says one of the letter symbols in each box and the child circles what he hears (N—P—B—D).*

(N) M R	B (P) D	S C (B)	T B (D)

B. *The teacher pronounces one word in each series (flap, cap, tap, went) and the child underlines that word.*

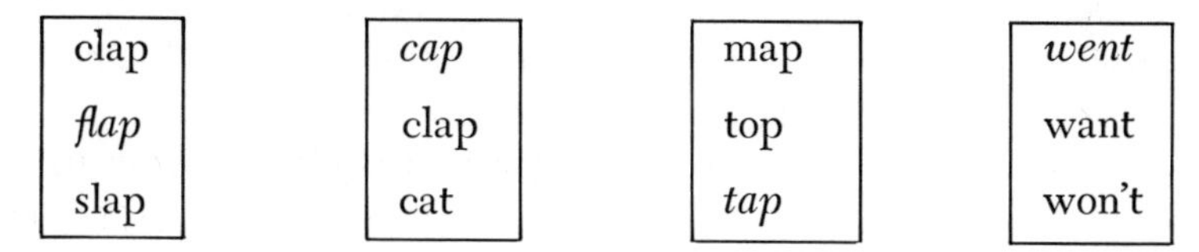

C. *The child marks the word in each box which rhymes with the stimulus word the teacher pronounces (am, land, jump, day).*

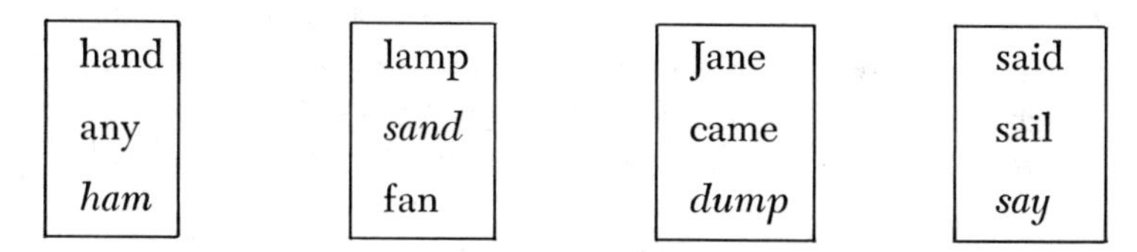

SUMMARY

Learning to read is (in one sense) an extension of language skills which the child has already developed. Yet reading calls for several skills which are very much different from those previously learned. Specific examples include visual discrimination of word forms and auditory discrimination of speech sounds. Failure to make adequate progress in these skills will inevitably slow or derail the entire developmental process of reading. Despite the importance of these factors, preparing for reading involves many other skills and capacities. Growing into reading is part of the child's total growth pattern. Certainly social-emotional factors are the key to success or failure in beginning reading for some children. These factors are not measured on reading readiness tests, and possibly this may be one reason why the predictive value of these tests is not higher.

The readiness period should not be thought of as ending with a calendar date or dealing with a limited number of specific skills measured by readiness tests. The length of the readiness period should vary for different children, since no pre-determined school schedule could possibly fit all children's development. The readiness program does not attempt to remove individual differences among pupils. It does give the school the opportunity to work with children who have deficiencies in skills which are believed to be important to progress in reading. No part of the readiness period should be thought of as a waiting period. Preparing for reading implies activity on the part of the child and a deliberate structuring of experiences on the part of the school.

Concern for a child's readiness to read is highly justifiable. Expecting a child to read before he is ready violates an important principle of teaching reading. The chief aim of the readiness period is to assure that children get off to a good start in learning to read. Experiencing failure in the early stages of learning to read can lead to attitudes which have far-reaching influence on later development.

YOUR POINT OF VIEW?

What is the basis for your agreement or disagreement with each of the following propositions?

1. Reading readiness tests could also be defined as intelligence tests.

2. The extent to which pictures are used in beginning reading materials is unsound since some children form the habit of depending on the picture clues rather than mastering words as sight words.

3. Language usage is the best single indicator of a child's mental ability.

4. Teaching children to listen is in general neglected in the American elementary school.

5. "Context clues" are of little importance in first grade when instruction centers around a basic reader series because of "controlled vocabulary." (Be sure to use a representative basic reader series to illustrate your point of view.)

BIBLIOGRAPHY

Anderson, Irving H., and Dearborn, Walter F. *The Psychology of Teaching Reading.* New York: The Ronald Press Co., 1952, Chap. 2.

Baker, Emily V. "Reading Readiness Is Still Important," *Elementary English,* XXXII (January, 1955), 17-23.

Banham, Katherine M. "Maturity Level for Reading Readiness: A Check-list for the Use of Teachers and Parents as a Supplement to Reading Readiness Tests," *Educational and Psychological Measurement,* XVIII (Number 2, 1958), 371-75.

Betts, E. A. "Practical Considerations Based on Research," *Elementary English,* XXXIII (October, 1956), 357-71.

Bigelow, Elizabeth. "School Progress of Underage Children," *Elementary School Journal,* XXXV (November, 1934), 186-92.

Bond, Guy L., and Tinker, Miles A. *Reading Difficulties: Their Diagnosis and Correction.* New York: Appleton-Century-Crofts, Inc., 1957, 84-92.

Bremer, Neville, "Do Readiness Tests Predict Success in Reading?" *Elementary School Journal,* LIX (January, 1959), 222-24.

Broom, M. E., Duncan, M. A., Stueber, J., and Emig, D. *Effective Reading Instruction* (2nd ed). New York: McGraw-Hill Book Co., Inc., 1951.

Buros, O. K. (ed.). *Mental Measurement Yearbook.* Brunswick, New Jersey: The Gryphon Press.

Cappa, Dan. "Kindergarten Children's Spontaneous Responses to Storybooks Read by Teachers," *Journal of Educational Research,* LII (October, 1959), 75.

Carter, Lowell Burney. "The Effect of Early School Entrance on the Scholastic Achievement of Elementary School Children in the Austin Public Schools," *Journal of Educational Research,* L (October, 1956), 91-103.

Deputy, E. C. *Predicting First Grade Reading Achievement,* Columbia University Contributions to Education, No. 426, New York, Bureau of Publications, Teachers College, Columbia University, 1930.

Durrell, Donald D., and Murphy, Helen A. "The Auditory Discrimination Factor in Reading Readiness and Reading Disability," *Education,* LXXIII (May, 1953), 556-60.

Edmiston, R. W. and Peyton, Bessie. "Improving First Grade Achievement by Readiness Instruction," *School and Society,* LXXI (April, 1950), 230-32.

Gans, Roma. "How Do We Know When Children Are Ready to Read?" *Childhood Education,* XXVI (December, 1949).

Gates, Arthur I. *The Improvement of Reading* (3rd ed.) New York: The Macmillan Co., 1947, Chap. 6.

Gates, A. I. "The Necessary Mental Age for Beginning Reading," *Elementary School Journal,* XXXVII (March, 1937), 497-508.

Gilbert, Luther C. "Genetic Study of Eye Movements in Reading," *Elementary School Journal,* LIX (March, 1959), 328-35.

Goins, Jean Turner. *Visual Perceptual Abilities and Early Reading Progress.* Chicago: University of Chicago Press, Supplementary Educational Monographs Number 78, 1958.

Gray, Lillian, and Reese, Dora. *Teaching Children to Read* (2nd ed.). New York: The Ronald Press Company, 1957.

Gray, W. S. "Summaries of Research in Reading," *Journal of Educational Research.* (February issue each year.)

Hackett, Herbert. "A Null Hypothesis: There Is Not Enough Evidence," *Education,* LXXV (January, 1955), 349-51.

Harrison, M. Lucile. *Reading Readiness.* Boston: Houghton Mifflin Co., 1939.

Heilman, Arthur. "Listening and the Curriculum," *Education,* LXXV (January, 1955), 283-87.

Henig, Max S. "Predictive Value of a Reading Readiness Test and of Teacher Forecasts," *Elementary School Journal,* L (September, 1949), 41-46.

Hester, Kathleen B. "Teaching Every Child to Read." New York: Harper & Brothers, 1955, Part 2.

———. "A Study of Phonetic Difficulties in Reading," *Elementary School Journal,* XLIII (November, 1942), 171-73.

Hildreth, Gertrude H. "The Role of Pronouncing and Sounding in Learning to Read," *Elementary School Journal,* LV (November, 1954), 141-47.

Hilliard, G. H., and Troxell, Eleanor. "Informational Background as a Factor in the Reading Readiness Program," *Elementary School Journal,* XXXVIII (December, 1937), 255-63.

Karlin, Robert. "The Prediction of Reading Success and Reading Readiness Tests," *Elementary English,* XXX (May, 1957), 320-22.

Kottmeyer, William. *Teachers Guide for Remedial Reading.* St. Louis: Webster Publishing Co. (1959), 49-64.

Lee, J. M., Clark, W. W. and Lee, D. M. "Measuring Reading Readiness," *Elementary School Journal,* XXXIV (May, 1934), 656-66.

McCracken, Glenn. "Have We Over-Emphasized the Readiness Factor?" *Elementary English,* XXIX (May, 1952), 271-76.

McKee, Paul. *The Teaching of Reading in the Elementary School.* Boston: Houghton Mifflin Co., 1948.

Monroe, Marion. *Children Who Cannot Read.* Chicago: University of Chicago Press, 1932, 9.

Moreau, Margaret. "Long Term Prediction of Reading Success," *California Journal of Educational Research,* September, 1950, 173-76.

Morphett, Mabel V., and Washburne, Carleton. "When Should Children Begin to Read?" *Elementary School Journal,* XXXI (March, 1931), 496-503.

Mulder, Robert L., and Curtin, James, "Vocal Phonic Ability and Silent Reading Achievement: A First Report," *Elementary School Journal,* LVI (November, 1955), 121-23.

Peck, Leigh, and McGlothlin, Lillian E. "Children's Information and Success in First Grade Reading," *Journal of Educational Psychology,* XXXI (December, 1940), 653-64.

Poling, Dorothy L. "Auditory Deficiencies of Poor Readers," *Clinical Studies in Reading.* Supplementary Educational Monographs, University of Chicago. Chicago: University of Chicago Press, 1953. No. 77, 107-11.

Pratt, Willis E. "A Study of the Differences in the Prediction of Reading Success of Kindergarten and Non-Kindergarten Children," *Journal Educational Research,* XLII (March, 1949), 525-33.

Prothro, E. T., and Teska, P. T. *Psychology: A Biosocial Study of Behavior.* Boston: Ginn & Company, 1950, 468.

Ragan, William B. *Modern Elementary Curriculum.* New York: Holt, Rinehart & Winston, Inc., 1953, 4.

Reynolds, Maynard C. "A Study of the Relationships between Auditory Characteristics and Specific Silent Reading Abilities," *Journal of Educational Research,* XLVI (February, 1953), 439-49.

Robinson, Helen M. "Factors which Affect Success in Reading," *Elementary School Journal,* LV (January, 1955), 263-69.

Rose, Florence C. "The Occurrence of Short Auditory Memory Span among School Children Referred for Diagnosis of Reading Difficulties," *Journal of Educational Research,* LI (February, 1958), 459-64.

Stone, Clarence R. *Progress in Primary Reading.* St Louis: Webster Publishing Co., 1950, Chap. 7.

Vernon, M. D. "The Development of Visual Perception in Children," *Education,* LXXVIII (May, 1958), 547-49.

Wachner, Clarence. "Listening in an Integrated Language Arts Program," *Elementary English,* XXXIII (December, 1956), 491-96.

Washburne, Carleton. "Individualized Plan of Instruction in Winnetka," *Adjusting Reading Programs to Individuals,* ed. Wm. S. Gray. Chicago: University of Chicago Press, 1941, 90-95.

Wepman, Joseph M. "Auditory Discrimination, Speech, and Reading," *Elementary School Journal,* LX (March, 1960), 325-33.

Wheeler, Lester R., and Wheeler, Viola D. "A Study of the Relationship of Auditory Discrimination to Silent Reading Abilities," *Journal Educational Research,* XLVIII (October, 1954), 103-13.

Williams, Gertrude H. "What Does Research Tell Us about Readiness for Beginning Reading?" *The Reading Teacher,* VI (May, 1953), 34-40.

Wilson, Frank T., and Flemming, Cecil W. "Correlations of Chronological Age, Mental Age and Intelligence Quotient with Other Abilities and Traits in Grade I," *Journal of Genetic Psychology,* L (June, 1937), 323-37.

Wilt, Miriam E. "A Study of Teacher Awareness of Listening as a Factor in Elementary Education," *Journal Educational Research,* XLIII, 626-36.

Witty, Paul A., and Sizemore, Robert A. "Studies in Listening I," *Elementary English,* XXXV (December, 1958), 538-52.

———. "Studies in Listening III," *Elementary English,* XXXXI (February, 1959), 130-40.

———. "Studies in Listening II," *Elementary English,* XXXXI (January, 1959), 58-70.

Yoakam, Gerald A. *Basal Reading Instruction.* New York: McGraw-Hill Book Co., Inc., 1955, Chap. 7, 103-19.

chapter 3

BEGINNING READERS

The following discussion deals with the relationship between the cultural and educational environment of beginning readers and the formation of attitudes toward self and reading. The environment in which beginning reading takes place has a vital influence on potential learners. This educational and cultural environment should never result in standardized instruction. Pupils are not interchangeable parts within a classroom; each learner is a separate psychological component.

There are critics of American education who believe our schools have a laissez-faire attitude toward learning the three R's. The fallacy of this premise is nowhere so strongly apparent as in the case of beginning reading. Children become eligible for reading instruction on the questionable basis of chronological age. During their first year of formal instruction, whether ready or not, they are expected to achieve an arbitrary level of competence in reading. If a child shows no interest or ability, then the home and school either consciously or unconsciously use coercive means of social control and pressures to motivate the child to achieve. This cultural behavior grows out of the extremely high value our society places on reading ability. This high value in turn determines to some degree the attitudes of both parents and school. The following is an illustration.

A group of teachers and administrators were discussing the problem of how to deal with retarded readers when it was established that low intelligence was not the causative factor. Various proposals for remedial teaching were discussed. Suddenly the tenor of the meeting was changed when a speaker made the following statement:

"We all know that there are tremendous individual differences among pupils in every type of skill performance—music, athletics, composition, creativity, oral expression, computation, reasoning, and achievement in all subject matter courses. We accept individual difference in these areas, but not in reading. Although we find great differences in reading skill in every classroom, we insist that all children should be reading at an arbitrary level which we refer to as grade level. The inferior reader must 'be taught' to read at this arbitrary level whether or not we can teach him, whether or not he can learn, and whether or not he is interested. Do we really believe that we never meet a child, even though he is not below average in intelligence, who is just not going to learn to read?"

The idea was promptly rejected with practically no discussion. Discussion of other ideas followed but after a period of time the moderator asked the group to consider the question expressed above —"Do we have a tendency to reject the idea of individual differences in reading ability and accept those differences in every other facet of human growth and development?" In the discussion it was finally suggested that the community will not entertain the idea that children may lack the maturity to deal with the reading process once they have been accepted by the school for instruction.

Books on psychology and the teaching of reading stress the large range of individual differences among children in reading achievement. Educators, bolstered by additional evidence from classrooms, have nevertheless been unable to convince the community at large that differences among learners are instrumental in producing differences in learning. The pressure from the community and the fact that the curriculum is based on reading skill may partially explain certain school practices. The curriculum of the school rests on the premise that children in a given classroom read at or near a particular level. Once the curriculum and graded reading materials have been determined, the tendency is to try to fit the learner to the materials. It is much easier to cling to an original false premise than it is to revise the curriculum and the grade level system to fit the facts of learner variability.

The reaction of the school and the home to reading skill has a very pronounced effect on the beginning reader. Children cannot help seeing the importance which is attached to learning to read. Many beginning readers must fail because success is measured by an arbitrary criterion, grade level achievement. We will look briefly at the way in which attitudes and later behavior are influenced during the beginning reading period.

ATTITUDES TOWARD SELF AND ADJUSTMENT

Among educators, parents, or psychologists there would be few dissenters to the proposition that "getting the right start" in learning to read is of the greatest importance. For some children who experience difficulty, a poor start is often the key to later reading difficulty as well as a factor in maladjustment. The fact that some children can fail in the beginning stages of reading and still develop into adequate readers and well-adjusted individuals does not in the least militate against the fact that the beginning stage in reading is extremely important. It is during this period that the child develops attitudes toward self, toward reading, and toward competition. These attitudes, in turn, are related to the motivations which may arouse anti-social behavior.

The child's attitude toward self is influenced by the attitudes of others toward him. There are parental reactions toward him as their child and as a learner, possibly complicated by an unconscious comparison of him with siblings. The teacher in turn reacts to the child as a learner, to his home and parents, and to the child as a problem if he develops behavior not condoned by the school. The child senses that his parents and teacher feel that learning to read is extremely urgent. Pressures from home, school, and self do not always result in learning. There are many activities which may call for intense competition, but in most cases it is optional with the individual whether he elects to compete. In the elementary schools there is not a choice of curriculums, one including reading and the other not. The curriculum is *based* on reading. The non-reader has no place to hide except behind the defenses he can devise. Unfortunately, the defenses he develops are not honored by the society in which he lives as substitutes for reading. Examples of these defenses are:

I'm too dumb to read
Don't-care attitude
Aggression
Withdrawal, daydreaming
Compensation

Self-confidence is very important for the beginning reader. The child who lacks confidence in his own ability is likely to over-react when he encounters difficulty in learning reading. It is true that the type of home the child comes from and the relations he has had with parents or adults will have already affected his confidence before he gets to school. It is the teacher's task to structure school experiences in such a way that the classroom will be an area of safety rather than a threat. This is one of the most difficult tasks confronting the teacher; it is also one of the most important. The task is difficult because the school is only one of several institutions which parcel out failure and success, ego-satisfaction and frustration. It has no control over the home, neighborhood, or community. Children entering school have patterns of behavior which reflect experiences of rejection, overprotection, success, personal inadequacy, and the like.

Today there are few educators who question that these experiences relate to learning. It is true that the school cannot undo the past of each child, nor can it control the present in the community and home. A child may come to school with feelings of inadequacy so strong and so reinforced by the home that the school cannot satisfy his need for attention and acceptance. But the school can, in many cases, compensate to some degree for the unfulfilled needs of children. Chapter 1 deals with practices found in many schools which militate against effective education. Even if teachers take the position that their only job is to teach, they must still understand that they teach potential learners. Factors which diminish this potential among learners are teaching problems.

An alert and observant teacher can see many clues which suggest how a particular child fits in with, or is accepted by, the peer group. Four children are playing in the sand box. Eddie approaches with the intention of joining the group, but is met with: "Get away from here!" "You can't play with us." "There's no more room—let us alone." These responses in themselves are not atypical of six-year-olds. What the teacher has to discover is whether this is just a group of "haves" protecting their domain, the sandbox, from a "have not," or whether this is an illustration of the group's rejection of Eddie.

There are two types of behavior, over-shyness and aggression, which pose special problems for the teacher and special threats to the learning situation. These behaviors are vastly different, yet it is safe to conclude that the same drives are often behind these apparent opposites in behavior. The shy and the aggressive child both desire responses from others. Each has learned the behavior patterns which he uses in an attempt to cope with his environment. Each will also need some help in learning to use behavior that will be likely to lead to group acceptance rather than group rejection.

ATTITUDES TOWARD READING

Most first grade teachers would agree that one of the most important aims of the beginning reading period is to help the child develop a positive attitude toward reading. Failure in reading is likely to produce the opposite attitude. When the school sets an arbitrary goal or level of achievement, namely, the reading of first grade material, the child feels that non-success in achieving this arbitrary standard is failure regardless of promotion policies.

A number of experienced teachers were given a conventional checklist of reading difficulties. This was a one-page list of difficulties which appear frequently among retarded readers. The teachers were asked to select the two problems which they thought would:

a) Be most likely to be present in remedial reading cases.

b) Be likely to be the most serious problems present.

The majority of teachers gave as their first choice "aversion to reading." If one thought only in terms of the actual mechanics of reading, he might not include aversion as a reading problem. However, it *is* a problem in working with most reading failures. Once a child has developed a dislike for reading, stemming from failure, he is not likely to give up his aversion as a result of persuasion based on the authoritarian statements that reading is fun, pleasant, or important. The child's dislike of reading is a most logical reaction. The fact that the child in our culture will be told it is an unfortunate response will have little influence on its removal.

LATER DEVELOPMENT IN READING

Attitudes and habits acquired by children during the beginning reading period influence later reading behavior. According to the experience of persons working with impaired readers in the upper elementary and intermediate grades, it is not safe to assume that children will outgrow ineffective reading habits. Poor reading habits seem to feed on themselves and multiply. Common but serious pitfalls which threaten the beginning reader include:

1. Word-calling without comprehension; the mere mechanics of reading is equated with reading.
2. Failure to use punctuation properly. Unless the weakness is overcome, the child can never enjoy reading because he will continually distort or destroy meaning.
3. Failure to develop and use methods of attacking unknown words, i.e., structural analysis, phonic analysis, and context clues.
4. Development of crutches which become substitutes for actual sight recognition of words when the sight-word method is used. An inadequate stock of sight words accompanied by pressure to read beyond one's present ability can lead to numerous bad reading habits such as:
   a) Guessing at unknown words
   b) Miscalling words
   c) Substituting words
   d) Inserting or omitting words
   e) Slow reading

These habits tend to be reinforced with practice rather than to disappear with time.

DEVELOPING INDEPENDENT WORK HABITS

This topic is of considerable importance in beginning reading and is related to attitudes toward reading, later development in reading, and emotional maturity. At the present time there is some concern with whether children are developing independence in work habits and self-responsibility.[1] Despite this concern, it is quite possible that

Habits of working independently, assuming responsibility, and finishing tasks can be developed in all areas of the curriculum. These habits are extremely important, and the school should provide guidance in these facets of social-emotional growth. *(Courtesy of Bexley Schools, Bexley, Ohio; photographer: Arthur Burt, Inc.)*

[1] Most of the March 1956 issue of *Childhood Education,* XXXII, is devoted to the topic "Children Learn Responsibility." *Discipline,* Bulletin 99, Assoc. for Childhood Education, Washington 5, D. C., 1957. This is an informative pamphlet dealing with how self-discipline is achieved by children. Contributions by six authors.

the importance of the relationship between independent work habits (or self-responsibility) and success or failure in reading is underestimated. The data on emotions and reading strongly suggest that learning to read cannot be reduced to a perceptual or associative process, even though reading cannot take place without these functions. Reading is more than the sum of the skills required in reading. There are also psychological factors which are much more difficult to analyze. This supports the hypothesis that reading is a part of the total development of the child.

In any discussion of reading readiness one invariably meets the term *immaturity*. An immature child has not attained a specific level of behavior associated with his chronological age. Lack of responsibility or self-dependence is universally cited as evidence of immaturity. The child of six who has avoided or who has been prevented from developing independence and self-reliance is not likely to become self-reliant and independent in school unless he receives some specific guidance. The point is that immaturity, in the psychological sense, has been learned. The child's behavior may have developed out of the parents' needs to keep the child dependent. It should be kept in mind that one of the easiest things to learn in early life is a pattern of abdicating responsibility. The child who learns this pattern has become accustomed to social controls from without. He will naturally find it difficult to develop self-discipline or controls from within. In this connection, Staiger suggests that some children fail to learn to read because they have never had to do anything and therefore feel that they do not have to learn to read.[2] Delays, procrastination, and lack of self-responsibility can only increase the difficulty of learning to read. In other situations where this behavior was learned, the parents can eventually make a response which resolves the problem. They can hang up the clothes, pick up the toys, write an excuse for the child when he is tardy, and take him to school in the car if he misses the bus. But learning to read is a task which no parent can perform for the child.

The aim of instruction in beginning reading is to make the child an independent reader. It is here that the child will develop habits of reading and study which will help or hinder him throughout his

---

[2] Ralph C. Staiger, "Self Responsibility and Reading," *Education*, LXXVII (1957), 561-65.

academic career. Independent work habits and self-responsibility are essential for children in today's schools because of group instruction in which children have to work out their own problems. Grouping practices create a problem since the teacher must divide her time among several different groups, thus leaving the child on his own during a good part of the time devoted to reading instruction. A recent summary of the literature on development of responsibility in children suggests a number of principles, some of which are abstracted and presented below.[3]

1. Training for responsibility begins early.
2. The child needs guidance from adults.
3. Children can learn responsibility only by practicing it.
4. Intelligent training for responsibility should be different for different children.
5. The child needs to know what is expected of him. This need demands consistency from adults.
6. No child should be expected to achieve perfection.
7. Adult attitudes toward responsibility influence its development in children.
8. Too much as well as too little responsibility can be harmful.

The child who develops independence and self-direction in his work habits early in the process of learning to read is not likely to become a severely retarded reader. The child who loses, or never gains, confidence in himself, the child who cannot work alone, complete tasks, and in general assume some responsibility for learning, is not well prepared to weather a learning crisis. There are a number of ways in which a teacher can help pupils get off to a proper start in developing good work habits.

Give responsibility to all children and not just those who are already confident and at ease. Collecting workbooks or readers, stacking them neatly, cleaning up after art work, arranging chairs after group work, and stopping or beginning a task when requested to do so help develop self-discipline. It should be remembered that children learn best through experience.[4]

---

[3] Betty L. Minton and Dale B. Harris, "The Development of Responsibility in Children," *Elementary School Journal*, LIV (1954), 268-77.

[4] Calvin Reed, "A Sense of Responsibility: Are Classroom Activities Nourishing It?" *Elementary School Journal*, LVIII (1958), 394-97.

When plans have been well laid, children work independently while the teacher is busy with a group activity not involving the entire class. *(Courtesy of St. Paul Public Schools)*

Do not give a child tasks that he does not understand or cannot do. He will lose interest, procrastinate, daydream, and soon conclude that this is what one does in school.

The teacher should never tell her students that she will look at their work when it is finished and then fail to do so. The child wants a reward, and the teacher's approval of the completed task is interpreted as a reward. Set short-term goals which can be readily achieved. The child will then have many experiences of success which he associates with the reading situation.

It is stated above that children should learn to begin and stop activities when requested to do so. If a child is engrossed in a task, such as coloring, printing, or working a page in a readiness book, permitting him to complete it might be better than interrupting and insisting that he join a group to do something else. When grouping is flexible and a good learning climate exists, he will be able to join the group in a few minutes without disrupting the activity. Furthermore, children have a relatively short attention span and become tired even of tasks they enjoy.

If a child works slowly on an activity that the teacher feels should be completed, she can give a moment's help and then praise the child for completing the task, thus instilling the idea that this is the standard of performance which she expects from him. Children's reading behavior should be observed very closely so that no child experiences too much failure and frustration with reading. Children should be praised when they try, even if their accomplishment falls short of arbitrary standards.

EXAMPLES OF BEGINNING READERS

We have discussed the social-educational environment in which beginning readers operate; we will now look briefly at the beginning readers themselves. Experienced teachers understand that the children who constitute any first grade class are tremendously different from each other, and few teachers would subscribe to the notion that a brief period of readiness experience in first grade appreciably narrows the range of individual differences. It is not an objective of the first year of formal schooling to remove individual differences. All children cannot be moved up to the level of the more advanced pupils, and it is educationally indefensible to attempt to hold the advanced pupils on a learning plateau until the slower ones have advanced. Although it is impossible to remove these individual differences, the teacher and school should be aware of them and concerned with them.[5]

The fact that children are so different when they come to school makes it imperative that the teacher discover those differences which are important factors in learning to read. Then she must develop a program of teaching which at its maximum effectiveness will help each child to grow at a rate commensurate with his ability. The teacher must guard against practices and classroom experiences which may damage the child psychologically and inhibit learning in the future. The discussion which follows attempts to show how differences among pupils are related to instruction. The cases used as illustrations were found in one first grade class.

---

[5] See Margaret McKim, *Guiding Growth in Reading* (New York: The Macmillan Co., 1955), 33-4, for an excellent treatment of this problem.

S. W. was a boy of average intelligence who gave the appearance of being shy. He was reluctant to respond in class or to join in the playground activities for fear that he would fail. He would give up easily and make no effort to get help from the teacher when it was needed and was showing no progress in reading. He was socially immature and inadequate in the group. Within three or four months he had, in general, been rejected by the group. On the surface, he seemed to accept this, yet he harbored intense hostility.

He did not manifest this hostility through overt attacks on other children but through such immature behavior as scribbling on another pupil's drawing, breaking another child's pencil, and putting his own coat on a hallway hook in place of another, which he then dropped on the floor. He displayed a tendency to tattle and call the teacher's attention to other pupils' shortcomings. Whatever form his aggression took, he always seemed to get caught.

J. L. was a boy of above average intelligence and, according to the teacher, just the opposite of S. W. She characterized him as being pushy in class, attempting to be the center of everything that went on. He was able to achieve leadership status among the class but still had an insatiable need to be the center of attention and to dominate others. Physically he was more mature than the other boys and extremely well co-ordinated. He was not a problem in the sense of being a bully simply because his superiority in things physical was never questioned.

Despite high ability he made a poor adjustment in class. He was unable to work alone or carry any project through to its conclusion. Instead of doing assigned seat work he would wander around the room in an attempt to get an audience. He got off to a very poor start in reading, as did S. W.

D. P., a girl of high average intelligence, was one of the most mature children in the class. Her language facility was above average and, while not the brightest child in the class, she was as well informed as any. She was accepted by both boys and girls as a leader and yet did not insist on the leadership role. Her social adjustment was excellent both in and out of class. She enjoyed reading from the start and made better than expected progress in beginning reading and continued this same level of performance in the following years.

What were the real differences between these pupils? On the basis of C.A., I.Q., and M.A. they were fairly well equated. All came from homes of higher than average socio-economic status. Each child had been read to a great deal prior to school and since early infancy. Each had rich and varied experiences prior to entering school, which included visits to large cities, to farms of relatives, zoos, and parks, family picnics, rides on trains, long trips by car, and eating out with their families. Each had many books at home. How did they differ?

S. W. was the older of two boys. Both parents set very high standards for him. His parents were perfectionists, and he could never quite measure up to their expectations. He became very aware of this. It was impossible to do anything exactly right. He was always nagged at when he attempted anything, and withdrawal was a most logical response. This response he soon learned and eventually overlearned. His ego was threatened by this inability to please his parents. When he really did wrong he was not rejected or severely punished. In fact, he was treated as an individual, for his parents tried to discover "Why did S. do this?" The closest his psychological needs ever came to being fulfilled was when he was caught in some misbehavior which was a threat to his parents. School simply became a new and different arena, and he used the same weapons and approach, even though, from an adult standpoint, his responses were not the most logical ones available.

Reading became a threat to him very early in school. Like most parents, his were concerned about reading. They wanted him to get a good start. His confidence in himself and in his ability was already undermined, and he started from the premise that he would fail in reading. It is not surprising that with this emotional conflict he was unable to bring his energies to bear on the reading task. As tension from failure mounted, he used responses which further alienated him from people—his parents, peer group, and teacher. Needing acceptance more than anything else, and being denied it, he withdrew from any situation which in his mind might further jeopardize his status.

J. L. was the only child of parents who had both finished college, done graduate work, and acquired professional standing. They were quite concerned with status, but unconsciously. They never verbalized comparisons between J. and members of his peer group. In their own minds such invidious comparisons were a sign of immaturity. Yet their need for J. to succeed, to be the best participant in all types of endeavor, while not perceived by them, was so close to the surface that it was somehow not lost on J. His security became tied up with excelling, with dominating others. Success was the safety region for him. Through it, he could dominate the home; it was the price paid for love, affection, and acceptance. As he grew to school age most of his endeavors were rewarded by success. He was "superior."

Reading was a different story. He did not start school with a superiority in this skill. He found himself in a group where, in one particular skill, he was only average. He seemed never to be interested in reading. As other pupils' superiority in reading became marked, reading became a threat to J. A frontal attack on the problem was not the solution he chose. He elected to compensate. He withdrew from reading, disrupted class activities, interfered with others' learning, and tried to capture attention and maintain his status in numerous ways, none of which seemed logical to adults.

The needs and motives of the two boys were strikingly similar, as were their attitudes toward the reading situation. Yet their overt reactions to a frustrating situation were quite different, so much so that the teacher identified the boys as being "just the opposite." Would knowing the background of each boy, as related here, help the teacher in dealing with their reading problems?

Our third case (D. P.) was not a reading problem. This girl was a well-adjusted, thoroughly accepted child. She was the youngest of several siblings, adored by her family, but not spoiled. She did not have to compete for affection. An outward appearance of the home lives of all three children appeared to be similar. Yet only one of the three had found security at home. Could this factor have had an important relationship to reading?

The three children just described were members of the same first grade class. This class contained over twenty other children, some of whom would merit an equally extensive individual analysis if they were to be understood as beginning readers. Here, only an important fact or two concerning these twenty children will be mentioned; teachers' knowledge or experience will show why these facts are important in beginning reading.

Some of the children were barely old enough to enter school. Others were eight or nine months older. Some had attended kindergarten the previous year, others had not. Three children had attended nursery school since they were three years old. Two of the mothers worked outside the home during those years.

The I.Q.'s of children in this group ranged from 76 to 130. Three children measured 85 or below. Mental age varied as much as 24 months within the group. Education of parents ranged from one year in high school to graduate work in college. Occupation of the parents ranged from manual laborer to physician. Two children had medical records showing excessive illness during childhood. One child wore glasses. There were emotional problems other than S. W. and J. L., mentioned above.

These and many other factors are definitely related to learning to read and to the differences in reading ability which will inevitably emerge in any first grade class. Being able to detect differences and understand their significance is an invaluable aid to the teacher as she plans experiences and sets goals for individuals in her group. From the potential learner's position, having a teacher with this ability to detect subtle but important differences is a form of insurance against being pushed too fast, losing self-confidence, and forming an aversion to school and to reading.

EGO-INVOLVED BEHAVIOR IN THE CLASSROOM

Understanding the term ego-involvement, as used here, does not call for an extensive background in psychology. Teachers, like pupils and parents, have egos and know what it is like to have one's ego crushed. They also know the satisfaction felt when one's abilities and accomplishments are recognized by others.

Pupils like to do those things which are ego-satisfying and tend to dislike and resist doing those things which threaten the ego or the self. Previous discussion has centered around the interaction between the learner and instruction. To posit that this interaction is important is to recognize the importance of the learner's ego. The first grade teacher starts with one advantage that should be exploited to the fullest: *The child is potentially ego-involved in learning to read.* At this stage of his career the child has usually been conditioned to enjoy books and stories. The sense of accomplishment felt when he reads a pre-primer for the first time is probably as great as for any subsequent academic accomplishment. When the child becomes engrossed in the process of learning to read, the effect is to minimize many of the interferences to learning found in the average classroom.

Ego-involvement, if it is not centered on the learning task, can work against the teacher. The following examples of behavior observed in classroom situations will call to mind parallel incidents which teachers have observed. Each incident occurred in a classroom

When reading is a pleasant experience, the child is drawn to the world of books and positive attitudes are formed toward reading. Successful reading fulfills ego needs and can help children in the socialization process. *(Courtesy of Three Lions)*

where the teaching was excellent, preparation of pupils for class discussion was thorough, and motivation of the group was above average.

In a first grade class the children had been divided into several groups, each of which practiced reading a story in a supplementary primer not being used by the class. Each group was to read its story to the class. In order that every pupil could make a contribution, one of the poorer readers was to show the pictures accompanying the story. In one group, a pupil other than the duly appointed one usurped this privilege and was slyly showing the picture from *his* book. The victim of this duplicity promptly and loudly called attention to the infringement. The disruption of the learning activity resulted from the importance the child attached to the ego-satisfying activity of showing the pictures.

A similar situation occurred in another class where five pupils had practiced reading a story in which they each read a predetermined number of lines. When they read this story to the class, one child paused a moment in his reading and the next pupil started to read his remaining lines. The injured party interrupted and loudly asserted, "No, it isn't your turn yet." This behavior interfered with the learning process for the entire class and shows that no child likes to be deprived of his "performance time," with its attendant ego-satisfaction.

In another first grade class a film strip was being shown. The teacher selected children, one at a time, to walk up to the screen and indicate certain words by using a pointer. A motivational peak was reached each time a pupil was to be selected, followed by a lapse in interest until a new selection was to be made. Achieving the role of "demonstrator" was such a strong status-building activity that it worked against the intended learning situation of mastering the content of the film.

In a second grade discussion of pioneers and how they cleared the land to plant crops, one pupil seemed extremely eager to make a contribution and pumped his hand up and down quite vigorously. When called on, his contribution to the topic was nil, but he produced a lengthy story which cast him in the central role: "I looked at some seed yesterday at home, and I remember I said to myself: 'this looks just like the cotton seed we had yesterday in school.' I said it looks just like it and I wondered if it was cotton seed. I was going to bring it to school today. . . ."

One third grade class had studied a particular unit and was now ready to discuss it in class. Prior to the actual discussion, the teacher and pupils had worked out an outline of major points to be discussed and the teacher had listed these points on the board. The outline was to serve both as a stimulus and as a means of keeping the discussion from wandering. One boy near the rear of the room held up his hand to make a contribution on item one, but since the entire class was prepared and responsive, all could not be called on. The discussion moved on through item two and was well into item three when this boy was finally called on. He gave an immediate answer which was in no way related to the question under discussion, but his response was logical and correct for item one.

The response was too spontaneous to support the hypothesis that he was caught without an answer for the question and simply talked to cover up. It was quite apparent that he had a contribution to make during the discussion of item one, and became so emotionally involved in this situation that he failed to make the shift to items two and three. His ego-involvement became a barrier to his own learning and interfered with the group learning situation.

No teacher, regardless of her skill and experience, can prevent such incidents from occurring in her classroom. From such incidents, however, the wise teacher will learn much about the needs of various pupils in her class. She will attempt to harness the children's egos to the reading tasks so that they will work for her instead of against her. She will realize that the more closely the beginning reading materials are related to the child and his interests, the easier it will be for him to become ego-involved in the reading situation. Illustrations of this point were observed in the same classrooms which provided the examples cited above.

John, a bright boy but a poor reader, could not read from the basal readers being used by the class. The teacher had John tell her a story involving one of his recent experiences. The teacher typed this story, using the easiest vocabulary possible. After reading it several times for him, she had John practice reading it. A flash card was made of each word he had difficulty in learning. John's progress in mastering the sight words was slow, but he did make progress. The last step was to fold a page of construction paper and fasten the typed story inside. On the front of this booklet John printed the words *John's Book.* He clutched his book tightly as he rushed out at the close of school. He would now earn praise and acceptance and restore some measure of self-esteem. Reading was less of a threat at that moment than it had been for many weeks.

Another teacher, whose practice it was to secure many different books for her second grade class, was able to help a very poor reader by finding for him a large colorful book with exciting, full-page pictures and very little reading text. Many pupils in the class showed interest in this book and asked if they might have it when Fred finished reading it. Fred was credited with reading a book and this experience attracted him, at least for the present, to books and reading. Every teacher knows how important these experiences are to the child involved. In the previous chapter it was noted that in the pre-reading stage the child's name is probably the first word he learns. In addition *his* birthday is announced on the board, and he learns the words used to designate *his* school, *his* street, *his* town. These relatively difficult words are learned after fewer exposures than are most words he learns during this period and illustrate the importance of ego-involvement in learning.

CONCLUSION

There are marked differences among children as they begin learning to read. Teachers are generally aware of this fact, but classroom practices and habits of thought prevailing in the school and community sometimes tend to slight the significance of these pupil differences. Our society places a high value on reading ability, and as a result all children in the group are expected to progress at a somewhat uniform rate. Failure to do so is a very noticeable failure. When some children in the group do not meet fixed arbitrary standards of achievement, pressures from both school and home increase. Reading is particularly sensitive to pressure because it involves learning a complicated symbol system.

Children as beginning readers are quite pliable, yet there are many who cannot adjust to or profit from a lock-step educational philosophy which treats pupils as interchangeable parts in the classroom. These children may have an initial desire to learn to read, but the type of experience they have can affect their goals and behavior. Reading and other learning tasks prescribed by the school can be interpreted as threatening rather than rewarding.

Ego-involvement is extremely important in learning. A child who fails to meet arbitrary group standards will not experience satisfaction from reading. Even when failure is not present, ego-involvement in learning tasks may lead the child away from the structured activity and thus disrupt learning for himself or others. Too much uniformity of instructional method used with a group that includes a wide range of interests and abilities will not be equally motivating or equally appropriate for each member of the group. This is the sole reason why instruction must be concerned with individual differences.

YOUR POINT OF VIEW?

Would you prefer to defend or to attack the following statements?

1. The teacher, the school environment, and the curriculum inescapably function as barriers to or means of fulfilling the psychological needs of children.

2. If every child in the class were ego-involved in the learning tasks, there would be practically no discipline problems in the classrooms.

3. Early experiences in learning to read have a considerable influence on pupils' later work habits and attitudes toward the school.

4. Despite grouping practices and educators' expressed concern for individual differences among pupils, the grade-level system inevitably results in "teaching to the mean of the group."

5. American schools' emphasis on reading readiness is more apparent than real. The concept of readiness is verbally embraced, but a large number of pupils are subjected to reading instruction before they are ready.

BIBLIOGRAPHY

A. C. E. Bulletin No. 99, *Discipline*. Washington, D. C., 1957.

Anderson, Irving H., and Dearborn, Walter F. *The Psychology of Teaching Reading*. New York: The Ronald Press Co., 1952, Chap. 1.

Blair, Glenn M. *Diagnostic and Remedial Teaching*. New York: The Macmillan Co., 1956, Chap. 13.

Childhood Education, XXXII (March, 1956).

Hymes, James L. Jr. *Behavior and Misbehavior*. Englewood Cliffs, N. J.: Prentice-Hall, Inc., 1955.

McKim, Margaret G. *Guiding Growth in Reading*. New York: The Macmillan Co., 1955, Chap. 3.

Milner, Esther. "A Study of the Relationship between Reading Readiness in Grade One School Children and Patterns of Parent-Child Interaction," *Child Development,* XXII (June, 1951), 95-112.

Minton, Betty L., and Harris, Dale B. "The Development of Responsibility in Children," *Elementary School Journal,* LIV (January, 1954), 268-77.

Preston, Mary J. "Reading Failure and the Child's Security," *American Journal of Orthopsychiatry,* X (1940), 239-52.

Reed, Calvin. "A Sense of Responsibility: Are Classroom Activities Nourishing It?" *Elementary School Journal,* LVIII (April, 1958), 394-97.

Russell, David H. "Reading and the Healthy Personality," *Elementary English,* XXIX (April, 1952), 195-200.

Spache, George D. "Personality Characteristics of Retarded Readers as Measured by the Picture-Frustration Study," *Educational and Psychological Measurement,* XIV (1954), 186-92.

Staiger, Ralph C. "Self Responsibility and Reading," *Education,* LXXVII (May, 1957), 561-65.

Witty, P. A. "Reading Success and Emotional Adjustment," *Elementary English,* XXVII (May, 1950), 281-96.

Woolf, Maurice D., and Woolf, Jeanne A. *Remedial Reading Teaching and Treatment*. New York: McGraw-Hill Book Co., Inc., 1957, Chap. 2.

Zolkos, Helena H. "What Research Says about Emotional Factors in Retardation in Reading, *Elementary School Journal,* LI (1951), 512-18.

chapter 4

BEGINNING READING

Beginning reading is that phase of formal instruction in which children first use reading materials, such as experience charts, pre-primers, primers, and first readers. In this initial stage of reading the child associates the written word symbol with the object it represents.[1] Since beginning reading is the logical extension of a readiness program, there is no break between the two, no point where one ends and the other begins. In a well-organized first grade the transition is so gradual that the children hardly perceive it. The use of pre-primers is seen simply as an extension of work done yesterday and last week. The period of beginning reading should provide intelligent, systematic guidance in activities which make learning to read a meaningful and natural growth process.

OBJECTIVES OF THIS PERIOD

It is understandable that any process as complicated as beginning reading must have many objectives. Some of these objectives have

[1] Kathleen B. Hester, *Teaching Every Child to Read* (New York: Harper & Brothers, 1954), 296.

been dealt with in previous discussions: to structure experiences so that the child feels accepted and develops desirable attitudes toward reading and toward self; to provide for group participation, development of verbal facility, listening ability, and auditory and visual discrimination; to teach left-to-right sequence; and to encourage contact with books, stories, and pictures. Despite the fact that these activities are very appropriate in the reading readiness program, it is apparent that the teacher must not neglect any of these goals when instruction in reading becomes more formal. In addition, the teacher will concern herself with other specific objectives:

1. Arouse and sustain interest in reading.
2. Expand sight recognition vocabulary.
3. Help the child develop means of working out unknown words, using all clues available, such as pictures, configuration of words, context, and structural and phonic analysis.
4. Provide practice in both silent and oral reading.
5. Stress that reading is getting meaning.
6. Provide experiences for developing and extending concepts.
7. Help the child develop smoothness in the mechanics of reading, such as heeding punctuation, reducing the number of regressions, reading with expression, and using correct pronunciation.
8. Encourage the development of independent work habits.
9. Provide individual instruction when needed, based on continuous diagnosis.
10. Keep goals and procedures flexible for individual children.

THE EXPERIENCE CHART

The experience chart is a means of capturing the interests of children by tying their personal experiences to reading activities. The chart, which tells about a shared activity, is a story produced co-operatively by the teacher and the class. This is a natural extension of earlier and less difficult experiences wherein the teacher wrote single words or short sentences on the chalkboard. Examples, cited in a previous chapter, included days of the week, names of months, the seasons, children's birthdays, holidays, captions for pictures, and objects in the room. The experience chart provides practice in a number of developmental skills which are closely related to reading. For example:

1. Oral language usage in the group planning prior to a trip and in recounting the experience, for chart building, after a trip.
2. The give-and-take of ideas as the experience is discussed.
3. Sharpening sensory acuity, particularly visual and auditory, while on excursions.
4. Expanding concepts and vocabulary.
5. Reinforcing the habit of reading from left to right.
6. Experience in learning words as wholes, thus building sight vocabulary.
7. Reading the sentence as a unit.
8. Reading about one's own experiences, emphasizing that reading is getting meaning from printed words.

All of the points cited above are appropriate both to readiness and to beginning reading, and the experience chart should not be thought of as belonging exclusively to one stage of development. The experience chart has merit in proportion to the degree to which certain logical practices are followed. For instance, vocabulary must be simple, and sentences short; a minimum of sentences must be used, and each sentence must contribute to the story. There should be deliberate repetition of common sight words.

PREPARING AN EXPERIENCE STORY

The teacher and children plan for a visit to the zoo, a nearby farm, or the library. Let us assume that the teacher has been able to make all of the necessary arrangements for a trip to the community library. She has arranged for the use of the school bus and has spoken to the librarian who has volunteered to read the class a story and who has set up a display of children's books. When she has the attention of the entire class, the teacher might say, "I talked to Mrs. Winters, the librarian, the other day and she invited all of you to come to the library and look at the new books—maybe some of you would want to take a book home with you. I wonder if it would be fun if we took a trip to the library?"

Experience charts vary as to purpose and difficulty level. Here, early in grade one, children work with a simple chart which stresses sight recognition of a very limited number of words. *(Courtesy of San Diego City Schools)*

CHILDREN: "Let's go!"
"I'd like that."
TEACHER: "If we go, we'll have to make plans first—what are some things we should decide first?"
BILLY: "Can we go today?"
TEACHER: "Billy asks when can we go? We can't go today, we have to make our plans first."
CHILD: "Let's go tomorrow."
TEACHER: "How many would like to go tomorrow?"
(General agreement)

TEACHER: "How shall we get to the library?"
MIKE: "Let's walk."
MARY: "Can we go in a car?"
TEACHER: "Mike suggests we walk, but it's quite a long way from here; Mary suggested we go in a car, but it would take a lot of cars for all of us. Maybe we could go in the school bus."
(Excitement heightens in the class)

The class and the teacher talk about what they should do and what they should not do at the library. Following each discussion, the teacher writes the decision on the board; from this activity an experience chart emerges. The chart itself may not be the most important outcome of this educational endeavor. The children have experienced how the group process works; co-operative planning and individual contributions have resulted in identifying and structuring a goal. The children are now ego-involved in a trip to the library. Their experience chart follows:

PLANS FOR OUR TRIP

We will go to the library.
We will go tomorrow.
We will go in the school bus.
This will be fun.
We can look at books.
We will sit in our chairs.
We will hear a story.

The children enjoyed the trip to the library. Mrs. Winters, the librarian, had three tables of children's books available; she showed where the children's books were kept on the shelves and on a book rack. She talked about how to treat books—not to fold pages or tear the paper cover. The children were permitted to look at the books and the pictures. Finally, Mrs. Winters read them the story *Stone Soup.*[2] The children clapped their hands when Mrs. Winters finished the story. They thanked her and then returned to their classroom on the school bus.

[2] Marcia Brown (New York: Charles Scribner's Sons, 1947).

As children grow in reading skill, the content of experience charts can be expanded and used for many purposes. Charts made earlier in the year are sometimes displayed around the room. Examples above list the characteristics of good listeners and good readers. ***(Courtesy of Bexley Schools, Bexley, Ohio; photographer: Arthur Burt, Inc.)***

That same day they discussed their trip and the things they saw and did and heard. The natural outcome was to "write a story" about their experience. The teacher asked questions and occasionally substituted words to keep the vocabulary reasonable. The following discussion developed the title for the story.

TEACHER: "What shall we call our story?"
BOB: "What we did at the library."
TEACHER: "That's a good suggestion; does anyone else have a name for our story?"
MARY: "I think it should be called 'We have a nice time at the library.' "

TEACHER: "Fine—anyone else?"
RUTH: "Things we did on our trip to the library."
TEACHER: "Those are all fine—we did have a very nice visit, we did learn many things and we did enjoy the story Mrs. Winters read us. Would it be all right to call our story 'Our Trip to the Library'?"

Since the children agreed to the title, she printed it on the chalkboard, saying each word as she wrote it and then reading the entire line, being careful to move her hand slowly from left to right as she read. Next, she inquired what incidents should be related in the story and accepted the various suggestions while attempting to keep the vocabulary as simple as possible. Each line of the story was developed in much the same way as the title was. The teacher was careful to see that all of the students participated. The following chart is the result:

OUR TRIP TO THE LIBRARY

We rode in the school bus.
The bus took us to the library.
We looked at many books.
We sat at tables.
We looked at books and pictures.
Mrs. Winters read us a story.
The story was *Stone Soup.*
We thanked Mrs. Winters.
Our trip was fun.

The teacher read each line as soon as she printed it on the board, again being careful to move her hand under the line from left to right as she read. The teacher and children then read the complete story. Next, a child was asked to point out the line that told how they had traveled to the library, the line that told the name of the story they had heard, the line that told where the children sat in the library, and so forth. In each case the child pointed out the desired line and attempted to read it.

The same chart may be used in other ways. Each line in the chart may be duplicated on a strip of heavy paper: *We thanked Mrs. Winters.* A child is handed a sentence and is asked to find this line on the chart. Individual words may also be placed on oaktag or cardboard and held up by the teacher and a child selected to point out that particular word on the chart: *books, us, bus.* Word cards may be prepared for each word in a particular line. These are handed to a child in mixed order and he is to arrange them in proper order to correspond with the line on the chart. These tasks can be either seatwork or boardwork. The experience chart can be used with the class as a whole and also with various reading groups. After its main use with a unit, it may be referred to incidentally when certain words used on the chart come up in other contexts and in other activities.

THE EXPERIENCE METHOD

The experience chart can be used in any method of teaching reading. But when it is advocated as the chief means of teaching the early stages of reading, the resulting method is designated as the *experience method* or the *experience approach.* Any procedure may have both merits and limitations, and this seems particularly true of the experience approach to teaching reading. Some of the major strengths and weaknesses of this approach are listed below.[3]

ALLEGED ADVANTAGES

1. Reading materials are related to the child's experiences, making for a high degree of motivation.
2. Reading for meaning is stressed.
3. Complete sentences are used, allowing for emphasis on context clues.

---

[3] For a further discussion of the origin, history and detailed analysis of this procedure the reader might consult the following:

Nila B. Smith, *American Reading Instruction* (New York: Silver Burdett Co., 1934), 229-63.

Irving H. Anderson and Walter F. Dearborn, *The Psychology of Teaching Reading* (New York: The Ronald Press Company, 1952), Chap. 7.

C. R. Stone, *Progress in Primary Reading* (St. Louis: Webster Publishing Co., 1950), Chap. 2.

L. A. Lamoreaux and D. M. Lee, *Learning to Read Through Experience* (New York: Appleton-Century-Crofts, Inc., 1943).

Paul McKee, *The Teaching of Reading in the Elementary School* (Boston: Houghton Mifflin Co., 1948), 216-30.

4. Charts permit flexibility in content of reading materials. (Types of desirable experiences usually associated with the method have been cited in the discussion of experience charts.)

ALLEGED DISADVANTAGES

1. It is difficult to control vocabulary. Too many words may be introduced at one time.
2. Basic sight words may not be repeated often enough to insure mastery.
3. When used exclusively as a *method* it puts too much of a burden on the teacher, demands much time and a high level of training.
4. It is difficult to adapt this type of instruction to the needs and abilities of *all* children.
5. It encourages memorization rather than mastery of sight words.

The strengths and weaknesses of the experience method are relative and not inherent in the method itself. Under certain conditions, all of the advantages of the method might be lost through over-emphasis, misuse, or lack of understanding. In other situations the effects of certain of the cited disadvantages could be held to a minimum through a teacher's skill, experience, and clear understanding of objectives. In the writer's opinion, the experience approach is most vulnerable when advocated as a complete method in itself. Most teachers prefer to use the experience chart as a supplement to a basal reader series. This permits certain of the weaknesses to be minimized. The basic readers provide drill on sight vocabulary and control over the introduction of new words. The use of experience charts adds flexibility and interest to the program.

THE BASIC READER APPROACH TO TEACHING READING

The use of a basic reading series is the foundation upon which most of the reading instruction in American schools is built. Basic reader series start with book materials at the readiness level and provide graded materials for each grade level up to the seventh or eighth grade.

READINESS BOOKS

At the readiness level one might find picture books in which a picture or series of pictures suggests a child-centered story. From the pictures the teacher and the pupils develop a story. The more skillful the teacher is in providing background and involving the pupils in participation and interpretation, the more successful the use of these materials will be. Other readiness books may call for children to identify and mark similar objects, letters, or words, to facilitate the development of visual perception. To strengthen auditory discrimination the child will identify two pictures in a group which will rhyme when named. Identifying other pairs of pictures which start with the same sound gives practice in the discrimination of initial sounds.

PRE-PRIMERS

The readiness books are followed by a series of pre-primers, two or three in number, in which the characters are the same ones the children met and talked about in the readiness books. The pre-primers introduce pupils to printed words *along with pictures.* The first few pages may have single words which are "naming words" to go with the picture. Gradually more words and sentences per page are used.

PRIMERS

The primer is the first hard-back book the child uses in school. It carefully builds on what has gone before, using the same characters the children are familiar with and reviewing the words already met, while it introduces 90 to 150 new words.

FIRST READERS

Some series contain a single first reader; others have two (1^1 level and 1^2 level). Different series vary as to vocabulary load introduced, but a range between 315 and 400 words for first grade is representative.

SUPPLEMENTARY MATERIALS

It is becoming more common at all grade levels for basic reader series to include some supplementary books to be used in conjunction with the regular graded series. There has always been an abundant supply of these supplementary materials available at the intermediate level. Recently, good supplementary books have appeared at the early primary level, where they are sorely needed. Some of these are easy reading, introducing very few words other than those already met in the regular basal texts. Others are designed for the more advanced readers and are more difficult and more challenging than the regular graded series.

Other supplementary materials include large poster-size wall charts or spiral-book charts which exactly duplicate a pre-primer. The large picture and large print have obvious advantages for classroom use. There has been considerable emphasis on film strips designed for use with basic reader series. The reading gains reported as resulting from the systematic use of film strips and other visual aids are exceptional.[4]

WORKBOOKS

The readiness books mentioned above actually resemble workbook materials. A separate workbook which parallels each level (pre-primers, primer, and first reader) is available. Seatwork, in the form of workbook exercises, can deteriorate into nothing more than "busy work" if teachers are not careful in its use, or if they do not have time to use it properly. On the other hand, the proper use of workbooks can have considerable educational value. They can be used as diagnostic instruments in that they identify those children who do not understand or who are, at the moment, incapable of doing certain tasks in the reading process. Some children may not have mastered a concept and the workbook will reveal to the teacher what she should emphasize. The workbook can be an aid in helping the child develop self-reliance and independence in work habits.

---

[4] See Glenn McCracken, "Have We Overemphasized the Readiness Factor?" *Elementary English,* XXIX (1952), 271-76; Gerald A. Yoakum, *Basal Reading Instruction* (New York: McGraw-Hill Book Co., 1955), 84-7. Kathleen B. Hester, *Teaching Every Child to Read* (New York: Harper & Brothers, 1955), Chap. 19.

TEACHERS' MANUALS

One of the greatest advantages in using a good series is the availability of excellent teacher guides. These guides are carefully worked out by the authors with the total reading program in mind. Sound laws of learning are followed, specific techniques are suggested, lesson plans are given in great detail, and the reasons for using certain approaches are explained. The beginning teacher would be remiss in not following the teacher guides and in not becoming very familiar with the rationale and concrete suggestions they contain. Experienced teachers might find the detail of these manuals a bit tedious, but they know that they can take what is offered and adapt it in light of their own experience.

The thoroughness and extensive treatment typical of teacher guides is exemplified in the manual for *Getting Ready,* a sixty-four page readiness book.[5] This manual contains a full page of instruction for each page of text whether it is a single picture or a series of letter- or word-matching exercises. In the Gray, *et al.,*[6] series a 256 page teacher's guide is available for use with the pre-primers alone. Considering that these pre-primers contain approximately sixty different words, it is obvious that the guide is thorough and goes beyond the mechanical aspects of instruction at the readiness level. The guide for the first reader in this series also contains approximately 250 pages.

With this type of meticulous concern for every facet of the reading program, the various guides can be excused for sometimes stressing the inevitable as if it were a deliberately planned virtue of the basic readers. It is common practice to find teacher guides making much of the fact that pre-primers, primers, and first readers "do not require children to deal with concepts beyond their experience level." Considering the small number of words found in these materials, it would be a challenge, using only this vocabulary, to confront the child with concepts beyond his experience level. He uses twenty to thirty times this number of words and understands many more.

---

[5] Paul McKee and M. L. Harrison (Rev. ed.; Boston: Houghton Mifflin Co., 1957).

[6] W. S. Gray, A. S. Artley, M. H. Arbuthnot, and L. Gray, "The New Basic Readers," "Curriculum Foundation Series," *Guidebook* to accompany *The Three Pre-Primers.*

The foregoing discussion has touched on the alleged major weakness of the basic reader series. The concern for controlling the introduction of new words puts a limit on the variety of reading material which can be accommodated within the framework of the controlled vocabulary. The teacher must motivate children to identify themselves with the characters and the situations depicted, even though these may be somewhat alien to children of certain socio-economic groups. Without identification, the vicarious experiences gained from reading about a set of middle-class siblings, their parents, and their dog, may not seem half as fascinating as television. If one reads the guides carefully, it will be obvious that a major portion of their content is devoted to suggesting ways and means of bringing in background and of extending the concepts and the meanings actually found in the reading materials. This is important because the child's interest must not be permitted to lag.

SIGHT WORD METHOD

Basal reader series in wide use today embrace two major premises: (1) that the child should learn a number of words as "sight recognition words" before attempting any type of word analysis[7] and (2) that the introduction of new sight words should be systematically controlled. At the present time, most children in American schools are taught by the "word method," sometimes called the sight method or the look-and-say method. They learn words as units even before they are deliberately taught the names and the sounds of the letters making up the words. The aim of instruction is to have the child learn a number of words as sight words before attention is paid to the analysis of words.

A number of reasons have been advanced in support of the educational practice of teaching reading through teaching words, as sight words, rather than starting with the sound of the letters constituting words.

---

[7] C. E. Sloop, H. E. Garrison, and M. Creekmore, *Phonetic Keys To Reading* (Atlanta, Ga.: Economy Co.), is an exception. This system is basically a phonetic approach and is discussed in a later chapter.

1. If a child knows a number of words as sight words (instant recognition), he can be taught to *see* and to *hear* similarities between these known words and the new words he meets. Having a sight vocabulary is an invaluable tool in helping him unlock other words.
2. Learning words as units leads to "whole word perception" as opposed to seeing a word made up of a number of letter parts.
3. Early in the child's career as a reader it is easier for him to learn a number of sight words than it is to learn a set of complicated rules of sounding—and the numerous exceptions to each rule.
4. Many words in English violate one or more rules of sounding. These are often the so-called service words which comprise a large number of the words found in all reading material from primers through college textbooks.
5. Teaching the child to analyze *each word* slows the reader and detracts from the pleasure of reading. This procedure can result in the habit of word-by-word reading or word analyzing if the child develops the idea that "this is reading."
6. Learning words as wholes should condition children to look at all of the word, beginning with the first word and glancing on through.
7. Learning words and reading them in logical combinations makes reading meaning-centered.

If the child learns the words in his pre-primers, he will be prepared for some of the first steps in the process of recognizing new words. In beginning reading the child knows both the meanings and the sounds of the words studied as sight words. It is the printed symbol that he is attempting to associate with the meaning and sound.

Since the sight word method is so widely used, it is obvious that a child who fails, for any reason, to master a number of sight words is at a considerable disadvantage in learning to read. A characteristic of practically all basal reading series in use today is that the same words are repeated line by line and page by page. Reading is simple for children who master these words since they know all but one or two words on each succeeding page. If they master the new words, the next page will be relatively easy. It makes little difference to the child who does not master the words as sight words whether the next page is all new words or all review, since he does not know the words in either case.

No matter how carefully vocabulary is controlled, the beginning reader who does not recognize sight words is a *non-reader.* To illustrate this point, let us look at an excellent and widely used basal reader series as it takes the child through the first grade. The Gray, *et al.,*[8] first grade series consists of three pre-primers: *We Look and See, We Work and Play, We Come and Go;* a junior primer, *Guess Who;* a basic primer, *Fun With Dick and Jane;* and a first reader, *Our New Friends.* Table 3 illustrates the number of word symbols the child is expected to deal with in each step of the first grade reading program, as outlined in this particular series.

A child who does not learn the sight words introduced in the pre-primer is not equipped to proceed to the more difficult books in the series. Success in reading each new book in a series is posited on mastery of the words previously introduced. Those who have mastered the process of reading are likely to lose sight of the many factors which must mesh at a given moment if success in reading is to be achieved. It is much easier to describe how to teach reading than to state specifically how children *learn* this process.

LEARNING A SYMBOL SYSTEM

In order that we may partially recapture the challenge of learning a symbolic process like reading, let us look at a number of symbols known to us and a number which are new. Below on the left are pairs of short word-symbols which are very much alike. For an adult it is extremely simple to distinguish between them. On the right are the

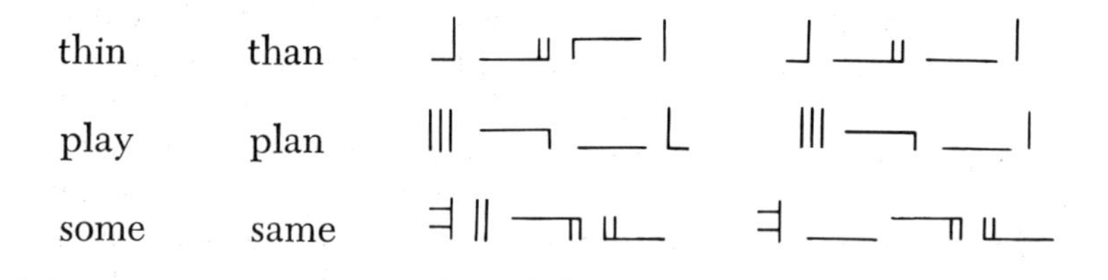

[8] William S. Gray, A. Sterl Artley, May Hill Arbuthnot, and Lillian Gray, *The New Basic Readers,* "Curriculum Foundation Series" (Chicago: Scott, Foresman & Co., Inc., 1951).

TABLE 3

AN ANALYSIS OF ONE BASAL READER SERIES, PRE-PRIMER THROUGH FIRST READER, SHOWING NUMBER OF DIFFERENT WORDS, NUMBER OF NEW WORDS, AND NUMBER OF PAGES AT EACH LEVEL*

	Different words	New words added to previous level	Pages in book	Words introduced in first four books
1st Pre-Primer *We Look and See*	17	—	44	*look, oh, Jane, see, Dick, funny, Sally, Puff, jump, run, Spot, come, Tim, up, and, go, down*
2nd Pre-Primer *We Work and Play*	38	21	60	*work, can, play, father, mother, help, little, big, is, baby, the, my, I, something, blue, make, red, yellow, can, find, boat*
3rd Pre-Primer *We Come and Go*	58	20	88	*said, for, want, here, we, one, three, a, two, you, it, not, to, me, ball, where, in, house, away, cookies*
Junior Primer† *Guess Who*	68	10	88	*now, who, what, get, do, pretty, this, will, with, guess*
Primer *Fun with Dick and Jane*	158	90	151	
First Reader *Our New Friends*	335	177	190	

* "The New Basic Readers" (Chicago: Scott, Foresman and Company, 1951).

† A supplementary book recommended for children who need more experience with the pre-primer level.

same word symbols built from a different alphabet which at this point is unknown to the reader. The new word symbols are no more alike than the words on the left, but it is much more difficult to distinguish between them.

The unknown symbols on the right are actually easier to learn than the ones on the left, for these reasons:

a) All letters are composed of three or fewer straight lines.

b) The lines are always horizontal or vertical (no slanting lines like *A, X, K, M;* no curved lines like *S, C, U;* no combinations of straight and curved lines like *D, B, P,* etc.).

c) The first thirteen letters of this alphabet are composed of long horizontal lines and short vertical lines and the last thirteen letters are composed of long vertical and shorter horizontal lines.

This new alphabet, with its equivalent in English, is found in Figure 12.

FIGURE 12

	A		N
	B		O
	C		P
	D		Q
	E		R
	F		S
	G		T
	H		U
	I		V
	J		W
	K		X
	L		Y
	M		Z

Two short reading passages using this new symbol system are presented below. The purpose is not to present a situation precisely analogous to beginning reading, since the reader will have to study the new alphabet (Figure 12) prior to reading. Attempting to read the passages will illustrate the difficulty of mastering a symbolic task in which the symbols are unknown. In this respect, the task is similar to beginning reading.

There are eleven different letter symbols and twelve word symbols in Passage A. Among the twelve words there are only six different words. Thus the vocabulary was carefully controlled. All of these words are found in the first few pages of pre-primers and have been used thousands of times by the reader. These factors might suggest that this reading exercise will be quite easy. Passage B should be extremely easy to read since, in this sixteen word passage, only four new letters and four new words are introduced. Seventy-five per cent of the words are repeated from the first lesson.

PASSAGE A

PASSAGE B

If you had a little trouble reading these simple passages (translations below*), then the experiment was worth the effort. The objective was to demonstrate that any symbolic process is potentially difficult and that when the symbols appear very much alike it becomes doubly so. Before the child is confronted with a task as exacting as reading passages A or B (above), he will have had many hours of practice aimed at helping him make finer and finer visual discriminations. He will also have had many experiences with the printed form of words in readiness books, in experience charts, and on bulletin boards.

---

*Passage A: look oh look
see baby play
look at baby
play baby play

Passage B: baby likes to play
look at baby play
oh oh see baby
play with me baby

USING BASAL READER SERIES

The purpose here is to deal with the framework of basal programs as designed for the first year of instruction. The major advantages of using a good series include:

1. Modern reader series are characterized by excellent use of pictures and art work.
2. A number of the first books used deal with the same characters, giving children a feeling of familiarity with the material and adding to their confidence in reading.
3. The books are graded to provide systematic instruction from the pre-readiness level through the upper elementary grades.
4. These graded materials permit teachers a great deal of flexibility in dealing with individual differences and in working with children grouped according to attained reading skill.
5. Excellent teacher guides are provided for each book or level. These provide suggestions for a step-by-step teaching program.
6. If used properly, the basic reader series deals with all phases of the reading program, guarding against overemphasis on some aspects and neglect of others.
7. Practice of new skills is introduced at the proper time and in the proper sequence.
8. A great deal of review is provided in deliberate, well-thought-out procedures.
9. To prevent frustration in reading the vocabulary is rigidly controlled.
10. Use of prepared materials saves teachers considerable time.

A WELL BALANCED PROGRAM

Providing a well balanced program is a virtue of basal series, particularly in the beginning reading stage. Provision is made for silent and oral reading, and by means of grouping and through individual work, the teacher can vary the emphasis for different pupils. The preparation of pupils for tasks is thoroughly outlined in the teacher's manual. During the readiness period the children have used a pre-reading book which included a number of pictures. Through these pictures the children were introduced to the characters that they will meet again in the pre-primer, primer, and first reader. The teacher acquaints the children with the names of these characters and prints their names on the chalkboard, thus preparing them for the first words they will encounter in the pre-primer. The pictures are specific in that they represent *particular* persons, but they are general in that the characters in them are doing things that most children understand. Out of these picture situations, discussion can grow and can provide an introduction to formal reading from books.

The first few pages of the pre-primer may be only pictures, but very soon words are introduced. These will probably be the names of the boy and girl who have been met previously in pictures—Jane, Sally, Ted, or Jack. The teacher will probably use the chalkboard and flash cards for both teaching and reviewing words. During seatwork, the children will draw a line from the word (*Sally, father, Ted,* etc.) to a picture the word represents. They might be asked to underline one of three sentences which describe a picture:

Sally rides in the wagon.
Sally plays with Spot.
Sally plays with Father.

Such exercises help children learn words in the first pre-primer. Soon, more than one familiar word will appear on each page but rarely more than one *new* word.

The repetition of words in beginning reading can dull the child's appetite for reading. The teacher must guide the pupils into both imaginative and reminiscent "building of ideas and stories." The book may contain the words "Look, Mother" under the picture. These words, with the help of the picture, can serve as the basis for a great number of interesting and logical questions and conjectures. Perhaps from the following one might easily visualize the picture that accompanies "Look, Mother."

"Who is in the picture?"
"Yes, what is Tom doing?"
"Does Spot like to wear Tom's hat?"
"What is Tom's mother doing?"
"Is she watching Tom?"
"Would he like for her to see Spot?"
"Does Spot look funny?"
"What does Tom say to his mother—who will read what he says?"

Many other points could have been discussed—pets in general, kindness to pets (Tom was not hurting Spot, but playing). Why wasn't mother watching? (Sometimes mothers are busy.) Why was she picking flowers? (Innumerable good responses.) What season of the year was this? As the child learns more words, he has less need for pictures which suggest the context or hold attention. As the pupils move through the basal series and master sight words they need less story analysis by the teacher.

Comprehension and meaning are emphasized as children select the best titles for paragraphs or short stories or as they recall sequences of events. Concepts of time, number, size, and direction are developed through seatwork which calls for children to follow directions, to perceive relationships, to grasp main ideas, and to anticipate events. Auditory discrimination exercises are provided in the form of rhyming exercises and an emphasis on the initial sounds of words. Motor co-ordination of small muscles is developed in exercises such as tracing, coloring outlined forms, drawing connecting lines between matching words, and copying words from a model.

Economy of Time. Economy of teachers' time is a major factor in the widespread use of basal series. This is closely related to the previous point of a balanced reading program. No teacher would ever have the time to match the meticulous planning that is reflected in the total program of a good basal series. When a teacher has materials available for teaching and drill on every facet of reading, she will have more time to prepare supplementary exercises as needed. It will still be necessary to prepare these for certain pupils, since the basal program cannot possibly meet all individual needs. However, it is easier to prepare supplementary lessons for a few than it is to build the entire program for all pupils.

Individual Differences. Individual differences are provided for in basal series even though the program will not be adequate for some few pupils who have special problems. A great number of levels of reading skill are encompassed in these materials. The teacher who understands her pupils, who understands the basal reading materials, and who is not compulsive in her teaching, will be able to use these materials to great advantage. Figure 13 attempts to illustrate the different levels one is likely to find among children in a given first grade and the correlative materials available in a basal reader series.

FIGURE 13

A Graphic Representation of the Reading Levels Which Could Be Expected for a Given Class Near the End of Grade One.

1. Readiness work, auditory discrimination, beginning sound in words, rhymes, etc., visual discriminations, has not learned enough sight words to read pre-primer
2. Making progress in PP^{2-3}
3. Successful reading of primer
4. Successful first readers
5. Can read in 2^1 readers
6. Can read in 2^2 readers
7. Third readers or above

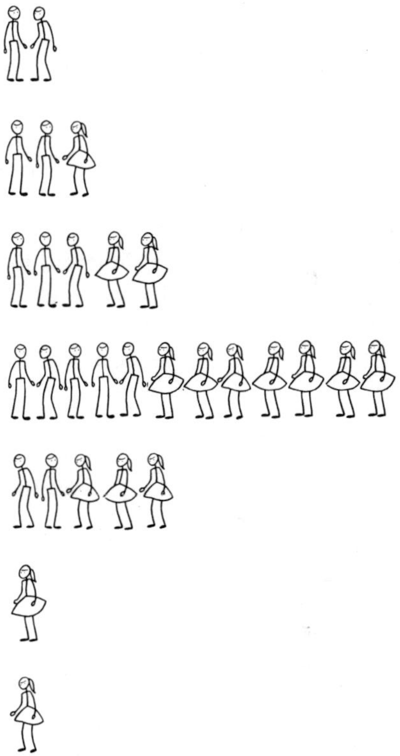

From the standpoint of the busy teacher, one of the major contributions of any good basal series is the well-thought-out seatwork which is provided in workbooks. A separate workbook is available at every level—readiness, pre-primer, primer, and first reader. Many exercises are tied to particular stories in the reading text; others are independent of actual stories but closely parallel or supplement the new tasks.

Some teachers use supplementary workbooks in addition to those provided with the basal series. The extra workbooks might stress a particular facet of reading or language, such as phonics. There is some potential danger in widespread use of these materials: first, the work itself can easily deteriorate into busy-work; second, this in turn can produce poor work habits among pupils; and third, the balanced reading program may be disrupted. Often additional seatwork is used because the teacher hopes to buy time for use with reading groups. However, intelligent use of the specialized workbook also takes time. Providing extra work in phonics has been very popular in recent years, and some writers feel that it is a mistake to combine a basal system with some independent phonic system.[9] It is true that any material may be used in such a way as to violate sound principles of teaching, but this is not inherent in the materials themselves. Materials can be used effectively if a child's needs have been ascertained and if exercises are selected which meet them.

Review. Adequate review is systematically provided in basal series. Children do not learn sight words, the sound of letters, initial blends, inflectional endings, and the like, as a result of one or two experiences. The introduction of new words is carefully controlled, and once a word or concept is introduced it will be repeated many times. Tests, designed to show pupils' mastery of all skills previously introduced, are provided in workbooks. These workbooks, when used properly, can serve as diagnostic tools to indicate where more teaching or review is needed.

The previous discussion is not meant to imply that basal reader series *are* the reading program. A teacher may rely quite heavily on these materials and still teach reading through the use of bulletin boards, labeling objects, drawings and pictures, experience charts, and reading stories and poetry. These reading experiences are not incidental but are deliberately planned.

WORD ATTACK SKILLS

If reading is to be enjoyable, children must rapidly expand their sight vocabulary so that they can deal with concepts and reading

---

[9] Lillian Gray and Dora Reese, *Teaching Children to Read* (2nd ed.; New York: The Ronald Press Company, 1957), 158.

situations which will hold their interest. Methods by which beginning readers acquire an initial stock of sight words have been discussed. (Readiness exercises, bulletin board and chalkboard work, filmstrips, experience charts and pre-primers.) Initial procedures must be supplemented with new techniques for arriving at the pronunciation of unknown words. Word analysis is an inclusive term which covers all methods of solving the pronunciation of words not known as sight words, and includes the following:

1. Word form or the unique appearance of words.
2. Structural analysis.
   a) Prefixes and suffixes.
   b) Inflectional endings of words: *-s*, *-ed*, *-ing*, etc.
   c) Compound words.
3. Context clues.
4. Phonic analysis.
5. Methods in combination.

WORD FORM

Word form or the unique appearance of words is undoubtedly a factor in distinguishing between words. Although some words look alike, it is obvious that they have distinctive characteristics and that no two words are so much alike that they cannot be distinguished in context. It is generally agreed that the configuration of words is a major help to some children but apparently not to all children. Gates suggests that "many failures in reading result from the pupil's habit of looking at the word in a careless or passive way."[10] The ability to see special characteristics of words is suggested as one of the first steps in visual discrimination as it relates to reading.[11] For example, the words *like* and *different* might suggest the configurational patterns  and  . Very little is known about the variety of clues children use in discriminating between words. It probably would not be useful to attempt to teach all children to be guided by the same unique features of words, such as the dotted *i*,

[10] A. I. Gates, *The Improvement of Reading* (3rd ed.; New York: The Macmillan Co., 1947), 242.

[11] Kathleen B. Hester, *Teaching Every Child to Read* (New York: Harper & Brothers, 1955), 60.

double letters such as *ee, tt, oo, ff*, or irregular heights of letters in a word. Calling attention to such characteristics may be of help to some students who possibly have not worked out any such helps. If word form, or unique appearance of words, was the chief method of mastering new words during the elementary years, the process of learning to read would be much slower, more time-consuming and more frustrating than it now is for most learners. Yet, in the very early stages of beginning reading, this is an important method for many children. When a child does not master the skills necessary to move on to other more efficient methods of structural analysis and phonic analysis, he becomes lost as a reader. He cannot progress because the problems of visual discrimination increase in proportion to the rate of the introduction of new words. Most children cease to rely, to any great extent, on unique configuration as a means of solving words after the beginning reading period.

STRUCTURAL ANALYSIS

Structural analysis refers to the recognition of new words by noting known roots and:

1. Inflectional endings to root words (*-s, ed, -ing*).
2. Words combined to produce a different word (compound word).
3. Prefixes or suffixes added to root words (derivatives).

Some inflectional endings are taught in first grade along with a few compound words. Prefixes and suffixes are introduced at a later period.

The pre-primers in a series will introduce approximately sixty different words. There will be few compound words or inflectional endings included. The primer of the series will introduce the *-s* ending on approximately twenty of the root words found in the pre-primers (*comes, looks, plays, knows, likes, wants, gets, boys, girls*). These will not be considered new words in figuring vocabulary load. The first reader will present about the same number of inflected words, using the *ed* and *ing* endings (*looked, played, playing, liked, pulled, riding, going, walking, wished, running*). A few common contractions and a number of compound words will also be found (*something, somebody, anything*). Workbook exercises will parallel the introduction of these new word forms. Teacher-made exercises can be developed that help the child see the structural changes which take place in words. Examples of simple inflectional endings and compound words are found in Figure 14.

FIGURE 14

A. Teaching endings: *s, ed, ing*
Notice how new words are formed when we add s, ed, *or* ing *to words.*

Word we know	Add *s*	Add *ed*	Add *ing*
walk	walks	walked	walking
ask	asks	asked	asking
call	calls	called	calling
look	looks	looked	looking
jump	jumps	jumped	jumping
show	shows	showed	showing
cover	covers	covered	covering

B. Teaching sight recognition of compound words
Notice how words under A and B are put together to make a new word. Say each word and notice the word under C very carefully.

A	B	C
any	one	anyone
up	on	upon
some	thing	something
in	to	into
when	ever	whenever
him	self	himself
snow	man	snowman
her	self	herself

Phonic Analysis. Phonic analysis is extremely important in solving unknown words. A misconception among laymen is that if children in beginning reading do not drill on isolated sounds, no phonics instruction is taking place. If children spent a period every day drilling on material such as:

ba - be - bi - bo - bu
la - le - li - lo - lu
ma - me - mi - mo - mu

it would at least be obvious that phonics had a part in early reading instruction and no doubt some parents and critics of the schools would be happy. Phonics instruction in the schools today starts in the readiness period and extends through all stages of reading instruction. The child has had experience with speech sounds all his life. He hears the difference between words such as *both, bath, bomb, bird; sell, silk, sick, send; much, milk, many, most.* The teacher works with the children to make sure that they hear the similar beginnings or similar endings of these words. The next step is instruction on seeing that letter combinations correspond to the similar sounds in the beginnings or endings of words.

If the child recognizes *m*ine and *m*any, he is then led to perceive that *m*ilk and *m*ud begin with the same symbol and thus the same sound. While he is learning sight words, he is also learning the sounds that initial letters contribute to words. If he knows the words *tell* and *sell,* he may be able to work out the word *bell,* since he also knows the words *b*e, *b*y, *b*oat, and *b*oy. Gray calls this process "initial consonant substitution" and points out that this process can work only in relation to other *known* words.[12] In addition to the clues just mentioned, if the child knows all of the words in the sentence except the one new word *bell,* the context in which the new word is found will also aid him in arriving at the correct choice.

CONTEXT CLUES

Context clues can be most useful aids in solving unknown words, provided that the child demands meaning from what he reads. The sight word method lends itself to reading for meaning almost from

[12] W. S. Gray, *On Their Own In Reading* (Chicago: Scott, Foresman, and Co., 1948), 96.

the start. After learning a few words the child reads from the first pre-primer. This book will contain not more than two dozen different words, but these words will be used in meaningful sentences and thought units. If a child masters sight words as he moves through the early stages of reading, he should have little trouble when new words are introduced. Each new word will be used in a meaningful context which will suggest the right word or at least limit the possible choices.

If the child knows the meaning of a word but does not recognize it as a sight word, he may select the correct word as he attempts to make sense from the sentence.

"The boy waved good-by as the train left the _______." Even when the sentence has a blank line substituted for the word, there is no problem in supplying the right word in order to make sense. If the child notices that the word starts with *s*, this in itself might suggest the word *station*. In the sentence "The girl waved good-by to her _______," there are a number of words which could be inserted. Some will be more logical than others, depending on what has happened in the story prior to this sentence.

COMBINATION OF METHODS

Methods in combination merits discussion even though it would not ordinarily be classified as a separate method of solving unknown words. Word form, structural analysis, phonic analysis, and context clues have been discussed as separate techniques, but in many instances they naturally operate together and complement each other. Sometimes it is impossible to determine what clue or which particular skill resulted in a successful attack on a new word. In the example "The girl waved good-by to her _______," words which meet the test of meaning would include *friend, parents, mother, father, teacher, brother, sister,* or *family*.

Assume that the reader has developed the habit of looking at the beginning letter of the unknown word for a clue to its pronunciation. This would now structure the problem differently. "The girl waved good-by to her f_______." If the reader uses the initial consonant as an aid, some guesses, which were logical before this initial consonant was used, are eliminated. We still have the choice between *friend, father,* and *family*. A reader who looks at more than just the initial consonant and has noticed and can sound *fam* is virtually assured of correctly identifying the word. The context plus this much phonic analysis should suggest the word *family*.

In the following sentence the word in parentheses is unknown to the child. "The boy was (looking) for the kitten." If no attention is paid to the word itself, the context would permit several logical guesses, such as *reaching, looking, waiting, hoping*. However, the child has had experience with the root word *look*. The recognition of this familiar root word permits no other choice except the correct one. Structural analysis helps the child eliminate all incorrect responses which are plausible in this particular context.

In the next example the first word is unknown. It is also one of the longest words the child has met in his reading. "'*Somebody* must get the ball,' said Billy." The sentence does not stand in isolation as it does here. In the story the children have been playing ball. The ball has rolled under the fence into Mrs. Brown's yard and the game has momentarily come to a halt. Something logical must be done and Billy suggests something. Previously the children had learned the word *some* and, prior to today's reading lesson, they had had a workbook exercise dealing with compound words, such as *sidewalk, playground, anyone, into,* and *anything*. If the child recognizes *some,* this much analysis plus the context should assure him of getting the word correct.

PICTURES

Pictures, which are used quite profusely in beginning reading materials, are of considerable help in arriving at unknown words. Some children become too dependent on pictures, but these readers are usually experiencing trouble in mastering sight words. The child should learn that he can help himself through the use of this formula:

What does the picture suggest?
What has just been read?
Use the "sense of the sentence" which contains the unknown word.
Heed the initial sound of the unknown word.

In each of the examples above we see the child using something he already knows as a tool to attack the unknown word. In the sight word method of teaching reading each new step in word analysis is built on some generalization from known words. When a number of sight words are mastered, new words met will have phonetic or structural characteristics identical with or similar to the known words. Context will be of major importance because instruction has stressed that reading involves getting meaning.

SPECIAL VISUAL APPROACH (The New Castle Plan)

A report of rapid progress on the part of beginning readers is found in various accounts of the New Castle reading experiment.[13] In 1947 a long term experimental program was inaugurated in the schools of New Castle, Pennsylvania. Colored film strip materials were developed for use with a basal reader series. The content of the filmstrips closely parallels, but is not identical to, the material covered in the basal series. The projected pictures measure approximately forty by fifty inches. All initial reading instruction for each new lesson occurs at the screen or chalkboard upon which the pictures are projected. Each frame of film attempts to clarify the lesson it accompanies.

A first report of the project states:

> "The basic principle behind the entire program was the idea that, because of the obvious value of a visual approach, every textbook lesson could best be introduced and taught from a large image projected on a screen, with the textbooks themselves serving as testing and practice material."[14]

The reading achievement reported for the children participating in this program is exceptional, particularly for the first year of instruction. Data for thirty-seven classes indicate reading achievement scores have been 40 per cent higher than national norms.[15] The director of the program states that other schools have reported much the

---

[13] Glenn McCracken, "Have We Overemphasized the Readiness Factor?" *Elementary English*, XXIX (1952), 271-76.

———, "New Castle Reading Experiment: A Terminal Report," *Elementary English*, XXX (1953), 13-21.

———, "The Value of the Correlated Visual Image," *The Reading Teacher*, XIII (1959), 29-33.

[14] Glenn McCracken, "The New Castle Reading Experiment," *Elementary School Journal*, LIV (1954), 385. Copyright 1954 by the University of Chicago.

[15] Glenn McCracken, "The Value of the Correlated Visual Image," *The Reading Teacher*, XIII (1959), 29-33.

same results and that corroboration is found in some reported research.[16]

The factors credited with effecting this reported improvement in reading are summarized below.

1. There is high pupil interest in the projected image.
2. High interest leads to longer attention span.
3. The large colored projection is vivid and the child needs fewer repetitions for learning.
4. There are fewer distractions. The room is semi-dark and there is nothing else to attract pupils' attention.
5. The fact that everyone's attention is focused on the same thing leads to a better climate for group discussion.
6. Shy pupils have an opportunity to participate without being singled out.
7. The size of print on the screen is better adapted to immature nervous systems than close-range book print.
8. When the text is projected on a clean chalkboard, the teacher and the pupils can work on it together, underlining capital letters, punctuation, or particular words.

The available data leave several questions unanswered, including how much time was spent in teaching reading under this method and, in general, how adequate the controls were. Nevertheless, as Yoakam points out, "The data . . . cannot be easily dismissed as insignificant."[17]

INDIVIDUALIZED READING

Characteristic of teacher willingness and eagerness to accept change in instructional method is the widespread interest in "self-selection" of reading materials in the individualized reading program. In essence, such a program is a highly desirable method of meeting individual reading differences which are inevitably found in the classroom. A number of books, at various difficulty levels, are made

---

[16] Jack Lichtenstein, "The New Castle Reading Experiment in Cleveland Heights," *Elementary English*, XXXVII (1960), 27-8.

[17] Gerald A. Yoakam, *Basal Reading Instruction* (New York: McGraw-Hill Book Co., Inc., 1955), 84.

available in the classroom. Each child selects a book he wants to read and which he can read. The teacher has individual conferences with each child, usually of four to ten minutes duration. The child reads to the teacher during this individual conference period, which serves for both diagnostic and instructional purposes. Six to ten such conferences could probably be held each day. Numerous reports of individualized programs have appeared, only a few of which are cited below.[18]

Some of the major advantages of this plan are summarized below:

1. Self-selection of reading materials keeps interest and motivation high.
2. Classroom management is much easier.
3. Individual differences are taken care of on an absolutely individual basis.
4. Children actually do a considerably larger amount of reading under the self-selection basis.
5. A close personal relationship between child and teacher is developed during the individual conferences.
6. The more advanced readers are not held back by group instruction techniques.
7. Children are not directly compared with each other as to reading level achieved.
8. Independent work habits and self-direction are fostered.

Veatch's book attempts to set out the goals and the philosophy of individualized reading. Two identifying features emerge: the renunciation of basal reader series as the foundation for reading instruction, and ability grouping as an acceptable method of dealing with individual differences. Of the former she states: "Seldom are two children ready to be taught reading from the same material at the same time. . . . It is doubtful that any one book can serve the common

---

[18] N. D. Evans, "An Individualized Reading Program for the Elementary School," *Elementary School Journal*, LIV (1953), 157-62.

Lorene K. Fox and Constance M. McCullough, "Individualized Reading," *NEA Journal*, XLVII (1958), 162-63.

Jill Bonney and L. B. Hanigan, "Individualized Teaching of Reading," *National Elementary Principal*, XXXV (1955), 76-82.

William S. Gray, "Role of Group and Individualized Teaching in a Sound Reading Program," *The Reading Teacher*, XI (1957).

The teacher-pupil conference is ego-satisfying to the child who completes a book as an independent reading project. Also, this brief individualized conference helps the teacher arrive at an appraisal of the child's reading and thus determine instructional needs. ***(Courtesy of Bexley Schools, Bexley, Ohio; photographer: Arthur Burt, Inc.)***

purpose of even two children for more than a day or two."[19] Ability grouping comes in for considerable criticism, yet one of the strengths of individualized reading is pointed up as follows: "A skill should be taught as each child reveals his need for that skill. Once a teacher knows what is needed he can proceed to teach it singly to a group or to the whole class."[20]

---

[19] Jeannette Veatch, *Individualizing Your Reading Program* (New York: G. P. Putnam's Sons, 1959), 7.

[20] *Ibid.* 31.

There are undoubtedly a number of advantages in individualized reading. One of the important contributions of this movement is the enthusiasm with which teachers attempt to make available to pupils a wide array of reading materials. The literature on this program contains many sound suggestions on how books may be obtained. The emphasis on the fact that the reader should be ego-involved in his reading is another sound contribution. The caution to refrain from over-reliance on a single basal reader series is also highly commendable. However, there is little point in breaking completely with basal instruction on the ground that these materials are sometimes

The amount of independent reading children do will depend to a large degree on the availability of interesting books and materials at the child's reading level. *(Courtesy of Bexley Schools, Bexley, Ohio; photographer: Arthur Burt, Inc.)*

poorly used. Creative teachers have for a long time recommended having supplementary reading materials available to be used in conjunction with basal instruction. In this respect individualized reading is not a new technique, but a new emphasis.

Witty has summarized the views expressed by a number of writers as to the definition of and the philosophy of individualized reading programs. He stresses the fact that while the recent individualized reading movement is not synonymous with individual instruction, these two concepts are not completely unrelated. The merits of individualized reading can be retained without proscribing all group instruction, and evaluation of individualized reading as an instructional approach would of necessity have to be program by program. Philosophy, practice, materials, and teacher skill will vary widely among different schools. (See Paul Witty, "Individualized Reading—A Summary and Evaluation," *Elementary English*, XXXVI (October 1959), 401-12.)

Several reservations arise from a serious review of the literature thus far available on the topic of individualized reading. First is the apparent (while probably not intended) lack of emphasis on how reading skills may be systematically developed. The vagueness on this topic is illustrated by statements such as: "Individualized reading is a special way of teaching in the classroom." "The child is taught the skills he needs as he needs them." "Individualized reading is based on the psychology of success." "It [individualized reading] is a developmental program with specific aims and definite procedures. Reading is taught fundamentally as well as 'incidentally.'" Nowhere in the articles from which the above statements are taken is there any discussion of how skills are taught.

It is undoubtedly true that a creative teacher can work successfully with this approach. The great danger, from the educational standpoint, is that *systematic instruction* in reading mechanics and skills can quite easily be slighted. The implication is not that such an outcome is inevitable, but rather that this is one of the major pitfalls in the individualized reading approach. After a careful reading of a number of articles which describe "self-selection" programs in first grade, one is left wondering how all of the children developed adequate skills to read a large array of books. If the mere presence of varied and interesting books accomplished this end, teachers are more or less superfluous. If the children happened to start *a priori* with adequate reading skills, this should be reported. The issue is that a vast majority of the descriptions of individualized reading programs convey the impression that it is a method of teaching reading.

A second reservation, related to the first, is the lack of rigidly controlled experimentation to determine the results of individualized reading programs. Observations by teachers and favorable comments by parents and pupils may lead to insights, but data on achievement are essential in evaluating any program.

A third caution is that the literature on individualized reading contains considerable criticism of the basal reader method which seems to be based on the assumption that certain illogical procedures are inherently a part of this method. It is implied, for example, that the backbone of basal reading is the reading circle in which children take turns reading from the same book; that all children in a class are reading from the same book; that each lesson in developing a skill is taught to the entire class, whether or not every child needs this instruction. Furthermore, there is often more than a hint that the basal reader method precludes the use of supplementary reading materials and that one of the often reported outcomes of individualized reading is that children read more books. This may be primarily because books are made easily available in such programs. Providing interesting books in all classrooms and making a conscientious effort to arouse pupil interest in these books would undoubtedly show some increase in pupil reading under any method of teaching. Providing supplementary reading materials is not a *method*, although it is advocated in most methods.

GROUPING

The practice of grouping pupils on the basis of reading ability is common in our schools. It should be kept in mind that grouping is not a teaching method. It is simply one of the organizational mechanics which may help the teacher do a more effective job of teaching because grouping permits the teacher to deal with a narrower range of reading ability than is found in a given classroom. Ability-grouping provides the framework in which an alert teacher may meet individual pupil needs.[21] There are always practical considerations which limit the degree to which this can be done. Thus, many authorities suggest that the class be divided into three groups. Five or six groups might well overtax the teacher, dividing her time with pupils in blocks too small to be effective. Two groups would undoubtedly leave her with too heterogeneous a collection of pupils in both groups.

Grouping practices should be extremely flexible. Good teachers are always more conscious of the goals of grouping than they are of the mechanics of the practice. They do not think of equal numbers of pupils in each group or of groups being rigid and final or that every pupil can be accommodated equally well within a three-group structure. They know from experience that one or more pupils may not fit logically into any of three groups. This point is best illustrated by the extreme cases found in every classroom—the very poor reader and the very accelerated reader.

Harris points out that different classrooms at a given grade level will differ to such a degree that it is impracticable to outline any particular plan of grouping with the expectation that it will be equally appropriate for all.[22] Factors other than the abilities of the pupils also influence grouping practices. These include class size, space for activities, and the availability of supplementary books, film strips, recordings, and the like. The teacher's method is also a factor. Relying heavily on basal readers may call for a structure different from the widespread use of the unit or project approach.

The Psychological Impact of Grouping. Grouping is sometimes discussed as being potentially threatening to pupils. There are various points of view as to how the grouping within a classroom is to take place so as not to introduce comparisons between children. The most frequently repeated suggestions include calling the groups group one, group two, and group three on the basis of reading ability; giving the

---

[21] For an historical account of the development and rationale of grouping practices found in schools since 1900 see Kathleen B. Hester, *Teaching Every Child to Read* (New York: Harper & Brothers, 1955), Chap. 17.

Further discussion of grouping practice may be found in *The Reading Teacher*, II (1957). This entire issue is devoted to the theme "Classroom Organization: Differing Viewpoints."

[22] Albert J. Harris, *How To Increase Reading Ability* (3rd ed.; New York: Longmans, Green & Co., Inc., 1956), 134-35.

groups some irrelevant titles such as bluebirds, redbirds, robins, the teacher knowing which is the superior group; referring to the groups by the names of children in the group. The latter has the merit of being a straightforward approach. No one is being humiliated on the basis of reading ability, and it is not made to appear that the teacher thinks every pupil should have a certain ability in reading. Psychologically, it is inadvisable for a teacher to attempt to hide differences among beginning readers. It is impossible to fool the children about their reading, and when the poorer readers see through the bluebirds versus the blackbirds they too start attaching a stigma to poor reading ability. This of course is what the teacher has done, but she did not do it openly.

A wise teacher has had different groups of children doing different things at the same time throughout the year, and no significance was attached to this by either the teacher or the pupils. This teacher probably did not start all children reading from the pre-primer on the same day. She observed children closely and identified those who were ready. When she started this group on a pre-primer, other groups worked on reading also. Some children worked in a readiness workbook, some worked on teacher-prepared readiness materials, and some did preparation for making an experience chart. The teacher, in a natural way, had planted the idea that groups of pupils would be reading from different books and would be working on different pages of workbooks. The teacher who is successful in doing this helps her pupils in many ways.

1. She helps children build a foundation for independent work habits.

2. Competition and feelings of failure are reduced, since children are not arrayed against each other on the same reading tasks.

3. Tension and bad attitudes toward reading are held to a minimum.

4. Each child is permitted to progress at his own rate, and intergroup rivalry is minimized.

5. The teacher is prevented from embracing, consciously or unconsciously, a grouping system that is too rigid.

6. The teacher is granted flexibility in reducing the size of a group she works with by having some children work independently while she works intensively with others.

The teacher who handles this problem in a natural, offhand manner and who makes no effort to hide facts will create fewer problems in her classroom. She indicates her acceptance of poorer readers, and they, in turn, can accept themselves without reservation.

The Ungraded Primary. The concept of grouping and the various practices of grouping have grown out of the recognition of pupil differences. The ungraded primary usually embraces the first three years of formal instruction but does not break this period down into grades one, two, and three. During these first three years of formal schooling, the children are designated as being in the primary school or at the primary level. They are not promoted or non-promoted at the end of years one and two. A recent study indicates that neither promotion nor non-promotion is in itself a very satisfactory solution to low achievement in reading. It is suggested that more flexible curriculums, methods, and materials are needed "in a type of school organization which encourages continuous pupil progress." (See Walter H. Worth and J. Harlan Shores, "Does Nonpromotion Improve Achievement in the Language Arts?" *Elementary English,* XXXVII (Jan. 1960), 49-52.)

While instruction in the conventional grade-level system is geared to the mean, experience tells us that pupils do not cluster closely around an achievement mean. Differences in achievement are marked, and they increase with instruction. The ungraded primary starts from the premise that each child should progress at his own rate, and the instructional program centers on each child's need at the moment. This is accomplished by breaking the primary years into a number of units of accomplishment or levels of competency. As each child develops competency at one level, he is moved on into work at the next level. The number of levels and the skills to be mastered at each level are worked out co-operatively by teachers in the program.

Austin describes an ungraded primary school that was eminently successful from the standpoint of both teachers and parents. No official reference is made to grade level; all primary grades, which cover the first three years of school, are simply designated primary rooms. Parents are always kept informed of their children's progress. Teachers are encouraged to work with the same group of children for more than one year, and new teachers are initiated into the program with a workshop held before the opening of school.[23]

No single learning curve fits first grader's achievement, and pupil variability in achievement increases in succeeding grades. There is evidence that if the children are allowed three years of instruction to achieve the third grade level, there will be fewer failures than there would be if all of the children had had to meet arbitrary standards at the end of grades one and two. Maturity and growth cannot be forced, and growth is characterized by both spurts and plateaus. The ungraded primary encourages continuous pupil progress without specifying precise amounts of growth which are to take place in a given year. Such a plan has particular merit for the child who starts slowly but later shows rapid progress.[24]

Some of the educational advantages believed to be inherent in the ungraded primary plan are summarized below.

1. It is easier to provide for the child's reading growth *early* in his reading career if one is not thinking of "grade level norms" the first year.

2. There is likely to be less failure and frustration in the reading situation if there is less emphasis on comparison and promotion.

3. A teacher often stays with the same group of students two years or longer. This gives her an opportunity to know pupils better. She is less likely to push a student beyond his ability during the first year, since she expects to work with him the next year.

4. Students always work at the level on which they need instruction; i.e., they are not likely to miss some facet of instruction because they were absent several weeks.

5. The slower learner will not repeat the first or second grade, but he may take four years to move up from the primary level.

---

[23] Kent C. Austin, "The Ungraded Primary School," *Childhood Education,* XXXIII (1957), 260-63.

[24] For further discussion of the ungraded primary see John I. Goodlad, "Ungrading the Elementary Grades," *NEA Journal,* XLIV (1957), 170-71; "More About the Ungraded Plan," *NEA Journal,* XLIV (1955), 295-96; Florence C. Kelly, "Ungraded Primary Schools Make the Grade in Milwaukee," *NEA Journal,* XL (1951), 645-46; Ada R. Polkinghorne, "Grouping Children in the Primary Grades," *Elementary School Journal,* L (1950), 502-08; and Ethel Thompson, "The Ungraded Plan," *NEA Journal,* XLVII (1958), 16-18.

6. The ungraded plan is flexible in allowing pupils to cover some phases of learning quite rapidly when they are capable of doing so and in giving them more time when it is needed.

7. Bright pupils would not "skip a grade" and possibly be deficient in some skill taught there. They would simply go through the entire primary curriculum at a faster rate.[25]

No method of grouping will automatically solve all instructional problems, and the ungraded primary plan is certainly not a panacea. If a shift to the ungraded plan is not accompanied by sympathy for and understanding of the goals to be achieved, none of the potential benefits are likely to be realized. If teachers or parents continue to think in terms of a grade-level system, the plan is doomed from the start. On the other hand, if the philosophy of the plan is believed sound and the chief reason for adopting it is to help children grow in reading, problems which do arise will not be insurmountable.

YOUR POINT OF VIEW?

Would you prefer to defend or attack the following premises? Why?

1. If you want a child to hear the speech sounds in words, it would be more logical to teach these sounds in each word before teaching the word as a sight word.

2. The reading material found in basic reader series is equally appropriate and meaningful for children regardless of home environment and socio-economic status.

3. A justifiable criterion for judging good teaching in beginning reading is the extent to which a teacher uses different methods in her classroom. (Basic readers, experience method, individualized reading, etc.)

4. "In-class grouping" has not helped teachers in dealing effectively with individual differences.

5. The ungraded primary is in essence an attempt to break away from grade-level standards of achievement.

---

[25] For a thorough discussion of the ungraded plan see John I. Goodlad and Robert H. Anderson, *The Non-graded Elementary School* (New York: Harcourt, Brace & Co., 1959).

BIBLIOGRAPHY

Anderson, Irving H., and Dearborn, Walter F. *The Psychology of Teaching Reading.* New York: The Ronald Press Co., 1952, Chap. 7.

Artley, Sterl A. *Your Child Learns to Read.* Chicago: Scott, Foresman & Co., 1953.

Austin, Kent C. "The Ungraded Primary School," *Childhood Education,* XXXIII (February, 1957), 260-63.

Betts, Emmett A. *Foundations of Reading Instruction.* New York: American Book Co., 1946.

Bohnhorst, Ben A., and Sellars, Sophia N. "Individual Reading Instruction *vs.* Basal Textbook Instruction: Some Tentative Explorations," *Elementary English,* XXXVI (March, 1959), 185-90.

Bonney, Jill, and Harrigan, L. B. "Individualized Teaching of Reading," *National Elementary Principal,* XXXV (September, 1955), 76-82.

Bremmer, Neville. "First-Grade Achievement under Different Plans of Grouping," *Elementary English,* XXXV (May, 1958), 324-26.

Burns, Paul C. "A Re-Examination of the Role of Experience Charts," *Elementary English,* XXXVI (November, 1959), 480-83.

Dawson, Mildred A., and Bamman, Harry A. *Fundamentals of Basic Reading Instruction.* New York: Longmans, Green & Co., Inc., 1959.

DeBoer, John J., and Dallmann, Martha. *The Teaching of Reading.* New York: Henry Holt & Co., Inc., 1960.

Dickhart, Audry. "Breaking the Lock-Step in Reading," *Elementary English,* XXXV (January, 1958), 54-56.

Dolch, E. W. "Phonics in the First Grade," *Elementary English,* XXXII (December, 1955), 514-18.

Evans, N. D. "An Individualized Reading Program for the Elementary School," *Elementary School Journal,* LIV (November, 1953), 157-62.

Fox, Lorene K., and McCullough, Constance M. "Individualized Reading," *NEA Journal,* XLVII (March, 1958), 162-63.

Gates, A. I. *The Improvement of Reading* (3rd ed.). New York: The Macmillan Co., 1947, 242.

Goodlad, John I., and Anderson, Robert H. *The Nongraded Elementary School.* New York: Harcourt, Brace & Co., 1959.

Goodlad, John I. "Ungrading the Elementary Grades," *NEA Journal,* XLIV (March, 1955), 170-71.

———. "More about the Ungraded Plan," *NEA Journal,* XLIV (May, 1955), 295-96.

Gray, Lillian, and Reese, Dora. *Teaching Children to Read* (2nd ed.). New York: The Ronald Press Co., 1957, 158.

Gray, William S. *On Their Own In Reading*. Chicago: Scott, Foresman and Co., 1948.

———. "Role of Group and Individualized Teaching in a Sound Reading Program," *Reading Teacher,* XI (December, 1957), 99-104.

Hampleman, Richard S. "A Study of the Comparative Reading Achievements of Early and Late School Starters," *Elementary English,* XXXVI (May, 1959), 331-34.

Harris, Albert J. *How to Increase Reading Ability* (3rd ed.). New York: Longmans, Green and Co., Inc., 1956.

Hester, Kathleen B. *Teaching Every Child to Read.* New York: Harper & Brothers, 1954.

Kelly, Florence C. "Ungraded Primary Schools Make the Grade in Milwaukee," *NEA Journal,* XL (December, 1951), 645-46.

Kingsley, Marjorie. "An Experiment in Individualized Reading," *Elementary English,* XXXV (February, 1958), 113-18.

Lamoreaux, L. A., and Lee, D. M. *Learning to Read through Experience.* New York: Appleton-Century-Crofts, Inc., 1943.

Lichtenstein, Jack. "The New Castle Reading Experiment in Cleveland Heights," *Elementary English,* XXXVII (January, 1960), 27-28.

McCracken, Glenn. "Have We Overemphasized the Readiness Factor?" *Elementary English,* XXIX (March, 1952), 271-76.

———. "The New Castle Reading Experiment: A Terminal Report," *Elementary English,* XXX (January, 1953), 13-21.

———. "The New Castle Reading Experiment," *Elementary School Journal,* LIV (March, 1954), 385.

———. "The Value of the Correlated Visual Image," *Reading Teacher,* XIII (October, 1959), 29-33.

McCullough, Constance M. "Groping or Grouping?" *Elementary English,* XXXI (1954), 136-38.

McKee, Paul. *The Teaching of Reading in the Elementary School.* Boston: Houghton Mifflin Co., 1948.

McKim, Margaret. *Guiding Growth in Reading.* New York: The Macmillan Co., 1955.

Newman, Robert E. "Building Each Child's Desire to Read," *Elementary English,* XXXVII (May, 1960), 310-15.

Picozzi, Adelaide. "An Approach to Individualized Reading," *Elementary English,* XXXV (May, 1958), 302-4.

Ploghoft, Milton H. "Do Reading Readiness Workbooks Promote Readiness?" *Elementary English,* XXXVI (October, 1959), 424-26.

Polkinghorne, Ada R. "Grouping Children in the Primary Grades," *Elementary School Journal,* L (May, 1950), 502-8.

Reeve, Olive R. "The Vocabulary of Seven Primary Reading Series," *Elementary English,* XXXV (April, 1958), 237-39.

Roswell, Florence G., and Chall, Jeanne S. "Helping Poor Readers with Word Recognition Skills," *Reading Teacher,* X (April, 1957), 200-4.

Sharpe, Maida Wood. "An Individualized Reading Program," *Elementary English,* XXXV (December, 1958), 507-12.

Sister Mary Alice R.S.M. and Adma d'Heurle. "New Ventures In School Organization—The Ungraded School and Use of Teacher Aids," *Elementary School Journal,* LVII (February, 1957), 268-71.

Smith, Nila B. *American Reading Instruction.* New York: Silver Burdett and Co., 1934, Chap. 8, 229-63.

Staiger, Ralph C. "How Are Basal Readers Used?" *Elementary English,* XXXV (January, 1958), 46-49.

Staufer, Russell G. "Individualizing Reading Instruction—A Backward Look," *Elementary English,* XXXVI (May, 1959), 335-41.

Stone, C. R. *Progress in Primary Reading.* St. Louis: Webster Publishing Co., 1950, Chap. II.

Thompson, Ethel. "The Ungraded Plan," *NEA Journal,* XLVII (January, 1958), 16-8.

Veatch, Jeanette. *Individualizing Your Reading Program.* New York: G. P. Putnam's Sons, 1959.

———. "In Defense of Individualized Reading," *Elementary English,* XXXVII (April, 1960), 227-34.

Whipple, Gertrude. "Good Practices in Grouping," *Reading Teacher,* VII (1953), 69-73.

Witty, Paul. "Individualized Reading—A Summary and Evaluation," *Elementary English,* XXXVI (October, 1959), 401-12.

Yoakum, Gerald A. *Basal Reading Instruction.* New York: McGraw-Hill Book Co., 1955.

Young, Marion. "A Report on Self-selection in Reading," *Elementary English,* XXXV (March, 1958), 176-81.

chapter 5

TEACHING READING IN THE PRIMARY GRADES

The term *primary reading* refers to the first three years of formal instruction. Having already discussed beginning reading, we are here concerned only with the later primary years. Primary reading is not to be thought of as a stage in the learning process which has fixed or rigid boundaries. It does not start with one particular aspect of the curriculum and end with another, but rather overlaps and blends with what we have previously discussed as beginning reading. The teacher in the later primary grades will stress the same fundamental skills but with the goal of expanding and broadening them. As pupils learn and master basic skills, new ones will be introduced.

A book on reading may be organized so as to discuss objectives, materials, and instructions grade by grade. This has value in that it gives a logical continuity to the steps of teaching reading in the order in which they are usually introduced. The disadvantage is that this method of organization reinforces the illusion that children in given grades have abilities which parallel the curricular materials designed for those particular grades. It is easy to embrace the idea that the second grade teacher teaches second graders and that third grades are populated by third graders. Experience in the classroom indicates that this idea is not very useful for instructional purposes since the classification of second or third grader does not define pupil achievement but merely identifies the room which certain pupils are currently occupying. Betts calls the evolution of the "graded school" the coming of the lock step in American education.[1]

OBJECTIVES OF THIS PERIOD

The primary grades find the majority of pupils making rather rapid progress in reading. This period is often referred to as the period for gaining independence in reading. Significant changes which have an impact on reading are taking place among children. They develop abilities which are prerequisites for improving reading and interests which enhance the value of reading ability. Pupils in the primary years acquire a large store of general information, a wider interest in events not directly involving their own lives, and an increasing ability to deal with the abstract. They are now mature enough to concentrate for relatively long periods, developing capabilities for both independent work and teamwork.

An almost unlimited number of objectives for primary reading instruction could be advanced.[2] Many of those listed here cannot be thought of as belonging exclusively to the primary period. Some were important in beginning reading and others will continue to be important throughout the intermediate, junior high, and secondary school levels. These objectives are to help the child:

1. Develop a large sight vocabulary.
2. Expand his stock of concepts and word meanings.
3. Learn and apply phonic principles for sounding out unknown words.

---

[1] E. A. Betts, *Foundations of Reading Instruction* (New York: American Book Co., 1946), Chap. 2.

[2] See Paul McKee, *The Teaching of Reading in the Elementary School* (Boston: Houghton Mifflin Co., 1948). McKee cites nine "instructural jobs" (p. 285). Also see Clarence Stone, *Progress in Primary Reading* (St. Louis: Webster Publishing Co., 1950), Chap. 10; Broom, *et al., Effective Reading Instruction* (New York: McGraw-Hill Book Co., 1951), Chap. 5.

4. Review and extend knowledge of language sounds associated with vowel and consonant combinations.
5. Use punctuation for smooth meaningful reading.
6. Develop the skill of reading several words together as thought units, either phrases or sentences.
7. Reduce the number of occurrences of reading errors such as hesitations, regression, repetition, substitutions, or omissions.
8. Develop the ability to recognize known root words in new word forms which include prefixes or inflectional endings.
9. Further develop the attitude that reading is always purposeful and that he must clarify his purpose in specific reading tasks.
10. Use the context as an aid in attacking unknown words.
11. Enjoy and appreciate the vicarious experiences which are open to him in reading.

THE INSTRUCTIONAL PROGRAM

READING GROWTH IS DEVELOPMENTAL

The instructional program in grades two and three closely parallels the program of beginning reading. Skills previously introduced are reviewed and extended. For instance, there will be continued emphasis on such skills as discrimination of initial consonant sounds and consonant blends, building sight vocabulary, profiting from pictures, and using context. Recognition of word endings *s, ed, ing,* taught in grade one, is followed by systematic instruction in extending this developmental task. In grade two, other suffixes will be dealt with including *er, y, est, ly, iest, less, ful;* later instruction will deal with *ment, tion, tive, sion,* and others.

Study in grade one of initial consonant blends, such as *cl, br, bl, scr, gr, str,* will be extended. Work on recognition of the contractions *aren't, I'll, won't, they're, can't, we'll, you'll,* etc., and of numerous compound words will receive attention.

In addition to a systematic effort to extend skills previously introduced, many new developmental tasks are undertaken. Particular emphasis is placed on phonic and structural analysis. The short and long sounds of vowels are taught as are a number of prefixes with attention paid to both structural and meaning changes involved.

Silent consonants (*k*nife, com*b*, i*s*land, li*gh*t) and the sound of *ph* will receive attention as will syllabication and simple alphabetizing.

Comprehension skills are developmental also and should be developed systematically in the primary grades. Context clues become more important as unknown sight words are met more frequently. It is essential to learn new connotations for many words and literal meanings cannot be insisted on for figurative expressions. The reader must follow the sequence of ideas and see their relationship to each other. The ability to analyze the meaning of sentences must be extended to paragraphs and larger units so that the main ideas of these larger units of material can be grasped.

The pace at which reading skills are taught in the primary grades is increased and the progress expected of pupils in a given period of time, such as a semester or year, is practically doubled when compared with the goals of beginning reading. The program necessarily includes simultaneous emphasis on the development of the mechanics of reading and the development of those comprehension skills which make reading rewarding and satisfying. To attain the many objectives of the primary period, instruction must focus on four main activities:

1. Selection of materials and the teaching schedule.
2. Diagnosis of pupil achievement and instructional needs to serve as a basis for classroom organization and instructional emphasis.
3. The systematic expansion of skills in the mechanics of reading.
4. The development of comprehension skills and emphasis on recreational reading.

MATERIALS AND TEACHING SCHEDULE

USE OF BASAL MATERIALS

The relation of basal reader series to the total reading program is much the same in grades two and three as in beginning reading. Growth in reading is developmental and basal reader materials are designed with this fact in mind. All facets of instruction are provided for in a logical sequence and each receives proper emphasis. The essence of primary-level instruction is continuity and a systematic building of skills. When a child's growth does not parallel the materials found at his grade level, it is the pupil's achievement and rate of growth, not the materials, that must determine the instructional program. The basal reader materials at this level not only stress the mechanical skills of reading but also emphasize comprehension, cultivating in the reader an attitude that demands comprehension from reading. While vocabulary is still controlled, the expansion of the reading vocabulary at this level permits practice in reading for information, organization of data, and interpretation and appreciation of literature.[3] These skills systematically taught in reading instruction should easily transfer to all reading situations involving subject area materials and textbooks. Instructional procedures for developing the mechanics of reading and comprehension skills are discussed later in this chapter.

EXPERIENCE CHARTS AND OTHER SUPPLEMENTARY MATERIALS

While basal reader series can provide the foundation for systematic instruction at this level, these materials should not be thought of as *the* reading program. Certainly the continued use of experience charts is justifiable in grades two and three.[4] Experience stories written by individual pupils, as well as charts produced by the class as a whole, can be used extensively at the primary level. Since the sight vocabulary of pupils has been enlarged, this particular problem in the use of experience charts is minimized in the upper primary grades.

Bulletin boards also have many potential uses since children can now engage in independent reading and find materials which bear on topics under discussion. Pictures and newspaper and magazine articles offer interesting sources of material. When children know that there is a certain space in the room reserved for use of such materials, they are motivated to do outside reading to find appropriate display materials. The bulletin board can be particularly effective when the teacher is working with units. The unit approach may be used successfully at this level if enough supplementary reading material is

---

[3] Guy L. Bond and Eva Bond Wagner, *Teaching the Child to Read* (New York: The Macmillan Co., 1960).

[4] An extensive discussion of the use of experience charts is found in Chapter 4 and will not be repeated here.

available at the pupils' reading level. (For a discussion of the unit approach, see Chapter 8.) If such materials are not available in the various content areas, there is little reason why a wide array of materials cannot be provided for recreational reading.

TEACHING SCHEDULE

Teachers in the primary grades must have definite daily periods of time devoted exclusively to reading instruction. In addition to this regularly scheduled time other periods may occasionally be used for reading instruction with particular groups. For instance, a number of poorer readers may be given extra practice in word-attack skills while those pupils fairly proficient in this skill read independently in a subject area text or for recreation. At other times the teacher may participate in the discussion of a story with a group of advanced readers while other pupils do seat work on teacher-prepared lesson sheets.

There is no one specific amount of time per day which can be said to be ideal for systematic reading instruction. Factors such as class size, pupils' achievement, the teacher's skill, and classroom organization would have to be considered in arriving at a schedule. In grade two, an hour each morning and possibly a slightly shorter period in the afternoon would certainly be considered a minimum amount of time for scheduled instruction. Other short periods throughout the week should be devoted to particular reading problems as they arise in other instructional activities. Problems in word meaning, word attack, punctuation, and exploration of concepts all involve reading instruction and should take place in any context whether the curricular task is in the area of arithmetic, health, or language arts.

RECREATIONAL READING

Reading for pleasure and satisfaction should be considered in any discussion of reading materials and schedules.

By providing vicarious experiences that help them gain insight into their own problems, recreational reading is a means through which children can attain greater maturity. Maturity, which is determined by the response that an individual makes in attempting to deal with his social and psychological needs, is never achieved once and for all. A child who is socially and emotionally mature at six may not be equally well adjusted at puberty. Thus, recreational reading should be continually encouraged throughout the primary and intermediate grades. All the *potential* resources residing in reading will go unrealized unless the individual *reads.* Teachers must help children see reading as a resource for intellectual, social, and emotional growth.

There are many factors which influence the success of a recreational reading program. First, any child's participation in recreational reading will be determined by the degree to which he has mastered reading skills and habits. The child deficient in these skills is not likely to turn to reading, because reading will not be satisfying. Second, the variability in pupils' skills, needs, and interests makes the teacher's task difficult. She will have to be familiar with a great deal of reading material and she will have to know something of the social and emotional environment of pupils if she is to have the right book at the right time for each pupil. At the very time the child is developing into an independent reader and might find great pleasure in reading, the school channels most reading experiences into textbooks and assigned reading in content areas. There is no doubt that in some instances the school's preoccupation with textbook subject matter may have a tendency to stifle outside reading for pleasure.

A third factor jeopardizing the success of recreational reading programs is the fact that many schools fail to provide supplementary reading materials at all reading levels. Today there are no areas of interest in which there is not a vast amount of reading materials. These materials parallel and supplement all subject matter found in the present-day curriculum. In science there are books devoted to subjects varying from rocks to rockets or snakes to satellites. There are biographies of men and women in such fields as medicine, exploration, invention, social work, statesmanship, nursing, and sports. Well-written stories can be found that deal with other countries and other peoples. These must be made available to children in the schools.

Despite all of the values inherent in wide and wisely selected reading, recreational reading seems to be a declining art. This is certainly true among adults and appears to be a growing problem among

Getting the right book and child together is one of the instructional tasks at all levels of teaching. ***(Courtesy of San Diego City Schools)***

adolescents.[5] The school has the responsibility of guiding the growth of children and cannot possibly wait for a child's needs to drive him into recreational reading. Recreational reading is a special instructional problem because of the discrepancy between the tremendous

[5] Alice R. Wickens, "A Survey of Current Reading Interests in Grades Seven through Nine." *Developing Permanent Interest in Reading,* edited by Helen M. Robinson (University of Chicago Press: Supplementary Educational Monographs, No. 84, 1956).

potential residing in recreational reading and the actual values presently achieved in our schools.

MOTIVATING CHILDREN TO READ

There are many ways in which teachers can help children develop an interest in recreational reading.

1. One way to make reading attractive to children is to read to them. In many instances a teacher will want to read a book or story in its entirety. Sometimes she might read just enough to whet appetites, and children will want to read the book for themselves. When the teacher reads, she will have to be well prepared. She must read with expression and feeling so as to provide a model interpretation.

2. Teachers must be prepared to guide children in selecting books which they are capable of reading and which they will enjoy. Nothing kills interest in reading so quickly as material for which one does not have an adequate background or in which one has no interest. Often the teacher can help supply these prerequisites. If the child is reading a biography, he should know something of the central character's background, accomplishments, and contributions. In dealing with fiction or historical works he should be aware of events and conditions which would make the story more meaningful.

3. To guide the child toward wide reading is a worthy objective, but at the same time a balanced diet is not necessarily the first step. Children should be permitted to read what they enjoy. The teacher's preference does not always coincide with the child's interest. A child may not be ready for the classics or for great literature. If he reads extensively, he will soon become satiated with "series" books, mysteries, westerns, myths, or whatever he is currently engrossed in. Recreational reading is by definition an individual matter. There is little cause for fear that the avid reader will not gradually broaden his interests and taste. He should be guided in this direction but not pushed.

4. In some situations it may be necessary to use extrinsic motivations. Librarians and teachers have found that some children are favorably influenced by keeping a record of the books they read. Charts or graphs can be used to reflect the number of books or stories

read. This extrinsic motivation is educationally justifiable, but teachers must remember its limitation. It can work for only a limited time. While it is being used and while it is serving as an ego satisfaction for the child, the real aim is to have the child develop a love for reading which in time becomes the reward itself. When this occurs, the child will no longer need the show of accomplishment in the form of a *record* of books read. Some children will need overt approval from the teacher as a reward for their effort in recreational or outside reading. These children should be permitted to tell the teacher or a group in the class about the story they have read. Acceptance and teacher approval then become associated with reading. If a child is adequately prepared, he may be permitted to read to a group during a free reading period or as part of a unit. This practice is certainly one of the chief uses of oral reading in the classroom.

ORAL READING

Although oral reading has not been treated as a separate topic in previous chapters, its role in beginning reading has not been slighted. Instruction in oral reading must be considered in light of the purposes for which it is used, the materials used, and how it is incorporated into the total reading program.

Teachers of beginning reading will use oral reading for a number of purposes. Opinions as to the relative value of teaching oral reading have changed considerably during the present century. At one time oral reading was widely practiced without much attention to the justification of the classroom procedures that were followed. Oral reading was equated with the school's reading program.[6] The term *oral reading* may call to mind children in a circle reading round robin from the same book with each child in the group reading silently along with, behind, or ahead of the child performing orally. The poorer reader took his turn along with the rest and sighed, mumbled, and coughed his embarrassed way through the allotted paragraph.

The evils that result from a particular educational practice may be remembered long after the practice has either been discontinued

---

[6] O. N. Darby, "The Place of, and Methods of, Teaching Oral Reading in the Elementary School," *Elementary School Journal,* LI (1951), 380-88.

or substantially modified. In some cases oral reading was overemphasized and children spent most of their time reading aloud. As a result, they read slowly, putting all the emphasis on the mechanics of reading and little emphasis on meaning. Gray and Reese tell of a boy reading a long passage orally. He read with expression and good interpretation. The teacher asked him a question about the content of what he had just read. His reply was that he could not answer because he "wasn't listening."[7]

Another abuse was that oral reading was often advanced as an end in itself rather than a means to several desirable ends. Oral reading was practiced in artificial situations with little thought given to creating a true audience situation. As these abuses were pointed out in the literature on teaching reading, a reaction against oral reading took place. The disadvantages and potential weaknesses were stressed to the point where many teachers may possibly have thought that the issue was oral reading versus silent reading, rather than the *intelligent use* of oral reading. At the moment the most popular position is the middle ground which embraces the position that a proper balance should be maintained between silent and oral reading. It is difficult to argue with the logic of this latter position; nevertheless, it is almost impossible to find what constitutes a proper balance. What is adequate and desirable for one teacher with a particular class may be an improper diet in another situation. Many writers do point out that there are close relationships between the development of abilities in silent and oral reading.[8]

The values of oral reading can be found in many natural classroom situations. The most common situation is one in which a child reads aloud in order to convey information or pleasure to an audience of his classmates. Regardless of the situation, oral reading can be justified only when the purposes are logical, the goals educationally sound, and the preparation adequate to the occasion. There is much written in teacher's manuals about the preparation of students for

---

[7] Lillian Gray and Dora Reese, *Teaching Children to Read* (2nd ed.; New York: The Ronald Press Co., 1957), 244-45.

[8] Guy L. Bond and Miles A. Tinker, *Reading Difficulties: Their Diagnosis and Correction* (New York: Appleton-Century-Crofts, 1957), 342.

reading tasks, but there are no reading tasks which make more justified demands for adequate preparation than does oral reading.

Reading in an audience situation can be an ego-building experience for the reader. Personal and social growth as well as self-confidence can be achieved. But the child must be able to read satisfactorily in order to elicit approval from others, and he should not be expected to read to a group unless adequately prepared. Furthermore, reading aloud from a book while children follow the same passage in their books minimizes the audience situation. Oral reading should, insofar as possible, make use of materials other than basal series used for instructional purposes with the class.

Oral reading can be an excellent means of teaching reading skills such as good phrasing, use of punctuation, reading with expression, and fluent reading without hesitations or repetitions. Oral reading is a logical extension of the language usage characteristic of children as they enter school. Practice in oral reading can help the child associate printed words with their speech equivalents.

McKim sees oral reading as a potential aid to comprehension in reading. "Some youngsters seem to need a little of the reinforcement of their own voices to help them in understanding what they read."[9] She also feels that oral reading while learning to read is not necessarily a handicap in acquiring an adequate rate of silent reading because vocalizing actually does not slow the *beginning* reader. On this same point Gray and Reese cite data which shows that for grades one and two the oral reading rate and silent reading rate are about equal. Beyond this level, of course, silent reading enjoys a distinct advantage as far as rate is concerned.[10]

It is often stated that oral reading provides an excellent opportunity for the diagnosis of reading skills and the discovery of pupils' reading weaknesses. This diagnostic function is a pupil-teacher situation centered around a teacher purpose and probably would not involve the child's reading to a group. It could be argued that this is not a true oral-reading situation since pupil purpose, informing an audience,

---

[9] Margaret G. McKim, *Guiding Growth in Reading* (New York: The Macmillan Co., 1955), 140.

[10] Lillian Gray and Dora Reese, *Teaching Children to Read* (New York: The Ronald Press Co., 1957), 247.

In the classroom the child who reads orally to others must be adequately prepared as a reader. Both his reading and their listening must be purposeful. Here the reader is making a contribution. The material he is reading is not found in the text used by the group. *(Courtesy of Bexley Schools, Bexley, Ohio; photographer: Arthur Burt, Inc.)*

is not paramount. It cannot be denied that oral reading provides many clues to the actual weakness in a child's reading. A child's response after reading silently may indicate that he is a poor reader, or that he is performing below a certain grade level. Such a diagnosis may not disclose *why* the child reads poorly. If the teacher can *hear* and *observe* the child's reading, she can discover important clues to his competence in sight vocabulary, attacking unknown words, use of context, use of punctuation, and whether he views reading as getting meaning. The teacher will not rely on only one sample of oral reading as an adequate diagnosis, but each instance of oral reading will be seen as a part of an ongoing diagnosis.

It is generally agreed that oral reading is a more difficult task than silent reading. Kovas emphasizes this, pointing out that in oral reading the reader must know all the words and must get the author's point and mood so that he can convey it to the listeners. To do this he must use proper phrasing, paying heed to punctuation while at the same time reading loud enough to reach all his listeners.[11] Children will inevitably face situations which call for reading aloud. Since almost all purposeful oral reading takes place in a social setting, these instances will be important to the reader, whose performance will place him in the position of being judged by others.

In summary, considerations which should be observed when using oral reading include:

1. The reader must have a purpose for the oral reading. He must have interesting data which he wishes to share with others.
2. The reader must be prepared. He must have mastered the mechanical skills required and have arrived at an acceptable interpretation of the author's intent.
3. Children are not always well trained in our schools to *listen.* When children cannot listen critically, the primary justification for oral reading is missing.
4. Instruction during the actual oral reading situation will usually destroy the value of oral reading.
5. Too much oral reading can diminish its effectiveness. The stress should be on good oral reading not on an endurance contest for either readers or listeners.
6. Oral reading must not become so artificial or mechanical for the reader that he forgets that he is reading for meaning.
7. The teacher should be ready to provide a good model of oral reading when such a model is needed by the group or an individual child.
8. It should be remembered that the larger the group involved, the more the problems.
9. Oral reading may be a considerable threat to some pupils. These cases should be handled with sympathetic understanding.

---

[11] Helen Kovas, "The Place of Oral Reading," *Elementary English,* XXXIV (1957), 462-66.

DIAGNOSIS OF PUPILS' READING ABILITY

It has been pointed out that throughout the primary years ever-increasing differences are found among pupils in the same classroom. If some children in a second grade read at the primer or first-reader level, their teacher must function as a first grade teacher. Some pupils in the same class will have mastered skills sufficient to read third grade materials. To teach these children where they are, the teacher, in effect, will be a third grade teacher. Very few second grade teachers enjoy the luxury of a group more homogeneous than depicted here. Third grade teachers are confronted with even more heterogenous groups as far as reading ability is concerned. Figure 15 is a graphic representation of the overlap between grades and the range of reading abilities found in the primary grades.

FIGURE 15

GRAPHIC REPRESENTATION OF READING ABILITIES IN THE PRIMARY GRADES. (Note that the *Range* of abilities increases at each succeeding grade level.)

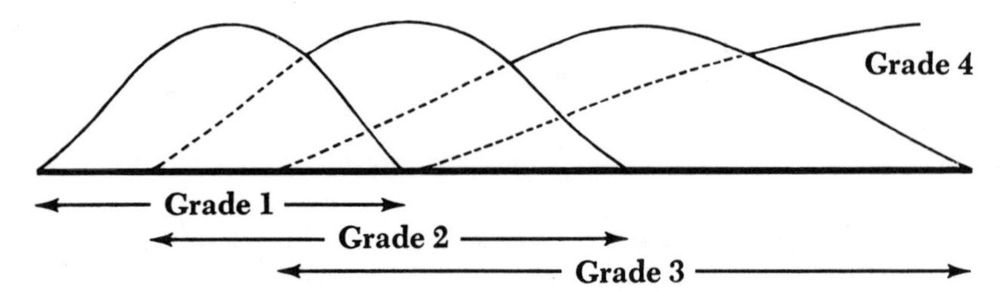

Teachers will have to be alert to differences among pupils in order to follow sound principles of teaching. Only through diagnosis will the teacher be able to assess needs and plan instruction for children whose needs vary considerably. Diagnosis should be thought of as continuous since children are changing rapidly. A diagnosis in September may be followed by a breakthrough on the part of the child in some vital skill or by a child's failure to master some new step in the reading process. In either case, the earlier diagnosis is obsolete.

Reading weaknesses and reading achievement can be assessed by either standardized or informal teacher-made tests. Although tests are designed for use at every grade level, no purpose would be served in a reading textbook by a separate discussion of tests each time a different instructional level is under consideration. The following discussion of tests and testing applies to the various levels of the elementary school with the exception that reading readiness tests are dealt with in Chapter 2.

STANDARDIZED TESTS

These are commercially printed tests which fall into two classes: those designed for group administration, and those designed to be administered individually. In both, credits are given for acceptable responses, and the child's score is determined by his correct responses, lack of errors, and rate of reading. Norms are usually provided, and any child's score can be translated into a grade-level equivalent. Usually sub-tests are scored separately, permitting the plotting of a profile which will indicate the areas of pupil strengths and weaknesses. Standardized tests are widely used in our schools and a larger number of them are becoming available each year. Most of these have real merit, yet it is doubtful that reading instruction is improving as a direct result of these tests. This is paradoxical. If tests have real merit, how could their widespread use not result in appreciable improvement in reading instruction?

The answer to this question is to be found in the way the tests are used. As pointed out in Chapter 1, the only justifiable purpose for the use of reading tests is to secure data about an individual's reading ability so that a reading program for the child can be built from the data secured. In actual practice some schools and some teachers gain comfort from the use of tests because they are convinced that testing programs per se have educational value. Testing becomes an end in itself rather than a basis for instruction. In some communities a metal filing cabinet "with a folder for each pupil" is interpreted as prima facie evidence of good teaching practices. This reaction suggests that the school has lost sight of the principle that diagnosis alone has no salutary effect on the pupil diagnosed.

GROUP TESTS

Tests designed for groups have some very obvious weaknesses. A second grade teacher testing a large number of children at one time

An entire class is being administered a reading achievement test. One child is seeking a further explanation of the task. As the teacher moves about the classroom, she will make a note of certain of her observations. The score made by each child will be of less value to the teachers than knowledge of the type of errors made by each pupil. Following study of the test results, there will be some pupils about whom the teacher will need more data. She will administer individual oral-reading tests to these pupils. *(Courtesy of Bexley Schools, Bexley, Ohio; photographer: Arthur Burt, Inc.)*

cannot hope to find out much about any individual child's reading needs or weaknesses. Such a test will differentiate between poor and good readers, but using a formal testing situation may not be the most economical method of securing this data. A considerable amount of teacher time must be spent in learning the precise procedure for administering and scoring the test and in analyzing the results. The skilled teacher who uses equal time and effort in informal reading situations will certainly arrive at an equally reliable division of pupils. In addition, she will also have a better idea of what particular weaknesses certain children have developed. From the standpoint of instruction this is more important than simply knowing which children are impaired readers.

Another drawback to the use of group tests is that pupils' scores can be influenced by such factors as the misunderstanding of directions, guessing answers, and confusion in marking responses. If these go undetected in the group-administration process, the analysis of test scores will result in a distorted picture of the child's reading ability.

All achievement batteries designed to test pupils in the elementary school contain reading tests. Often these reading subtests are available in individual booklets which can be secured and administered independently of the rest of the battery. (The *California*, *SRA* and *Metropolitan* achievement batteries and the *Co-ordinated Scales of Attainment* are examples.) Since there are so many different reading tests, it is to be expected that many of them will measure virtually the same aspects of reading. Nevertheless, there are major differences among tests as to what they measure, the level of difficulty for which they are designed, the care which went into their construction, and their ease of administration. Each of these factors affects two important attributes of reading tests—the consistency with which they measure reading skills, and the degree to which they actually measure the skills that they allegedly measure.

No full-time elementary teacher would have the time or the need to become thoroughly conversant with all standardized reading tests. However, it might be well to know where one can go for information about tests when that information is needed. Probably the most authoritative source for such information is *The Mental Measurement Yearbook*, edited by Buros.[12] Information regarding tests can also be secured from publishers of tests and sample sets of tests can be purchased. A number of publishers who issue descriptive test catalogues are cited at the end of this chapter. In addition, many universities and colleges maintain testing bureaus which are equipped to advise teachers and administrators concerning tests and testing programs.

STANDARDIZED INDIVIDUAL TESTS

Individual tests can minimize some of the shortcomings attributed to group tests. Teachers can observe one child quite closely during the administration of the test. This permits much more precise knowledge of reading errors made and whether or not the child understands the test directions. Individual standardized tests range in content from a single paragraph of oral reading at each grade level to a number of subtests including silent reading, oral reading with

---

[12] Oscar Krisen Buros, (Ed.), *The Fifth Mental Measurements Yearbook* (New Brunswick: Rutgers University Press, 1959). The fourth and third editions of the volume were published in 1953 and 1949 respectively.

A particular child may be administered a reading achievement test at any time. Members of this class have grown used to the idea that all pupils will not be engaged in the same task at the same time. *(Courtesy of Bexley Schools, Bexley, Ohio; photographer: Arthur Burt, Inc.)*

comprehension questions, spelling, letter recognition, sounding of blends, word meanings, and rapid recognition of sight words in isolation. The most significant subtests are the oral reading passages at each grade level. These are usually relatively short reading passages upon which the grade norms are based and as a result tend to rate pupils higher than their actual reading level on sustained reading material. Table 4 presents data on the number of running words (total number of words in the reading passage at each grade level) found in several reading tests designed for use in the elementary grades.

TABLE 4

NUMBER OF RUNNING WORDS FOUND ON REPRESENTATIVE READING TESTS, GRADES 1-6

Grade Level	Running Words Found on:		
	Durrell Analysis of Reading Difficulty*	Gray Oral Reading Paragraphs Test†	Gilmore Oral Reading Tests*
1	21	49	26
2	51	49	50
3	55	49	51
4	72	62	67
5	78	62	107
6	97	62	107

* World Book Co., New York
† Public School Publishing Co., Bloomington, Indiana

REPRESENTATIVE TESTS

A brief description of a limited number of both group and individual tests follows. These tests are selected because they illustrate different types of reading tests and because, in most cases, they are recent publications or recent revisions.

Representative Group Tests

1. *American School Achievement Tests* (Part I Test of Reading)
   A. Primary Battery, Grades 2-3
   B. Intermediate Battery, Grades 4-6
   C. Advanced Battery, Grades 7-9

Reading skills measured (all levels): Sentence and word meaning, paragraph meaning, and total reading score.

Four forms: D, E, F, G

Publisher: Public School Publishing Company.

2. *California Achievement Test Batteries* (1957 edition)
   - A. Lower Primary, Grades 1-2
   - B. Upper Primary, Grades 3-4
   - C. Elementary, Grades 4-6
   - D. Junior High, Grades 7-9
   - E. Advanced, Grades 9-14

Reading skills measured: Reading vocabulary and reading comprehension are tested. Each is covered by several subtests which yield part scores. The reading tests, which are part of the achievement battery, are available as separate tests under the title *California Reading Test.*

Four forms: W, X, Y, Z

Publisher: California Test Bureau

3. *Doren Diagnostic Reading Test of Word Recognition Skills* (Grades 1-9). This test is primarily for use in remedial diagnosis in the area of word recognition. The eleven subtests include the following: recognition of letters, sounds of initial consonants, blends, rhymes, speech consonants, word endings, vowels, sight words, and words within words.

The test is available in one form only and requires approximately three hours for administration. It is a group diagnostic test limited to word-recognition skills.

Publisher: Educational Test Bureau

4. *Gates Reading Tests* (1958 edition)
   - A. *Gates Primary Reading Tests:* Grades 1-2^1
     - Type PWR: A test of word recognition
     - Type PSR: A test of sentence reading
     - Type PPR: A test of paragraph comprehension

Each of the above tests is available in three alternate forms (1-2-3). Each takes approximately fifteen minutes to administer.

   - B. *Gates Advanced Primary Reading Tests* (Grades 2^2-3)
     - Type AWR: Word recognition
     - Type APR: Paragraph reading

Each test available in three alternate forms (1-2-3).

C. *Gates Basic Reading Tests* (Grades 3^2-8)

Type GS: Reading to appreciate general significance
Type ND: Noting details
Type LD: Understanding directions
Type LC: Level of comprehension
Type RV: Reading vocabulary

D. *Gates Reading Survey* (Grades 3-8)

Three tests (level of comprehension, word knowledge, and speed of reading) are included in one test booklet. Administration time is approximately one hour.

Publisher: Bureau of Publications, Teachers College, Columbia University.

5. *Iowa Silent Reading Test,* Elementary (Grades 4-8). This test is available in four alternate forms and measures the following reading skills: word meanings, comprehension of paragraphs, comprehension of sustained reading, rate of reading, study skills and locating information.

Publisher: World Book Company

6. *Iowa Tests of Basic Skills* (Grades 3-9). This achievement battery yields eleven separate scores in the following major areas: vocabulary, reading comprehension, language skills, work-study skills, and arithmetic skills.

All of the subtests for each grade, three through nine, are included in one spiral booklet of ninety-six pages. These booklets are re-usable since responses are made on separate answer sheets.

The reading comprehension test requires approximately one hour for administration at *each* grade level. It consists of a number of stories of graduated length and difficulty. Comprehension is tested by means of multiple choice items, the reader selecting the one best answer from among the four available. As noted above, the reading comprehension test is available only as part of the entire Basic Skills Battery.

Publisher: Houghton Mifflin Company (3 alternate forms)

7. *Metropolitan Achievement Tests* (Grades 1-9). Separate achievement tests are designed for each of the following levels. Reading is one of the major subtests at each level:

Level	Subtests
Primary I, Grade 1^2	
Primary II, Grade 2	word knowledge
Elementary, Grade 3-4	word discrimination
Intermediate, Grade 5-6	paragraph reading
Advanced, Grade 7-9	

The reading tests are available as separate tests at the elementary, intermediate, and advanced levels. These cover comprehension, word recognition, and vocabulary. Two comparable forms are available at each level.

Publisher: World Book Company.

8. *Nelson-Lohmann Reading Test* (Grades 4-8). This is a paragraph test using multiple-choice questions to measure the pupil's grasp of central ideas, word meanings derived from context, and details, and the pupil's ability to integrate ideas. There are separate tests for each grade level 4-8 and two comparable forms are available.

These tests are also part of the battery: *Co-ordinated Scales of Attainment.*

Publisher: Educational Test Bureau, Educational Publishers, Inc.

9. *Primary Reading Profiles* (Revised edition). Grades 1-2, one form.

This is a battery of five subtests which yield separate scores and a total test score. The areas covered are reading aptitude, auditory association, word recognition, word attack, and reading comprehension.

One of the excellent features of this test is the subtest measuring auditory association. Few standardized tests attempt to measure this skill. This is particularly useful to teachers of grades 1-2.

Publisher: Houghton Mifflin Company.

10. *SRA* Achievement Series* (Grades 1-9). This achievement series offers separate tests, each designed for one of the following levels:

Grades 1-2. The reading test contains 4 subtests:
Verbal-picture association, language perception, comprehension, and vocabulary. A separate test measures arithmetical skills and number concepts.

Grades 2-4. The reading test consists of two subtests:
Vocabulary and comprehension. (Two alternate forms.)

In the following levels, tests are available both as achievement batteries covering the complete academic program or as separate tests in four major areas: reading, language arts, arithmetic, and work study skills.

Grades 4-6. (Two alternate forms)
Grades 6-9. (Two alternate forms)

**Publisher:* Science Research Associates, Inc.

11. *Stanford Achievement Tests.* Four separate batteries cover grades 1-9. Each battery contains a substantial subtest on reading which consists of several parts.

Primary Battery, Grades 1.9-3.5
Elementary Battery, Grades 3-4
Intermediate Battery, Grades 5-6
Advanced Battery, Grades 7-9

Separate reading tests are also available for the elementary, intermediate, and advanced levels. Alternate forms are available and each test requires approximately forty minutes to administer.

Representative Individual Tests

1. *Durrell Analysis of Reading Difficulty* (Grades 1-6). Major subtests include a separate series of paragraphs for oral reading and recall, silent reading and recall, and listening comprehension. Other subtests measure visual recognition of letters and words, ability to give sounds of letters and blends, and spelling. Each individual test folder contains an extensive checklist of potential reading difficulties. This test has several limitations: only one form is available, grade level norms are based on rate but not on comprehension; and comprehension questions rely heavily on recall of detail, thus slighting other facets of comprehension.

Publisher: World Book Company

2. *Gates Reading Diagnostic Tests* (Grades 1-8, although majority of subtests are most appropriate at lower levels). Subtests measure: Oral reading (without comprehension check), auditory comprehension of word meanings, phrase reading, sight word recognition, word attack skills, oral spelling and visual-auditory perception of speech sounds.

The limitations of this test are that excessive time is needed for administration and that examiners must have access to, and be familiar with, *The Improvement of Reading.*[13]

3. *Gilmore Oral Reading Test* (Grades 1-8). This test consists of ten paragraphs, arranged in order of difficulty, which form a continuous story. Each paragraph, representing a grade level, is followed by five comprehension questions. There are two forms of the test, both of which are included in the same spiral-bound booklet. The test yields separate scores on rate of reading, comprehension, and accuracy (pronunciation of vocabulary). The individual record blank permits a detailed record of reading errors.

Publisher: World Book Company

4. *Gray Standardized Oral Reading Paragraphs Test* (Grades 1-8). A series of paragraphs which serve as a basis for determining rate of reading and reading accuracy as measured by such criteria as mispronunciation, omission, insertion, substitution, and repetition.

This is a single-form test which can roughly establish a child's reading level while calling the examiner's attention to certain mechanical aspects of reading.

Publisher: Public School Publishing Company

5. *Leavell Analytical Oral Reading Test* (Grades 1-10). A continuous story divided into nine paragraphs which vary in difficulty from beginning reading to beginning high school level. Comprehension questions follow each paragraph. Each paragraph contributes three scores based on comprehension, mechanical errors, and rate.

---

[13] Arthur I. Gates, *The Improvement of Reading* (3rd ed.; New York: The Macmillan Co., 1947).

These are summated and the scores on all paragraphs read are converted into a grade-level score. Norms are not provided for rate, comprehension, and reading error scores.

INFORMAL TEACHER-MADE TESTS

Teachers can devise informal tests for any classroom purpose. The simplest screening test might consist of having a child read a paragraph or two from a book to determine whether he can successfully read that particular book. More thorough informal tests will yield important data about children's reading, and these tests have certain advantages for classroom use. First, they are simple to construct since the teacher has available graded reading materials from the pre-primer level through the upper grades. Second, the child can be tested over longer passages of sustained reading than are characteristically found on standardized tests. Third, the use of teacher-made tests avoids the formality of the usual test situation. Informal testing is not likely to arouse the pupil tensions which sometimes accompany testing and which occasionally influence pupil performance. In this respect, the informal test more closely parallels the actual reading situations which the child encounters in the classroom. Finally, the teacher-made test is inexpensive and demands no more teacher time for administration and analysis than do other tests. At the same time it yields very specific data on each child's weaknesses and needs, as do the individual standardized tests. The following steps might serve as a guide in the construction of an informal test.

Step I. Devise a checklist of reading behaviors. This is usually one page upon which the teacher can rapidly record reading errors and observations of related behavior. Figure 16 is an example which could be duplicated and filled out for each child in the class. The checklist can be used with any graded reading materials.

FIGURE 16

READING BEHAVIOR RECORD

Name________________ Age____ Grade____ Date________
School________________ Teacher________________
Examiner________________

I. *Word Analysis* — Yes — No

A. Knows names of letters.
B. Attacks initial sounds of words.
C. Can substitute initial sound.
D. Can work out initial blends.
E. If root word is known, can get words formed by adding prefixes and suffixes.

II. *Sight Words* — Yes — No

A. Knows words in context, but misses them in isolation.
B. Knows a word one time, misses it later.
C. Guesses at unknown words.
D. Does not attempt unknown words.
E. Frequently adds words.
F. Omits words not known, reads on.
G. Occasionally omits or skips words he knows.

III. *General Reading Habits*

__________word by word __________does not utilize punctuation
__________poor phrasing __________points with finger
__________(other) __________(other)

IV. *Informal Reading Analysis*

	Book	*Grade Level*	*Approx. Number of Running Words*	*Number of Errors*
1.				
2.				
3.				

V. *Highest Level Child Can Read Successfully*

	Excellent	*Average*	*Below Average*
Attitude toward reading			
Self-confidence			
General background experience			
Language facility			
Recall or comprehension			

Step II. Construct a simple test of sight words in isolation. The Dolch Basic Sight Word Test[14] could be used or a typed list of approximately one hundred words taken from pre-primers, primers, and first readers, omitting proper names. Almost any list made will contain words found on the Dolch list. Testing sight words in isolation will sometimes reveal that a child knows more words in actual reading than he does in the sight recognition of words in isolation. Often a child miscalls small words in sustained reading situations which he may be able to correct immediately. This indicates that he has not *mastered* these small "service words" as instant recognition sight vocabulary. The following 100 words are common to the pre-primers and primers of a number of widely used basal reader series. A child who has trouble with many of these words will find reading a frustrating task.

we	horse	they	boat
with	a	jump	to
yes	an	big	walk
stop	look	come	want
like	was	go	on
help	find	think	house
very	little	and	my
all	best	could	can
this	old	boy	talk
some	try	may	girl
the	see	again	said
ball	mother	pretty	will
friend	any	which	father
went	over	then	small
did	wagon	live	blue
good	not	run	had
in	play	arm	she
me	what	up	your
hat	do	each	after
man	ran	his	clean
that	new	got	many
saw	wish	red	most
you	dog	there	around
here	under	please	open
sure	ride	name	every

[14] Garrard Press, Champaign, Illinois.

Step III. Secure materials for testing children on sustained reading. Short passages of 100 or more words from pre-primer through sixth grade level can be used. Pages from books can be cut out and placed in order of difficulty in a teacher-made booklet, or the basal readers themselves can be used. Comprehension questions should be carefully developed for each passage. The child should not be permitted to read from a book which he is using in class or which he has used extensively in the recent past. Some teachers prefer to have typed copies of these passages so that they can mark the copies, showing each error and weakness observed while the child is reading. The checklist mentioned above is also used to its fullest advantage during this step of the informal analysis.

Judging the pupil's reading level for basal materials can be accomplished quite accurately by carefully noting his reading behavior on the sustained material test. Failure to pronounce as high as 7 or 8 different words per 100 running words at a given level would indicate this basal material is too difficult for independent reading. On the other hand, few reading errors on basal material at a given level does not assure that the reader will be successful in reading subject textbooks at this grade level. Textbooks in content areas are as a general rule more difficult than the basal-reader materials because in the former the vocabulary is not so rigidly controlled and more unknown concepts appear. A sustained reading test similar to that just described can be devised using representative passages from a geography or science text. Such a test should include carefully prepared comprehension and vocabulary questions.

Step IV. Include a subtest which deals extensively with word analysis skills. Attention has already been paid to these skills in the sight word test and the sustained reading, but further information will often be desired on a child's word-analysis skills. The sight word test included no inflectional endings but only common root words such as *look, run, walk, go, talk, come, like, want, see, play,* and *stop.* The child may now be tested with a series of cards containing these root words plus the common endings (Figure 17A). If the child reads at a level of difficulty above first grade, he can be tested with a number of derived forms, contractions, and compound words. (See Figure 17B.) Performance on these tasks would determine whether the child should be tested on breaking words into syllables. Figure 17C uses words taken from spelling books at various grade levels. Separate duplicated work sheets can be made up for each grade level or one page might be developed which covers several grade levels. The child is asked to break the stimulus word found in Column A into syllables and write it in Column B.

FIGURE 17

Test of Word Analysis Skills

A. *Easy root words plus endings* s, ed, ing

running	seated	playing	comes	played
asks	talking	lived	wanted	going
looked	wants	jumps	talks	sees
helps	coming	lives	walking	helping
wanting	likes	pleased	talked	looks
sits	helped	finding	runs	sitting
living	stops	plays	seeing	jumped

B. *Contractions, compound words, and derived forms usually learned at second grade level*

happily	belong	I'll	slowly	behind	hadn't
bakery	didn't	friendly	report	surely	himself
princess	outside	loudest	I'd	everybody	believe
quickly	snow plow	return	herself	you'll	politely
I've	it's	really	suddenly	everyone	shouted
isn't	quickly	everything	doesn't	couldn't	yourself
beside	anything	can't	between	into	wasn't

Contractions, compound words, and derived forms usually learned at third grade level

expect	explain	disappear	comfortable	rapidly
afternoon	ourselves	happiness	halfway	sawmill
you've	discover	invite	safety	invisible
family	they'll	include	upward	Thanksgiving
enjoy	unless	gentleman	peaceful	eyebrow
funniest	experiment	foolish	enchanted	
finally	we've	contentment	bathroom	

C. Words taken from spelling books at 3rd, 4th, and 5th grade level to test child's ability to break words into syllables. Pupil writes words in Column B. First word serves as sample.

3rd Grade Level		4th Grade Level		5th Grade Level	
A	B	A	B	A	B
yesterday	yes ter day	grandfather	grand fa ther	citizen	cit i zen
money		beautiful		terrible	
birthday		lessons		interesting	
yellow		history		difference	
Easter		remember		medium	
stockings		arithmetic		average	
only		studying		frightened	
afternoon		geography		electric	

If the pupil's performance indicates a lack of ability in attacking words through phonic analysis, a most important step is to determine whether the child actually hears the different speech sounds in similar sounding words. Teachers can prepare auditory discrimination exercises consisting of three- or four-word series to check the pupil's ability to hear *initial sounds, initial blends, vowel sounds,* and *word endings.* The teacher pronounces each word in the series, and the child repeats the one word which does not belong or does not rhyme or begin with the same letter or letter blend. (See Figure 18.)

FIGURE 18

TEST OF AUDITORY DISCRIMINATION

(The teacher pronounces the four words in each series.)

A. TESTING ABILITY TO HEAR INITIAL CONSONANTS

Child repeats the one word that begins differently from the first word.

toy	pat	did	wind	dark	farm
tall	pet	kid	went	drink	warm
hall	cot	doll	bend	dash	find
tack	put	dull	well	bark	full
ball	hard	lack	kick	march	rode
pull	yard	lock	pick	much	load
back	hunt	lamp	kill	met	right
burn	hurt	damp	kind	net	race

B. Testing Ability to Hear Endings of Words

Child repeats the one word which does not rhyme.

pig	bake	ball	wet	bug	bag
dig	make	full	bet	hug	rug
big	bark	tall	pet	did	rag
bag	wake	wall	sat	mug	sag
pot	lick	leg	cut	fell	then
not	stuck	peg	hit	fill	hen
got	stick	lap	hut	sell	thin
God	kick	keg	but	bell	pen

C. Testing Ability to Hear Initial Blends

Child repeats the word which does not begin with the blend sound.

chair	sled	blue	step	tree	plan
champ	sack	blow	sack	truck	pain
cow	slip	bank	stop	train	place
chicken	slap	black	steep	turn	play

D. Testing Vowel Sounds

Child repeats word having short vowel sound.

mate	fan	fight	joke	cute	tall
mail	fame	mile	lock	dull	team
mad	table	fine	note	true	see
take	flame	skim	snow	tube	peck

USING TEST RESULTS FOR GROUPING AND INSTRUCTION

The results of diagnosis based on either standardized or informal tests can be used for various instructional purposes. The obvious uses are instruction based on pupil needs as disclosed by the diagnosis and grouping practices which might facilitate this instruction. Pupils of widely varying achievement in a classroom will not profit equally from the same procedures applied to the group as a whole. Grouping, as stated previously, is a device which permits teachers to work with a smaller number of pupils who have similar instructional needs. Several factors which relate to grouping in the primary grades should be kept in mind. First, it is to be expected that some pupils will make substantial gains in reading during a period of weeks or months in the primary years. Therefore, neither reliance on a single initial diagnosis nor a rigid grouping arrangement would be desirable. Diagnosis must be ongoing and grouping practices flexible.

Second, the range of pupil abilities will inevitably place some children at the extremes of the achievement continuum outside of the conventional three-group or even a four-group structure. Fitting instruction to these extreme individual differences will call for a supply of materials at many difficulty levels and a variety of approaches to any given instructional objective. Third, since the total reading process is composed of a great number of related but specific skills, it is likely that some children will belong in one group when achievement in one skill is the criterion and in other groups for other instructional purposes. Few children, for example, will be equally deficient—or proficient—in phonic analysis, comprehension of what is read, and appreciation of literature.

The facets of primary reading dealt with in this chapter include the objectives of primary reading and its instructional program from the standpoint of materials, teaching schedule, recreational reading, oral reading, and formal and informal diagnosis. The two major tasks of dealing with the development of the mechanical skills of reading and the expansion of comprehension skills are discussed in the following chapter.

A representative list of test publishers from whom descriptive catalogues or brochures may be obtained.*

Acorn Publishing Company, Inc., Rockville Center, New York City, N. Y.

Bureau of Educational Measurements, Kansas State Teachers College, Emporia, Kansas.

Bureau of Educational Research and Service, State University of Iowa, Iowa City, Iowa.

Bureau of Publications, Teachers College, Columbia University, New York City (27), New York.

California Test Bureau, 5916 Hollywood Boulevard, Los Angeles (28), California.

---

* Source: *The Fifth Mental Measurements Yearbook,* Oscar Krisen Buros, Editor. The Gryphon Press, Highland Park, New Jersey, 1959.

Consulting Psychologist Press, 270 Town and Country Village, Palo Alto, California.

Co-operative Test Division, Educational Testing Service, 20 Nassau Street, Princeton, New Jersey.

Educational Test Bureau, Educational Publishers, Inc., 720 Washington Avenue, S. E., Minneapolis, Minnesota.

Educational Testing Service, 20 Nassau Street, Princeton, New Jersey.

Gregory, C. A. Company, 345 Calhoun Street, Cincinnati (19), Ohio.

Houghton Mifflin Co., 2 Park Street, Boston (2), Massachusetts.

Institute for Personality and Ability Testing, 1602 Coronado Drive, Champaign, Illinois.

Ohio Scholarship Tests, Ohio State Department of Education, Columbus, Ohio.

Oliver and Boyd Ltd., Tweeddale Court, Edinburgh (1), Scotland.

Psychological Corporation, 304 East 45th Street, New York (17), New York.

Public School Publishing Co., 345 Calhoun Street, Cincinnati (19), Ohio.

Scholastic Testing Service, Inc., 3774 West Devon Avenue, Chicago (45), Illinois.

Science Research Associates, Inc., 57 West Grand Avenue, Chicago (10), Illinois.

Sheridan Supply Co., P. O. Box 837, Beverly Hills, California.

Stoelting (C. H.) Co., 424 North Homan Avenue, Chicago (24), Illinois.

Western Psychological Services, 10655 Santa Monica Boulevard, Los Angeles (25), California.

World Book Company, Yonkers-on-Hudson, New York.

(Bibliographical references for primary reading are found at the end of Chapter 6.)

chapter 6

TEACHING READING IN THE PRIMARY GRADES (continued)

Following diagnosis, plans can be made for teaching both mechanical and comprehension skills. Since every skill is developmental, once it is introduced the skill must be extended. For example, auditory discrimination is extremely significant in beginning reading and becomes even more essential when major emphasis is placed on teaching phonic analysis. Instant recognition of words is stressed in beginning reading, but the need for this skill becomes more acute when new words are introduced with increased frequency in the primary and intermediate grades.

In other contexts throughout this book the point is stressed that mechanical skills and reading habits are closely related to comprehension. This relationship is reaffirmed here because in the following discussion mechanics and comprehension skills are discussed separately. Nevertheless, many of the exercises and examples emphasize both skills simultaneously.

DEVELOPING AND EXTENDING THE MECHANICAL SKILLS OF READING

The term *mechanics of reading* is used to refer to such skills as:

1. Extension of sight vocabulary
   a) Learning recognition of new words prior to silent reading
   b) Use of experience charts and pictures
   c) Picture-word cards
   d) Completing sentences by choosing proper word
   e) Rapid recognition of vowels in medial position
   f) Combining phrases into meaningful sentences
   g) Identifying root words and inflected forms
2. Word recognition skills
   a) Structural analysis
   b) Kinesthetic method
   c) Phonic analysis
3. Profiting from punctuation
4. Alphabetizing skills
5. Syllabication

EXPANDING SIGHT WORD VOCABULARY

Developing sight vocabulary is one of the most important goals in the primary reading program. The pupil who fails in this ability is in trouble as a reader. The child in the first grade will meet several hundred words on experience charts, on bulletin boards, and in basal readers. If he masters as sight words all the words he meets in the pre-primer, primer, and first reader of a given basal series, he will know between three and four hundred words, although this figure is too high to be used as an estimated average for all pupils beginning their second year of school. At the end of second grade if a child knew only the words met thus far in any one basal reader series, he would know between 800 and 1000 sight words. In the third year he would again double his stock of sight words. Throughout the primary period pupils read from a variety of sources, but it is probably no exaggeration to say that the basal reader series will provide the backbone of the *formal instruction* in reading and word getting. This is true because the systematic teaching of skills is provided within the framework of these materials.

A number of procedures and exercises for helping children extend sight vocabulary are found in basal reader workbooks. In many instances, teachers can devise additional seat-work lessons for pupils who need added experience. A few typical techniques are cited below:

1. Chalkboard work on new words which are introduced in the day's reading assignment. It is considered desirable to study these new words prior to having children read the story silently. The new words are pronounced as they are printed on the board *(stump, footprints, suddenly, ocean).* Similarities to other words previously learned are pointed out, i.e., the *st* in *stump,* the word *foot* in the compound word *footprints,* the root word *sudden* in *suddenly.* Learning *ocean* as a sight word is stressed because of the difficulty of sounding it.

2. Using experience charts and personal experience records, labeling objects in the room, and matching captions with pictures. A series of pictures can be displayed and appropriate titles consisting of words, phrases, or sentences can be prepared on oak tag or cardboard. Children then match the proper written caption with each picture:

"The box is empty"	"A jet plane"
"Evergreens"	"Children in a school bus"
"A brown cow"	"Two boys"
"The tree has no leaves"	"A boy and a dog"

3. Using picture-word cards to teach "naming words." A picture of an object is pasted on one side of the card and the word for the picture printed on the other side:

house, car, tractor, bridge, shirt, television, giraffe,
piano, dress, swing, policeman, cowboy, hammer, etc.

4. Introducing exercises which call for pupils to select the proper word to fill in a space left blank in a sentence. These exercises stress both meaning and differentiation between similar appearing words.

The kittens were asleep on the ______________.
stay - straw

The bird built its nest in the ______________.
tree, tray

They made a ______________ for the puppy.
bad, bed
Mr. Brown sells ______________ in his store.
hats, hates

A more difficult task is illustrated below where two similar appearing words are to be placed in two blanks in a sentence.

It was their _______ to go by _______. (plane - plan)
The _______ is about a _______ from here. (mile - mill)
The dog took the _______ to the _______. (bone - barn)
The train whistle went _______ _______. (toot-toot - two-too)
We must _______ to write on the _______. (line - learn)

5. Using word-drill periods and work sheets for seat work which stress seeing the difference between similar appearing words.

a) The easiest drill usually involves "family" phonograms in which the initial letter or initial blend is the important visual cue:

*l*ake, *t*ake, *m*ake, *c*ake, *r*ake
*h*at, *c*at, *m*at, *f*at, *p*at, *r*at
*f*all, *c*all, *t*all, *b*all, *h*all, *w*all

b) A child is to supply a word containing the same phonogram as a pair of cue words.

make lake
They used a boat to cross the l_____.
told fold
The teacher showed them how to f_____ the paper.

c) Practice may be provided in discriminating between common service words which have marked similarities.

their, there; where, when, which; stay, stop;
must, much; many, may; than, then, thin;
horse, house; every, very; think, thank.

d) Practice may be given in rapid recognition of vowels in medial position. (To be read orally):

pin, pen, pan, pun
men, tan, fun, fin, son
sack, sick, sock, suck
duck, kick, back, lock, neck
fell, fall, full, fill
bat, fit, hut, got, let

6. Combining phrases to form meaningful sentences. This exercise forces attention on both the configuration of words and their meanings. In a *finish the sentence* exercise, children draw a line from the phrase in Column A to the phrase in Column B which completes the meaning:

A	B
The car	is on his head.
Around the house	give us milk.
The horse	is a beautiful lawn.
A straw hat	moves down the road.
Cows	drinks milk.
The cat	has a beautiful saddle.

7. Identifying root words in inflected forms. The child writes the root in the space provided.

taken	_______	using	_______
carried	_______	goes	_______
earlier	_______	laziest	_______
parties	_______	angrily	_______
reaching	_______	wagged	_______

DEVELOPING WORD RECOGNITION SKILLS

As mentioned above, many reading activities are related to several objectives, such as mastering sight words, identifying unknown words, and getting meaning. Word identification is one of the more important mechanical skills of reading. *Word analysis* includes all methods of arriving at the pronunciation of unknown words. Gaining independence in reading implies a mastery of those techniques which will permit a child to read a passage containing words which he does not recognize instantly as sight words. The reader in the primary grades will continue to use all methods of word analysis discussed in beginning reading, deducing words from pictures, word configuration, context, and structural and phonic analysis. However, in the primary grades phonic and structural analysis become more important because of the reading tasks dealt with.

As taught in the primary grades, *structural analysis* involves a review and extension of the child's experience with:

common word endings
compound words

- doubling consonants before adding endings beginning with a vowel
- adding *es* to form some plurals
- forming plurals of words ending with *y*
- contractions
- recognizing prefixes and suffixes added to root words
- syllabication

Compound words will not be difficult for the child who forms the habit of examining unknown words. The compound words he meets will be composed of shorter words that he has already learned. Basal

Children practice using phonic clues as a means of arriving at the pronunciation of words which they must eventually learn as sight words. Instruction in larger groups preceded this seat work. Each child works with specific materials which relate to his individual instructional needs. *(Courtesy of Bexley Schools, Bexley, Ohio; photographer: Arthur Burt, Inc.)*

reader series introduce a few compound words at first grade level and provide drill on recognition and analysis at each succeeding grade level. Plurals formed by *s, es,* and *ies* are usually not introduced until after the child has learned the root words.

There are a number of rules which apply to inflectional endings: an apostrophe followed by an *s* is used to form possessives; when root words end in *y*, the *y* becomes *i* in forming plurals; *e* is dropped before adding a suffix beginning with a vowel; some single consonants preceded by a single vowel are doubled at the end of root words before adding suffixes beginning with a vowel. The words and inflected forms are learned as sight words before any of these rules are taught. After the child has had a number of experiences with each of the procedures described above, the rules or generalizations are taught. Exercises dealing with some of these changes which take place in words are illustrated in examples 1 through 5 below. Each exercise can be extended to a full-page lesson sheet to be used by those pupils who need such drill.

1. Noticing the structure of compound words.

a) The two words in columns 1 and 2 can be placed together to form one word. Write the two words together under 3 and say the compound that is formed.

1	2	3
after	noon	afternoon
with	out	________
every	one	________
club	house	________
air	plane	________
door	way	________
some	time	________

b) Each word under 1 can be placed with a word under 2 to make a compound word. The first one is done for you.

1	2	3
*after	way	afternoon
with	time	________
every	plane	________
club	one	________
air	*noon	________
door	out	________
	house	________

2. Doubling the final consonant.

A number of one-syllable words ending with a consonant are given below. Double that consonant before adding the endings which begin with a vowel.

can	canned	canning
plan	________	________
skip	________	________
pop	________	________
drag	________	________
stop	________	________
slam	________	________
chop	________	________

3. Forming plurals by adding *es.*

Many plurals are formed by simply adding s, *as in* boys, girls, trees, farms, cats. *In many words* es *is added to form plurals.*

fox	foxes	inch	inches
box	________	dress	________
dish	________	lunch	________
brush	________	mix	________
potato	________	match	________
class	________	fish	________

4. Forming the plural of words ending in *y.*

Change the y *to* i, *then add* es.

funny	funnies	body	bodies
fly	________	army	________
baby	________	party	________
puppy	________	cherry	________
lady	________	family	________

5. Recognizing contractions.

The two words in column A are often combined to form a different word found in column B. The apostrophe (') in these words indicates that a letter or letters have been omitted in forming the new word.

A		B
I am	=	I'm
I will	=	I'll
he will	=	he'll
he is	=	he's
has not	=	hasn't

I have	=	I've
have not	=	haven't

(In follow-up work sheets only column A is presented and the child writes the contraction.)

do not	________
was not	________
they have	________
you will	________
it is	________
does not	________

Children use prefixes and suffixes in spoken language long before coming to school. Words formed with prefixes and suffixes are taught as sight words before the meanings of specific prefixes or suffixes are taught. The structural characteristics of any word are changed by a syllable added either at the beginning or at the end of that word. A child may know the symbol *load* as a sight word, but the first few times he sees *unload, reload,* or *unloading* he may not see what is familiar but may see the whole new configuration as unfamiliar. Thus, recognizing common prefixes will be an aid in learning new words where the root word is known.

Instruction cannot deal exclusively with the structural changes resulting from the addition of prefixes or suffixes. Exercises should force attention both to the structural change and the modification of meaning. Workbooks of all basal series have lessons devoted to the study of prefixes, but the teacher does not have to wait for a particular time or page in a workbook. The curriculum of the modern school does not impose such rigidity. It is just as appropriate to show pupils that prefixes change the meanings of words in a science, arithmetic, hygiene, or geography class as it is to discuss this point during the period devoted to reading instruction.

Figure 19 illustrates exercises which teachers can develop and duplicate. Introductory exercises can deal with one prefix. These can be followed by exercises using all of the prefixes taught thus far. Having the pupil make a sentence using the base word, then a sentence with the same word plus the prefix, emphasizes the meaning of the prefix.

FIGURE 19

1. *Make a sentence with each of the following words. What happens to the meaning of each word lettered* b*? What can you say about the prefix* un*?*
   a) clean
   b) *un*clean
   a) fair
   b) *un*fair
   a) load
   b) *un*load
   a) kind
   b) *un*kind

2. *Make a sentence with each of the following words. What happens to the meaning of each word lettered* b*? What can you say about the prefix* re*?*
   a) fill
   b) *re*fill
   a) read
   b) *re*read
   a) visit
   b) *re*visit

3. *Make a sentence with the following words. Each lettered* b *has a prefix. Explain what each prefix does to the word meaning.*
   a) view
   b) *pre*view
   a) ability
   b) *in*ability
   a) agree
   b) *dis*agree

Suffixes are word endings which give root words different shades of meaning (*er, or, ist, an, al, ure, ty, ment, ism, age, is, en, el, ive, ish, ant, ful, ly, less,* etc.). Since there are a great number of suffixes and very few have an absolutely fixed meaning, an attempt to teach concrete meanings for the majority would probably produce more confusion than learning. If a child develops the habit of *seeing* the more common endings so that he is not prevented from recognizing known root words, the new word is not likely to cause trouble. Composing sentences using the different forms of a word is a better method of teaching than having the child attempt to tell the precise difference between words like joy*ful*, joy*fully*, joy*ous*; depend*ent*, depend*able*, depend*ency*.

The English language is rich in the number of prefabricated units that can be attached to any number of root words to form new words:

Heat: heated, preheated, reheat, preheating, heatedly
War: postwar, warlike, warring, prewar, wartime
Luck: lucky, unluckiest, luckily, unlucky
Place: placing, displace, replaced, replacable

Assume that the word *happy* is a known sight word. Identifying the word *unhappily* theoretically calls for these skills: recognizing the prefix *un* and the suffix *ly* as units, perceiving the root word *happy*, applying the rule that words ending in *y* change *y* to *i* before adding an ending, and understanding syllabication—i.e., prefixes and suffixes usually stand as syllables and two like consonants usually divide, thus giving the pronunciation *un hap pi ly*. It is doubtful, however, that any reader goes through all of these mental steps since the process would be most uneconomical. The reader also has the context to suggest the word, and after he has met a word on several occasions, he will probably have mastered it as a sight word and will not have to resort to analysis.

The Kinesthetic Method. The kinesthetic method is sometimes used to help children recognize words. This approach is also referred to as the *tracing method* or a *visual-motor method*.[1] In this approach the sense of touch is added to sight and hearing in an effort to help the child who has extreme difficulty in learning to recognize words. The method usually employs the following steps but could be varied with individual children.

a) A word is written or printed on a card.
b) The teacher says "This is the word *farm*—say it with me."
c) The child traces his finger over the word one or two times saying, "the letters *f-a-r-m* is *farm*."
d) With the stimulus card out of sight the child attempts to write the word from memory.

---

[1] Donald D. Durrell, *Improving Reading Instruction* (Tarrytown-On-Hudson, New York: World Book Company, 1956), 202-04.

e) The child compares his efforts with the original and repeats the tracing and sounding until the word is mastered.

In addition to use with severely impaired readers the kinesthetic method could be used with any child who consistently confuses certain words (*these, those; were, where*) or who reverses words (*was, saw; no, on*). It can also be used in learning difficult spellings. As a method of teaching reading this approach would probably not be used except in extreme remedial cases. Since it is very time-consuming, it would be uneconomical to use the method with children who could learn by faster methods. The kinesthetic approach as a remedial technique is discussed at length by Fernald.[2]

PHONIC ANALYSIS

Phonics instruction may well be the most important of the mechanical skills taught in the primary grades in helping the child expand his sight vocabulary and become an independent reader. Basal series differ as to when particular phonic tasks are introduced. There is no uniformity of opinion as to what phonics instruction should and what should not be included in the curriculum of grades one or two. The practice of teaching more phonics rules and applications in beginning reading seems to be emerging. However, all steps taught at any given grade level must be reviewed and retaught in the following grades. It is therefore important that teachers not associate particular phonics instruction too closely with a particular grade level. In order to present an over-all view of the phonics program in the primary grades, Chapter 7 is devoted to this topic.

In addition to reviewing all skills previously taught, the major steps in the phonics program which are characteristically stressed in the primary grades include the teaching of:

1. All initial consonant blends not taught previously
2. Short sound of vowels
3. Long sound of vowels
4. Vowel digraphs (two vowels together)
5. Role of silent *e* at the end of words
6. Vowel sounds modified by consonant controllers (*r, l*)

---

[2] Grace M. Fernald, *Remedial Techniques in Basic School Subjects* (New York: McGraw-Hill Book Co., Inc., 1943).

7. Diphthongs
8. Syllabication (discussed briefly below)

These and other facets of phonics are discussed in the following chapter, which is devoted entirely to phonics instruction.

CONTEXT AND METHODS IN COMBINATION

At practically all points on the reading continuum the one ability that sets the good readers apart from poorer readers is the degree to which the context helps the reader get unknown words. When children do not profit from context clues, this weakness is easy to detect by observing their reading behavior—either they do not "try" words or they insert words which do not belong. On the other hand, when a passage is read correctly, it is difficult for an observer to determine to what degree dependence on context clues contributed to the successful reading.

The good reader keeps in mind what has been read and how the sentence he is reading builds on this meaning. If context is not enough, he glances through the word to detect a prefix, the root word, or an inflectional ending. When no prefix is found, the first syllable is isolated. This may unlock the word. If not, he will work further through the word. These operations are performed so rapidly by a good reader that there may be no perceptible pause between the different modes of attack. If the word is not solved by this attack, the reader may go on past the word for additional context clues. This step may call for rereading the sentence, but if it is successful, meaning will have been reached.

When each method of attacking unknown words is discussed and examined separately, one might conclude that in a given situation a reader uses only one method. The exclusive use of one method in this way makes for slow and inefficient reading, although some children approach reading in this manner. The more ability a reader has in profiting from structural, phonic, and context clues, the less likely it is that he can tell which one was the key in helping him solve a particular word. The smooth, facile reader is one who attacks an unknown word simultaneously on every front on which it is vulnerable to analysis. Early in the first grade the child learns to sound the initial letters of words. This skill, plus pictures and context clues, makes it possible to eliminate many of the words that might otherwise have been plausible choices.

The more difficult the level of the material, the less likely it is that the immediate context alone will be an adequate tool for getting unknown words, but often with the smallest additional clue the word is easily solved. Assume that the pupil meets a sentence containing an unknown word: "Jack was sure his ______ would let him go." This is the opening line of a story and the author has yet to unfold the plot or background. There are many words which might complete an idea when this is all we know. Is Jack being held a prisoner? The word could be *captors*. Is he thinking of "getting permission"? The word might be *mother, father, friends, teacher*. If the reader notes something about the unknown word, he may get a valuable clue. For instance, "Jack was sure his p______ would let him go." *Mother, father, teacher, friends* are eliminated if the reader can use initial sounds. Several possibilities remain, such as *pal, playmates, principal, parents*. The word *play* is known as a sight word. It is not found in this unknown word, so playmates is not suggested. It is possible that word configuration (length of word) might help the reader decide between *pal* or *parents*. With enough skill at phonic analysis to work his way through the first syllable, the reader is almost assured of arriving at the correct response. If he should try PA rents or PAR ents, either pronunciation will be close enough to suggest the correct word.

"It's my ______," said Jimmy. Here a number of possibilities occur to the reader: my *idea, turn, guess, opinion* or any number of possessions. This sentence alone does not provide enough context, but rarely does such a sentence stand alone. As we take into consideration the context supplied by several previous sentences, the unknown word falls into place.

> The boys searched everywhere but they did not find the little lost puppy. "I hope Blackie doesn't get hit by a car," said Billy. Jimmy was very sad. He had been thinking all afternoon about not closing the gate when he had gone to mail the letter. The puppy must have gotten out when he left the gate open. "It's my _____," said Jimmy. Then he told about the gate.

Since a later chapter deals with phonic analysis, it should be emphasized that phonics is only one of many skills needed for facile reading. For instance, when a child does not know the meaning of a word, arriving at its *exact* pronunciation through phonic analysis will not help him. In the following sentence there is an unknown symbol:

The man was attacked by a marbohem.

Everyone reading this page can sound out *mar-bo-hem,* but no one knows what attacked the man since saying *mar-bo-hem* does not convey meaning to the reader. Words can be substituted for *marbohem* and some readers would still have trouble with the meaning even though they successfully analyze the speech sounds in the words. For example:

1. The man was attacked by a peccarry.
2. " " " " " " freebooter.
3. " " " " " " iconoclast.
4. " " " " " " fusilier.
5. " " " " " " hypochondriac.

Analysis is only a tool for use in the reading process and should not be confused with the process. It is a valuable technique in reading, but is not in itself a method of teaching reading.

PUNCTUATION

Learning to profit from punctuation in reading is a mechanical skill which greatly influences comprehension.[3] The lack of ability to use punctuation in making reading a smooth and meaningful process appears with surprising frequency among impaired readers. Experience in working with poor readers indicates that this habit is not exceptionally difficult to eradicate. Ignoring punctuation is one of the easiest defects to detect on any reading analysis, a fact which suggests that the importance of learning to use punctuation is underrated in reading instruction.

One of the most effective methods of dramatizing the utility of punctuation is through the use of a tape recorder. On the playback

[3] John J. DeBoer, "Grammar in Language Teaching," *Elementary English,* XXXVI (1959), 413-21.

the reader follows the reading passage as he listens to his recorded version. Errors are easily detected and insight comes a little easier when the child acts as his own critic.

Another procedure is to deliberately displace punctuation in a passage and thus illustrate how the meaning becomes lost. The same passage can be reproduced several times with varying degrees of distortion. The pupil sees how difficult it is to get meaning from a passage so treated. In Figure 20 the first copy completely obscures the meaning, the second copy is frustrating but not impossible, and the third is reproduced correctly.

FIGURE 20

How Punctuation Helps the Reader

Billy listened, carefully as the teacher. Explained how punctuation helps. The reader commas periods exclamation marks and question marks? All help a reader get meaning. From the printed page. Billy wondered what would happen. If the printer got the punctuation marks mixed. UP it was hard for him to imagine. What this would do to a story.

Billy listened carefully as the teacher explained. How punctuation helps the reader. Commas periods, exclamation marks and question marks all help. A reader get meaning from the printed page. Billy wondered. What would happen if the printer got the punctuation marks mixed up. It was hard for him to imagine what this would do. To a story.

Billy listened carefully as the teacher explained how punctuation helps the reader. Commas, periods, exclamation marks, and question marks all help a reader get meaning from the printed page. Billy wondered what would happen if the printer got the punctuation marks mixed up. It was hard for him to imagine what this would do to a story.

SIMPLE ALPHABETIZING

In the primary grades the initial steps in developing this mechanical skill are dealt with. Only the basic alphabetizing skills needed in using the dictionary are taught.

These include:

1. Teaching the alphabet in order.
   Exercises might include:
   a) having the child write the alphabet in sequence.
   b) fill in the letters which are missing:
   AB__ DEF__ IJK__ NO__ QR__ UV__ X__Z.
   c) write the letters which come before:
   __ D; ____K; ____N; ____T; ____W.
2. Arrange a series of words in alphabetical order using the initial letter only:
   In column B write in alphabetical order the words found in column A.

A	B
almost	______
earth	______
puppy	______
rain	______
milk	______
drive	______
change	______
geese	______
few	______

Later instruction will deal with alphabetizing by the first two letters, three letters, and through the entire word.

SYLLABICATION

The ability to break words into the syllabic components is one of the mechanical skills which receives attention at various levels of instruction. A limited number of rules of syllabication are introduced at the primary level. The major emphasis on syllabication is found in the intermediate grades where dictionary skills are stressed. Pupils have a number of experiences with words from which they might generalize a number of rules. Whether or not these rules are memorized, most children will learn more effectively if the rules are presented verbally. How well a child masters the basic pattern of syllabication will influence his progress in independent reading. The first step in the process is the ability to hear the number of distinct sounds in a word, or the number of syllables it contains. A few rules and illustrations follow.

1. Every syllable contains a sounded vowel. (Exceptions are the syllables *dle, ble, zle, tle, cle,* etc., at the end of words. These particular endings are syllables but do not contain one of the conventional vowel sounds.)

2. The number of vowel sounds in a word determines the number of syllables in the word.

3. A syllable may be a single vowel such as *a*-ble, *o*-boe, vi-*o*-let, ed-*u*-ca-tion; or a syllable may contain a vowel digraph plus one or more consonants—*rain, meet, see.*

4. In general, when two consonants fall between the two vowels the division of syllables is between the two consonants: *af-ter, sis-ter, win-dow, gar-den, pen-cil.*

5. Double consonants are usually separated: *lit-tle, val-ley, let-ter, sum-mer, cot-ton, din-ner.*

6. Prefixes and suffixes which are syllables should be learned and recognized as units—*un, ex, pre, ment, tion, tive, ly.*

7. Consonant blends are usually not divided when breaking words into syllables: tea-*cher,* ta-*ble,* wea-*ther,* re-*ply.*

COMPREHENSION SKILLS

The mechanics of reading are of necessity closely related to the comprehension of material read. Learning to use punctuation might appear to be totally within the framework of mechanics, yet nothing can more quickly distort meaning than the inability to profit from the clues that punctuation provides. Word-by-word reading has implications other than just in the skills area. In addition to slowing the reading rate this habit tends to force attention on words rather than larger units. It is the sentence which carries meaning, and when a child spends too much time on word units, he may easily lose the thought of the sentence unit.

In the transition from beginning reading to independent reading, quite noticeable changes take place in the materials which children read. Pictures will still be found in basal readers, but there will be fewer of them and the decline of the importance of pictures in providing context clues will be quite obvious. Stories will be much longer, will be more interesting, and will include more concepts.

These will not be built around the "one family" theme. There will be fairy tales and tales of animals who think and talk and have feelings. There will be stories of children who live in different lands and do unusual things. The lives and contributions of great men and women will be studied. Materials at this level call for the reader to make interpretations. He must detect clues to the mood of characters, see the relationship between events, and grasp the intended meaning of figurative or idiomatic expressions. Humor may not always be overt, and inferences may have to be drawn in the absence of absolute statements. The ability to read each word in a passage is not the only criterion of reading. The child must also be able to tell "if grandfather was serious or just playing a joke on the boys" or "if Jerry was frightened by what he overheard" or "how the storm affected the plans for a vacation."

MISCONCEPTIONS

During the latter stages of the primary years many children will encounter a number of words and concepts which will puzzle them. Many such instances will occur in subject-matter texts as well as in basal readers. Whereas the child comes to school with the "meanings" which are adequate for dealing with beginning reading, he is by no means familiar with the various connotations of the words with which he must cope in the primary and intermediate grades. A lack of concepts and insufficient knowledge of various connotations of words is not the only problem with which the teacher must deal in expanding meaning. A related problem is that of misconceptions harbored by pupils. The school cannot be held responsible for misconceptions which children have picked up elsewhere. It may be impossible in overcrowded classrooms to prevent misconceptions from arising or going undetected. Nevertheless, the extent to which this problem exists should motivate teachers to seek ways of modifying instructional techniques, for the confusion of meanings is a barrier to reading and learning.

One of the axioms of teaching reading is that "new" words in a lesson should be mastered both as sight words and as to meaning before the child is expected to read that lesson. Often little attention is given to mastering shades of meaning, and too much is taken for granted when the child is able to "call the word." As a result, many teachers would be shocked at the misconceptions still harbored by some children in their classes. The following responses on vocabulary tests illustrate some rather striking misconceptions, even though it is not difficult to imagine how some of these arose. The responses are given verbatim.

regard- *a*) like you were guarding something
b) to think of someone as a cousin
c) to re-do your work

priceless- *a*) something that doesn't cost anything
b) you want to buy something and you think it's not worth it

brunette- *a*) a kind of permanent
b) a girl that dances
c) a prune

shrewd- *a*) when you're not polite
b) being kind of cruel
c) guess it means rude

lecture- *a*) 'lected for president

When asked to give the meaning of "conquer," one boy volunteered, "It means like to *konk her* on the head." Another, when meeting the written word *mosquitoes* for the first time, concluded it was the name of a fairy—"most quiet toes." A first grade teacher recently provided a classic example of a child's misconception:

> At Christmas time all of the children were drawing and coloring a Christmas scene. One little boy drew a pretty picture of a Christmas Night scene with stars and snow and trees. Over in one corner was a very short, fat little man. I asked the boy to tell me about his picture. He said, "This is a picture of Silent Night." I was still somewhat at a loss and asked, "Who is the person over on one side?" He looked quite amazed that I didn't know and said very firmly, "That's Round John Virgin."

An eight-year-old listening around Christmas time to a choir on television asked, "What does the word *si door im* mean?" His parents were at a loss until he repeated the line, "Oh come let us si door im."

A three-year-old hearing an older sibling make some reference to a dinosaur immediately responded, "I like to go to the *dime store.*"

Some of these examples illustrate what takes place when a child is confronted with concepts beyond his present grasp. He usually changes them to a more concrete meaning which is known to him. Although illustrating how the child deals with unknown words which he *hears,* these examples can also provide us with insight into what happens when a child *reads* unknown words.

EXPANSION OF MEANINGS

Children's development of concepts cannot be left to chance. The school deliberately seeks to provide an environment which will lead to the development and expansion of concepts in every area of the curriculum. The following procedures can be used in helping children develop meanings. They are not limited to a particular grade level. While many of these techniques are used in the formal reading program, they are appropriate for teaching terms and concepts in all subject areas.

Using Pictures. The use of pictures is an excellent method of expanding concepts and clearing up misconceptions. The role of pictures in beginning reading has been discussed previously in relation to helping pupils master sight words by suggesting context. Here we deal with the utility of pictures in developing and expanding concepts. A picture of an eroded hillside is much more effective in fixing the concept of *erosion* than is a word definition of the term. Early basal readers rely heavily on pictures, but it is actually in the content areas that pictures have greatest value. Pictures are more likely to fix accurate concepts of *colonial architecture,* the *iron-plated Monitor,* an *anteater,* a *Chinese junk, terrace farming* or the *human circulatory system* than is language alone.

The same picture can be used at different levels for teaching words and meanings. For example, let us imagine a picture which would be available to almost any teacher. The picture is a downtown scene in a small city. We see a bus, a Western Union boy on a bicycle, various store fronts and offices, a policeman directing traffic, a fire hydrant,

Children expand their stock of sight words and their arithmetical concepts while studying the pictures and values of coins. The class as a group worked with the chart shown. It remains available so that individual children can check or review the concepts covered. ***(Courtesy of Eastern Illinois University)***

the city hall across from a parking lot.[4] Without going into more detail, we might build a hierarchy of concepts.

> "*Where is the policeman?*"
> "In the *street.*"
> "Yes, he is really standing in the middle of where two streets cross—what is that called?"
> "That's an *intersection.*"
> (The class level will determine whether the teacher should explain the term intersection.)

---

[4] This is a description of the poster picture "The City" found in *Readiness Pictures* (New York: The Macmillan Co.).

"How many kinds of travel or transportation do we see?"

"Some people are *walking.*"
"A boy on a *bicycle.*"
"What does the boy do?"
"He delivers telegrams."
"How do you know?"
"I can tell by his hat."
"There's a *bus.* It's a city bus."
"There are lots of *cars.*"
"I see an *airplane* above the city."

"What kinds of transportation are not seen in the picture?"

"Trains."
"Don't see any *boats.*"
"There are no big *trucks*—big trailers."

(Teacher points to the symbol which identifies the telephone company office.)
"What is in this building?"

"That must be the telephone office."
"What's this sign across the street?"
"City Water Company, it says."

"What do we call these types of businesses?"
(no response)
"Did you ever hear the term *utilities* or *public utilities?*"
(The teacher prints the word on the board.)
"What other *utilities* do you think this city has—what others besides telephone company and water company?"

"Electricity."
"That's right—what other name might it have?"
"Light Company"
"Power Company"

"Do you think of any other *utility* companies? Would there be a gas company?"

Other meanings the teacher can lead into are:

"Four stories high"
"This canvas over the sidewalk is an *awning* or a *canopy.*"
"This is a parcel post truck. Its purpose is to serve the people. How is it like the power company? How is it different?"

The picture we have attempted to visualize is a simple one which could be used at various grade levels. Through its use the teacher can stress:

1. Noticing details.
2. Symbols standing for things (picture of Western Union boy's hat and the telephone symbol on window).
3. Many different *names* standing for the same things.
   a) Power company, public service company, utility company, etc.
   b) Canopy, awning.
4. The same word having different meanings according to usage (i.e., *meter:* parking meter, gas meter, electric meter; meters in cars: speedometers, gas meter, and mileage meter).

The value of pictures lies in their wealth of detail and the fact that they stay in focus or can be referred back to after a discussion has led away to other things.

DEVELOPING DIFFERENT MEANINGS FOR THE SAME WORD

The child's early language development is characterized by mastery of the concrete first and then a gradual moving up the ladder of abstraction. He may know such words as *air, blue, mine, broadcast, fence,* and he may know several meanings for each word; yet he will not be familiar with all the meanings of these words. The child will probably have mastered a number of meanings for the word *air.*

1. My daddy put *air* in the tires.
2. We hang clothes outside to *air* them.
3. We breathe *air.*

The same child may be confused by the following:

1. If asked to "*air* his views."
2. To hear that "his older brother gave his girlfriend the *air.*"
3. That Mrs. Jones is disliked in the neighborhood because "she puts on *airs.*"

The child may understand what is meant by *blue* in the sentence, "The boy had a *blue* boat." He may not be familiar with: "The boy felt *blue* when his aunt left." He may understand "Grandfather rode the *horse*," but not have a concept of "The coach warned the boys not to *horse* around" or the expression "That's a *horse* of a different color" or "The mayor accused the council of beating a dead *horse*."

He may know one or two meanings of *mine* but some of the usages or concepts involving the word *mine* will undoubtedly be beyond him.

a) "The book is *mine*."
b) "Joe's father worked in the coal *mine*."
c) "That corner store is a gold *mine*."
d) "The tank was damaged by a land *mine*."
e) "Don't under*mine* the confidence of the people."
f) "Our break is over, let's get back to the salt *mine*."
g) "He was stationed aboard a *mine* sweeper."

The above examples point up how difficult it is to measure "size of vocabulary," for each child has several different kinds of vocabularies. The word *mine* would be in a child's meaning, speaking, and reading vocabularies if he could read sentence (a) above, even though that was the only usage which was familiar to him. And in some instances, if the child could "read"—that is, correctly say all the words in sentence (d) above—it would be concluded that *mine* was in his *reading vocabulary* whether or not he could explain the sentence. Inability to explain the usage would indicate only that the child did not understand this particular concept.

Adult's meaning vocabularies are larger than their speaking, writing, or reading vocabularies. The sounds "klee-shay" may conjure up meaning for an individual when he hears the word used in context, yet the written symbol cliché may be meaningless if he sounds "clish." The word *cache* may be mispronounced in reading but still produce meaning in the sentence "The bandits, under cover of darkness, returned to the mountain cache for their stolen loot." Meaning may escape the individual when the T. V. badman says, "Let's go, boys, we have to beat the posse to the *kash*."

Learning meanings is a fascinating and highly motivating experience for children. The teacher can point out that most words carry several different meanings according to how they are used. She might illustrate with simple words like *can, stick, run,* or *set*. As the teacher asks for different usages, she will write the children's responses on the board at the same time attempting to fix the various meanings by using other known words.

"I *can* spell my name."—*can* means *able*

"I bought a *can* of beans."—*can* means a *container*

"Put the garbage in the *garbage can.*"—another type of *container*

"My mother said, 'tomorrow I will *can* the peaches.' "—*can* means to *preserve food.*

The last example may not be given by any child in an early elementary grade in an urban locality, but this usage may be known to almost every child in the same grade in another locality. Some other usages of the word *can* may not be appropriate for an early grade level, but would be at a higher grade level.

"Can it, Mack."—an order to stop talking

"If you leave now the boss will can you."—dismiss from job

"Why don't you trade in that old tin can and get an automobile?" —a battered old car

After several group exercises which stress that the objective is to supply different meanings of a word, not simply different sentences, the teacher can suggest a written game Each child works independently, selecting his own words for illustrating different usages. In order not to handicap the poorer spellers, the teacher may offer to spell any words the children want to use in their sentences. "Just hold up your hand and I'll come to your desk and write out the word you want to use." This exercise has considerable diagnostic value in that it yields data on spelling ability, language facility, legibility of hand writing, ability to follow directions, and ability to work independently.

Some specific findings reported by one teacher include:

1. Despite what appeared to be a thorough explanation of the objective, a number of pupils missed the point of the exercise and wrote different sentences using the same meaning of the word selected.

2. Several pupils misspelled words which they could spell correctly when the teacher pronounced or dictated these words. (The pupils slurred or omitted syllables when they said these words silently.)

3. The papers revealed many words misspelled *which the pupils thought they spelled correctly.* This data served as a basis for spelling review.

4. The handwriting was inferior to that which the child would do on a writing test.

5. This exercise disclosed great differences among pupils in their ability to use expressive language as well as exposing a paucity of concepts among some pupils.

6. Misconceptions were found on many pages. These could be corrected individually with the pupil.

SYNONYMS

The pupils are reminded that words which have the same meaning are called *synonyms.* "Give me another word that means the same as *big, work, fast*" will as a rule elicit responses from everyone in the group. Exercises that permit group participation can be followed by individual work involving a series of three-by-five cards each containing the directions "Go to the board and write the word ______. Under it write as many synonyms as you can." Another series of cards may include a number of words some of which are synonyms for the stimulus word. The pupil selects the synonyms and writes them under the stimulus word. This latter task is the easier of the two and permits pupils of differing ability to participate. (See Figure 21.)

FIGURE 21

EXPANDING MEANINGS THROUGH PRACTICE WITH SYNONYMS AND ANTONYMS

Write on the board the word *timid.* Under it write as many synonyms as you can.

On the board write the word *rapid.* Under it write any word in the following group which is similar in meaning.

quick	speedy
shave	light
fast	fleet
grasp	throw
inquire	reduce
hastily	swift

On the board write the word *release* and under it write any word in the following group which is nearly the *opposite* in meaning.

grasp	trap
relief	free
hold	captive
clutch	repeat
dismiss	catch
receive	keep
mistake	

Another exercise might call for the child to underline two words in a series which are similar in meaning:

almost	together	certainly	*nearly*
thrilling	spinning	exciting	frightening
nonsense	terrible	scolding	awful
matches	money	penny	postcard

Work sheets of varying difficulty can be used with pupils of different ability levels in a class. Similar exercises are applicable to expanding word meanings by teaching words of *opposite meanings.* The objective should always be to work out lesson plans that will assure that the pupils:

See the words.
Hear them pronounced.
Experience their use in sentences.

Sentence comprehension exercises can be used in which the child reads to determine whether two sentences carry the same meaning:

Read the two sentences marked A. Do they have the same meaning? If so, write *S* in the box to indicate they have the Same meaning. Write *D* if the sentences have a *D*ifferent meaning. Do the same for sentences B, C, D, etc.

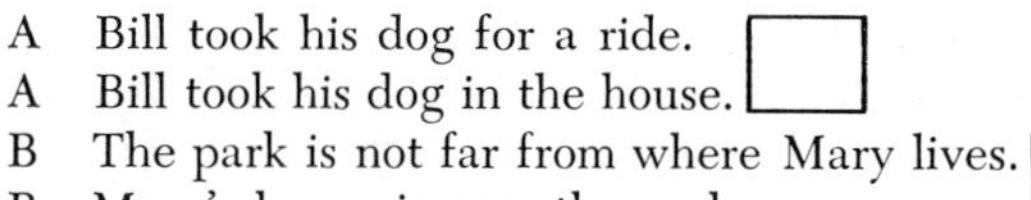

A Bill took his dog for a ride.
A Bill took his dog in the house.
B The park is not far from where Mary lives.
B Mary's house is near the park.
C Tom has a cat and a pony at the farm.
C Tom has a pet goat at the farm.

HOMONYMS

Homonyms are words which sound exactly alike and are spelled differently. They are potential sources of trouble to young readers since both sight recognition and meanings may be confusing. Many common homonyms look very much alike (*their, there; see, sea; hear, here; beat, beet; dear, deer; course, coarse*). The reader in the primary grades gets meaning from hearing the following sounds in these combinations, but he may not recognize all of the written symbols.

1. *Their* coats are over *there.*
2. The *plane* landed safely on the *plain.*
3. *Would* you please carry in some *wood?*
4. He felt *weak* for a *week* after he was sick.
5. "*Oh,*" he said, "how much do I *owe* you?"
6. The boy *ate eight* pieces of candy.
7. *See* the ship on the *sea.*
8. *No,* I do not *know* where it is.

One method of expanding both sight and usage vocabularies is to list homonyms in columns with the word the child is most likely to be familiar with on the left. An exercise calling for the use of each word in a sentence will provide a check on the mastery of meanings.

The words in columns A and B are pronounced the same.

A	B	A	B
do	dew	sail	sale
dear	deer	hair	hare
way	weigh	made	maid
hall	haul	one	won
pair	pare	poor	pour

For children who have trouble with these words, simple card games can be devised for two or more players in which one word of each pair is included in a draw pile and the other words shuffled and dealt to the players. When a card in the draw pile is turned up, whoever has the homonym for it in his hand pronounces the word on the stack and gives its meaning, then gives the meaning for the word in his hand. If he does each without help, he "takes" both cards. There are many variations which can be used with such cards.

Following is a list of easier homonyms which the child usually meets in the primary grades.

beat	beet	red	read
know	no	ring	wring
do	dew	would	wood
dear	deer	whole	hole
to two	too	sail	sale
knew	new	hall	haul
mail	male	pair	pare
road	rode	tail	tale
wait	weight	steal	steel
there	their	birth	berth
sun	son	ate	eight
oh	owe	some	sum
waist	waste	pain	pane
rap	wrap	so	sew
bee	be	by	buy
one	won	not	knot
see	sea	hear	here
hair	hare	our	hour
week	weak	maid	made
fair	fare	piece	peace

FIGURATIVE LANGUAGE AND IDIOMATIC EXPRESSIONS

Figurative language and idiomatic expressions are quite widely used both in basal readers and in subject texts.[5] These expressions pose virtually no problem for some readers, but can be stumbling

---

[5] Hulda Groesbeck, *The Comprehension of Figurative Language by Elementary Pupils: A Study of Transfer.* Unpublished Doctoral Thesis, Oklahoma University, 1961.

blocks for other children in getting the meaning. This occurs because some readers have developed the habit of expecting the words they read to have literal meanings. It has also been noted that some children can both use and understand such expressions in oral communication but are still confused or misled when they attempt to read them.[6]

Some examples of expressions that will be met in the primary or elementary grades follow. The mere fact that a child can read these correctly is not assurance that he interprets them correctly.

"The old sailor *spun a yarn* for the boys."
"Soon *night fell.*"
"Don't *throw your money away* at the circus."
"Before long they were driving through *rolling hills.*"
"The *rich earth; thin as a bean pole.*"
"He returned *heavy-hearted.*"
"The waves *pitched the boat* up and down."
"Give me a *lift.*"
"They *picked themselves up.*"
"*Made his mark.*"
"The captain *barked* his orders."
"A *finger* of light"
"*Water*-tight"

Workbooks have a limited number of exercises which attempt to give practice in interpretation of figurative language. The teacher must be on the alert when these exercises are used, for a pupil may check the correct response without clearly understanding the intended meaning. When a child makes an error in interpretation and his response is marked wrong by the teacher, all he has to do is erase his X and place it in the remaining choice, thus "correcting his error." Learning may not have taken place even though the exercise is corrected.

Although teachers understand that some pupils will need extra practice in developing skills, they often do not find the time to con-

---

[6] Elizabeth Ann Holmes, *Children's Knowledge of Figurative Language,* Unpublished Masters Thesis, Oklahoma University, 1959.

struct teacher-made work sheets. If exercises are duplicated, one preparation can be used with successive classes, and if several teachers at various grade levels co-operate, they will find work sheets designed for use at one grade level are appropriate for particular children in other grades. Pooling their effort will save time, add variety, and enhance the teaching in that school. Figure 22 contains examples of exercises designed by teachers in grades three through five in one elementary school. These were then made available to all teachers.

FIGURE 22

WORKING WITH EXPRESSIONS

What is the meaning of the words that are underlined? Write "same" before the sentence which explains the underlined words.

1. Father said: "I was walking through the park and Mr. Brown *gave me a lift.*"
   ________ picked father up in his arms.
   ________ lifted father off the ground.
   ________ gave father a ride home.

Finish the sentence with the one group of words (phrases) that makes the best meaning.

1. The stones in the show case were ________.
   as big as watermelons.
   as high as a mountain.
   as shiny as diamonds.

Can you tell in your own words what each of the following expressions means? If any puzzle you, ask the teacher for help.

1. A wolf in sheep's clothing
2. Keep the wolf from the door
3. Flew into a rage
4. The ship was water-tight.

DEVELOPING APPRECIATION FOR READING

Closely related to comprehension is the problem of purposeful reading. Children need guidance in discovering the values inherent in meaningful reading. While a large number of values could be cited, the one we are concerned with at the moment is the pleasure and growth potential to be found in this activity. There is no denying that pleasurable and purposeful reading is dependent upon the development of mechanical and comprehension skills. Yet millions of individuals attain satisfactory proficiency in these skills without ever finding a deep personal satisfaction in reading. Persons who love to read find this fact difficult to believe. However, studies of the reading interests and activities of a great number of high school and college graduates demonstrate its truth.

No doubt the school shares the responsibility for this outcome. Perhaps the degree of emphasis that is placed on *learning* to read leads pupils to see this accomplishment as an end in itself rather than the means to many desirable ends. Whatever the cause, too many children experience an uncritical, unimaginative growth in reading. Reading should never deteriorate into a ritual but should serve as a means of awakening the senses and stirring the imagination and the emotions. Whether the child is exploring one of the man-made wonders of the world or one of nature's wonders, such as the functioning of an ant colony or the metamorphosis of the monarch butterfly, reading can feed the senses with raw material for building concepts. Feelings and images aroused by reading can also stimulate emotions. A poet speaks to his love:

"I never think of you
but what some new virtue
is born in me."

A leader in the American Revolution, having been chided for a long absence from America, writes a friend a few observations in 1789:

> A thousand years hence, perhaps in less . . . the ruins of that liberty which thousands fought for, or suffered to obtain, may just furnish materials for a village tale. . . .
>
> When we contemplate the fall of empires and the extinction of nations of the ancient world, we see but little to excite our regret. . . . But when America shall fall, the subject for contemplative sorrow will be infinitely

> greater than crumbling brass or marble can inspire. It will not then be said, here stood a temple of vast antiquity, here rose a Babel of invisible height, or there a palace of sumptuous extravagance, but here, oh painful thought! The noblest work of human wisdom, the grandest scene of human glory, the fair cause of freedom rose and fell. Read this and then ask if I forget America.[7]

It is true that children in the primary grades do not read Cyrano De Bergerac or the letters of Thomas Paine. But the point is that they may never read these authors or Blake, Milton, Oliver Wendell Holmes, Hawthorne, Mark Twain, Dostoievsky, Whitman, or Lincoln if they do not learn to read for pleasure and develop an appreciation for reading. The primary grades are not too early to awaken the senses and emotions through reading.

There are many ways in which a creative teacher's enthusiasm becomes contagious. Such a teacher is a good storyteller, with the ability to become completely engrossed in the stories she tells or reads to children. She will understand children's capacity to be drawn out of their immediate environment by becoming involved in a story. For instance, the story of the first day in school of a child from another land can arouse a strong feeling of empathy. Children sense the feeling of loneliness, strangeness, and fear. They see that the children in the story also sense this and accept the newcomer and help in various ways to make him feel accepted and at home.

Analyzing Stories. Some stories need to be analyzed and discussed. The discussion should not be conducted from the standpoint of "who remembers something from the story" but by skillfully leading the children to see how the author is able to picture each character and show the type of person he is, how he conveys the characters' attitudes toward each other and toward themselves, how the reader is led to see the difference between unkindness and thoughtlessness, to see how people feel after making mistakes, what they do about them, and why it is not always possible to do exactly what one wants. Analysis of stories is not a testing period or a time for the recitation of facts. Analysis should lay the foundation for the type of insight Emily Dickenson developed before she could write, "There is no frigate like a book to bear us lands away."

---

[7] *The Complete Writings of Thomas Paine.* Ed., Philip S. Foner (New York: The Citadel Press, 1945), II, 1274.

A unit on harbors, ships, and the sea has combined the learning of a "specialized vocabulary," an interesting room display, and a meaningful group reading activity. Reading for meaning will animate any group and provide passage to many interesting ports. *(Courtesy of San Diego City Schools)*

Dramatizing Stories. Dramatizing stories or incidents from stories helps children develop understanding, imagination, and appreciation. To dramatize a story or scene, children must read the material critically and understand the author's purpose and the feelings he wishes to convey. In the dramatization these would find expression through tone of voice, emphasis, gesture, facial expression, and the like. In selecting material to be acted out, children will have to make correct judgments on the dramatic potential of various stories or situations. A story about a man lost on a mountain might be extremely interesting reading, but it is not well suited to a third grade dramatic production. One drawback is that only one character is involved.

Choral Reading. Choral reading is sometimes thought of as an activity reserved for expert readers. Actually, choral reading can be used at a number of instructional levels. The reading ability of the participants simply determines the materials which might be used successfully. For example, a teacher discovered quite by accident that choral reading had extremely high motivational value for her third grade class. She was showing a text-film of a story that the class had not read before. Each frame consisted of an attractive picture in color and two or three lines of text. She would call on individual children to read this material but would occasionally say "let's all read." The response was so enthusiastic that she printed on chart paper poems such as "The Wind," "Watching Clouds," "Railroad Reverie," "The Owl and the Pussy Cat," "Hold Hands," or any number of limericks. Later she prepared duplicated sheets which contained several pieces of material appropriate for choral reading. She observed that choral reading was always the motivational peak of the day's activity.

Choral reading has many justifications—possibly the chief one being that it is enjoyable. Other values often cited are that choral reading:

1. Is a good technique for getting all children to participate.
2. Can be a means of motivating children to want to read. The shy child or the poor reader is not likely to experience failure or frustration in this type of group reading experience.
3. Provides an opportunity to teach good pronunciation and reading with expression.
4. Permits the use of different materials for emphasizing different objectives such as phonic analysis, profiting from punctuation, and proper phrasing.
5. Can be a creative experience since children can suggest different ways a poem or passage can be interpreted.
6. Helps develop an appreciation for fine literature or poetry.

CONCLUSION

Reading instruction in the primary grades is extremely important because of the nature of the learning tasks found there and because of the variety of growth patterns characteristically found among children during this stage of their development. In order to provide pupils with the instruction they need, it is necessary to reach a thorough individual diagnosis of reading achievement based on either standardized or informal tests or both. Diagnosis as the basis for a program is quite essential at this instructional level because children are going through a stage of rapid development and are entering into independent reading. Furthermore, the curricular materials are used and designed with the assumption in mind that pupils have achieved a certain level of competence in reading.

In the primary grades children meet a number of concepts in their reading which are strange or unknown. They encounter an increasing number of words not in their sight vocabulary, a fact which calls for a higher level of word recognition skill. The accelerated pace at which new tasks are introduced makes it essential that sound principles of teaching reading be followed. Growth in reading must be treated as developmental. Practically all skills previously taught must now be reinforced and extended. Mechanical and comprehension skills must be developed simultaneously and at a rate of growth which is considerably beyond that found in beginning reading. To prevent both gaps in learning and overemphasis of particular skills, instruction must be systematic and planned.

The primary grades are a period in which children's experience with reading will mold their later attitudes and reading habits. Great damage can be done to some children by expecting them to read materials which at the moment they are incapable of handling. Other children may form mal-attitudes if they are forced to perform mechanical activities when they are capable of wide and extensive reading for pleasure and profit. Thus, a successful program in the primary grades, probably as much as at any instructional level, depends on the right combination of instruction in all facets of reading.

YOUR POINT OF VIEW?

1. Informal teacher-made tests can yield as much data about an individual child's reading as can standardized tests.

2. Misconceptions are more likely to arise in the content areas than in materials used for reading instruction.

3. Oral reading has little educational value in the primary grades.

4. One of the inherent dangers of the sight word method is that a child may progress satisfactorily in beginning reading and fail at succeeding levels when new words are introduced more rapidly. This is because he has learned to be too dependent on configuration and context clues and does not make the shift to dependence on word analysis.

5. One of the strengths of American schools is their success in arousing and maintaining pupil interest in recreational reading.

BIBLIOGRAPHY

Betts, E. A. *Foundations of Reading Instruction.* New York: American Book Co., 1946.

Bond, Guy L., and Tinker, Miles A. *Reading Difficulties: Their Diagnosis and Correction.* New York: Appleton-Century-Crofts, Inc., 1957.

Chall, Jeanne S. "Interpretation of the Results of Standardized Reading Tests," *Evaluation of Reading* (Helen M. Robinson, Editor), University of Chicago Press. Supplementary Educational Monographs, Number 88 (December, 1958), 133-38.

Darby, O. N. "The Place of and Methods of Teaching Oral Reading in the Elementary School," *Elementary School Journal,* LI (March, 1951), 380-88.

Dawson, Mildred A. "The Role of Oral Reading in School and Life Activities," *Elementary English,* XXV (January, 1958), 30-37.

DeBoer, John J., and Dallmann, Martha. *The Teaching of Reading.* New York: Henry Holt & Co., Inc., 1960.

Dolch, E. W. "Comprehension in Reading," *Education,* LXXVI (May, 1956), 536-40.

Dolch, E. W., and Leeds, Don. "Vocabulary Tests and Depth of Meaning," *Journal of Educational Research,* XLVII (November, 1953), 181-89.

Durrell, Donald D. *Improving Reading Instruction.* Tarrytown-on-Hudson: World Book Co., 1956.

Everhart, Rodney W. "Teaching Language in the Elementary School," *Elementary School Journal,* LIX (March, 1959), 336-39.

Fitzgerald, James A. "Prefixes in Child Writing," *Elementary English,* XXXVI (December, 1959), 576-80.

Gray, Lillian, and Reese, Dora. *Teaching Children to Read* (2nd Ed.). New York: The Ronald Press, 1957.

Gray, William S. *On Their Own in Reading* (Rev. Ed.). Chicago: Scott, Foresman and Co., 1960.

Harris, Albert J. *How to Increase Reading Ability* (3rd Ed.). New York: Longmans, Green and Co., 1956.

Hunt, Lyman C. Jr. "Can We Measure Specific Factors Associated with Reading Comprehension?" *Journal of Educational Research,* LI (November, 1957), 161-72.

Jarolimek, John, and Foster, Clifford D. "Quantitative Concepts in Fifth Grade Social-Studies Textbooks," *Elementary School Journal,* LIX (May, 1959), 437-42.

Kastner, Marie A. "Instructing and Motivating Pupils in the Light of Test Results," *Catholic Educational Review,* LVII (February, 1959), 106-10.

Kovas, Helen. "The Place of Oral Reading," *Elementary English,* XXXIV (November, 1957), 462-66.

Larrick, Nancy. "How Many Words Does a Child Know?" *Reading Teacher,* VII (December, 1953), 100-4.

McKee, Paul. *The Teaching of Reading in the Elementary School.* Boston: Houghton-Mifflin Co., 1948.

McKim, Margaret G. *Guiding Growth in Reading.* New York: The Macmillan Co., 1955.

Otterman, Lois M. "The Value of Teaching Prefixes and Word Roots," *Journal of Educational Research,* XLVIII (April, 1955), 611-16.

Piekarz, Josephine A. "Getting Meaning from Reading," *Elementary School Journal,* LVI (March, 1956), 303-9.

Reading in the Elementary School, Forty-eighth Yearbook, Part II, National Society for the Study of Education, University of Chicago Press, 1949.

Rinsland, Henry D. *A Basic Vocabulary of Elementary School Children.* New York: The Macmillan Co., 1945.

Russell, David H. *Children Learn to Read.* Boston: Ginn and Company, 1949.

———. "Primary Reading Programs in England and Scotland," *Elementary School Journal,* LVII (May, 1957), 446-51.

Sheldon, William D. "Reading: Instruction," *Review of Educational Research,* XXV (April, 1955), 92-106.

Sister Josephina CSJ. "Reading Accomplishment of Gifted and Average Pupils," *Educational and Psychological Measurement,* XVIII (1958), 867-71.

Smith, Nila B. "What Research Tells Us about Word Recognition," *Elementary School Journal,* LV (April, 1955), 440-46.

——— (and others). *Graded Selections for Informal Reading Diagnosis.* New York University Press, 1959.

Stone, Clarence R. *Progress in Primary Reading.* St. Louis: Webster Publishing Co., 1950.

Stroud, James B. "Background of Measurement in Reading Improvement," *Eighth Yearbook National Reading Conference 1959,* Fort Worth, Texas. Texas Christian University Press, 1959, 77-88.

Sutton, Rachel S. "The Effect of Vocabulary-Building on Reading Skills," *Elementary School Journal,* 1953, 94-97.

chapter 7

PHONICS INSTRUCTION

Phonetic analysis is probably the most important of the methods of learning words not known as sight words. Even so, the teaching of phonics should be integrated with the teaching of other techniques for learning unknown words. Each word is then seen in proper perspective.

In previous chapters phonics was discussed in relation to other facets of reading instruction. This section deals exclusively with phonetic analysis, and is an attempt to present an overview of the total primary program. The justification for discussing phonics in isolation lies in the premise that there is considerable confusion and insecurity among a number of elementary teachers with regard to teaching phonics. This premise is supported by investigations which indicate that teachers consistently state that their greatest instructional need is an understanding of phonics.[1]

Journal articles with titles such as "Am I Teaching Phonics Right?" "Some Misconceptions Concerning Phonics," and "Is English a Phonetic Language?" indicate some degree of confusion about the use of

[1] J. Kendall Haggard, "Phonics in Directed Reading Activities," *Reading Teacher,* IX (1955), 90.

phonics. Gertrude Hildreth writes that "Recent controversies over methods of teaching reading indicate that misconceptions concerning phonics and methods of teaching sounding are fairly common."[2] E .W. Dolch says, "Teachers everywhere are uncertain whether they are doing the right thing about phonics. Their question, spoken or unspoken, is 'am I teaching phonics right?' "[3]

If the above premise is true, there is definite advantage in having the phonics program set aside for treatment in its own chapter. This permits the teacher to see the program as a whole, rather than exclusively as a grade-level breakdown. There is logic in this point of view, since no step in phonics instruction is restricted to a particular grade level. Yet, because of the nature of available instructional materials, many teachers feel less prepared to teach all steps in phonics than they do those steps stressed at their particular grade level.

Following a brief discussion of past practices in phonics instruction, a number of steps in teaching phonetic analysis will be discussed below.

BRIEF REVIEW OF PAST PRACTICES

Some knowledge of the history of phonics teaching in American education would undoubtedly be helpful in understanding some of the problems, attitudes, and misunderstandings observable in education today. The following discussion is a very brief summary of phonic practices advocated in the past.[4]

Beginning around 1890 and continuing for a period of thirty or forty years, the cornerstone of reading instruction in American schools was a synthetic phonics method. Previous to this era much time

---

[2] Gertrude Hildreth, "Some Misconceptions Concerning Phonics," *Elementary English*, XXXVI (1957), 26.

[3] E. W. Dolch, "Am I Teaching Phonics Right?" *Elementary English*, XXXIV (1957), 227.

[4] The reader who wishes a more detailed account of past practices will find the following sources helpful:

Nila B. Smith, "Phonics Then and Now," *Education*, LXXV (1955), 560-65.

W. S. Gray, *On Their Own in Reading* (Chicago: Scott, Foresman & Co., 1948), Chap. 1.

E. A. Betts, "Phonics: Practical Consideration Based on Research," *Elementary English*, XXXIII (1956), 357-71.

was spent on the rote learning of the ABC's. Emphasis now shifted from drill on "letter names" to drill on the "sounds of the various letters." Here we have a form of phonics drill unrelated to meaning and in some instances unrelated to words in English. Children drilled on isolated sounds as illustrated below:

da ha la ma pa ra
be se te ne le re
pi mi ti si li ri

This drill was not in context with reading, since the drills preceded the child's learning of words. It is easy to see that this type of introduction placed little if any emphasis on reading as a process of discovering meaning.

Rebecca Pollard's synthetic method, introduced about 1890,[5] advocated reducing reading to a number of mechanical procedures, each of which focused on a unit smaller than a word. Reading became very mechanistic and, when mastered, often produced individuals who were adept at working their way through a given word. The result among both teachers and pupils was that facile reading became equated with "facility in calling words." A few of the recommended procedures of this method were:

1. Drills in articulation were to precede any attempt at reading. The child was to drill on the "sound of letters." Then he would be able, it was reasoned, to attack whole words.

2. Single consonants were "sounded." Each consonant was given a sound equivalent to a syllable. Thus *b, c, d, p, h,* and *t* were sounded *buh, cuh, duh, puh, huh,* and *tuh.*

3. Drill on word families was stressed. This was unrelated to meaning. Sometimes children memorized lists of words ending in such common family phonograms as *ill, am, ick, ate, old, ack.*

4. Diacritical markings were introduced in first grade, and children drilled on "marking sentences." For example,

> "The gh̸ōst wăs ā cŏmmŏn sīg̸h̸t near the w̸rĕc̸k. He knew the īs̸lănd was ĕmpty."

A number of widely used reading texts adopted the suggestions of Pollard, and in many cases extended them. For instance, if a unit

---

[5] Rebecca S. Pollard, *Pollard's Synthetic Method* (Chicago: Western Publishing House, 1889).

was attempting to teach the phonogram or "family" *ick,* a story might be built primarily from words in that family, regardless of meaning or lack of it in the passage. The following example is illustrative and, it is hoped, exaggerated.

> "Nick, flick the tick from the chick with a stick. Prick the tick from the chick with a thick stick. Nick, do not kick the brick, kick the stick."

Since some of the family phonograms are also words (*am, is, and, ate, an, all, old, it, at, eat*) the practice of "looking for small words in large words" was advocated. The justification for this practice was that the little words were familiar to the child and he could pronounce them. If he found little words he knew in larger unknown words, he had a start toward mastering the unknown larger word.

The procedure of looking for small words in larger words fails for two reasons. First, there is little logic in having the child see the word *ill* in the monosyllabic words *will, Bill, fill, mill, kill,* and *pill,* unless it is the association of *ill* with *pill,* which leaves much to be desired. In teaching reading today the clue will not be the word *ill* but the sound of *ill* in conjunction with the sounds of various initial letters: *w, b, f, m, g, k, p,* and *h.*

The second charge against "finding little words" appears to be so serious as to remove the practice from the list of justifiable procedures. Many of the little words which retain some degree of pronouncable autonomy in single syllable words lose this characteristic in words of more than one syllable. In *pan, can, man, fan, tan, ran* or in *ham, jam, Sam,* noting the little words *an* and *am* would not destroy the pronunciation of the words. However, seeing or pronouncing the *am* in *am*ong, *am*end, *am*en, *am*use, *am*ass would prevent a correct phonic analysis. Likewise, seeing or saying the word *as* in *as*hore, *As*ia, *as*ide, *as*leep; *it* in *it*em; *at* in *at*omic and *at*hlete; or *all* in *all*ow, or *all*ege would hinder attempts at word analysis.

The "total emphasis" on phonics brought the method into disrepute during the 1920's. Reform was not advocated, but rather discarding the teaching of phonics. It was commonly alleged that the abuses of phonics teaching were responsible for the reading problems found at that time. Thus, what was *pre*scribed at one moment was *pro*scribed the next. There was much confusion among teachers, and this confusion seems not to have abated perceptibly today. Phonics is the most written-about topic in the area of teaching reading and, possibly, the least understood.[6] There are several reasons why teachers are confused about how to incorporate phonics into everyday teaching practices. Let us assume a teacher feels the need of help. She will want to read what others have to suggest, and here we run into our first problem.

Writings on Phonics. Much professional writing on phonics is vague and of little help to a classroom teacher. Many articles, although justified in themselves, do little more than touch the periphery of how to teach phonics. They deal with phonics as if it were a philosophical issue. To illustrate, let us look at a number of questions about phonics which apparently never grow too old to be asked again. Some of them, although they appear to be justifiable and logical, are fuzzy or nebulous. "Should I teach phonics?" or "Should phonics be taught in our schools?" Many authors and readers feel these are legitimate questions for discussion. The real issue is whether knowledge of, or skill in, the use of phonics is valuable in learning to read. Once the results of adequate and germane experiments have established the fact that sounding is an honored and efficient means of gaining independence in reading, we need not question whether it should be taught. Most educators agree with the axiom advanced by Ernest Horn "that if a thing is worth learning it is worth teaching."

Another favorite question is, "When should phonics instruction begin?" This is a straightforward question which should lend itself to a straightforward answer. It appears that this question aims at finding a place where two continuums intersect—the child's readiness and the school curriculum. This is an illusion, because the term "phonics" in this question demands a clear definition. Yet, in this question, and usually in the discussion which follows, the term "phonics" lacks a precise meaning. Does it mean teaching a child to discriminate between initial sounds or word endings? Does it mean teaching short vowel sounds, long vowel sounds, syllabication, or the rule of final *e* in short words? Even if separate questions are made of each step in phonics, different pupils in the same class will be ready for each step at different times. To pick a particular grade level or

[6] See previous references in this chapter (Haggard, Hildreth, Dolch, Smith, Gray, and Betts).

even a particular mental age and arbitrarily say phonics should not be taught prior to the child's achieving that mental age, still leaves as an open question what precisely is meant by phonics.

Our second point has to do with the negative approach to phonics; authors are often explicit in what they oppose but much less articulate about the practices they advocate. Opposition is voiced against most of what was practiced during the so-called "phonic age." In the literature on phonics, a great deal of stress is placed on the evils of past practices or methods of teaching phonics. Often the indictment should be against the misuse of a practice rather than against the practice itself.

MISCONCEPTIONS

The controversy over the teaching of phonics has produced a widely accepted myth that all practices followed during this earlier period are inherently suspect and should be avoided by good teachers today.

This often leaves teachers confused, and may nourish misconceptions about teaching phonics. As late as the present decade it was possible to find teachers who felt insecure about deliberately teaching first grade children the names of the letters of the alphabet. They had read many times that "this was a common practice during both the era of emphasis on phonetic methods and the earlier era of emphasis on the A B C method." The issue is teaching the alphabet *in sequence* in grade one which is not in any way connected with the first grade curriculum. Recognizing and knowing the names of the various letters is a different matter. Teacher confusion grew out of the fact that much of the writing on the topic lacked clarity.

A second misconception is that teaching word families is an indefensible practice. This idea may stem from the fact that many critics of the earlier synthetic methods belabor the manner in which these were once taught. The criticism might be justified if it were made on the basis that drill on a column of words entirely unrelated to meaningful reading is a poor learning technique. On the other hand, when children have learned the words *make* and *take* as sight words, and they meet the new word *lake* in a reading exercise it would not be poor instruction to point out that this word and certain others whose meaning is known, contain the common speech sound *ake* (*cake, bake, wake, snake, rake, shake*).

There is little point in opposing the teaching of "family groups" on the basis that a relatively small number of English words contain these families. This is not a sound argument because so many small, often used words *are* formed from some thirty such families, and these words are among those most frequently occurring in beginning reading materials (specifically such families as *an, at, it, am, in, as, ate, ake, et, ick, eat, arm, en, ing, ot, est, un, all, ell, and, ame*). There are enough common or service words which are *not* phonetic and which must be learned as sight words. Any clue, such as word families, which a child can pick up early in learning to read can be useful.

A third misconception which has been repeated so often that it has finally achieved the status of a "law" is that no work or drill on phonics should ever take place except when it relates directly to what the child is reading. It is stated that the need for instruction must arise out of what the child is reading at the moment; otherwise phonics instruction will be divorced from meaning. This concept is a reaction against the old practice of long periods of drill on phonic elements before any reading of meaningful units was practiced. This type of phonics drill was not only divorced from learning to read for meaning but even from reading itself, since the child had as yet not been exposed to reading.

The concept that phonics instruction should be related to what the child is reading at the moment is a good rule to keep in mind when introducing a new step or phonic concept, but the individual differences among pupils in any classroom make it highly unlikely that all will need the same instruction at any given moment. Even after deliberate and systematic classroom instruction, not all children will have learned specific phonic principles and skills. If after instruction a child has not mastered the initial sound of consonants, it is a defensible procedure to see that he receives instruction or drill. When a child has not mastered certain consonant blends, the teacher does not have to wait until such words as *bl*ack, *sl*eep, *tr*ain or *br*eak are met in a reading lesson before she works on this problem.

Once the child is reading, any practice, technique, or procedure that helps him attack words independently is related to reading. When a child comes to a word that lends itself to phonic analysis and he cannot independently solve the pronunciation of the word, he is ready for a lesson in phonics. Any technique that will not damage his efficiency as a reader is a good technique if it helps him.

STEPS IN PHONICS INSTRUCTION

There are a series of instructional tasks which, when taken as a whole, constitute a phonics program. This discussion outlines a phonics program consistent with the *sight-word method of teaching reading* followed in most basal reading texts in use today. While the following tasks are arranged in a logical sequence, it is not to be inferred that this arrangement is the only sequence with merit. To be consistent with the practice of basal reader series, consonant sounds are treated before vowel sounds.[7] The steps in phonics instruction are to teach:

1. Auditory discrimination of speech sounds in words.
2. Learn a number of sight words. This step is not phonics instruction but must not be lost sight of, since all following steps are based on the child's knowing sight words.
3. Sounds of initial consonants in words which have been learned as sight words.
4. Mental substitution of initial consonants.[8]
5. Substitution of final consonants.
6. Initial consonant digraphs (*th, ch, sh, wh*).
7. Initial consonant blends.
8. Vowel sounds.
   a) long vowel sounds
   b) short vowel sounds
   c) double vowels
      (1) digraphs
      (2) diphthongs

---

[7] This chapter concludes with a brief discussion of a phonetic method which advocates the teaching of vowel sounds prior to the teaching of consonant sounds.

[8] This term is used by William S. Gray, *On Their Own in Reading* (Rev. Ed.; Chicago: Scott, Foresman & Company, 1960).

d) vowels followed by *r*
e) effect of final *e*
f) final *y* sounded as long *i*

9. Silent consonants.
10. Syllabication.

It should not be inferred that each of the above steps is of equal importance in learning to read, or that each should receive the same amount of instructional time. The steps listed are simply the framework, since some steps include many specific tasks. For instance, under syllabication one would deal with such teachings as "prefixes and suffixes are usually syllables; there are as many syllables as sounded vowels; two consonants coming between vowels usually divide (*gar·den*); double consonants usually divide (*let·ter,sum·mer*); the letter combinations *cle, ble, gle, dle, kle,* and *tle* at the ends of words are single syllables." There is no agreement as to the number of such rules or principles that should be taught in the reading process. Even a summary of all the suggestions found in the literature of teaching reading would be beyond the scope of this book.

The actual learning of phonics as it relates to reading usually begins quite early in the pre-school years.[9] The child learns a sound like *mommy,* and can easily differentiate it from similar sounds. He may have a pet *kitty* and a playmate *Kathy* and will differentiate if asked "where is *Kathy*?" even though the kitty is also present. Phonics instruction begins when an adult talks with an infant, thus providing the child a model.

When a child associates sounds with objects and does not confuse sounds that are very similar such as *mommy, money, monkey,* and *maybe,* he is mastering auditory discrimination, which is a prerequisite for phonic analysis in the reading process. None of the later "steps" in learning phonics can take place in the absence of mastery of this basic language function. Beginning reading instruction in the school builds on the child's previous language experiences. In reading, the child will have to make visual discriminations between written word symbols and learn that the written symbols represent the speech sounds of words he speaks and understands.

---

[9] See Chap. 4.

Sight Words before Analysis. Using the sight-word method, the teacher builds on the pupil's previous language experience and teaches him to recognize whole words. That is, the child is taught the sight symbol *man* before he is taught the sounds of symbols *m, a,* and *n*. The word *man* is much more meaningful than the three symbols of which it is formed, because the child:

1. Understands the meaning of the sound *man*.
2. Can make this sound himself and associates it with its referent.
3. Can recognize a picture (sight symbol or representation) of a *man*.

Thus, it is easy to move from what is known to the new and unknown—the printed word *man*. Earlier chapters in this book include a discussion of the methods and procedures used to help children learn sight words: name cards for familiar objects in the room, the child's name on books and drawings, experience charts, exercises such as finding two words in a series which are alike or which begin with the same letter, pictures with the name of the object depicted, readiness workbooks, pre-primers, and bulletin boards. As a result of these pre-reading experiences and the mastery of a series of pre-primers, the beginning reader soon learns a number of words as sight words. Once this is accomplished, the foundations for word analysis have been established.

Sound of Initial Consonants. Next, the child's attention is directed to the sounds associated with the initial consonants in these words. This is simply taking one short step from the known to the unknown. For example, assume that included among the sight words a child knows are the words *be, back,* and *ball*. He is now ready to associate the sound of *b* in these words with the written symbol *b*.[10]

The teacher prints a capital *B* on the chalkboard and says, "Today we will learn all about the letter *B*. Next to the big *B* I will print a little *b*. This big *B* is called a capital *B*. Now I am going to write some words which begin with *b*." (She writes *be, back,* and *ball*). "Who can give us another word that begins with the *b* sound? Yes,

[10] Many children are already able to recognize a number of letters. They have written their names; the teacher has spelled words as she printed experience charts, and large wall charts which display capital and lower case letters have been used to teach letter names.

bear, boat, big—Bobby we write with a large (or capital) *B* because it is somebody's name."

When a number of examples have been given, the teacher asks, "What do we notice about the sound of each of these words?" "That's right, they all begin with the sound of *b—bear, ball, boat, bat, big, bomb.*" As the words are called out by the children, they are added to the list on the board and the teacher asks, "What do we *see* that is the same in all of these words? That's right, they all begin with *b*." It should be noted that in no instance were the children asked to sound the letter *b* in isolation, although it may have been emphasized without distortion.

In addition to the group work just described, there will be workbook exercises giving each child an opportunity to do seat work which parallels the concept taught. These exercises use both visual stimuli and sounds associated with pictures, letters, and words. A few typical examples are:

1. In the row of pictures below, the child is to mark pictures of objects whose names begin with the same sound as the name of the object in the picture on the extreme left. (See Figure 23.)

FIGURE 23

2. A picture of a familiar object is shown along with the word represented by the object in the picture. The example is a bell (Figure 24). Here the child can see and hear the *b* sound. He is then to mark all the other words in a supplied list which begin with the same sound.

FIGURE 24

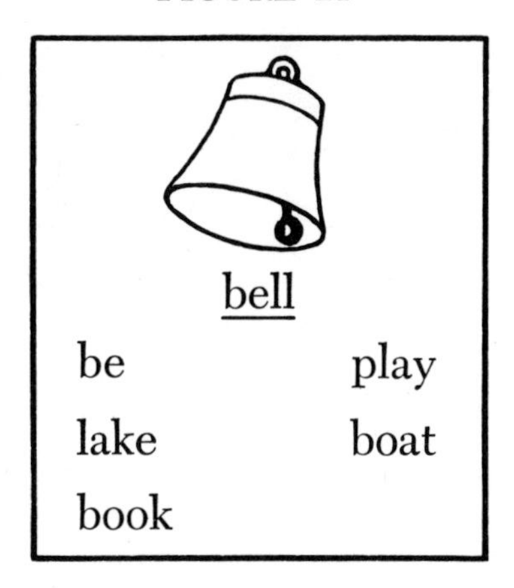

3. Figure 25 shows a series of words in columns, some of which begin with the same sound and the same letter. The child is to draw a line from the word in column *A* to the word in column *B* which begins with the same sound.

FIGURE 25

A word of caution should be injected here to point out that many exercises found in workbooks which aim to provide auditory practice can result in nothing but visual discrimination exercises, unless the teacher is careful to see that each child actually *sounds* the word symbols which are given as stimuli. To illustrate, the following exercise is patterned after the one above and can be correctly marked using only visual clues. Incorporating auditory practice would require associating sounds with each initial symbol.

FIGURE 26

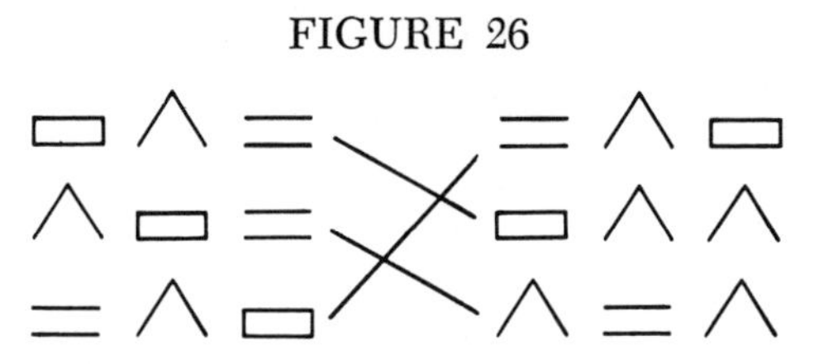

4. A pictured object is shown, followed by four words, none of which stand for the picture, but one or more of which begin with the same sound as the name of the pictured object.

FIGURE 27

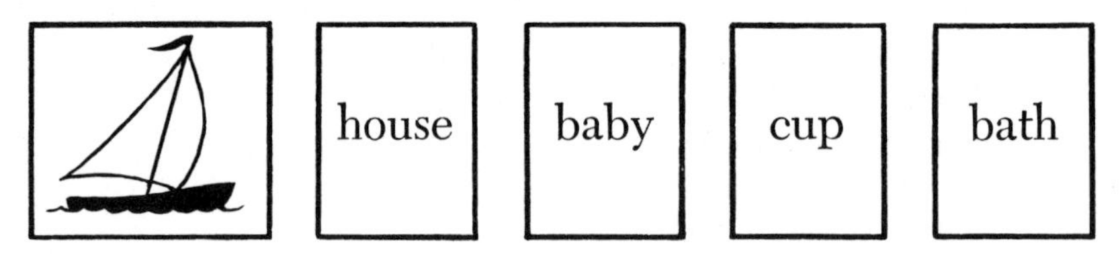

5. A series of boxes is shown, each containing three words. The teacher pronounces one of the words and the pupil underlines the word pronounced. (See Figure 28.) He need not know all of the words as sight words, provided he is familiar with the initial sound of each. In the following example, the teacher could pronounce *bank, tell, bill, may, bat.* There are many other types of exercises and many variations of those illustrated.

FIGURE 28

1	2	3	4	5
call *bank* play	*tell* sell fell	hill fill *bill*	*may* pay say	hat show *bat*

Substitution of Initial Sounds. The next important skill to be learned is to substitute known letter sounds in attacking unknown words. Assume the child knows the words *take* and *make* and meets the unknown word *rake.* He should be able to combine the *r* sound (which he knows in words like *run, rain* or *ride*), with the sound of *ake* in *take.* By this process of "thinking the sounds," he should unlock the new word.[11] If the reader has mastered the steps in phonics previously introduced, this step also starts from that which is known, i.e., sight words and the sounds initial consonants contribute to words.

In beginning reading it is a common practice to teach a number of monosyllabic words which contain frequently used phonograms. Practically all workbooks use these "word families" as a means of teaching new words. Work on the substitution of initial consonants parallels the primers and first readers. Moving through the primer, the child meets such words as *back, came, day, fun, gate, hand, just, king, lake, met, not, pin, rest, sun, tall,* and *wet.* Each of these words contains a familiar and often occurring phonogram. Children should not receive drill on these word endings in isolation (*ack, ame, ay, ate, est, ust, ing, ake, et, ot, in, un, all, et*). Nevertheless, a number of important words can be solved independently when the child knows some sight words containing often used letter combinations and can substitute initial letter sounds.

Substitution of Single Consonant Sounds at the Ends of Words. Some teachers prefer to teach consonant sounds at the ends of words at the same time that they deal with a particular initial consonant sound. Other teachers work through the initial sounds and then work on single consonant sounds at the end of words. Regardless of which procedure is followed, the child is taught to notice visually and auditorily the final consonants in short words. He knows words such as *men, log, pen, bold, leg* and the sounds of letters, including *t.* He is now asked to substitute the *t* sound at the end of the words to get *met, lot, pet, bolt,* and *let.*

Initial Blends. In dealing with many words that the child will meet early in the process of learning to read, sounding only the initial consonant will result in confusion. These words fall into two

---

[11] For an excellent discussion of the "substitution" principle, see W. S. Gray, *On Their Own in Reading* (Rev. Ed.; Chicago: Scott, Foresman & Company, 1960).

classes: simple consonant blends, and a smaller group of two-consonant combinations representing special speech sounds in English (*th, sh, ch, wh*). The consonant blends include *st, sw, sm, sp, sk, sn; br, cr, dr, fr, gr, pr; bl, cl, fl, gl, pl, sl; scr, str, spr, spl.* Teaching these blends and special consonant sounds parallels closely the teaching of single initial and final consonant sounds.

There is a great deal of variance among teachers as well as among basal readers as to (a) when blends are dealt with, (b) which are taught first, and (c) how rapidly the blends are covered. One basal series teaches several consonant blends in the primer level and the majority during the first reader level. Another series teaches many words containing blends as sight words during the first grade, but reserves teaching the blend sounds for second grade. Some materials suggest teaching initial blends first and later stressing blends and special consonant sounds at the ends of words (chur*ch*, tra*sh*, che*st*, che*ck*, fla*sh*, fre*sh*, fro*st*, smoo*th*, whi*ch*, thi*ck*).

WORKING WITH VOWEL SOUNDS

Teaching vowel sounds is a challenge, because these sounds in English are not consistent. When an attempt is made to advance rules which cover all vowel situations, the resultant list is lengthy and exceptions to the rules are numerous. Oaks has analyzed the vowel situations occurring in the primer-through-third-grade materials in fourteen basal reader series. She presents eight principles that apply often enough in vowel situations to merit their being taught. In her study, the eight rules were applicable in only about 50 per cent of the total vowel situations, and exceptions to the rules occurred in approximately 25 per cent of the total vowel situations.[12]

Many children arrive at a correct application of a phonic principle before it is deliberately taught and before they are able to verbalize the rule. That is, after many contacts with *e* on the end of short words, children come to the conclusion that the *e* is not sounded. They might also learn to "try" the long sound of the vowel that comes earlier in words containing a final *e*. Some children will notice that

---

[12] Ruth E. Oaks, "A Study of the Vowel Situations in a Primary Vocabulary," *Education*, LXXII (1952), 604-17.

the final *y* in small words containing no other vowel has the long sound of *i* (*my, cry, fry, by*). However, having the rule "verbalized" is often a big help to learning. The purpose and function of the teacher and school are to provide guidance, and most children gain proficiency in phonic analysis more quickly and more surely with guidance that leads to insights. To require rote memorization of a great number of rules will hinder some children in understanding the relationship between the rule and their reading. They may become so involved with learning the rules that they miss the application.

In most basal readers the deliberate teaching of vowel sounds is reserved until late in the first year or until the second year of formal reading instruction. Some authors suggest that the long sounds of vowels be taught first, since the long sound is the name of the vowel. Others suggest that beginning with the short sound is the most logical, since the majority of words learned thus far have the short sound, particularly the smaller, one-vowel words. Another suggestion is to teach both the long and short sound of a vowel together, since the child can compare and contrast these sounds in words he has already learned. Suggestions vary as to the order in which the vowel sounds are to be introduced. When teachers have a clear concept of the aims of phonic instruction, it is doubtful that practices involving the variables just mentioned would of themselves materially influence reading achievement as it is measured at the end of the third or fourth grade.

When teaching vowel sounds, a teacher should follow the same pattern as in each preceding step in phonic analysis—moving one short step from what is already known to what is unknown. The child knows a number of words having the short sounds of vowels, and some having the long sounds. At this point the objective is to focus on these sounds, causing the child to notice the vowel symbol and hear its various sounds. Using the vowel *a*, illustrations of teaching the long sound of vowels, short sound of vowels, and vowels followed by *r* and *l* are given here.

First, attention is directed to the vowel *a* in words which the children know as sight words. A column of words containing the long sound of *a* as the initial letter is placed on the chalkboard (Figure 29, column A). Children are asked to say each word and listen to the sound of the *a* in these words. The teacher explains that the vowel "saying its name" is called the long sound, and long vowels are marked *ā*. The class is now asked to supply other words which begin with the long sound of *a* as heard in *age, able,* and *ape.* Probably not many words of this kind will be suggested. The teacher can then emphasize that most words learned so far have the short sound.

Another column of words beginning with the short sound of *a* can be placed on the board (Figure 29, column B). As the words are pronounced, the children listen in order to distinguish between the short and long sounds. Next, known sight words containing the vowel in medial position are put on the board and children are asked to tell which sound of *a* they hear (Figure 29, column C).

FIGURE 29

Teaching long and short initial vowels; short vowels in medial position.

A	B	C
āble	ănd	hăd
āge	ăct	căn
āid	ăpple	flăg
āgent	ăsk	băck
āpe	ăt	lămp
ācorn	ădd	măn
ā	ăny	măd
āte	ăbsent	cămp
Āpril	ăm	căp
āim	ăbout	hăt

Pupils are now invited to give other words which contain only the single vowel *a* in the middle of the word. Many such words can be suggested (*had, cap, bag, sand, pack, rat, plan, dad, flag, has, bad, cat, fast, hand, sack, mad, fat, than, sad, band,* etc.). At this point a rule can be stressed:

"One vowel in the middle of a word (or syllable) *usually* has its short sound."

The Effect of the Final *e*. To teach the effect of the final *e* on vowel sounds, the words *name, came, take, made, grade, place, gave, make, game, hate,* and *cane* may be placed on the board. All of them contain the vowel *a* in medial position, have a final *e*, and should have been learned previously as sight words. Children say the words and listen to the sound of *a* in each word. The fact is stressed that in each word the long sound of *a* is heard. Pupils are then led to observe that each word ends with the vowel *e*, but that the final *e* is not sounded when the word is pronounced. The rule is then stated: "In short words containing final *e*, the *e* is silent, and the previous vowel usually has its long sound."

A concrete method of illustrating the role of the final *e* is to use words having the short vowel sound and which (upon addition of final *e*) become different words now having the long vowel sound.

hat	*hate*	*hop*	*hope*
mad	*made*	*not*	*note*
can	*cane*	*rob*	*robe*
rid	*ride*	*cut*	*cute*
fin	*fine*	*hug*	*huge*
hid	*hide*	*tub*	*tube*

Some words will be suggested by the children that do not follow the rule (*love, come, give, some*). These words can be used as a means of pointing out that there are some words that are exceptions.

Long Vowel Sounds at the Ends of Words. Children will have learned a number of sight words containing a single vowel at the end of the word. In such cases the vowel sound is usually long (*go, me, my, so, no*). Vowels which end syllables are usually sounded long (*ti* ger, *mo* tel, *fa* tal, *to* tal); the generalization to be taught is, "A vowel at the end of a one-vowel word or syllable usually has the long sound." Final *y* at the end of a word containing no other vowel has the long sound of *i* (*my, dry, cry, try, why, by, fly*). This principle can be taught either in conjunction with long vowel sounds at the ends of words, or when dealing with the long and short sounds of the vowel *i*.

Adjacent Vowels. When two vowels come together and stand for a single sound, they are referred to as vowel digraphs. When two adjacent vowels are both sounded in the same syllable, they are called diphthongs. The most widely advocated generalization to cover vowel digraphs is: When two vowels come together the first is usually long and the second is silent. Although this rule seems to cover all two-vowel situations, there are about as many exceptions as instances when it applies. However, when the rule is applied for specific vowel situations (*ai, ee, oa, ea, ay*), it will hold more frequently.[13]

Pupils can be reminded that the vowel sound is usually short in one-vowel words where the vowel does not end the word. Figure 30 shows a column of familiar sight words which follow this rule.

FIGURE 30

A single vowel with a short sound.	Two vowels together. First is sounded long; second is silent.
cot	coat
mad	maid
lid	lied
men	mean
fed	feed
set	seat
got	goat
met	meet
did	died
pan	pain

In the second column a vowel is inserted in each word, making a new word containing two adjacent vowels. The first vowel has the long sound and the second is silent. Lest the child over-generalize from this rule, the instances where it does not apply should be reviewed. This would include the vowel digraphs *au, eu, aw, ew, oo,* where two vowels result in a single sound but not the long sound of the first vowel. For example:

au: haul, cause, haunt, caught
eu: feud, neutral, deuce, neutron
aw: lawn, hawk, draw, trawler
o͞o: goose, tooth, spoon, broom
o͝o: good, took, look, wood

[13] For a discussion of this point see E. W. Dolch, *The Teaching of Sounding* (Champaign, Ill.: The Garrard Press, 1951), 35-6.

Diphthongs are two adjacent vowels, each of which is sounded, as the *ou* in *house, oi* in *oil, oy* in *boy, ow* in *how* (but not the *ow* in *blow, grow, throw,* or *sow,* where the sound is long *o*). It is doubtful that teaching diphthongs is of major importance in the total phonics program. These sounds are met in a number of words that are learned as sight words, and certain of these words can serve as key words to help the pupil hear the sound (h*ou*se, *oi*l, b*oy*, h*ow*).

Vowels Affected by Particular Consonants. The long and short vowel sounds are by far the most important phonic clues in helping children unlock the pronunciation of words. In addition, there are other vowel situations which should be explained, even though they may be of lesser importance in phonic analysis. When a vowel is followed by *r,* the sound of that vowel is affected by the *r.* Usually a blend results, which is neither the long nor the short sound of the vowel (*car, curl, fir, for, park*). When the vowel *a* is followed by *l* or *w,* the resultant sound is a blend (*awl, tall, awful, talcum, awning, ball*). These particular instances of vowel controllers are of minor importance.

SUMMARY OF RULES RELATED TO VOWEL SOUNDS

1. Long vowel sounds are usually identified as the names of the vowel letters *a, e, i, o, u.*
2. A single vowel followed by a consonant in a word or syllable usually has the short sound: *can* in *cancel.*
3. A single vowel which concludes a word or syllable usually has the long sound (*me, ti ger, lo co mo tive*).
4. In the vowel digraphs *oa, ea, ee, ai, ay,* the first vowel is usually long and the second is silent (*coat, reap, lead, wait, play*). The digraphs *oo, au,* and *ew* form a single sound which is not the long sound of the first vowel (*food, good, haul, few*).
5. In words containing two vowels, one of which is final *e,* the final *e* is usually silent and the preceding vowel is long.
6. Single vowels followed by *r* usually result in a blend sound (*fir, car, burn, fur*). The vowel *a* followed by *l* or *w* usually results in a blend sound (*awl, tall, claw, awful*).
7. The letter *y* at the end of words containing no other vowel has the long sound of *i* (*my, try, sky, shy*).

8. Diphthongs are two-vowel combinations in which both vowels contribute to the speech sound (h*ou*se, bo*y*, c*ow*).

CONSONANTS WHICH ARE NOT SOUNDED

Having learned several hundred words as sight words, the child has met many words containing silent consonants. Such words, which have a high frequency of usage, must be learned as sight words. In the late primary and early intermediate grades these words appear with increased frequency and it may be desirable to prepare lessons for teaching certain of them. Instruction can stress the fact that the pronunciation of many words does not involve sounding all of the letters. Both new and familiar words within the child's meaning vocabulary may be taught or reviewed. Pupils are invited to look carefully at the words and listen to the beginning sound as each word is pronounced:

know	knee	knot	knowledge
knight	knife	knapsack	knob
knew	knit	knock	kneel

After the silent initial *k* has been studied, other silent letters should be taken up so that the pupil does not associate silentness only with the initial *k*.

know	knife	thumb	comb
knight	wrote	ghost	wreck
knee	sight	island	salmon

Silent letters in words do not constitute a major problem for most children in their reading. Many of these words contain structural clues which make them fairly easy to remember as sight words. After a child meets the words *knight, island,* or *knee* a given number of times, he is more likely to recognize them than he is such words as *their, there, these, those, when, where* after an equal number of experiences. Thus, it is likely that unsounded letters are more a threat to the learner in spelling than in reading. Study of silent consonants leads logically to a further generalization: (1) "In many words beginning with *kn,* the *k* is silent. (2) The letters *gh* in many words are silent (*light, night, right, sight, blight*). (3) *b* at the end of many words is not sounded (*thumb, comb, limb, lamb, climb*).

Silent letters in many words have no apparent function, but this is not universally true. An interesting lesson can be built around instances of a silent letter distinguishing one word from another when both words are sounded exactly alike. William Gray writes that "Silent consonants often enable us to discriminate between the meanings of printed words that are spelled differently but pronounced alike."[14]

Some examples for board work might include:

know—no	hour—our
to—two—too	but—butt
knot—not	in—inn
wrap—rap	knew—new
buy—by	whole—hole

If certain words did not contain silent vowels, we would in many cases have to depend on diacritical markings to distinguish between these words. The silent letters give us a visual clue to the meaning and pronunciation of these words.

1. We āt ăt āt.
2. He broke the window pān with the păn.
3. The fĭr forest was destroyed by the fīr.
4. He hĭd when they played hīd and seek.

SYLLABICATION

A syllable is a vowel, or group of letters containing a vowel, which forms one speech sound. A child must be able to break unknown polysyllabic words into syllables if he is to approximate the pronunciation of these words. This ability grows out of knowing both the structural and the phonetic features of words.

Structural analysis involves a deliberate attempt to see and recognize familiar units or parts of a word such as prefixes, endings, and root words: *re* read *ing*, *pre* heat *ed*, *bi* week *ly*, *un* wholesome *ness*, *dis* appear *ance*. Children should learn to recognize those word beginnings and endings, which are usually pronounced as units: *bi, re, dis, pre, in; ly, ness, ing, tion, ment, ful, tive, less,* and others.

---

[14] W. S. Gray, *On Their Own in Reading* (Rev. Ed.; Chicago: Scott, Foresman & Company, 1960), 99.

A knowledge of vowel behavior within words is the second major aid in breaking words into syllables. The sounds of vowels and letter combinations are not as consistent as prefixes and suffixes. Nevertheless, many phonetic generalizations are useful. Although the following examples are not words, the letter combinations can be broken into syllables: *comration, ragmotex, obsebong, fasnotel, debloman.* The likely syllabication is: *com·ra·tion, rag·mo·tex, fas·no·tel,* and *deb·lo·man.* Most facile readers would pronounce these nonsense words in substantially the same way. These readers probably would not recite rules to themselves before attempting to pronounce the above words, but they would probably be subconsciously influenced by rules they had learned.

When generalizations applicable to syllabication are taught, children should be provided with a number of examples and then led to see for themselves what happens. Out of this experience rules can develop. Starting with the question, "What usually happens when two consonants come between vowels?" the teacher can place on the board a number of words such as:

af ter	win dow	rab bit	let ter
gar den	can dy	din ner	sum mer
fas ter	pen cil	lit tle	cot ton

The generalization will then emerge that "when two consonants come between vowels the syllable division comes between the consonants" or "one consonant goes with each vowel." It should be pointed out that this rule will not always hold, but that it is the best guess to make when trying to pronounce an unknown word. In the case of double consonants (le*tt*er, su*mm*er), there are few exceptions to the rule.

To teach what happens when one consonant comes between two vowels, a list of known sight words may be placed on the board:

be gin	fe ver	to tal	de cide
o ver	di rect	ti ger	me ter
fa tal	mo ment	pu pil	ho tel

From these examples children will both see and hear that "the single consonant goes with the following syllable." They will also note that when "the syllable is a vowel or ends with a vowel, it usually has the long sound." These two generalizations should be taught together because they work together. In cases where the first of two vowels separated by a single consonant has its short sound, the single intervening consonant closes the first syllable (*cam el, mag a zine*).

A few generalizations about common word endings as they relate to syllabication might be taught. Children have had experience with prefixes and suffixes and may follow these rules even though they are not able to verbalize them.

1. Common endings which begin with a vowel such as *ing, est,* or *er* are usually sounded as syllables (look *ing,* long *er,* long *est*). This is not true of *ed* except when preceded by *t* or *d* (needed, wanted).

2. Most one-syllable words remain intact as syllables when endings are added. In many instances this violates the "divide between consonants" rule stated earlier. This is not a problem to children if they have learned to see prefixes and suffixes as units. Examples might include spell *ing,* want *ed,* tell *ing* (not spel *ling,* wan *ted,* tel *ling*).

3. Certain letter combinations, when found at the ends of words, are rarely divided and thus stand as the final syllable.

un *cle*	fa *ble*	bu *gle*	sad *dle*	an *kle*
cir *cle*	tum *ble*	sin *gle*	can *dle*	spar *kle*
bicy *cle*	mar *ble*	ea *gle*	nee *dle*	pic *kle*
mus *cle*	dou *ble*	strug *gle*	bun *dle*	twin *kle*

sam *ple*	gen *tle*	puz *zle*
tem *ple*	rat *tle*	daz *zle*
sim *ple*	whis *tle*	muz *zle*
pur *ple*	ti *tle*	

The generalizations are:

1. The letter combinations *cle, ble, gle, dle, zle, kle, ple, tle* at the end of words usually stand as the final syllable.
2. The final *e* is silent and the sound contains the *l* blended.
3. This final syllable is not accented.

DESCRIPTION OF A "PHONETIC METHOD"

The preceding discussion has attempted to present phonics teaching as incorporated with the sight-word method of teaching reading.

What follows is a brief description of *Phonetic Keys to Reading* which is a program for grades 1-2-3 described by its publisher as a new approach to teaching reading.[15] There are some major differences between the *Phonetic Keys to Reading* approach and the sight-word approach. In the former, the child learns the sounds of letters (and rules or generalizations which he is to apply in reading) before he learns words as sight words. The long and short sounds of vowels are taught first. These are also taught in the sight-word method but usually in grade two. The real difference between the two is the time at which these skills are introduced.

The second major difference between the two methods is the amount of phonic analysis found in the first grade curriculum. The word analysis skills usually taught in grade one in the sight-word method have been discussed in the chapter on beginning reading. For purposes of contrast, the phonetic analysis skills taught in first grade in the *Phonetic Keys to Reading* approach are summarized below. This summary deals separately with the audio-readiness, primer, and first reader stages. The phonic tasks are listed in the order in which they are presented.

1. The *audio-readiness pre-primer stage* is developed in the 96-page book *Tag*. This single book combines the readiness program and the pre-primer stage. The first step related to reading is teaching sight recognition and the long sound of the vowels. The specific tasks introduced during this period are:

   a) Recognition of capital and lower case vowel letters and the long sound of each vowel. (The vowel sounds are introduced in the order *O, A, E, I, U*).

   b) Recognition of the short sound of all vowels.

   c) Recognizing and learning the sound of the consonants *t, g, d, n, p, h, q, s, b, r, l, k, m, f*, and *c*.

   d) Recognition of the blend sounds *st, fr, pl*.

   e) Recognition of the consonant diagraphs *sh* and *th*.

   f) Recognizing and learning the sound of *w, v, j, y* as initial consonants, and the sound of *x* at the end of words.

[15] Cornelia B. Sloop. *The Phonetic Keys to Reading* program consists of the following books: First Grade—*Tag, Dot and Jim, All Around with Dot and Jim;* Second Grade—*Through Happy Hours, As Days Go By;* Third Grade—*Along New Ways, Wide Doors Open.* A teacher's manual is available at each grade level. Also available is a large number of word and phonetic flash cards. (Oklahoma City, Oklahoma: Economy Co., 1953).

g) Learning that the vowels *e*, *o*, and *y* at the end of short words have the long vowel sound (*me, be, so, no, my*).

h) Learning that the letter combination *ay* usually has the long sound of *a*.

2. *The Primer period* utilizes the book *Dot and Jim*. This 96-page primer introduces one hundred twenty-nine new sight words and reviews the thirty-nine previously taught as sight words. Phonic skills and rules taught in the pre-primer are reviewed. The new materials introduced in the primer are:

a) The sound of dipthong *ou* and *ow*.
b) The consonant blends *tr, br, spl, str*.
c) The rule of consonant controllers *ll* or *lk* following the vowel *a* (ta*lk*; ta*ll*).
d) The sound of *ng* (ha*ng*, ri*ng*, stri*ng*).
e) The sound of *nk* (pi*nk*, ta*nk*, su*nk*).
f) The sound of dipthongs *oi, oy* (*oil, boil, toy, boy*).
g) The letter combinations *kn, gn* (*knee, knife, gnat*).
h) The two sounds of *s* (*s* in bu*s*, *s* in new*s*).
i) The fact that the letter *c* followed by the vowels *e, i,* or *y* usually has the sound of *s* (*city, cycle, cellar*).
j) The two vowel sounds of double *oo* (*zoo, look*).
k) The sound of *aw* as in s*aw*.
l) The word-ending *ing*.
m) The dividing of syllables between double consonants (lit · tle, dad · dy).
n) The sound of the endings *ble, cle, dle, gle, kle, ple, tle, zle*. (The *e* is silent and the *l* sound is heard.)
o) The fact that each syllable in a word must contain a vowel sound.
p) The fact that a vowel at the end of a syllable usually has its long sound.
q) The sound of letter combination *ck*; digraph *ch* - *wh* and blend *cl*.
r) The sound of letter combinations *er, ir, ur*.
s) The ending *ed*.
t) The sound of the combination *ew* as in *new, grew*.
u) The fact that the letter combination *ear* may have the sound of *er* as in d*ear*, *ar* as in b*ear*, *ur* as in *ear*th.
u) The fact that syllable division usually comes between two consonants: *pic nic, win ter*.
w) The blend *sl*.

x) The fact that the vowel *o* preceding *ld* or *md* usually has its long sound (*sold, comb*).

3. *The First Reader* is the 96-page book *All Around with Dot and Jim,* which introduces the following phonetic skills:

a) Suffixes—helping the child to look for the root word plus the suffix *s, ing, ed, er, ly,* and *y* (*help* + *s, ed, ing;* farm *er,* firm *ly,* stick *y*).

b) The sound of the letter combination *tch* (ca*tch*, wa*tch*).

c) The suffix *es.*

d) The rule: In one-syllable words containing one vowel and ending with a single consonant the final consonant is doubled before adding endings which begin with a vowel (*running, hopping, hitting*).

e) The consonant blends *sm, cr, sp, squ, sw* (*sm*all, *cr*op, *sp*ell, *squ*eal, *sw*ing).

f) The rule: If a word ends with silent *e* the *e* is usually dropped before adding a suffix beginning with a vowel (*wake* = wak*ed,* like = lik*ed, shine* = shin*y*).

g) The suffixes *est, en.*

h) The rule: The vowel *i* before *ld, mb, nd* in one-syllable words is usually sounded long (*wild, kind, climb*).

i) The sound of *dr, gl, pr, sn, bl, gr, sc,* and *spr.*

j) The function of the apostrophe in contractions.

k) The fact that the digraph *ph* usually has the sound of *f* (*phone, Phillip*).

l) Compound words and the use of the hyphen.

m) The fact that words ending in *y* do not drop the y before adding *ing* (*frying, crying, trying*).

n) The fact that letters *igh* usually have the long sound of *i* (or the *gh* is usually silent, as in *bright, light, sight*).

o) The fact that when *ture* comes at the end of a word, the *t* usually as the sound of *ch* and the *u* has its long sound (*picture, mixture*).

p) The fact that when words begin with *wr,* the *w* is silent.

The above outline of the phonic skills introduced in the first year of the *Phonetic Keys to Reading* program is given here to contrast it with the phonics program characteristically introduced and taught in most basal readers. The major difference between the two systems is that approximately 70 per cent of all the learning-to-read phonics rules in the *Phonetic Keys to Reading* approach are introduced in the first grade. In the more widely used basal reader approach, only a small part of the total is introduced in grade one. They usually present only the sounds of initial consonants, a limited number of consonant blends, the special speech sounds *ch, th, sh, wh,* and the endings *s, ed, ing.*

In certain other facets of teaching reading, the two methods appear to be closely parallel. Both stress the importance of the child's experiences; both use experience charts, pre-primers, and primers; and both stress review of concepts and skills previously introduced.

RATIONALE FOR PHONETIC METHOD

The rationale for the sight-word method is found in Chapter 4. The most widely advanced justifications in support of the phonetic approach are listed here.

1. In learning to read, the child should develop analytic skills from the beginning. The sight-word method delays the introduction of phonic analysis too long.
2. Starting with vowel sounds is justified because the vowel is the key to sound words or syllables.
3. Children in the first grade can learn both the phonic elements in words and generalizations covering many situations. When they learn these, they have a valuable and useful tool in all reading situations.
4. It follows that, with these skills, children become independent in their reading much earlier, and there is less need for rigidly controlled vocabulary and constant repetition of the same words in text materials.
5. Data indicate that, after the first year, children taught by the phonic method perform a variety of reading tasks much better than do comparable groups taught in the sight-word method.

COMPARING RESULTS OF METHODS

There have been numerous studies comparing reading achievement attained by a phonic approach with that obtained by the sight-word approach. The phonic methods employed vary a great deal, and, unfortunately, the procedures used are rarely described precisely. General terms and descriptions are employed, such as the following: "A synthetic phonics system was employed." "Letter names and letter sounds were deliberately taught the experimental groups and taught incidentally in the control group." "The control group followed the regular basal program." "The control group followed traditional methods." "A modified phonetics approach was used." Evaluating all data reported the past few decades does not indicate a clean-cut superiority for either the phonetic or the sight word approach. Much data could be cited which support one or the other position.

In recent years there have been studies which purport to compare the *Phonetic Keys to Reading* method (described above) with sight-word reading programs which follow a particular basal reader series. One such report from the Champaign, Illinois schools, has received wide attention.[16] This study, covering several years, was begun in 1952. Five experimental classes were taught by the *Phonetic Keys to Reading* method, and five control classes followed a "traditional" basal reader program. The pertinent data from this study are summarized below.

TABLE 5

		Grade I		Grade II	
		Word Meaning	Para Reading	Reading Comprehension	Vocabulary
Experimental	*(Phonetic Keys)*	3.1	2.5	4.4	4.8
Control	*(Basal Reader)*	2.2	2.1	4.0	4.3

Artley, in reviewing the above report, raised several questions as to methodology and experimental controls.[17] The teachers in the experimental group volunteered; the method of selecting the control teachers is not clear. A class-size average of twenty pupils is given for the experimental group; data are less explicit for the control group. Probably the most serious question left unanswered is: was the amount of instructional time approximately the same for both groups?

[16] Margaret Henderson, *Progress Report of Reading Study 1952-1955,* Board of Education, Champaign, Ill.

[17] A. Sterl Artley, "Progess Report on the Champaign Reading Study, 1952-55: A Review and Discussion," *Elementary English,* XXXIV (1957), 102-5.

Kelly reported a study of achievement of two groups of second grade pupils, one taught by the *Phonetic Keys to Reading* method, the other by the Scott, Foresman basal reader series.[18] Pupils who were second graders in 1950, and who had received instruction in a basal reader series, served as the control group. The experimental group was drawn from pupils in the second grade in 1955 who had received two years of instruction in the *Phonetic Keys to Reading* method. The mean reading achievement is not given for the entire population of the 1950 and 1955 second grade classes, but rather for 100 pairs of students who could be matched on the basis of mental age. The mean reading achievement for the basal reader group was 2.9, for the *Phonetic Keys to Reading* group 3.7. The reading test which yielded this data is not given. No mention is made of whether equal amounts of instruction time were spent with both instructional methods.

Paul Sparks and Leo Fay reported a four-year study which also compares pupil achievement resulting from *Phonetic Keys to Reading* instruction with that of pupils receiving instruction within the framework of the Scott, Foresman basal reader program. Comparisons are made of over 400 pupils in each group at the end of grades one, two, three, and four. The class size and the time spent in teaching reading were kept as nearly equal as was administratively practical. The data are summarized below:

1. At the end of grade one, pupils receiving the *Phonetic Keys to Reading* instruction were superior in reading comprehension and reading vocabulary.
2. At the end of grade two, the same group was superior in reading comprehension, but there was no difference between the groups in reading vocabulary.
3. At the end of grade three, there were no differences in reading achievement.
4. At the end of grade four, there were no differences between the groups in reading vocabulary, reading speed, or spelling. However, in reading accuracy the basal reader group was superior (5 per cent

[18] Barbara Cline Kelly, "The Economy Method Versus the Scott, Foresman Method in Teaching Second-Grade Reading in the Murphysboro Public Schools," *Journal of Educational Research,* LI (1958), 465-69.

level of confidence). Neither method was superior with slow learners.[19]

John McDowell reports data on two groups, each consisting of 142 fourth-graders, which parallels the Sparks and Fay study. One group had received three years of instruction which stressed phonics. The other group followed a basal reader program in which phonics had been introduced gradually over the primary years. At the end of fourth grade the basal reading group was significantly superior in rate, paragraph comprehension, use of index, and total reading, as measured on the Iowa Silent Reading Test. The phonics group was significantly superior on alphabetizing and spelling. Comparative data is not available for each of the four years of instruction. However, the important fact brought out by the McDowell study is that even though special phonic instruction had resulted in superior reading in beginning reading, the balanced basal program, including phonics, had overcome the deficit and resulted in superior reading by fourth grade.[20] A complete discussion of the two methods is not given, and the variables of teacher proficiency and instruction time were not controlled.

The question of instruction time spent in teaching beginning reading is important in evaluating comparative studies. A number of experienced teachers who have at different times taught by both the basal reader approach and the *Phonetic Keys to Reading* approach have stated to the writer that they spend more classroom teaching time with the latter. This is, of course, a subjective conclusion. Most of these teachers believe that they are able to take their classes farther in a year with the phonic approach than they did with other methods, but they spend more time in teacher-preparation. These are, of course, not criticisms of the method, but if all these factors are valid, they should be carefully controlled in comparative studies. More time spent in teaching beginning reading may well be desirable, but this in itself is not a part of any formal method.

---

[19] Paul E. Sparks and Leo C. Fay, "An Evaluation of Two Methods of Teaching Reading," *Elementary School Journal*, LVII (1957), 386-90.

[20] Reverend John B. McDowell, "A Report on the Phonetic Method of Teaching Children to Read," *Catholic Educational Review*, LI (1953), 506-19.

Some conclusions which seem tenable, based on the above and other recent studies, are the following:

1. On the general question of which method is superior for teaching reading, studies thus far available are inconclusive, particularly if it is assumed that reading is a developmental process. Short-term studies cannot answer this question. If the question is phrased so as to deal only with a particular facet of reading, or with reading behavior measured over a limited time, more definitive answers are available.

2. Present data show conclusively that many children can learn much more in the area of phonic analysis in grade one than is at present included in most of the leading basal reader series. The data do not show what is sacrificed or neglected when the first year of reading instruction deals primarily with phonetic analysis. What we do know is that a group in grade one receiving deliberate and systematic instruction in both synthetic and analytical word analysis skills will measure higher on these particular skills than a group not receiving this type of instruction.

3. This points up the fact that the major issue is not a phonetic method *v.* a non-phonetic method; there are no non-phonetic methods in use in America today. Many critics of reading instruction would be amazed to learn that in essence phonetic methods do not teach any more basic phonic principles than do the leading basal reader series.[21] The real difference between methods is the point on the instructional continuum where emphasis on phonic principles is placed.

An interesting report relating certain phonic-visual skills to reading achievement in the first grade is found in *Success In First Grade Reading*, edited by Donald Durrell.[22] This study of more than 2,000 first grade children indicated that most reading difficulties could be prevented by early instruction in letter names and sounds and that

---

[21] This is basically true, although *Phonetic Keys to Reading* does teach some principles which have extremely limited application. Most of these situations are covered as sight-word exercises in basal reader series.

[22] *Success in First Grade Reading*. Boston University, *Journal of Education*, ed., Donald D. Durrell, CXL (1958), 1-48.

the best test for predicting success in reading achievement in the first grade is pupil knowledge of letter names.[23] An implied criticism in this study of basal reader series is found in the statement that "One of the major handicaps to the instructional program [using a basal reader series] was the necessity for teachers to build and exchange much of the instructional materials."[24]

The data from this study and from studies of the phonetic approach suggest that most basal reader programs might possibly be strengthened by more emphasis on phonic analysis in beginning reading. This does not imply, however, that a purely synthetic approach is necessarily the most desirable one.

CONCLUSION

Since there has been so much controversy about teaching phonics, and in order to show the continuity of the total phonics program in the primary grades, this chapter has dealt with phonic instruction separately from the other facets of word analysis and reading instruction. It should be emphasized that sound principles of teaching reading must apply to phonics as well as to all other facets of reading instruction. The fact that confusion and misconceptions are more prevalent in regard to phonics instruction than in other areas should not cause teachers to deviate from principles in which they believe, nor fail to apply the precepts of good teaching.

The principles of teaching reading most closely related to instruction in phonics are (1) complicated symbolic processes are sensitive to pressure; (2) children in groups learn to read as individuals; (3) instruction should be based on diagnosis; (4) a given technique will not work equally well with all children; and (5) reading is a process of getting meaning.

Phonics, which relates to the sounds which must be associated with letter-combinations in words, is by far the most complicated facet of the entire symbolic process called reading. Each child must hear, and be able to discriminate between, very similar sounds. In many workbook exercises, he can use his eyes to discriminate between

---

[23] *Ibid.*, 5, 24, and 42.
[24] *Ibid.*, 4.

similarities and differences in words where the authors and teacher wanted him to rely on auditory discrimination. By not keeping this fact in mind, a teacher may mistake ritual for teaching. For instance, a lesson on the short sound of *a* may be followed by a workbook exercise devoted to it. The teacher may diligently mark all errors, require that corrections be made, inquire if there is anyone who does not understand the lesson, and be greatly relieved to find that all pupils indicate that they understand. This can take place in a classroom where very few pupils have grasped the material, although some will have been most proficient in correcting errors made on the workbook exercise. Their "correcting" will have consisted of marking remaining choices. This type of response is indicative of intelligent behavior but not of having mastered the short *a*.

After a child has failed to master a number of steps in phonics, his reading ability may appear to deteriorate. That is, he now stands lower in relation to a fixed grade-level standard than he did some months ago. At this point, subtle and overt pressures are brought to bear. Uncompleted workbook pages and other evidence of bad work habits will appear. He may be assigned to a lower grade, which will bring pressures from home. The child himself will become overly concerned about his reading ability, thus adding more pressures, all of which may eventually seriously hinder his learning progress.

To discover what phonic skills a child needs, the teacher must rely on thorough diagnosis. If it is true that some teachers feel insecure in teaching phonics (a premise advanced earlier in the chapter), it is not likely that they will be expert in diagnosing pupil needs in this area. This could result in a tendency to follow mechanically the suggestions and tailor-made lessons found in workbooks or in phonetic methods. This, of course, does not make for creative teaching. There may also be further confusion as to the advisability of using practices which have been proscribed by an authority and indecision as to what practices are still in good repute. In short, there has been much written about phonics, and possibly too many fine lines drawn between the acceptable and the suspect. If any practice helps a particular child over a barrier in his reading and is not a threat to his future reading progress, that practice is, in his case, justifiable. Armed with this philosophy, teachers might dispel the fear of doing something wrong while teaching phonics.

Justifying a given technique on the ground that it helps a particular child does not violate any sound principle of teaching. However, it does not reduce the validity of the premise that any given practice or procedure is not likely to work equally well with all children. Therefore, the reading teacher must have a variety of approaches in order to deal with the problems she will meet or to achieve the goals she has set.

The one principle which would, if followed, prevent an overemphasis on phonics, or on any other mechanical aspect of reading, is that reading must be viewed as a process of discovering meaning. The good teachers of reading never lose sight of this fact. But becoming facile in discovering meaning depends on mastering certain fundamental mechanics in the reading process, and phonics *is second in importance to no other skill.*

YOUR POINT OF VIEW?

1. The significant difference between a phonetic method and the basal reader method is the number of phonic rules or generalizations taught in each program.

2. The significant difference between a phonetic method and the basal reader method is the point on the educational continuum where phonics instruction receives emphasis.

3. If experimental studies establish that children in first grade taught by a specific phonetic method are significantly superior in reading to children taught by other methods, all schools should adopt that phonetic method.

4. Reading experts would tend to agree that the vaguest term in the previous proposition is (select one):
   A. "Specific phonetic method"
   B. "Significantly superior"
   C. "Reading"

5. An admonition frequently found in the literature on reading is "never teach phonic analysis except in meaningful reading situations." A particular child in grade four cannot achieve independence in reading because he is very deficient in "sounding out unknown words." It would be completely justifiable to work with him for a number of reading periods on phonics in isolation, i.e., drill on letter sounds, syllabication, and the like.

BIBLIOGRAPHY

Agnew, Donald C. *Effect of Varied Amounts of Phonetic Training on Primary Reading*. Durham, North Carolina: Duke University Press, 1939.

Artley, A. Sterl. "Progress Report on the Champaign Reading Study 1952-55: A Review and Discussion," *Elementary English,* XXXIV (February, 1957), 102-5.

———. "Controversial Issues Relating to Word Perception," *Reading Teacher,* VIII (April, 1955), 196-99.

Bear, David E. "Phonics for First Grade: A Comparison of Two Methods," *Elementary School Journal,* LIX (April, 1959), 394-402.

Betts, Emmett A. *Foundations of Reading Instruction.* New York: American Book Company, 1946, Chap. 24.

———. "Phonics: Practical Considerations Based on Research," *Elementary English,* XXXIII (October, 1956), 357-71.

Bloomer, Richard H. "An Investigation of an Experimental First Grade Phonics Program," *Journal of Educational Research,* LIII (January, 1960), 188-93.

Burrows, Alvina Treut. *What About Phonics.* Washington: Bulletin No. 57, Association for Childhood Education, 1951.

———. "Applying Phonics Research to Classroom Teaching," *Childhood Education,* XXXII (February, 1956), 273-79.

Cordts, Anna D. "The Phonetics of Phonics," *Reading Teacher,* IX (December, 1955), 81-84.

Daniels, J. C., and Diack, Hunter. "The Phonic Word Method," *Reading Teacher,* XIII (October, 1959), 14-21.

Diack, Hunter. "On Seeing Words as 'Wholes,'" *Elementary English,* XXXV (October, 1958), 380-82.

Dolch, E. W. *The Teaching of Sounding.* Champaign, Ill.: The Garrard Press, 1951.

———. "Phonics in the First Grade," *Elementary English,* XXXII (December, 1955), 514-18.

———. "Am I Teaching Phonics Right?" *Elementary English,* XXXIV (April, 1957), 227-34.

Durrell, Donald D. *Improving Reading Instruction.* Tarrytown-on-Hudson: World Book Company, 1956, Chaps. 10, 11.

——— (ed.). "Success in First Grade Reading," *Journal of Education* (Boston University), CXL (February, 1958), 1-48.

Gray, Lillian, and Reese, Dora. *Teaching Children to Read* (2nd ed.). New York: The Ronald Press Co., 1957, Chap. 11.

Gray, William S. *On Their Own in Reading* (Rev. Ed). Chicago: Scott, Foresman & Co., 1960.

Haggard, J. Kendall. "Phonics in Directed Reading Activities," *Reading Teacher,* IX (December, 1955).

Harris, Albert J. *How to Increase Reading Ability* (3rd ed.). New York: Longmans, Green & Co., 1956, Chaps. 12, 13, and 14.

Hester, Kathleen B. *Teaching Every Child to Read.* New York: Harper & Brothers, 1955, Chap. 11.

Hildreth, Gertrude. "The Role of Pronouncing and Sounding in Learning to Read," *Elementary School Journal,* LV (November, 1954), 141-47.

———. "Some Misconceptions Concerning Phonics," *Elementary English,* XXXVI (January, 1957), 26-29.

———. "New Methods for Old in Teaching Phonics," *Elementary School Journal,* LVII (May, 1957), 436-41.

Kelly, Barbara Cline. "The Economy Method versus the Scott, Foresman Method in Teaching Second-Grade Reading in the Murphysboro Public Schools," *Journal of Educational Research,* LI (February, 1958), 465-69.

Lineham, E. B. "Early Instruction in Letter Names and Sounds as Related to Success in Beginning Reading," *Journal of Education,* CXL (February, 1958), 44-48.

McDowell, Reverend John B. "A Report on the Phonetic Method of Teaching Children to Read," *Catholic Educational Review,* LI, (October, 1953), 506-19.

McKee, Paul. *The Teaching of Reading in the Elementary School.* Boston: Houghton Mifflin Co., 1948, Chaps. 8-11.

Mills, Robert E. "An Evaluation of Techniques for Teaching Word Recognition," *Elementary School Journal,* LVI (January, 1956), 221-25.

Mulder, Robert L., and Curtin, James. "Vocal Phonic Ability and Silent-Reading Achievement: A First Report," *Elementary School Journal,* LVI (November, 1955), 121-23.

Oaks, Ruth E. "A Study of the Vowel Situations in a Primary Vocabulary," *Education,* LXXII (May, 1952), 604-17.

Russell, David H. *Children Learn to Read.* Boston: Ginn and Co., 1949, Chap. 10.

Smith, Nila B. "Phonics Then and Now," *Education,* LXXV (May, 1955), 560-65. (This entire issue devoted to Phonics.)

———. "What Research Says about Phonics Instruction," *Journal of Educational Research,* LI (September, 1957), 1-9.

———. "Phonics and Word Method: Origin and Development," *Education,* LXXVIII (May, 1958), 515-20.

Sloop, Cornelia B., Garrison, Harrell E., and Creekmore, Mildred. *Phonetic Keys to Reading: a Reading Program for Grades 1, 2 and 3*. Oklahoma City: The Economy Co., 1952.

Sparks, Paul E., and Fay, Leo C. "An Evaluation of Two Methods of Teaching Reading," *Elementary School Journal,* LVII (April, 1957), 386-90.

Waldman, John, and Triggs, Frances O. "The Measurement of Word Attack Skills," *Elementary English,* XXXV (November, 1958), 459-63.

chapter 8

THE INTERMEDIATE GRADES

The intermediate grades present a formidable challenge to the teacher of reading. The pitfalls are as numerous and as serious as those found at any instructional level. The most important challenge is achieving the proper balance between systematic instruction in reading and instruction in the subject areas of the curriculum characteristically found in these grades. Academic failures and loss of interest in school occur in the intermediate grades because school practices, curricular materials, and educational goals tend to accentuate reading instruction problems.

A TRANSITION PERIOD

Teachers agree that ideally the process of learning to read progresses smoothly without perceptible breaks through a series of grade levels. There are certain factors in the total school framework, however, which cause many teachers to feel that an abrupt transition occurs between third and fourth grades. The end of the third grade and the beginning of the fourth is often designated as the period of "independent reading." There is evidence in classroom behaviors that some teachers do succumb to the philosophy that the intermediate grades should be characterized by a shift in emphasis from "learning to read" to "reading to learn" in the various subject-matter areas. The use of a number of non-integrated textbooks in various content areas tends to substantiate the idea that this is a transitional period.

These factors form the basis for the generalization that reading skills are taught in the primary grades and applied in the intermediate and later grades. A further generalization is that since reading skills are taught in the primary grades, children who have been through these grades have mastered the skills. It is true that once pupils reach the intermediate level they are expected to do more reading grade by grade while less time is devoted to the actual process of learning to read. A study of the relationship between reading ability and a language-factor intelligence test at all grade levels indicated, however, that the correlation between these measures was lowest at grade four. The authors posited a "fourth grade hump in reading" which may be accounted for by the increased difficulty of concepts, style of writing, and specialized vocabulary found in reading materials at this level. A second hypothesis was that this finding might reflect a decline in the systematic teaching of reading at the fourth grade level.[1]

AN OVERVIEW OF THE INSTRUCTIONAL PROGRAM

The reading program of the intermediate grades includes both the reinforcement and the extension of the basic reading skills discussed in the chapter on beginning reading and the chapter on the primary grades. The need for expansion of reading skills does not cease with a given chronological age, grade level placement, or degree of competency attained. Because reading is a developmental process, competency in reading is a relative thing. Mastery of skills adequate for the second grade curriculum does not assure that one will be equally competent in dealing with the fourth or sixth grade curricular materials. Actually, maintaining reading competency consistent with grade placement may require more rapid growth in the intermediate grades than in preceding grades.

---

[1] George Manolakes and William D. Sheldon, "The Relation Between Reading-Test Scores and Language-Factors Intelligence Quotients," *Elementary School Journal,* LV (1955), 346-50.

In addition to working with the skills introduced in the primary grades, the intermediate-level teacher must provide guidance in a large number of even more complicated reading tasks. The application of skills previously taught also becomes more complex. For instance, visual discrimination taught in beginning reading involves perception of structural differences between whole word symbols. In grade four the child must perceive minute differences within words in order to use a dictionary. Also, in beginning reading getting meaning from context was relatively simple since the connotation of an unknown sight word was undoubtedly in the child's meaning vocabulary. In addition, the unknown sight word was probably the only new word on the page. In the intermediate grades a paragraph in a social science text may contain a number of new and difficult concepts as well as several unknown sight words.

OBJECTIVES OF INTERMEDIATE LEVEL INSTRUCTION

1. Individual evaluation should take place to determine the capacity of students and the present level of achievement in all facets of reading including:

a) sight word vocabulary
b) word attack skills
c) level of silent reading
d) meaning vocabulary and concepts
e) ability to profit from listening situations including oral directions
f) oral reading skills
g) facility in finding information, use of reference materials
h) work habits and attitudes
i) rate at which curricular materials can be read

2. Following diagnosis, the teacher should devise a flexible reading program to take care of individual differences and needs revealed in the initial diagnosis.

3. Reading instruction must be deliberate and systematic. Inestimable damage to children can result from the philosophy that "children learn to read in the primary grades and read to learn at the intermediate level." They must do both at each level.

4. The child should be helped to expand his stock of concepts. This is essential in all content areas.

5. Practice should be provided in various types of functional reading—in newspapers, magazines, and books—to supplement basic texts in subject areas.

6. Guidance should be supplied in reading for recreation, pleasure, and personal growth.

7. The child's reading interests should be widened to build a sound foundation for life-long personal reading activities.

8. Appreciation should be developed for good literature, poetry, and drama.

9. A wide selection of materials should be made available in all fields—science, literature, biography, current events, social studies, and the like.

10. A program should be devised for guiding the growth of intellectually gifted children.

11. Children should be helped to increase the rate at which they can comprehend printed word symbols in combination. This skill becomes increasingly important at this instructional level since the curriculum materials in the various content areas make ever-widening demands on readers.

12. Steps should be taken to improve critical reading skills such as:

a) Coping with figurative or picturesque language
b) Drawing inferences
c) Classifying ideas and selecting those that are germane to the reader's purpose
d) Evaluating ideas and arriving at the author's purpose or intent
e) Detecting bias and differentiating between fact and opinion

13. The following reading-study skills should be developed and extended:

a) Using books effectively—making maximum use of the index, table of contents, and appendix
b) Acquiring facility in the use of a dictionary
c) Using reference books effectively
d) Understanding graphs, maps, charts, and tables
e) Using library resources, card catalogue, and periodical indexes
f) Note-taking and outlining materials for a given purpose

14. Diagnosis (outlined above) should be continuous and ongoing throughout each instructional year. An initial diagnosis serves only for initial procedures.

SYSTEMATIC READING INSTRUCTION

The objectives listed above are illustrative of the broad reading program in the intermediate grades which has as its over-all goal the continuous growth of the child.[2] Before such a wide array of goals can be achieved all instructional activities must be well planned and systematically carried out. There are several ways in which a given objective can be achieved, but regardless of a teacher's preference for particular techniques she must make certain that no important reading skill is slighted or ignored. Reading instruction in the intermediate grades should consist of the proper combination of:

1. Review or re-teaching of essential skills taught at the primary level for those pupils who may not have mastered them there.

2. Introduction and systematic teaching of new reading skills characteristically emphasized in the intermediate grades. Figure 31 summarizes these skills at both the primary and intermediate levels.

FIGURE 31

A

READING SKILLS AND ABILITIES CHARACTERISTICALLY EMPHASIZED AT PRIMARY LEVEL

1. Stress readiness activities
2. Associate meaning with printed word symbols
3. Develop sight vocabulary
4. Build visual word discrimination skills
   a) Word configuration
   b) Context clues
   c) Structural analysis

[2] Gertrude Whipple, "Characteristics of a Sound Reading Program," *Reading in the Elementary School*, Forty-eighth Yearbook, Part II, National Society for the Study of Education, University of Chicago Press, 1949, 33-53.

(1) Inflectional endings
(2) Compound words
(3) Prefixes and suffixes

5. Build auditory discrimination of speech sounds in words
   a) Skills in listening
   b) Initial consonant sounds
   c) Substitution of initial and end sounds of words
   d) Blends and digraphs
   e) Vowel sounds
6. Teach expansion of meanings
   a) Use picture clues
   b) Work with roots or base words
   c) Work with synonyms and antonyms
7. Develop independent work habits
8. Teach simple alphabetizing

B

READING SKILLS AND ABILITIES CHARACTERISTICALLY EMPHASIZED AT INTERMEDIATE LEVEL

1. Review, re-teach, or teach all skills under *A* which child has not mastered
2. Continuously expand sight vocabulary
3. Expand word attack skills (phonics and syllabication)
4. Develop study skills in finding materials
   a) Dictionary skills
   b) Use of reference materials, development of independent work habits
   c) Facility in using index, table of contents, appendix, glossary, maps, and charts
5. Expand concepts in content areas
   a) Development of ability for critical reading
   b) Development of skill in evaluating what is read, perceiving relationships, and drawing inferences
6. Increase rate of comprehension
   a) Development of different rates of reading for different materials and different purposes
   b) Development of ability to scan material for specific information

7. Cultivate social understandings through reading
   a) Understanding one's immediate environment and its relation to the past
   b) Understanding other people, countries, and cultures
8. Encourage recreational reading for
   a) Pleasure
   b) Growth toward maturity
   c) Personal adjustment

It has been pointed out that the curriculum materials for the intermediate grades place major emphasis on the teaching of subject-matter content. At the same time the available data show conclusively that a great number of pupils at the intermediate level cannot cope with the content materials at their grade level because they lack the necessary reading skills. Thus, in the intermediate grades there is danger of a too literal acceptance of the old dictum that "a pupil learns to read by reading" or "nothing improves one's reading like more and more reading." This is true for readers who have mastered the necessary reading skills, but there is a fallacy in these statements when applied to any child who is deficient in reading skills. The more reading a pupil with poor reading habits does, the more he reinforces his poor habits. Reading with instruction and guidance aimed at improvement is the key. Learning in all content areas, from this point on in the grades, depends primarily on reading skill. The facts taught in science, geography, history, and mathematics are important, but the school's basic task is to teach each child the reading skills which will enable him to read independently in any of these content areas. Since many children still need instruction in reading skills, any reduction in emphasis on this facet of reading is a serious omission. McKee's insistence that definite time periods should be assigned for the teaching of reading fundamentals in the intermediate grades is valid.[3]

Using Basal Reader Series. The use of basal reader series is one proven method of implementing systematic reading instruction.

---

[3] Paul McKee, *The Teaching of Reading in the Elementary School* (Boston: Houghton Mifflin Co., 1948), 352.

Criticism of the use of basal readers at the intermediate grades often starts with the premise that these materials are not in themselves a complete reading program. One can agree with this premise without accepting the rather facile generalization that basic series have little instructional utility at this level. Ragan correctly points out that the problem of reading instruction is not solved by the elimination of basal readers at the intermediate level or by making the reader series the reading program.[4] These materials are designed to take the child through a developmental program which maintains a proper balance of instruction in all facets of reading. Other assets of basal readers include the following: they are graded as to difficulty level; they allow for review of skills previously introduced; workbooks provide seat work; most series include supplementary books for both the poorer and the accelerated readers; the content and interest level of basal materials at the intermediate level is often more appropriate for the group for whom it is intended than are the materials at the beginning reading level.

Basal readers can be misused or not used at their maximum effectiveness if the school attempts to have all pupils in a given grade use only materials designed specifically for that grade. This procedure will be ineffective with both the poorer and the more capable readers. The former may not be able to read the material at their grade placement, and the accelerated readers are often bored when they are forced to proceed at a tempo that is below their rate of growth. It should be remembered that these are not inherent weaknesses of basal readers but weaknesses resulting from the inept use of such materials.

Important reading tasks which are stressed in the basic reader approach at the intermediate level include:

1. Training in reading for different purposes
   a) Noting detail, possibly skimming for specific facts
   b) Drawing conclusions or inferences
   c) Detecting author's mood and purpose

---

[4] William B. Ragan, *Modern Elementary Curriculum* (Rev. ed.; New York: Holt, Rinehart & Winston, Inc., 1960), 208.

d) Evaluative reading or critical analysis which involves the weighing of facts, opinions, generalizations, analogies, and the like

e) Problem-solving through reading

2. Extension of word recognition skills· phonic analysis; structural analysis with emphasis on prefixes and suffixes
3. Practice in organization of data gleaned from reading
4. Development of general vocabulary and expansion of concepts
5. Development of all communication skills through integrating reading, listening, and composition
6. Broadening interests and reading tastes, helping to build a foundation for recreational reading and cultivating appreciation of poetry and good literature.
7. Workbook exercises which develop skill in the use of the dictionary
8. Graded books and workbook exercises which are excellent materials for use in a reading diagnosis

A Period for Reading Instruction. A definite reading instruction period should be incorporated into the program of the intermediate grades. Incidental teaching of reading in the subject areas, which is commendable in itself, will leave many children with inadequate instruction in fundamental reading skills. Using basic readers and the workbooks which are included in basal programs will assure systematic instruction in all skills and prevent serious instructional gaps which might occur in incidental teaching. A definite reading period does not imply that all pupils will be receiving the same instruction. As pointed out above, this practice is unjustifiably wasteful. Certainly in the use of workbooks good readers will not need all types of drill included and the poorer readers will need teacher guidance in this work, not merely the assignment of pages.

While the teacher works with a group of pupils who need review on word-attack skills, more advanced readers can be reading independently from supplementary sources. This reading can be influential in extending reading horizons and developing new reading interests. During some reading periods the teacher can work with the advanced group stressing appreciation or critical analysis of a poem or story while the skills group works independently on teacher-made or workbook skill-building exercises. At other times the teacher may not work with any particular group but will give hints on individual help where needed. There will be some situations where instruction can involve the entire class. For example, the teacher may deal with the entire class when giving instruction in the use of the dictionary, in group planning of a unit, in word meaning sessions, when reading to the group, or when giving instruction in how to find materials. These instances of class-wide instruction would undoubtedly be followed by grouping techniques based on pupils' present achievement and individual needs.

Skills in Word-Attack. Word-attack skills must be both reviewed and extended in the intermediate grades. The specific tasks to be dealt with include all those which have been discussed at the beginning and primary levels. Since instruction in these tasks has taken place in previous grades one of the real dangers at the intermediate level is the assumption that pupils are proficient in these skills. As a matter of fact many pupils will need review or reteaching of word-attack skills. Since it would be wasteful to teach these to the entire class, such instruction should take place on an individual or small group basis determined by pupil needs.

Experience indicates that lack of ability in phonic analysis will be a major stumbling block for many pupils at this level. Since most of the emphasis on teaching phonics falls in the primary grades, the curricular materials at the intermediate level may not contain enough practice for those pupils who are markedly deficient in this skill. Pupils in this category will have a variety of problems. Thus, to help all such individuals the teacher at the intermediate level should be familiar with the entire phonics program. So that the teacher may see the continuity of the total phonics program, Chapter 7 is devoted to this topic.

Prefixes and suffixes should be dealt with extensively at the intermediate level from the standpoint of both structural and meaning changes produced.[5] There is, of course, no limit to the prefixes or suffixes which should be taught at this level. The following prefixes

---

[5] James A. Fitzgerald, "Prefixes in Child Writing," *Elementary English*, XXXVI (1959), 576-80.

should not be neglected: *dis, de, ex, in, ab, pre, re, sub, un, co, trans, in, be, con, mis, auto, al, semi, en.* Suffixes: *ment, tion, able, ous, ly, er, ful, ward, less, or, en, ence, ance, ness, est, ible, ing, ist, ably, age, ed, ance.*

Syllabication is a dictionary skill which should be stressed in the intermediate grades. Breaking words into syllables is of considerable aid to the child in arriving at the pronunciation of words in reading and is also a real aid in spelling. Practice in breaking words into syllables is most helpful as a remedial technique (See Chapter 13).

SPECIAL INSTRUCTIONAL PROBLEMS IN THE INTERMEDIATE PROGRAM

Every instructional level in the school presents its own unique challenges to teachers. Undoubtedly it is not intentional that the intermediate grades constitute a break in the continuity of instruction in the elementary school. Nevertheless, the emphasis on separate textbooks in the various subject areas is one of the chief sources of instructional problems. These books call for a fairly high level of independent reading ability and special facility in a number of reading-study skills such as the ability to use the dictionary, reference materials, graphs, charts, and tables.

These curricular materials confront the reader with an ever-increasing number of unknown and relatively difficult concepts.[6]

In addition, much more complex sentence structure and a variety of organizational patterns are found which frustrate many pupils. It is necessary to know many new and more difficult connotations for words met previously and to understand a large number of idiomatic and figurative expressions. The amount of reading which is required is suddenly increased and pupils must develop the ability to read and comprehend at a more rapid rate. They must also develop flexibility in their reading so as to be able to adjust rate to both difficulty level and purpose. Instructional procedures for coping with these and other problems are discussed in the remainder of this chapter.

---

[6] Richard L. Carner and William D. Sheldon, "Problems in the Development of Concepts Through Reading," *Elementary School Journal,* LV (1954), 226-29.

VARIABILITY AMONG PUPILS

Individual differences in reading ability tend to increase with reading instruction. A given group of pupils will show greater individual differences at the end of four years of schooling than they did at the end of the first year. Good teaching aims at moving every child along at his maximum rate. The gifted child will move further in a given period of time than will the average child. Thus, the better the teaching, the greater will be the differences between children. By the time a group of children reach the intermediate grades, they are strung out over a considerable range of reading ability. Although different facets of the reading program receive varying degrees of emphasis at different grade levels, in the intermediate grades the emphasis almost has to be on what the individual child needs regardless of what is found in the curriculum guide of a particular grade. The need for individualized instruction in the intermediate grades grows out of the wide range of abilities found in children and their equally wide range of instructional needs.

Importance of Diagnosis. Diagnosis is essential to a successful reading program at the intermediate level. Principles of teaching reading do not vary with grade level or with the materials being used. The variability of pupils in the intermediate grades makes a number of principles, discussed previously, particularly appropriate to this period: (a) no child should be expected to deal with materials he cannot read; (b) instruction must be at the learner's present level; (c) a thorough diagnosis will single out the pupils needing special instruction and indicate the skills in which the student is deficient; (d) once weaknesses are discovered, instruction must be fitted to individual needs.

An illustration of the importance of following sound principles of instruction is provided by the pupil who has failed to master phonic-analysis skills. Experienced teachers know how unlikely it is that he will simply outgrow his inadequacy. The fact that the child has come this far without developing insights and techniques for overcoming his problem is in itself evidence that he is not likely to do so in the absence of skillful guidance and teaching. If a child has not developed the ability to hear the differences between the first syllables of words such as *dim*ple, *dem*onstrate, *dum*found, *domi*noes, *dam*sel; or *mar*ble, *mor*tal, *mur*mur, *mer*cy, *mir*acle, it is useless to attempt to teach him a number of rules regarding short vowels, long vowels, or vowels followed by varying numbers of consonants. The child must be taught to make auditory discriminations and the fact that this is ordinarily taught in first grade does not alter the fact that in this case it will have to be done now. Until the inability to discriminate between speech sounds is overcome, the student can make little real progress in gaining independence in sounding. The principle of going back to where the child is applies to every learning step in phonic analysis, such as learning initial consonant sounds, learning substitution of initial sounds, recognizing blends, distinguishing between long and short vowel sounds, and understanding syllabication.

Standardized tests and teacher-made informal reading tests appropriate for all of the elementary grades have been discussed in detail in Chapter 5. The reader may wish to refer to this discussion found on pages 151-167. A commendable practice in the intermediate grades is the use of teacher-prepared comprehension questions over the various subject materials covered. Such tests can serve two purposes. They are diagnostic from the teacher's standpoint, and they can provide excellent guidance for the reader. To devise tests which serve both these purposes is difficult and time-consuming. As a result, many attempts at preparing such tests tend to isolate facts and details. In this connection, it should be remembered that the pupil at the intermediate level needs practice in evaluating ideas, seeing relationships, and drawing inferences.

Grouping Practices. Grouping pupils for instructional purposes is essential in the intermediate grades if the teacher is to deal successfully with the needs of all pupils. The philosophy and aims of intraclass grouping have been discussed in Chapter 4 and will not be repeated here. However, the range of reading ability among pupils at this level and the great variety of reading materials available make possible a number of grouping practices which can be used effectively. Highly structured groups become less practical in the intermediate grades. Yet all the virtues of grouping can be achieved if a variety of tasks at varying levels of difficulty are devised for use in a given classroom.

While a majority of the pupils in a social science class may profitably use the assigned textbook, there are numerous other materials available at all levels of difficulty. Some of these lend them-

Children who have approximately equal reading skill analyze and discuss a story which they have all previously read silently. Interest is heightened because their discussion is being recorded. With the playback in mind, children will practice good habits of listening, remembering not to interrupt speakers or inject irrelevant comments. ***(Courtesy of San Diego City Schools)***

selves to use by the entire class; other materials and tasks will be more appropriate for either accelerated or impaired readers.

1. A film may be shown to the entire class.

2. Pictures which illustrate a particular concept appropriate to the topic can be gathered and placed on the bulletin board. Perhaps this project can be carried out by some of the less competent readers.

3. A special vocabulary lesson can be worked out using new terms children are likely to meet in their reading.

4. Each child can also make his own "new word list" which grows out of his reading on the topic.

5. Newspaper and magazine articles may be read by some pupils in the class.

6. Models, charts, or other illustrations which clarify some facet of the project may be prepared and displayed. With some guidance from the teacher, this task may be made quite appealing to poorer readers.

7. Better readers may report to the class on material found in reference or other books.

In teaching or reviewing certain reading skills, the teacher can use many procedures parallel to those used at the primary level. Many pupils are now independent readers, and they can, if materials are available, do profitable supplementary reading while the teacher stresses the mechanics of reading with a group of less competent readers. At other times poorer readers can work independently on skill-building exercises while the teacher checks the progress of, and gives suggestions to, the group of advanced readers.

Individualized Reading. Discussed in Chapter 4 as a *method,* individualized reading might be mentioned here as an extension of traditional grouping practices. An individualized program can help teachers cope with pupil variability. The wider the range of abilities and the wider the range of pupil needs in reading, the more apparent it becomes that three or four reading groups will not be adequate to meet the needs of all pupils in a given classroom. Some pupils will not fit logically into any one of these groups. It is an educational paradox that as pupil abilities within the classroom become more diverse, the textbook approach becomes more widely used and the basic curricular materials become more rigid and inflexible. The aim of individualized reading is to have each child read the materials he is capable of reading and in which he is interested. When these two requirements are met, reading is likely to become purposeful and profitable. An individual reading program can be initiated at any grade level.

The unit approach discussed later in this chapter depends to a high degree on individualized reading even among children working in the same group or on the same facet of a given project. Independent readers must be permitted to read on their own and to pursue their immediate interests. Average readers may work alone or in small groups according to the nature of the project. Pupils with special problems may be worked with individually. Only good teaching and sound administrative practices can make it possible to meet the varied needs of all pupils.

DEVELOPING PERMANENT READING INTERESTS

Developing permanent reading interests is closely related to pupils' motivation for reading. Maintaining interest in reading and healthy attitudes toward reading are special problems in the intermediate grades, particularly in schools which do not provide a wide range of reading materials in all areas. There are still too many instances where schools rely primarily on the one-textbook approach in the various subject-matter areas. The only justification for this practice would be a belief that all pupils in a given class read at the same level, that no children in the group lack the ability to read books at the designated grade level, and that no children are ready to move beyond these graded materials. In reality, a child who enjoyed a fair degree of success in primary reading may feel threatened by the much broader reading tasks demanded by the curricular materials of the middle grades. On this point Gates writes,

> There is evidence from various sources that children often need some help in breaking away from the primary reading habits to advance to the higher intermediate level. There are even cases in which perfection of the primary techniques presents a special danger, the danger that marked facility for reading at the primary level will induce a child to rest on his oars.[7]

When the child can read the words but meets many concepts he does not understand, his enjoyment of reading is curtailed. When the child senses that he is expected to read and understand, his inability to do so colors his attitude toward reading. Reading becomes a threat in that he cannot attain arbitrary goals set by the teacher or cope with the questions provided by the text. No sense of fulfillment, achievement, or success accompanies the daily reading tasks which are then

[7] Arthur I. Gates, *The Improvement of Reading*, (3rd. ed.; New York: The Macmillan Company, 1947), 35. By permission of The Macmillian Company.

neither pleasant nor rewarding. When reading does not fulfill these psychological needs which are so strong in children, interest in reading is likely to suffer.

Once the child discovers that reading is a satisfying experience, reading for many purposes should become a highly reinforced response.[8] The child should learn that he may read:

1. To gain information about countless interesting topics.
2. To realize a very important form of self-achievement.
3. To experience vicarious adventure and romance.
4. To better understand the world in which he lives.
5. To broaden that concept through understanding other people and other parts of the world (or universe).
6. To become familiar with and profit from the lives of great persons through the reading of biographies.
7. To keep informed about current advances in international relations, medicine, science, and new occupational opportunities.

All of the outcomes listed above depend on two factors: the child's ability to read, and the availability of interesting reading material.

Schools must assume the responsibility for making materials available including current publications such as newspapers, magazines, and brochures on special topics. In addition, of course, pupils must be encouraged to read. One of the best ways of doing this is to incorporate the use of supplementary materials into the daily curricular activities of the school. A daily newspaper which features national and international news is probably the most effective means of helping the student understand modern man's interdependence with others. The "news" is the most forceful illustration of this interdependence. An event which occurs any place in the world is read about or discussed freely that same day or hour anywhere in the world. Pupils should be led to appreciate our progress in communication, but they should also be taught to see and understand the cumulative effect of error, bias, or misunderstanding inherent in mass communication. The point here is that an event which is "reported"

---

[8] A. Sterl Artley, "Literature in the Language Arts Program," *Journal of Education,* CXXXVIII (1955), 9-13.

as having happened comes to be accepted as an event which happened. Further, the *way* it is "reported" may make it appear to have implications which do not necessarily follow.

This brings us to the point that building permanent reading interests can sometimes be obstructed by ignoring any topic which might be considered controversial. If the future allows us the luxury of retrospection, we may be forced someday to conclude that a most telling weakness of American education in the past has been the tendency of our schools to try to capture pupils' interests with watered down, expurgated versions of political, social, and economic issues. It has often been said that our schools have failed to teach the responsibility of good citizenship. Certainly schools have tried to teach abstract morality as it applies to citizenship, but often this teaching has been conducted in a sort of intellectual vacuum. Good citizenship in a free country rests on making choices. Free choice is an asset to society only where the issues are clearly seen and alternatives clearly understood. It is a tenable hypothesis that our schools from the intermediate to the college level have fostered immaturity among potential learners.

The school too must make choices. Units on topics such as the following are neither inherently good nor inherently poor:

"How the pioneers cleared the land, planted, and harvested crops."

"Agricultural advances in the U. S."

"A comparison of personal income in countries throughout the world."

"The effect of natural resources on the Westward movement in the U. S."

However, young citizens in the intermediate grades can also deal with:

"The effects on human health of chemical preservatives put in breads and the effects of poison insecticides used to control destructive pests."

"How poverty breeds political unrest."

"Is the waste of national resources an inevitable result of free enterprise?"

"Historical milestones in man's quest for personal (civil) liberties."

"The basic philosophical differences (aims) between various 'isms' or forms of government."

While it is true these topics might be controversial, error of opinion can be tolerated in the intermediate grades if reason (and reading) are left free to combat it. An excellent time and place for pupils to begin thinking on such topics is that point on the educational continuum where they are developing permanent reading interests and permanent attitudes toward reading.

THE INTELLECTUALLY CAPABLE

The problem of arousing and maintaining interest in reading is not confined to the less than adequate reader. The excellent student also faces certain educational hazards in our schools. Since we teach great masses of children in large groups by textbook methods, it is almost inescapable that the more facile readers will not always be stimulated by our standardized methods and materials. The intermediate grades can become a very critical period for gifted students as far as maintaining interest in reading is concerned. The challenge of the intellectually able student is present at all grade levels but becomes more pronounced at the intermediate level because the child's abilities and interests are often beyond the standard curricular materials. When bright pupils are expected to "adjust" to this condition, they often become satisfied simply to get by or, worse, to become uncritical readers. They may plod through required text-reading which requires no mental exertion on their part.

It is true that there are marked differences in reading achievement and needs among pupils who are classed as intellectually capable. Some of this group will need instruction in the fundamental skills of reading. Their ability to deal with concepts may be far advanced of their reading level. A larger group of the extremely capable will be advanced both in the mechanical skills and in the ability to deal with concepts. For these pupils, graded materials at their grade placement level will be mastered without as much drill repetition and guidance as is characteristically given to the class. The problem will not be alleviated by having these children do more work at this level, i.e., simply read other textbooks. This solution will not extend the talented, who will acquire little additional information by spending time with other texts.

While stating that every child should be educated to his maximum ability to profit from instruction, our schools have been relatively unsuccessful in achieving this goal with the intellectually capable. Regardless of high ideals, our mass educational structure has in many cases led us to gear instruction to the golden mean. This is not to be construed as an expression of disaffection for universal free education but rather as a recognition of the need to effect a solution for one of its obvious shortcomings. If pupils are helped to develop study skills which lead to independence in reading and are provided easy access to interesting supplementary reading materials, the school has at least fulfilled its obvious obligations. However, there are many other instructional responsibilities which should be fulfilled for all children but which are particularly acute in the case of the intellectually capable.[9]

The following procedures have been particularly successful in motivating the more able students.

1. If the school has a central library, pupils should be allowed to patronize it whenever the need arises and not be restricted to specified library periods.

2. Pupils should be given systematic instruction in the use of library resources such as encyclopedias, *Readers Guide to Periodical Literature*, bulletins, newspapers, and current magazines.

3. Time should be provided for independent reading, and the reading done at such times should always be purposeful. The gifted child, or any child, should never be kept occupied with busy work.

4. As a child develops interest in a particular topic or field, he should be kept supplied with challenging materials which will extend his growth. He should be praised for all serious effort and accomplishment.

5. Children should be encouraged to make plans and carry them out independently after the initial planning with the teacher.

---

[9] See *Promoting Maximal Reading Growth Among Able Learners*, ed., Helen M. Robinson, University of Chicago, Supplementary Educational Monographs (Chicago: University of Chicago Press, 1954), No. 81.

6. The teacher can afford to use more analysis of stories or literature with the more capable pupils. This might take place on an individual or small-group basis.

7. Those pupils capable of such work should be encouraged to participate in special creative activities such as:

a) writing biographies of famous persons from material they have gathered from many sources.

b) describing historical events based on wide reading about these happenings.

c) writing plays or dialogue involving historical personages.

d) making "resource maps" in social studies.

e) giving oral reports based on outside reading which will be a contribution to the knowledge of the group.

8. Children should be encouraged to gather resource materials on a topic on which the class is working. These would include pictures, current magazines, bulletins, books which deal with any facet of the topic, and films. Such materials could be used in developing an "interest corner" (See Chapter 14, p. 439, and Chapter 13 for further discussion of this procedure).

9. Pupils should be given access to professional recordings of plays, poems, or prose. Such materials, as well as films and books, may be borrowed from libraries, curriculum centers, or the local state department of education depository.

10. Children should be encouraged to do research on topics which help them see the social forces which shape their society. This type of activity will make "learning for responsible leadership" more than an empty phrase.

INTEGRATING READING INSTRUCTION WITH SUBJECT MATTER

In discussing the integration of reading instruction with subject matter, two concepts deserve attention. The first is that all reading instruction in the intermediate grades cannot logically be relegated exclusively to one scheduled period each day while the rest of the school day is devoted exclusively to teaching content subjects without concern for reading skills. The idea that various facets of reading must be taught concurrently with subject matter is constantly verbalized by teachers and educators. Even in schools which are departmentalized with one teacher responsible for social science, another for science, and so forth, a respect for the integration of reading and the content subjects emerges in the slogan "every teacher a teacher of reading." The nature of the reading materials and the great difference between pupils' instructional needs make it logical and even mandatory that some reading instruction be related to the social sciences, science, literature, arithmetic, and other subject areas.

Some discussions of this problem are couched in terms which suggest that the curriculum is seen as a series of separate tasks, one of which is instruction in reading. It is occasionally suggested that the duty of the school is to teach children to read as quickly as possible so that they can cope with other areas of the curriculum. In one sense, no one can disagree with this position, but in this setting reading can easily become thought of as an assortment of mechanical skills which the reader applies to subject matter. Here we have more than a hint of compartmentalization and this attitude is easily transferred to pupils who think they "read" reading one hour, "do" arithmetic another, and "study" social science, health, or science at other times.

The second concept pertinent to the integration of reading with the content subjects is the point frequently raised that the various areas require different types of reading and therefore call for different special types of reading instruction in social studies, mathematics, science, and English.[10] The point is made that certain skills are more identifiable with certain areas than with others. "It seems reasonable to expect that the reading skills required for science material will differ from those required for materials of history, mathematics, or other content areas, each of which requires its peculiar combination of abilities."[11] This point is carried further by some writers who list the various skills which they feel are most closely associated with each content area. The following skills are examples, each of which has been identified with reading in *one* of the areas—science, mathematics, social studies, or English:

---

[10] Dorothy Kendall Bracken, "Appraising Competence in Reading in Content Areas," *Evaluation of Reading*, ed., Helen M. Robinson, University of Chicago Press, Supplementary Educational Monographs (Chicago: University of Chicago Press, 1958), No. 88.

[11] J. Harlan Shores and J. L. Saupe, "Reading for Problem-Solving in Science," *Journal of Educational Psychology*, XLIV (1953), 149-58.

adjust rate to purpose	read for main ideas
attitude of the reader	noting and weighing details
drawing conclusions	using contextual clues
word attack skills	organizing ideas
getting main ideas	discriminating between relevant and irrelevant information
locating information	
specialized vocabulary	

Most teachers of reading would find it difficult to associate each of the skills listed above with just one of the content areas.

This leads us to the second point of view which holds that while there are a great number of reading skills which go toward making up the total skill called reading, it is doubtful that these skills divide along content or subject-matter lines. Granted there are a few specifics which are more likely to be needed in one area than in another, but these do not constitute the essence of reading. A few specific skills would include map reading in history, graphs and tables in geography, abbreviations of elements in science, understanding scale drawings or blue prints in shop work. The basic premise of this point of view is that reading ability is a total process involving the total person and that a reader functions in *any* reading situation under a given set of attitudes, interests, and skills. There are not several sets of principles, one applicable to reading, one to science, one to geography. Reading weaknesses or inabilities inevitably operate in all reading situations.

A further point would be that there are not several sets of principles and practices in reading which divide along subject area lines. Whether the teacher is attempting to develop adequate concepts for *congruent, parallel, equivalent,* or *isosceles* in arithmetic or *plateau, pole, delta,* or *isthmus* in geography, the problem is working with word meanings. Drawing inferences should not be thought of as belonging exclusively to one area of the curriculum. A pupil may in the course of a day be asked to draw inferences as to what happens when a decimal point is inserted between digits in two-digit numbers, what effect mountains, located between the sea and the plains, have on rainfall on the plains, and what happens to the circumference of a balloon placed in the freezer compartment of a refrigerator.

A factor which may lead to the hypothesis that certain essential skills of reading are more appropriate to one content area than another is the fact that many pupils can read successfully from basal readers and yet do poorly in subject areas. The reasons for this have been discussed previously. The basal readers present a controlled vocabulary; teachers are alerted to new words and difficult concepts found in each lesson, and systematic instruction is provided to help the pupil over these potential difficulties. Since all reading skills are developmental, the real issue may well be the difficulty level of the material in subject-area textbooks. These materials call for a more extensive development of essential reading skills rather than a different configuration of skills for each content area. When one carefully analyzes the content of history, science, arithmetic, and geography books, he finds it difficult to isolate particular reading skills which are more characteristically needed in one area than in another.

What will inevitably be found is that the vocabulary and concepts met in each field are roadblocks for some pupils. Background or lack of background, interests, attitudes, ability to note details, grasp main ideas, and use context clues, word attack skills, and the reader's purpose, are factors which operate in all reading situations. Reading which children are expected to do in many content areas is farther removed from their actual experiences than is the material in basal reader series. Textbooks which may be excellent from the standpoint of accuracy and breadth of content may be relatively poor from the standpoint of the reader's present vocabulary and concepts.

DEVELOPING CONCEPTS

Meaningful reading at the intermediate level depends on the acquisition and continual extension of concepts. Here, pupils are confronted with more difficulties per reading unit than they met in their primary reading. One of the major reading problems is coping with the gap which tends to develop between the child's store of meanings and the demands made by the curricular materials he is expected to read. In an earlier chapter it was pointed out that because of the rigid control of vocabulary in beginning reading materials, teachers had a special problem of arousing and maintaining interest in these materials. Children's concepts and experiences extended far beyond this basal reader material. By the time the intermediate level is reached, the teacher's problem has traveled full circle. Difficult words and concepts are introduced in the content textbooks in such profusion that many pupils are frustrated and in a sense lost.

Hildreth writes, "The middle-grade pupil can now expect to meet new words he has never seen before in the proportion of about 1 in 10, even in material prepared for his age group and a still larger proportion of strange words in difficult texts."[12] The problem of meaningful reading is complicated by the fact that in the intermediate grades, as well as at higher levels, there are found a great number of idiomatic expressions, abstract terms, figurative terms, and new connotations for words met earlier. In the primary grades, even though the occurrence of these is less frequent, teachers are alerted to them through the teaching manuals accompanying the basal reader series used. Also, deliberate instruction is provided in the workbooks which supplement the reader series. With the shift to separate textbooks in the content areas, there tends to be less emphasis on helping pupils with meaning difficulties precisely at the point where help is most needed. Examples of difficult concepts from fourth and fifth grade geography, science, and arithmetic books are cited below. Teachers found that many pupils did not understand these concepts even after the material had been assigned and covered in class.

Many years and great sums of money will be needed to *harness the river*.

It (blood) is carried through other *branching tubes* called veins.

When you are frightened, your *pupils get bigger*.

Check by doing each example again.

You bite and chew your food with the *crowns of your teeth*.

Ornithologists have examined the crops of many birds to find out what kind of food they eat.

Most of the *infections* and *contagious* diseases are caused by bacteria.

Birds help to keep the *balance of nature*.

We can use a *ruler* to subtract fractions.

Cloud formations make what is called a *mackerel sky*.

---

[12] Gertrude Hildreth, *Teaching Reading* (New York: Holt, Rinehart & Winston, Inc., 1958).

The *red corpuscles are racing through* the *capillaries.*

To solve problems like this, turn your *multiplication table of eights into a division table.*

The native city is *backward* and ugly.

The Mediterranean became a *melting pot* for surrounding civilization.

The people who lived in *fixed settlements* made far greater progress than the Nomads.

Now, as in ancient times, the Mediterranean is a great *connecting* highway.

There is plenty of *home-grown wool.*

Business and industry were *paralyzed.*

Science has *unlocked the greatest force in nature.*

China was not entirely *sealed off* from her neighbors.

A *belt of irrigated land* stretches almost all the way along the coast.

In time, *the front of Europe shifted* from the Mediterranean Coast to the Atlantic Coast.

As the *globe* shows, Europe and Asia really form one *land mass.*

The *shrinking world* and new inventions have made this possible.

If some day the river is controlled it will be a great *life-giver* instead of a *life-destroyer.*

Gradually the continent was opened up. Another "jewel" had *been added to the British crown.*

The top of the world will have a new meaning in the future.

Almost every farmer grows some *cash crop* besides food for his family.

Britain was busy for many years in getting *stepping stones* along the sea-ways.[13]

PRONUNCIATION AND MEANING PROBLEMS

Pronunciation and meaning problems can be dealt with in the context in which they are met, but there is nothing educationally unsound in reviewing or teaching a series of such words by means of either the chalkboard or a lesson sheet. One value of the latter procedure is that a given exercise can be used with only those pupils

---

[13] Unpublished data compiled by teachers in actual classroom situations. For further data the reader may consult: George G. Mallinson, Harold E. Sturm, and Robert E. Patton, "The Reading Difficulty of Textbooks in Elementary Science," *Elementary School Journal,* L (1950), 460-63. Paul Witty, "Reading of Social Studies Materials," *Elementary English,* XXVII (1950).

who reveal a need for it and may be used with them several times if needed. A list of words that are difficult to pronounce might include: *aisle, fatigue, coyote, exit, plague, sieve, cache, posse, gauge, corps, beau, feign, nephew, antique, bouquet, isthmus, agile, chaos, ache, plateau, quay, bivouac, czar, recipe, stature, reign, viaduct, suede.* A number of exercises can be devised to teach the pronunciation and meaning of such words. A few are listed below:

1. In the first column the difficult words are listed and adjoining columns contain the dictionary pronunciation and meaning:

cache	cāsh	a hole in the ground, or a hiding place
feign	fān	to imagine; invent, hence, to form and relate as if true
quay	kē	a stretch of paved bank or a solid artificial landing place made beside navigable water, for convenience in loading and unloading vessels
bivouac	bĭv ŏŏ ăk	an encampment for a very short sojourn, under improvised shelter or none.

2. Use the difficult word and a synonym in the same sentence:

As they reached the *plateau* the guide said, "It will be easier walking on this *flat level* ground."
"Climbing mountains is hard work," said the guide. "We will rest when you feel *fatigued* so tell me when you get *tired*."

3. Prepare a card for each word; one side of the card contains the difficult word and its pronunciation; the other side has a sentence using the word.

Card front	Card back
c h a o s (kā ŏs)	When a tornado strikes a community, *chaos* results. Houses are blown down, fires break out, fallen trees block the streets, telephone poles and wires are down, and the fire department cannot get through the streets.

4. Prepare a short paragraph in which the difficult word is used in several contexts.

From the aerial photographs it was difficult for him to *gauge* whether the railroad was narrow or regular *gauge*. He recalled that the day the picture was made the fuel *gauge* registered very nearly empty. He remembered attempting to *gauge* the effect of the tail wind on his chances of returning safely.

5. *Homographs* are words which are alike in form, but different in both sound and meaning. Words which fit these criteria present considerable opportunity for confusion when standing alone, for pronunciation and meaning are not indicated. It should be pointed out that it is only through context or usage that the proper choices are indicated.

The announcer stated, "Thus we *close* the broadcast of this very *close* game."

The director was not *content* with the *content* of the scene.

The old man stated he would *refuse* to let the health department clear the *refuse* from his property.

The teacher said she would not *object* if each pupil brought an interesting *object* to school.

Some people would *rebel* at being called a *rebel.*

Truck farms *produce* a variety of *produce.*

Many a *minute* was *spent* in giving *minute* details.

When you make a *record* of your sales, be sure to *record* them carefully.

Teaching word recognition, meanings, and concepts in all learning situations which call for reading is one excellent method of integrating reading instruction in all subject areas. A broader method for integrating reading instruction with the total curriculum is through the unit approach.

THE UNIT APPROACH

The unit method has been discussed in educational sources under many different labels.[14] Descriptive titles for this concept include *resource units, teaching units, activity units, core units,* and *survey units.* The unit method is a classroom procedure which attempts to organize and integrate a number of learning activities around a

---

[14] William B. Ragan, *Modern Elementary Curriculum* (Rev. ed.; New York: Holt, Rinehart & Winston, Inc., 1960), Chap. 5, 6.

particular theme. A unit may be devised for any subject area and can cover a time span of a few days during which pupils attempt to find the answer to a particular question or, as is usually the case, may extend over a period of weeks and may culminate in some class project. The culmination might be a play, a school program, or a science fair consisting of many individual and committee projects all related to the central theme. While the unit approach is not new, it is consistent with the aims of modern curriculum planning. Unit study can help avoid the tendency toward fragmentation of the curriculum into isolated, seemingly unrelated parts.

Units lend themselves to two types of major emphasis. The first type emphasizes pupil experiences built around a specific topic, such as *How We Get Our Food.* Experiences related to this topic might include visits to various types of farms, to a cannery, a cold storage plant, a meat packing plant, a dairy, or a bakery. Pupils may plant and care for a garden or a window box. The second major emphasis is on wide reading. It is likely that emphasis on the experience approach will come at the early elementary level, shifting to reading in the subject areas in the intermediate grades. These two methods are extremely compatible, and the proper combination of the two approaches undoubtedly makes for a better total learning situation.

The use of the unit approach that emphasizes wide reading is reserved for the intermediate grades because wide reading calls for pupils who have mastered the fundamentals of beginning reading. Also, it is difficult to secure a wide variety of interesting supplementary materials on a variety of topics at reading levels below the third grade. Finally, by the time they have reached the intermediate grades, pupils have had opportunities to learn to work both independently and co-operatively in small groups.

ADVANTAGES OF THE UNIT APPROACH

The potential advantages of the unit approach are quite varied. The actual benefits resulting from its use will vary with such factors as the teacher's skill, the reading ability and work habits of the pupils, and the amount of supplementary reading material available. Some of the more frequently mentioned advantages of the unit approach are summarized below.

1. The unit serves as the framework within which learning experiences are shaped into larger, more meaningful wholes. The unit permits more than the superficial study of a topic and encourages wide and varied reading.
2. Units can be used in any area of the curriculum.
3. The pupils learn that reading is the key to getting information on all subjects and not just an operation performed in the basal reader and accompanying workbooks.
4. The unit approach can and should include a great variety of experiences related to reading, such as excursions, field trips, and small group participation in working on various facets of the problem.
5. Units structure the learning situation so as to make reading more varied, more meaningful, and more interesting.
6. Units permit pupils of widely different reading abilities to work on different facets of the same project. Reading materials at many levels of difficulty can be used, and children need not be directly compared as readers.
7. The unit approach gives the teacher flexibility and freedom to work with a child or a group of children engaged in some reading activity at their own level. The retarded and the accelerated reader can be working independently and successfully on something that is challenging.
8. Units aid independent reading and help to foster independence in research reading.

EXAMPLES OF UNITS

A unit on weather designed for a fourth grade class may be used as an illustration. The teacher had aroused the interest of the class through an assignment of watching weather reports on television, finding interesting pictures of weather stations, and a class discussion of stories dealing with weather. Out of this grew the class decision to have a study unit on weather. Pupils worked co-operatively in identifying objectives, finding questions to be answered, and working on individual projects which fell within the limits of the unit. These are listed below:

1. Objectives of unit on weather
   a) To learn ways in which weather helps or harms man.

   b) To learn what causes various types of weather and changes of seasons.
   c) To learn the causes and effects of rainfall, temperature, fog.
   d) To become familiar with the instruments used in measuring or predicting weather changes.

2. Questions to be answered
   a) How is a thermometer constructed and how does it work?
   b) What is fog?
   c) What causes hail?
   d) What is lightning? Why is it followed by thunder?
   e) Why do we have seasons such as winter and summer?
   f) Why are some parts of the earth always hot and others always cold?
   g) Why is there very little rainfall in one part of a country and a great deal in another part?
   h) Why is it important for man to be able to predict weather?
   i) What is a barometer? How does it work?
   j) What is humidity?

3. Representative activities or projects, both individual and group
   a) Keeping a daily record of temperatures. Securing temperatures registered in cities in different parts of the country.
   b) Preparing charts and graphs which illustrate some aspect of weather.
      (1) Average rainfall for different states and countries.
      (2) The relationship between rainfall and the type of crops raised in a particular area.
      (3) The effect of rainfall on density of population.
      (4) Maps showing occurrence of tornadoes, hurricanes, or floods during past decade.
   c) Explaining and demonstrating a thermometer and barometer.
   d) Doing research on the work of the U.S. Weather Bureau in predicting weather—how it is done and why.
   e) Studying the effects of weather on human dress, shelter, or diet.
   f) Measuring rainfall during a rain.
   g) Securing pictures which illustrate any facet of weather or the effect of weather, such as floods, erosion, storms on land and sea, barren deserts, and permanent snows.

4. Culminating activity

It was decided that at the end of the unit the class would have a Weather Fair. All individual and group projects would be displayed, including posters, graphs and charts, picture series, pupil-made instruments for measuring weather, and all written projects. Parents were invited to visit the class on a particular afternoon, and other classes in the school saw the display at certain times that day. Children explained their projects and received a great deal of ego satisfaction from this culminating activity.

Units Integrate Work in All Areas. A well planned unit provides a variety of purposeful learning experiences, as illustrated below; the teacher had structured activities so that all facets of the curriculum received attention.

Spelling. Many words were learned incidentally as children printed them on their posters or charts. New words were assigned and studied as part of the unit (*weather, thermometer, mercury, rainfall, temperature, erosion, bureau*).

Health. One popular topic, *How Weather Affects Our Health,* almost became a unit within a unit. The entire class participated, and each pupil was asked to write a brief account of anything he had found in his reading that answered the question. The teacher had a few references for those children who needed help in finding material. What was ostensibly a health lesson also became a lesson in communication skills as the children worked on their written assignments. Practice in oral language usage also received attention as children discussed or reported their findings to the class.

Arithmetic. A lack of understanding of the problems to be solved is more of a stumbling block in arithmetic in the intermediate grades than is lack of computational skills. Failure to read problems critically will result in hazy concepts. In unit work the arithmetic problems which are met emerge from the immediate experience of the learner. Problems such as finding the average rainfall, average temperature, or total foodstuffs raised, are related to larger goals and become meaningful in the goal-directed activity. The need for accurate measurement becomes apparent in building a barometer or measuring a rainfall.

Science. Basically the unit was a science unit. One topic that received emphasis at this particular grade level was how science predicts and tracks weather and the scientific instruments used in the process. In studying the thermometer and barometer many scientific principles and questions evolved, such as the principle of expansion, the principles of gravity and pressure, and the questions of whether mercury is a metal, why it is used in these instruments, what the function of heat is in causing a thermometer to work.

Social Science. The discussion above on health led into social science topics. A discussion of diet in relation to health led to questions and discussion on how weather affects diet or the production of foodstuffs. A discussion of the economic value of climate would logically follow. The realtionship of climate to certain natural resources was discussed, i.e., to forestry, deposits of coal, and petroleum. The relationships between rainfall, temperature, winds, forests, and the types of crops were discussed. Methods of cultivation and crop rotation were studied in relation to erosion of the land.

Reading. Reading was the process which provided the raw material for all of the curricular activities mentioned above. The unit stressed, in the pupils' minds, that they were getting information for science, health, and geography. This reading was purposeful. Neither the reading nor the teaching of it were the compulsive "let's get this workbook page finished" approach. The teacher kept in mind all the principles of teaching reading. She had to be particularly careful not to expect all children to read the same materials and to provide a variety of supplementary materials at many grade levels. The following is a partial list of books which the teacher was able to assemble and make available. These are listed by grade level.

Grade II Level

1. "The Thermometer"
   "Winter Is Coming" — *Let's Look Around*
   "Under the Ice"
   "Water into Ice"
2. "Rain-Sleet-Snow" — *Busy World*
   "Changing Weather"
3. "How Spring Came" — *The Story Road*
4. "Jack Frost"
   "The Storm" — *Over a City Bridge*
   "What Time of Year"

Grade III Level

1. "The Thunderstorm"
2. "Spring Days" "The Storm"

3. "The Magic Rain Cloud" — *The Five-and-a-Half Club*
4. "Sing a Song of Seasons" — *Smokey the Crow*
5. "Adventures in Science" — *Just Imagine*
6. "The Wonderworld of Science"
7. "Little Wolf the Rain Dancer"

Grade IV Level

1. *Exploring in Science*
2. *Explaining Why*
3. *The How and Why Club*
4. *Everybody's Weather*
5. *Good Wind and Good Water*
6. *Between Earth and Sky*
7. *Everyday Weather and How It Works*

Grade V Level

1. *The World Around Us*
2. *The World I Know*
3. *Aviation Science for Boys and Girls*
4. *Life* magazine
5. *Everybody's Weather*
6. *Clouds, Rain, and Snow*

References for Teacher

1. *Science for Progress*
2. *Science in Today's World*
3. *Science for Better Living*
4. *Everyday Science*
5. *Earth Science*
6. *Doorways to Science*
7. *Exploring the World of Science*
8. *Life* magazine
9. *National Geographic Magazine*
10. U. S. Weather Bureau, *Collection of Weather Publications*

In developing a unit, the teacher may find that her first important task is to secure materials at various levels. The references available will vary from school to school. Basal readers at all levels could serve for such a unit as well as selected reading from subject-matter texts. *My Weekly Reader* files would provide material on many topics, and a child is often pleased to bring to school his own books on some special topic.

Throughout the unit the reading skills of pupils must be dealt with; use of the unit method in no way restricts the teacher in developing the reading skills of her pupils. In fact, once the preliminary planning of a unit is taken care of, the creative teacher will find that she has as much time and opportunity to help individual pupils or small groups as she had when working with a conventional grouping arrangement. Most unit work introduces a fairly heavy vocabulary load. It follows that some time must be spent on sight word recognition problems. As the teacher has different children read for her and as pupils ask for help with unknown words, she can prepare several word lists of new words to be studied during the course of the unit. One such list might be taken from the more difficult sources and be used exclusively with the advanced reading group. Lists of easier words can be used in sight word exercises with average and poor readers. Many new and unknown words can be used for teaching phonic analysis and for stressing the importance of context clues in solving meaning difficulties.

RATE OF READING

The rate at which one can assimilate meaning from printed symbols becomes a reading problem when students are expected to understand curricular materials for which their reading skill, habits, and abilities are inadequate. The intermediate grades are probably the first level at which a concern for rate of reading is justified since at this point emphasis begins to be placed on the various content areas. In recent years there has been considerable emphasis on the need for improving rate of reading. The impetus for this concern with rate undoubtedly came first at the college level, where, for the past several decades, considerable attention has been given to the improvement of reading ability with emphasis on rate. College reading improvement programs grew out of the conviction that many college students have the capacity to meet the demands of the college curriculum but that their reading habits make them poor academic risks. It is undoubtedly true that many teachers, ranging from high school to the intermediate levels, are convinced that this is also the case with many of their students.

Over the years the term *rate of reading* has been widely but not always wisely used. It has been a popular practice to speak of the rate of reading of the average high school senior, college freshman, or adult. The impression was often left that the figure quoted, such as 325 or 375 words per minute, had some real significance. The implication was that once an individual's rate for reading a given passage was established, this figure could be cited as though it were a constant for any reading situation. The emphasis on rate led some individuals to confuse the entire reading process with the number of words one could allegedly cover in a specified period of time. In an effort to lessen this tendency it became popular to talk about "rate of comprehension," a term which emphasized that reading is getting meaning. But this term was also subject to semantic confusion since several factors are always at work in determining one's rate of comprehension. A number of variables which influence the rate at which different reading materials can be assimilated are:

1. The reader's knowledge of the general subject matter
2. The vocabulary load, difficulty level of words and concepts
3. The reader's degree of motivation
4. The reader's purpose for reading the material
5. The physiological state of the reader, whether fatigued, etc.
6. The length of the reading period
7. Mechanical factors such as size of print and length of line
8. The readability of the material as determined by such factors as style of writing, sentence structure, and sentence length
9. The reader's mastery of the mechanical skills of reading, such as number of words known as sight words, ability to sound unknown words, ability to profit from punctuation, and freedom from the habit of inserting, omitting, or repeating words or phrases
10. The number of figures, illustrations, cross-references, and footnotes the material contains

Consideration of these factors reveals that no one sample of reading behavior can provide a valid basis for establishing a person's rate of comprehension. Any figure arrived at would be valid only for the particular material read under the precise conditions which prevailed while it was being read. Regardless of the fact that the term rate of reading is vague and may lead to confusion, there is little question that the rate at which pupils read curricular materials is an instructional problem which tends to become more acute as they move through the grades.

VARYING RATE ACCORDING TO MATERIAL AND PURPOSE FOR READING

A facile reader must develop several different rates for reading different types of printed matter.[15] This fact merits careful attention in the intermediate grades because here the pupil must read a great variety of materials in various content areas. The child should learn to adjust his reading behavior to the material and to the objectives he has for reading. A magazine article may be read with good comprehension at several hundred words per minute while the same reader may have to spend several minutes in reading a mathematical problem stated in forty words. Or assume that a pupil, having read a particular passage, is attempting to recall the five largest cities of the United States. He has tentatively settled for New York, Chicago, and San Francisco but the other two city names do not come to mind. As he rereads, it would be a slow and possibly wasteful effort to read carefully every word and sentence of the entire section which contains the desired information. If the pupil had mastered the technique of scanning material, it would be a speedy process to find the one or two sentences that contain the desired data; these could then be read carefully. Many readers find that they can read long descriptive passages in a novel much more rapidly than dialogue.

IMPROVING RATE THROUGH IMPROVING READING SKILLS

The problem of improving rate can be oversimplified unless one keeps in mind that rate is influenced by the reader's habits, skills, and attitudes toward the material being read. It would be unrealistic to attempt to improve slow rate of reading without dealing with those factors which are the basis for the slow reading. When slow reading is simply a habitual response stemming from a lack of basic reading skills, it can be dealt with by practice in those skills. Lack of skills, or the development of habits such as guessing, substituting or omitting words, adding words to salvage meaning, or ignoring punctuation, inevitably contribute to slow reading. Inadequate word-attack skills may prevent the child from arriving at the pronunciation of

---

[15] Lawrence W. Carrillo and William D. Sheldon, "The Flexibility of Reading Rate," *Journal of Educational Psychology,* XLIII (1952), 299-305.

words or cause him to arrive at the pronunciation very slowly. Word-by-word reading is usually related to these problems.

Reading in phrases is a skill which relates to rate of reading on two scores. Word-by-word reading is time-consuming and also tends to interfere with getting the meaning. A child who has been taught to read for meaning will have to repeat sentences and parts of sentences when he loses the thought because he has been so slow in piecing the various work units into a meaningful whole. When word-by-word reading is habitual—that is, when it has been reinforced by many thousands of reading experiences—it is sometimes advisable to give the reader practice on reading easy phrases. Gradually, more difficult reading material can be used. The teacher can make up drill exercises which use phrases in isolation, exercises which show logical phrases underlined, or short passages where the student underlines logical phrases. These three procedures are illustrated in Figure 32.

FIGURE 32

A. The following phrases or short sentences are designed to give practice in reading a number of words as one thought unit. Some pupils read one word at a time—that is, they pause after each word: up, the, mountain. *Since this is a logical thought unit it should be read:* up-the-mountain. *Read the phrases from left to right across the page.*

In the car   down the hill   at the farm   from the house
had to leave soon   in the big house   he will be   has gone away
the white horse   eat some cake   ran to the house   the show
can see it   the pretty dress   will look good   we can see
much too much   the tiny boat   on the paper   to the fair

B. In the following paragraph logical thought units have been separated. Be sure to read each phrase as a whole. There are many different ways we could read the same passage. The following is only one example.

Billy saw the car   coming down the road.   He said to himself,
I hope I can get a ride   to town.   He began to wonder   if he should
accept a ride   if he didn't know   the driver.   The car pulled up
and slowed down.   He saw a man   and two boys   about his age.
The boys shouted,   "Hi, Billy."   He recognized the twins.

C. Underline phrases which could be read as one unit. Remember that there may be several different ways to arrange words in thought units. Underline the way you think best.

The twins, Roger and Sandy, had moved to town several weeks ago. "Hop in the car," said Sandy. "Have you met my dad?" asked Roger. Billy shook hands with Mr. Farrell. As they neared town, Mr. Farrell said, "Can you come and play with the boys at our house or must you go straight home?"

Inadequate comprehension skills contribute to slow reading. If meanings are not readily grasped, a child may be forced to re-read a passage.[16] If he selects a wrong meaning, the misconception that results will probably not fit with the rest of the material and a re-reading will be called for. The reader's ability to adjust to sentence structure, style, and the author's organizational patterns are skills which influence rate as well as critical reading.

DEVELOPING STUDY SKILLS

The term *study skills* is used to designate a particular group of reading skills which include the following.

1. How to use a table of contents.
2. How to use the index, knowledge of what can be found there, how to use key words, and how to look under several headings for a topic.
3. How to read tables, figures, charts, and maps.
4. How to profit from clues which might indicate whether a book or source will be useful for particular purposes that the reader has in mind—title of the book, chapter headings, date published, and the level of difficulty.

---

[16] Helen M. Robinson, "Development of Reading Skills," *Elementary School Journal*, LVIII (1958), 268-74.

5. How to use references and encyclopedias effectively.
6. How to use a dictionary.
7. How to use a library, including the card catalogue and various indexes.
8. How to read to secure particular information for units or projects.
9. How to summarize data for oral or written reports.

Some important study skills deal with the effective use of books; others deal with locating books and materials which contain desired information. Knowledge of how to use the card catalogue and other reference materials effectively is a valuable asset to the independent reader. Once interest in a subject or unit is aroused, the reader will want to use all the tools available for finding pertinent data. *(Courtesy of Bexley Schools, Bexley, Ohio; photographer: Arthur Burt, Inc.)*

The intermediate grades are as important as any period in the entire educational process for the development of study skills. The increased need for study skills stems from the nature of the materials used in these grades, the need for wide reading, and the fact that supervision is not always instantly available. Reading ability is a prerequisite for the development of study skills, but this ability in itself does not assure that a pupil has mastered these skills. Extensive reading may not result in mastery of study skills. When a pupil fails to develop adequate study skills, the educational process may become dull and unpleasant. Therefore, guidance and specific instruction must be provided to help children develop these skills.[17]

Using books effectively implies a mastery of the first four skills above. Pupils must be taught how to use a table of contents, index, appendix, charts, graphs, and tables effectively. Some children will learn these things incidentally, but the skills are so important that they cannot be left to incidental learning. It should not be inferred that since the intermediate grades are under discussion these skills are not to be taught prior to the intermediate grades. At each grade level there will be some appropriate teachings which will help children use books more effectively. For instance, pre-primers contain a table of contents and this list of stories should be called to the attention of children. As more difficult books are used, more helps are provided within the book itself, yet many pupils go through grade after grade without knowing how to use these various aids.

As children become independent readers and attempt to find answers through wide and varied reading, they must understand and use all the hints and helps available in order to determine rapidly and accurately whether a particular book contains information in which they are interested. In other words, knowing how to use the book is a prerequisite for intelligent use of supplementary reading in the subject areas and in any unit work.

Workbook exercises are often provided to help pupils understand the function of an index, table of contents, or appendix. It is not uncommon to find pupils who can work out correct solutions to workbook problems which consist of sample lines from an index but who

---

[17] James M. McCallister, "Reading—Study Skills," *Evaluation of Reading*, ed., Helen M. Robinson, University of Chicago, Supplementary Educational Monographs (Chicago: University of Chicago Press, 1958), No. 88, 106-10.

When children feel at home in the library, it speaks well for the entire school. In such situations it is likely that children are developing some permanent reading interests, that they are learning to use books and resources effectively, and that their intellectual growth is being encouraged. *(Courtesy of Eastern Illinois University)*

still do not know how to get help from a real index. One of the best ways to teach children how to use a book effectively is to design a learning situation around a textbook which they will be using throughout the year. A social science, science, health, or other text would provide opportunities for teaching the functions of the table of contents, charts, indexes, or appendixes. The use of the child's actual text will give him something concrete to return to when he is in doubt. Skills learned in using one text should transfer to books in other areas.

An illustration of an exercise which can serve either as a teaching device or as a test to measure what children know about the use of the table of contents, indexes, appendixes, and the like, is found in Figure 33. This particular exercise was constructed for use with a fifth grade social studies text.[18] A similar exercise for higher or lower

[18] O. Stuart Hamer, D. W. Follet, B. F. Ahlschwede, and Hervert Gross, *Exploring Our Country* (Chicago: Follett Publishing Co., 1953).

grade levels would serve equally well and might be preceded by a review of the major parts of the book and how each can help the reader.

FIGURE 33

1. On what page is the table of contents? _______
2. How many chapters are there in this book? _______
3. What chapter tells about countries other than the U.S.? _______
4. On what page does the appendix begin? _______
5. List three types of information found in the appendix:

_______, _______, _______.

6. What key word do we look under if we wish information on Bonneville, Grand Coulee, and Hoover dams? _______
7. The index begins on what page? _______
8. There are how many pages in the index? _______
9. Finish this sentence: The index is found on pages 388- _______
10. What page contains the populations and capitals of each state?

____

11. What page of your book has a picture of a blockhouse? (use index) _______
12. Under the heading Civil War, you are told to see another heading, what is it? _______
13. How many subtopics are listed under the entry Great Ideas?

____

14. Are each of these listed somewhere else in the index? _______
15. Where do you find the definition of *erosion*? _______
16. On what page do you find data telling you which state has the largest and which the smallest area? _______
17. On what page will you find a picture showing erosion? _______
18. What is the pronunciation of Sault St. Marie? _______
19. Does your book contain a diagram showing how plywood is made? _______

A number of facts can be taught through the use of such an exercise. Question 3 points up the fact that chapter headings are much more specific than the book's title in telling what the book is about.

Questions 4, 5, 10, and 16 call for the reader to use the appendix. He will discover that the appendix is the source of much data. Questions 6 and 19 emphasize the use of key words. Question 9 contains the number 388-497 which means that the topic is covered on pages 388 to 397, while 103, 224, 435 are separate references to the same topic. Question 16 is not answered in the index but three previous questions have led the reader to the appendix which does answer the question.

The interpretation of graphs, charts, and tables must also be taught, reviewed, and re-taught. Interpretations and explanations must be made in the subject-area classes in which examples arise. Some pupils may successfully interpret graphs and tables in an arithmetic lesson but not see that the graph in the health book is related to skills learned and applied elsewhere. A graph comparing the number of doctors per unit of population in various countries may present problems of understanding. A series of symbols representing units of production may not be seen as an important source for comparing different regions or countries.

Students should be led to see that making a bar graph or a simple pie chart to illustrate facts gleaned in their reading will make the data very meaningful. The following are a few projects which might serve as examples.

1. A bar graph showing the population of the pupil's home state and all states which border on it.
2. A graph comparing the five largest oil producing states.
3. A graph showing average per capita income since 1900 at ten-year intervals.
4. A graph comparing salaries of teachers, doctors, and lawyers over the past fifteen years.
5. A graph showing the population of the world by race.

Tasks such as these call for finding and organizing data, selecting reasonable units to represent factors compared, making accurate measurements, and using reference books, indexes, and tables of contents. Such a project represents almost complete integration of reading, arithmetic, social studies, and other areas.

REFERENCE MATERIALS

Using reference materials is an important study skill which, as a general rule, is not thoroughly taught in our schools. Many students reach high school or even college with only a hazy idea of how to make a systematic search of available materials. McKee says, "Wherever the child, in or out of school, is confronted with a problem to be attacked by means of reading, the first task he faces is that of locating printed information which is pertinent to his problem."[19] Although a few children in the upper primary level are ready for limited use of instruction in the use of reference materials, it is in the intermediate grades that teachers have a major responsibility to teach these skills. The use of encyclopedias and other reference books should be deliberately taught. If a set is located in the room, different children or groups can be taught facility in their use at various times. Instruction here will parallel points already covered above—i.e., topics are arranged in alphabetical order, books are numbered in series, the alphabetical range covered is indicated on the cover, and cross listings and key words will have to be used. The teacher can make a set of card exercises, each card containing a question: "What book and what page tell about coal?" "About the Suez Canal?" "About Iron Deposits?"

Using the Dictionary. The use of the dictionary is another important study skill associated with reading instruction at the intermediate level. The three major tasks in learning dictionary usage are (1) learning to find a particular word, (2) learning to determine its pronunciation, and (3) learning to select the correct meaning of the word in the context in which it is used. Teaching dictionary skills is often neglected by teachers even when they acknowledge the value of these skills. This neglect might stem from a teacher's feeling of inadequacy about certain relatively difficult facets of dictionary usage such as diacritical markings or pronunciation keys. On the other hand, teaching may fall short of maximum efficiency when dictionary skills are taught as something extra rather than being seen as an intrinsic part of the regular reading instruction. The use of the dictionary should always be seen by both teacher and pupil as a means of getting meaning, not a form of rote drill or a penalty for making certain errors.

There are certain prerequisite skills which are essential for successful use of the dictionary. A few of these skills or understandings are:

---

[19] Paul McKee, *The Teaching of Reading in the Elementary School* (Boston: Houghton Mifflin Co., 1948), 425.

1. The knowledge of alphabetical order.
2. The understanding that a word can have many different meanings.
3. The knowledge of root words and the various inflected and derived forms of root words.
4. The understanding that letters and combinations of letters have different sound values in different situations and that some letters are silent.
5. The knowledge that *y* on the end of some words is changed to *i* before adding *es* for plurals.

William Gray states, "All major word perception abilities are fused in the use of the dictionary."[20]

Facility in the use of the dictionary paves the way for a number of potential breakthroughs in the struggle for independence in reading.

1. Unlocks the sound or pronunciation of words.
2. Discloses new meanings of words which may be known in only one or a limited number of connotations.
3. Confirms the spelling of a word when one can approximate its correct spelling.
4. Expands vocabulary through mastery of inflected and derived forms of known root words.

These skills are developmental in nature and must be refined and extended as the child moves upward through the grades. The alphabetizing ability which is adequate for successful fourth grade work will be inadequate for junior high or high school. The brunt of teaching dictionary skills falls on the intermediate grades simply because most of those skills are introduced during these years of instruction. The success the child feels and the utility he sees in dictionary usage can be most important factors in how he reacts to the dictionary as a tool for helping him in all facets of communication. Pupils must be shown that dictionary skills are permanently needed skills. Failure to master these skills can color the attitudes of pupils for many years to come.

---

[20] William S. Gray, *On Their Own in Reading* (Chicago: Scott, Foresman & Co., 1948), 121.

A number of developmental tasks are associated with dictionary usage and there is general agreement in the literature on what these tasks are and the order in which they should be presented.

DEVELOPMENTAL TASKS IN DICTIONARY MASTERY

1. Recognize and differentiate between letters.
2. Associate letter names with letter symbols.
3. Learn the letters of the alphabet in order.
4. Arrange a number of words by alphabetical order of their initial letter.
5. Extend above skill to second and third letters of words, eventually working through all letters of a word if necessary.
6. Develop facility in rapid, effective use of dictionary, i.e., where does H, P, V come in the dictionary; open dictionary as near as possible to word being studied.
7. Develop the ability to use accent marks in arriving at the pronunciation of words.
8. Learn to interpret phonetic spelling used in dictionary.
9. Use pronunciation key given somewhere on each double page of most dictionaries.
10. Work out different pronunciations and meanings of words which are spelled alike.
11. Determine which is the preferred pronunciation when several are given.
12. Select the meaning which fits the context.
13. Profit from guide words found at the top of each page to tell at a glance if the page contains the word being sought.
14. Use intelligently special sections of a dictionary: geographical terms and names, biographical data, foreign words and phrases.

Although particular skills are characteristically taught at a given grade level, what the individual child has learned or not learned should determine what is taught. Fortunately, dictionaries are available at all levels of difficulty from simple picture dictionaries to massive unabridged editions. The needs of the child and the goals of the teacher should determine how these differences in dictionaries will be utilized in the classroom. A child who is expected to use a dictionary successfully which calls for skills far beyond what he has mastered will profit little from the experience. Any classroom practice which puts the child in such a position has little if any educational justification.

CONCLUDING STATEMENT

In this chapter the reading program at the intermediate grades has been discussed with attention being paid to special instructional problems found at this level. These problems included the transition from primary-level reading to a major emphasis on reading in various content subjects; the increased variability in reading achievement among pupils; the need for developing permanent reading interests, and the need for providing guidance to help the intellectually capable child expand his reading horizons.

These and other special problems emphasize the need for deliberate and systematic instruction in reading. In addition, since reading problems arise in all subject areas and affect both instruction and learning, some responsibility for reading instruction must be assumed in classes devoted to subject content. Methods of achieving this integration of reading and subject matter were outlined in the discussion of the unit approach and reading-study skills.

The nature of the curricular tasks found in the intermediate grades calls for wide and extensive reading. To meet these demands successfully, pupils must continually extend a number of developmental skills, such as:

1. word meanings and concepts
2. word-attack skills
3. ability to use books efficiently including reference materials
4. flexibility in reading, particularly in the ability to adjust rate to the material and the purpose for reading.

Reading instruction in the intermediate grades is important because if growth in these and other developmental skills lags, the pupil and the curriculum are soon out of adjustment.

YOUR POINT OF VIEW?

What is the basis for your agreement or disagreement with each of the following statements?

1. There is little evidence in either the curriculum materials or instructional objectives to indicate that there is more of a transition between third and fourth grades than between other elementary grades.

2. Variability among pupils in the intermediate grades could be reduced by improved teaching in earlier grades.

3. Concepts are the basis for prejudice, misunderstanding, co-operation among people, successful problem solving, and cultural lag in our institutions.

4. Rate of reading or rate of comprehension is determined by such factors as intellectual level, background experience, and concepts held. Therefore, working directly on "speeding reading" will be ineffective unless these factors are dealt with.

5. One of the strengths of American schools is their thoroughness and effectiveness in helping pupils develop study skills.

6. The unit approach relies too much on incidental learning and slights systematic instruction in reading.

BIBLIOGRAPHY

Aaron, I. E., Goodwin, Frances, and Kent, Vada. "Fourth Grade Teachers Experiment with Cross-class Grouping for Reading Instruction," *Elementary English,* XXXVI (May, 1959), 305-307.

Berry, June, and Mercer, Winston. "Developing Library Skills—Every Teacher's Responsibility," *Education,* LXXVIII (October, 1957), 78-81.

Betzner, Jean. *Exploring Literature with Children.* New York: Bureau of Publication, Teachers College, Columbia University, 1943.

Bond, Guy L., and Tinker, Miles A. *Reading Difficulties: Their Diagnosis and Correction.* New York: Appleton-Century-Crofts, Inc., 1957.

Carver, Richard L., and Sheldon, William D. "Problems in the Development of Concepts through Reading," *Elementary School Journal*, LV (December, 1954), 226-29.

Elkins, Annice Davis. "The Problem of Reading Geography," *Education*, LXXVII (September, 1956), 37-44.

Harris, Albert J. *How to Increase Reading Ability* (3rd ed.). New York: Longmans, Green and Co., 1956.

Hildreth, Gertrude. "Interrelationship among the Language Arts," *Elementary School Journal*, XLVIII (June, 1948), 538-49.

———. *Teaching Reading*. New York: Henry Holt & Co., 1958.

Hillenbrand, Robert. "The Appreciation of Picturesque Language in the Intermediate Grades," *Elementary English*, XXXVI (May, 1959), 302-4.

Johnson, Lois V. "Language Activities and the Study Trip," *Elementary English*, XXXV (February, 1958), 108-11.

———. "The Process of Oral Reporting," *Elementary English*, XXXV (May, 1958), 309-13.

Kottmeyer, William. "Direct versus Incidental Teaching of Reading beyond the Primary Grades," *Reading Teacher*, VIII (April, 1955).

Lanning, Frank W. "Illusions of Unity," *Elementary School Journal*, LX October, 1959), 40-42.

Larrick, Nancy. *A Teacher's Guide to Children's Books*. Columbus, Ohio: Charles E. Merrill Books, Inc., 1960.

Letson, Charles T. "Speed and Comprehension in Reading," *Journal of Educational Research*, LII (October, 1958), 49-53.

McAulay, J. D. "Integrating the Social Studies," *Education*, LXXX (December, 1959), 239-42.

McKee, Paul. *The Teaching of Reading in the Elementary School*. Boston: Houghton Mifflin Co., 1948, Chaps. 11 and 12.

Murray, C. Merrill. "Selecting an Elementary School Dictionary," *Elementary English*, XXXIV (May, 1957), 293-97.

Ragan, William B. *Modern Elementary Curriculum*. New York: Holt, Rinehart & Winston, 1953.

Rinsland, Henry D. *A Basic Vocabulary of Elementary School Children*. New York: The Macmillan Co., 1945.

Roswell, Florence G. "When Children's Textbooks Are Too Difficult," *Elementary School Journal*, LX (December, 1959), 146-57.

Russell, David H. *Children Learn to Read*. Boston: Ginn and Co., 1949.

St. Mary, Maurice E. "Social Studies—A Way to Understanding," *Elementary School Journal*, LX (November, 1959), 93-96.

Smith, Nila B. "Teaching Study Skills in Reading," *Elementary School Journal*, LX (December, 1959), 158-62.

Sochor, Emma Elona. "Literal and Critical Reading in Social Studies," *Journal of Experimental Education*, XXVII (September, 1958).

Stroud, J. B. "Rate of Visual Perception as a Factor in Rate of Reading," *Journal of Educational Psychology*, XXXVI (November, 1945) 487-98.

chapter 9

CRITICAL READING

CRITICAL READING DEFINED

The term *critical reading* is undoubtedly meaningful to teachers, despite the fact that it might be difficult to find anywhere a definition which covers all facets of the term. One of the basic difficulties in attempting a definition is the fact that the concept in question has no fixed boundaries. Critical reading can take place on many levels. A high school student, a college sophomore, and a doctoral candidate in English, may all critically read *Macbeth*, though the performance of the high school student would be considered inadequate at the higher educational levels. Reading matter is distributed over a wide range of difficulty and complexity. Very few people explore the more difficult end of the continuum, yet the goal of formal education is to guide and direct each student to "explore to the maximum of his ability."

At a given moment a reader can comprehend at a level commensurate with his academic background, experience, and intellectual level. In the final analysis, the catalyst between writer and reader is the manner in which the latter uses his past experiences in the reading situation. Thus, it is fruitless to talk about getting *the* meaning of a passage, since most serious writing lends itself to a number of interpretations. As Triggs points out, the meaning which is attributed to written symbols in any reading situation is not intrinsic within the passage but is actually supplied by the reader.[1]

Critical reading is developmental in nature. It is an ongoing process. Some second graders may merit the designation *critical readers,* but no one would suggest that their interpretation of the Constitution is adequate for our society. Nevertheless, if children are to become adept at critical reading, they must be guided toward this goal from the beginning of their experience with reading. Helping the child develop ability to read critically is a problem and a challenge for teachers at all grade levels. Reading for meaning is emphasized by the authors of practically all basal reader series, and the emphasis is particularly noticeable at the beginning reading level. Pre-primers and primers contain instructions on building meanings around the few lines of print found in these books. Pictures are widely used to aid the child in extending concepts encountered at this level. One study of the degree of emphasis on critical skills found in a number of basal reader series lists thirty-three skills being stressed in the first six grades.[2]

As the child progresses in reading ability, the materials he reads increase in difficulty. The teacher's task becomes that of keeping children's concepts abreast of the material they are reading. This is easier in the prepared basal reading materials than it is in the content areas where more words and concepts are likely to be new to the child. In the stories children read there are many opportunities to sharpen critical reading powers if the teacher is able to take advantage of them. Children must develop the ability to interpret stories, determine whether places and characters are real or imaginary, discern moods of character, relate the sequence of events, and give plausible explanations of why persons felt and spoke as they did.[3]

---

[1] Frances O. Triggs, "Promoting Growth in Critical Reading," *Reading Teacher,* XII (1959), 158-64.

[2] Gertrude Williams, "Provisions for Critical Reading in Basic Readers," *Elementary English,* XXXVI (1959), 323-31.

[3] Edna Wilson, "Promoting Growth in Interpreting Different Kinds of Material," *Promoting Growth Toward Maturity in Interpreting What Is Read* (W. S. Gray, ed.), Supplementary Educational Monographs, No. 74, 1951, University of Chicago Press.

In the content fields the analysis is much the same, but the events perhaps deal with natural phenomenon rather than with story-book characters. (1) "What factors make it necessary for country X to import considerable food-stuffs?" (2) "There are a number of substances called minerals; each has a different boiling point." "What does this statement mean? What is its significance to man? Give examples." If the information necessary to answer these questions is gleaned through reading, critical reading has taken place.

Critical reading is not simply getting answers. Some exercises may get at certain facts but help very little in developing critical reading. Other types of questions are characteristically asked about material similar to that alluded to in the previous paragraph: "What are the main imports of country X?"; "list the minerals discussed in this chapter"; "what is the melting point of lead?"; "who discovered a process for making steel?"; and the like. Correctly answering these questions may not be evidence of critical reading. Seatwork or questions accompanying reading assignments are often dull. Some of these call for merely repeating sentences or words which answer questions or for scanning the entire article to find a synonym. Examples:

1. A story is read and a task is assigned. Fifteen statements, in jumbled order, are to be numbered to coincide with the order in which they appeared in the story.
2. Write a word that is used in this story for the word *large*.
3. Write the word which means a place where ships unload.
4. Copy the sentence that tells the number of lakes in Minnesota.

The appetite for critical reading is often dulled by thoughtless, time-consuming tasks such as these. Yet these and similar questions are referred to as aids to measuring or developing comprehension. Unfortunately, this type of busy-work is often encountered about the same time that the child is ready to do independent reading.

PREREQUISITES TO CRITICAL READING

A number of abilities must be dealt with in teaching for critical reading. When the student develops these abilities, his reading skill is enhanced; when they are neglected, the result is likely to be inept

Critical reading is a prerequisite to intelligent discussion. Small group participation permits pupils to paraphrase what they have read. In so doing they can demonstrate that they perceive the author's purpose, see relationships, detect humor, and draw warranted inferences. *(Courtesy of Bexley Schools, Bexley, Ohio; photographer: Arthur Burt, Inc.)*

and uncritical reading. Some of these abilities are listed below.[4]

1. The ability to recognize the meanings of words.
2. The ability to select the one appropriate meaning of a word which may have many meanings.
3. The ability to deal with figurative language, not insisting on literal meanings when the author does not intend literal interpretation.
4. The ability to determine the author's main ideas.
5. The ability to paraphrase, or restate, what the author has written.
6. The ability to see the relationship between one part and another and of all parts to the whole.
7. The ability to adjust to the author's organizational pattern.

---

[4] For an excellent summary of factors related to comprehension, see Frederick Davis, "Fundamental Factors in Comprehension in Reading," *Psychometrika*, IX (1944), 185-97.

8. The ability to determine the author's purpose, his intent in writing, his point of view, his biases, or whom the author is addressing and with what goal in mind.
9. The ability to draw inferences which are not specifically stated in the data.
10. The ability to recognize literary devices such as humor, satire, or irony, and to detect mood or tone.

RECOGNIZING WORDS

An example of a form of word paralysis is provided by the fourth grade boy who was quite adept at arithmetical computation, including division. He came to a page in his workbook in which the directions read "Write the quotients for the following problems." The boy did not attempt to solve a single problem on the page because the word *quotient* baffled him. The problems looked very much like the ones he had done previously, but surely this strange word instructed him to do something new and unknown. The teacher had assumed that everyone in the class knew the word, since it had been discussed at length. The concept had not been mastered, at least by this student.

The content areas, such as science, mathematics, health, and social studies, use hundreds of words which can inhibit learning if not fully understood. Examples are *ratio, proportion, respiration, longitude, exponent, photosynthesis, plateau, congruent, catalyst, inertia, delta,* and *contagious.*

Cole has a chapter on special vocabularies in her book *The Improvement of Reading.* She tells of a student in a chemistry class who asked his instructor for help in understanding the law: "The volume of a gas is inversely proportional to its density." The instructor tried without success to explain the concept embodied in the law. Finally, he asked the boy to define volume, volume of a gas, density, and inversely proportional. The boy had only one concept for *volume*—a book; *gas* was what is used in a stove; *density* meant thickness; he had no concept to go with *inversely proportional.*[5] The boy had actually "memorized" the law, a fact which emphasizes the futility of such effort in the absence of understanding.

---

[5] Louella Cole, *The Improvement of Reading* (New York: Farrar and Rinehart, Inc., 1938), 167. By permission of Holt, Rinehart and Winston, Inc.

The child's need for learning new words and concepts never abates, but sometimes the great mass of material to be taught may interfere with the effective teaching of meanings. In earlier chapters a number of procedures have been suggested for helping children master unknown words. Some of these procedures have merit for use in the upper grades and should be used when appropriate. A technique used with success by some teachers is the *word meaning period.* Ten- to fifteen-minute periods are used in which pupils present and discuss words whose meanings they had not known when they met them in their reading. A number of variations can be introduced to keep the period interesting. A pupil reads the sentence containing the word he has just learned and tells its meaning in that context. Other pupils can volunteer to use the word in different contexts, supply synonyms, or give other words which have the same root.

Another variation is a teacher-planned period devoted to learning important word roots and to demonstrating the possibilities of word building through the addition of prefixes, suffixes, and other roots. For example, *dict* is a root meaning "to say." To *pre*dict is to say in advance, and implies that an event is pre *dict* able. This same root permits one to say that if one is to *dic*tate, his *dic*tion *in dic*tating should be clear and that his pronunciation should not contra*dict* the *dic*tionary. The study of word meanings can be a fascinating and rewarding experience.

On the other hand, an assignment to learn a number of roots listed in one column and the common words made from each of these roots listed in an adjacent column may not be highly motivating because the drill is detached from a meaningful learning situation. In science, geography, or social science, however, words and concepts are met which need clarification. This provides an excellent opportunity for the integration of teaching meanings with teaching subjects. Terms and concepts, such as *photosynthesis, extracting minerals, geology, biology, plywood,* and *perspective,* can be used as a starting point for a study of word derivations.

The teacher might use the following exercise for teaching how some of our common words were built from words borrowed from other languages. *Auto* is a Greek word meaning *self; graph* is also Greek and means to *write;* when we put these two roots together we have our English word *autograph.* Do you see how the meaning of this word is related to the Greek word from which it is built?

Root		Root		
photo	= light;	*graph*	= to write:	photograph (to write with light)
tele	= far;	*graph*	= to write:	telegraph
phono	= sound;	*graph*	= to write:	phonograph
geo	= earth;	*graphy*	= to write:	geography
bio	= life;	*logy*	= to study:	biology
geo	= earth;	*logy*	= to study:	geology

Word meanings can be further explained by studying roots and prefixes, and roots and suffixes.

Prefix		Root		
con	= with, together;	*tract*	= to draw:	contract
re	= back;	*tract*	= to draw:	retract
ex	= out of;	*tract*	= to draw:	extract
im	= into;	*port*	= to carry:	import
trans	= across;	*port*	= to carry:	transport
re	= back;	*port*	= to carry:	report
Root		**Suffix**		
port	= to carry;	*able*	= capable of:	portable
dict	= to say;	*tion*	= act of:	diction
grat	= thanks;	*full*	= full of:	grateful

When pupils evince interest in word building (roots, prefixes, suffixes), the teacher can make available teacher-constructed exercises similar to the examples above. Knowledge of roots and prefixes will help a child work out the meaning of many words that at first glance may appear strange and difficult.

SELECTING THE APPROPRIATE MEANING

Teachers in one school tested the children in all grade levels, first through high school, on a few common words like *set, run, stick,* and *mine.* The word *set* elicited approximately ten different meanings in the first grade class. The number of different meanings associated with this word increased through the grades and reached twenty-eight correct usages in a third-year high school class. Yet the word *set* is considered a rather simple word.

The ability to select the appropriate meaning of a particular word which has many meanings is essential for critical reading. The word *base* has many meanings: third base, the base of a triangle, the base line of a graph, a naval base, base motives, and a number of others. *Dividend* does not have the same meaning in long division that it does when used as an increment from investments in stocks and bonds. The literal definition of *island* as "a body of land entirely surrounded by water" is not the meaning implied by John Donne when he states, "no man is an island entire unto himself—each is a piece of the continent, a part of the whole." Nevertheless, this conventional meaning would have to be known in order to understand the author's intended meaning. The child's learning of various connotations of words is complicated by the widespread use of figures of speech. Although these expressions may increase the difficulty of a passage, they also add to its beauty or forcefulness.

DEALING WITH FIGURATIVE LANGUAGE

Figurative language is a potential barrier to readers if they have a predilection for concrete meanings. Our language contains many colorful words which suggest vivid images, but, more important, our language is extremely flexible. Mutual agreement between persons using the language permits picturesque comparisons between things which are unlike. Cyrano De Bergerac, sword in hand but mortally wounded, describes the approach of death, "I stand—*clothed with marble, gloved with lead.*" Overstatements or gross exaggeration emphasize particular qualities—"He's as patient as Job," "strong as Hercules," "tall as a mountain." Likenesses are suggested through implied functions—"The ship *plowed* the waves," "The arrow *parted* his hair." Sometimes, in fact, words are used in such a way as to mean just their opposite. Obviously, understanding material containing such expressions depends on the reader's realization of the intended meanings.

As early as second and third grade, numerous figures of speech and idiomatic expressions appear in basal reader series. The following passage is filled with expressions which probably would pose no problem for adults but which might mystify a child who reads slowly or literally.

> Joe, *flying down the stairs, rested his eye* on the hawk. Grandfather *buried his nose* in a book and acted as if he were *completely in the dark*. Grandmother and Sue *put their heads together* and tried to figure out *which way the wind was blowing*. Joe *tipped his hand* by carrying the gun. On the *spur of the moment* Grandmother *hit the nail on the head. Cool as a cucumber,* she called to Joe, "*Freeze in your tracks* and put that gun back upstairs!" Joe's *spirits fell* as his grandmother's words *took the wind out of his sail*. He *flew off the handle* and told about the hawk. "*That's a horse of a different color,*" said Grandmother, satisfied that she had *dug up the facts*. "Let the boy alone," said Grandfather. "He will *keep the wolf from the door*." Outside, Joe thought, "I'd better *make hay while the sun shines,*" as he *drew a bead* on the hawk.

Although these expressions may not bother most children, more difficult figures of speech will constantly confront them. The children who are baffled by such expressions need more experience with them. For these pupils, the teacher should devise exercises over and above those which are found in workbooks at their grade level. If the reader is *thinking while reading*, he will probably develop the flexibility necessary to deal with this type of language.

IDENTIFYING MAIN IDEAS

The ability to arrive at the author's main ideas is often considered virtually synonymous with critical reading. Getting the main ideas from a passage is not an isolated skill that can be developed out of context with all other reading skills. This skill depends on the reader's mastery of the mechanics of reading, breadth of vocabulary and concepts, background, and attitudes. While the importance to the reader of getting main ideas is obvious, the reasons for the extreme difficulty of teaching this skill are not so self-evident.

Workbook exercises in the elementary grades attempt to deal with this problem. There are lessons in which the child reads a paragraph, and is asked to select the best title for the passage from among three suggested titles; or, after reading a paragraph, he is to select the best summary sentence from among the three listed. These exercises are designed to make the child conscious of reading for meaning or reading critically. Evidently, not enough of this type of drill is provided or such techniques are not sufficient for cultivating habits of reading critically. Many pupils do not become proficient in grasping main ideas or the author's purpose.

A pupil who can read every word and who knows the meanings of the words in a passage can fail miserably in identifying the important facts. Such occurrences emphasize what was pointed out previously, that reading is more than the sum of its parts. Always, there is the interaction between the reader (meaning such psychological factors as adjustment, attitudes, past experience) and the material to be read. A reader who may get the significant points while reading a science unit may be quite inadequate in his interpretation of a story or a unit on geography. Such performance can usually be traced to lack of interest, background, or failure to discern the purpose for reading. The critical reader is one who has attained smoothness and facility in reading skills and who does not let his previous experiences or attitudes interfere with the analysis and evaluation of what he reads.

One can understand why the pupil who lacks reading skills, word knowledge, or background, may fail to grasp important meanings. In the intermediate grades and above, getting the author's main ideas can be complicated by the special vocabularies of various subject areas, such as health, science, mathematics, and geography. Another problem is the increasing complexity of sentence structure met in materials at these levels. Difficulties are compounded in many instances because systematic instruction in reading has ceased in many schools by the sixth grade or junior high level, although, in reality, many pupils have considerable need for further systematic instruction in reading.

PARAPHRASING

The ability to paraphrase, or restate in one's own words, the author's main ideas is usually the criterion by which the pupil's critical reading ability or comprehension is judged. The inability to paraphrase often implies one of two things: either the pupil did not fathom what the author was trying to tell him, or he lacks the language facility to restate what he read. Paraphrasing is one of the most effective and, at the same time, one of the least used techniques available to teachers at all levels. Walpole states: "Paraphrasing provides a simple classroom technique which not only commits the pupil to a specific task of interpretation, but also enables him to study other versions and see how people interpret the same passage in widely varying ways."[6] Paraphrasing exercises provide an almost ideal example of a means of integrating all of the language arts. First, the student gets experience in interpretive reading. Second, by writing he gains experience in all facets of composition, such as sentence and paragraph construction, organization of material, and grammatical usage. This technique can be highly motivating to students if care is exercised in the selection of reading passages.

In order to paraphrase accurately or restate the essence of what an author has written, one must be able to grasp the meaning as he reads. Paraphrasing demands that one see the relationships between various parts of a passage and see how these parts are related to the total effect sought by an author. As a rule, good readers have developed the ability to read in "thought units." Thus, their reading habits lead them naturally into logical and meaningful phrasing. They have learned to see the relationships between words and how the author builds a pattern of thought units into a large whole. The point under discussion cuts across several factors which have been listed as related to critical reading: main ideas, paraphrasing, adjusting to author's organization, and seeing the relationship between a part and the whole.

The illustrations below have been used with high school groups. In each case, passage A was read by the student who was then asked to write a sentence or two restating what the author said. Immediately following this, each pupil was given passage B which was the same passage but was divided into meaningful thought units. All of the students stated that it was easier to get meaning from passage B. The point of the exercise was to help students see that in their reading for meaning they must do what was done for them in passage B, i.e., read in meaningful thought units. Such an exercise can be developed for use at practically any reading level.

---

[6] Hugh R. Walpole, "Promoting Development in Interpreting What Is Read in the Middle and Upper Grades," Supplementary Educational Monographs, No. 61, 1945, University of Chicago Press, 162-167.

Passage A

A man rises, sometimes, and stands not, because he doth not, or is not believed to fill his place; and sometimes he stands not, because he overfills his place: He may bring so much virtue, so much justice, so much integrity to the position, as to be a libel upon his predecessor, and cast infamy upon him, and a burden upon his successor.[7]

Passage B

A man rises, sometimes,
and stands not,
because he doth not,
or is not believed to fill his place;
And sometimes he stands not,
because he overfills his place:
He may bring
so much virtue,
so much justice,
so much integrity to the position,
as to be a libel upon his predecessor,
and cast infamy upon him,
and a burden upon his successor.

Passage A

Man, of whom David had said, (as the lowest diminution that he could put upon him), 'I am a worm and no man'—he might have gone lower, and said, I am a man and no worm.[8]

Passage B

Man,
of whom David had said,
(as the lowest diminution that he could put upon him)
'I am a worm and no man'—
He might have gone lower,
and said,
I am a man and no worm.

---

[7] Paraphrased from John Donne, *Complete Poetry and Prose of John Donne* (New York: The Modern Library, 1946), 338.

[8] *Ibid.*, 369.

DISCERNING RELATIONSHIPS AND ORGANIZATIONAL PATTERNS

Factors six and seven, seeing relationships between the parts and the whole and adjusting to the author's organizational pattern, are, to some degree, dealt with in any paraphrasing exercise. These skills should be deliberately taught; as a rule, they cannot be taught through a mere discussion of critical reading. The child needs concrete experiences and illustrations. These should be provided in all areas of the curriculum, since each subject matter calls for meaningful reading.

Many educators are of the opinion that pupils in American schools, at all levels, do not have enough experience in writing, and, as a result, lack opportunities to learn good habits of organization of paragraphs and larger units. Most of the practice pupils receive in analysis and organization in the elementary grades is found in reading and language arts. In the upper grades the responsibility for such instruction is usually associated with the teaching of English. Many exercises which aim at helping the pupil see how larger meaningful language units are built and logically held together fail because they can be solved or completed without critical thinking.

Keeping one narrow question in mind and rereading the passage as often as necessary will lead to the correct response on exercises, such as underlining key words or topic sentences, selecting the best of several suggested titles for a story, rearranging the jumbled steps in an outline, striking out sentences which do not belong in a paragraph, or discovering paragraphs which interrupt the thread of narrative. Each of these exercises attempts to teach something about organization and analysis which is useful in critical reading. But taken individually or together, these often fail if they are synthetic or artificial. One can master the tasks called for in these drills and still not be able to transfer any appreciable learning to other reading situations. Many pupils do not see the relationship between working on these exercises and reading textbooks in geography, history, or science. To see such parallels, the purpose must be clear.

It should be pointed out that the type of exercise mentioned above is not inherently poor. Pupils should be taught the significance of key words and phrases which authors use to indicate contrasts, comparisons and transitions. Critical readers profit from clues, such as

"There are *three* main points"—"First," "Next," "And in conclusion," "while on the other hand," "provided that," "differ in some respects," "as well as," and the like. One author has aptly labeled such clues as *signal words.*[9]

FURTHER PREREQUISITES TO CRITICAL READING

The last three factors can be discussed as a group. These include the ability to determine the author's purpose, to draw inferences, and to recognize literary devices such as humor, satire, and irony. In dealing with stories or literature, teachers are more likely to attempt to deal with these factors consciously and deliberately. Most literature teachers place more emphasis on analyzing the plot and the characters and on studying the author's style and organization. In fact, it is possible to have too much analysis of literature. An author of children's literature, Adele De Leeuw, has a word on this point: "As an author, I have a plea. Do not spoil reading by too much classroom analysis. Let the interpretation come of itself. . . . The sacred trust of teachers is to keep open that path to broader understanding, and not to close it by the insurmountable block of too much analysis."[10] This author's plea is no doubt warranted, but nevertheless children need a degree of guidance so that they can gradually become proficient in the interpretation and analysis of what they read.

Almost all the prerequisites for, and obstacles to, critical reading are related to the two skills of discerning a writer's purpose and of drawing inferences. The presence or absence of bias, a lack of background, the habit of accepting that which is in print or that which is allegedly backed by authority, and the lack of experience in dealing with controversial topics, all help to determine whether critical reading can take place. College students too have trouble discerning an author's purpose. Students in a reading improvement course, after

---

[9] Ken Macrorie, *The Perceptive Writer, Reader and Speaker* (New York: Harcourt, Brace and Co., 1959), 271-73.

[10] Adele De Leeuw, "Nobody's Doll," "With a High Heart," and "Linda Marsh," *Promoting Growth Toward Maturity in Interpreting What Is Read* (W. S. Gray, ed.), University of Chicago Press, 1951, 49-53. Copyright 1951 by the University of Chicago.

reading and discussing several serious paragraphs, were given the following passage by Mark Twain. Each student was to read the passage silently and to write a sentence or two answering these questions: "What is the author's purpose? How does he achieve it? What is the author's mood?"

> It was a crisp and spicy morning in early October. The lilacs and laburnums, lit with the glory fires of autumn, hung burning and flashing in the upper air; a fairy bridge provided by kind Nature for the wingless wild things, that have their home in the tree-tops and would visit together; the larch and the pomegranate flung their purple and yellow flames in brilliant broad splashes along the slanting sweep of the woodland; the sensuous fragrance of innumerable deciduous flowers rose upon the swooning atmosphere; far in the empty sky a solitary oesophagus slept upon motionless wing; everywhere brooded stillness, serenity, and the peace of God.[11]

Hundreds of students, and a smaller number of teachers and adults, have responded in essence: "It is a beautiful fall day. He describes nature, the beautiful colors, and the peace and quiet one finds in nature." Despite the first line a number of readers move the day into spring. Occasionally a reader says, "I wondered about the oesophagus, but thought it might be a tropical bird." However, once adults are shown the ridiculous nature of the passage they seriously doubt that others would be so easily taken in by it.

The ten abilities related to critical reading operate in all reading situations, not just in those that occur during the clock-hour devoted to formal instruction in reading. They operate whenever reading is used in the pursuit of knowledge, whether in history, geography, economics, health, mathematics, science, or literature. The reader must know the meaning of the words used and the different shades of meaning words have in different contexts. He must separate main thoughts or ideas from qualifications; he must detect the author's purpose, bias, and intent. From the first grade through college, the teacher has a major responsibility to structure reading situations so that these factors and many others are kept in proper focus.

---

[11] Mark Twain, "A Detective Story," from *The Man That Corrupted Hadleyburg* (New York: Harper & Brothers), 304.

KNOWLEDGE AND BACKGROUND

The absence of the skills discussed above is a major stumbling block to critical reading, but such factors as how long, how thoroughly, and how extensively they have been practiced also will have a bearing on one's level of critical reading. As Durrell points out, "The efficiency of transferring ideas from one person to another is seldom high," and there is an unavoidable loss for the reader in this process.[12] Eller lists a number of obstacles to critical reading found in the school, in society, or in both. Some of them follow:

1. Pupils form the opinion that anything in print is true.
2. Children are conditioned to accept authority blindly.
3. Schools have relied on single texts in the various content areas, and the teacher stresses "what the book says." Thus, children do not learn to look for differences of opinion or for interpretations.
4. Schools avoid controversial topics and emphasize uniformity.[13]

Each of these points is inevitably tied in with experience, and is thus affected by a person's background and knowledge. It is likely that the greatest barrier to critical reading is the reader's lack of background and experience. The teacher has to deal with this problem regardless of the level or the curriculum area in which she teaches. In reality, we are dealing with two questions. First, what does the reader bring to the reading situation in the way of experience and understanding? And second, what does he need in order to understand the particular reading he is attempting? Both of these points are related to one of Herbart's five steps in the learning process—the preparation of the learner for that which is to be learned.[14] As noted earlier, it is in beginning reading instruction that the teacher often does the best job of preparing the learner. The higher one goes through the grades, the more need there is for this type of preparation

---

[12] Donald D. Durrell, "Development of Comprehension and Interpretation," *Reading in the Elementary School,* Forty-eighth Yearbook, Part II, N.S.S.E., 193-204.

[13] William Eller, "Fundamentals of Critical Reading," *The Reading Teacher's Reader* (Oscar S. Causey, ed.), (New York: Ronald Press, 1958), 30-34.

[14] See J. B. Stroud, *Psychology in Education* (New York: Longmans, Green and Co., Inc., 1957), 446.

because the reading materials deal with concepts which are often beyond the present stock of concepts held by some students in the room.

A third grade class is reading a story about bees storing honey in a hollow tree. The facts that the bees "belonged to a farmer," worked for him in a hive he provided, and yet one day swarmed and left the hive, may call for a good deal of explanation by the teacher, or by bee experts in the class, before all aspects of this story are meaningful to every member of that third grade class.

A high school or college student reading *John Brown's Plea to the Court* can hardly be expected to arrive at a sound critical analysis of this passage unless some background facts are also known: who was John Brown?; when did he live?; what political-social issue was involved?; what experiences did John Brown have in Kansas prior to the Harper's Ferry episode?; was John Brown's attitude shared by a large number of people living at that time?; how would one describe John Brown's emotional maturity?; is the real issue here the question of whether the end justifies the means?

Critical reading has neither disappeared nor is it widely practiced. There is so much to read on so many important topics that no one can hope to read everything available on any topic. As a result, many people are content to settle for digests of magazine articles, condensations of books. This type of reading matter flourishes because so many people feel a need for at least a thin veneer of culture, but not a coating thick enough that it would require critical reading or thinking.

College students' and adults' reactions to the Mark Twain passage cited above are illustrative of behavior which would naturally occur in a society which has not been perturbed by the obstacles to critical reading and thinking which have gradually accumulated in its mass educational system. It is a rare day when millions of people are not taken in by some form of advertising which in the final analysis is as divorced from meaning as is the Twain passage. Also, on numerous occasions, people are faced with political arguments which are equally meaningless. Whether or not our schools will produce more critical readers is an issue which has great significance for a democracy's future. Probably the most devastating criticism of the schools, which bears on this point, is that "the schools reflect the culture around them."

WHAT THE SCHOOL CAN DO

There are a number of practices which, if followed, will have some impact on improving instruction. The following list of procedures can serve as a summary on critical reading.

1. Do not violate the principles of teaching reading, which apply particularly to critical reading.
    a) Diagnosis is essential in order to discover weaknesses before the child has a reaction formation against reading.
    b) Instruction should be based on pupil's needs.
    c) Reading is getting meaning.
    d) Many approaches and techniques are needed.
    e) Do not ask the child to read over his head. Asking a child to read something he cannot read is unjustifiable and asking him to read it critically is expecting the impossible.
2. Pre-teach difficult, new, or unknown words as they are encountered in any reading—particularly in subject areas. Work on both pronunciation and meaning.
3. Get rid of the idea that reading and the teaching of reading take place during the "reading period" and that during other periods subjects are taught.
4. There should be a deliberate effort to study the organization of sentences, paragraphs, and larger units.
    a) Stress the function of pronunciation for students needing this type of drill.
    b) Explain and analyze difficult sentence structure, dependent clauses, complex sentences, and inverted order.
5. Teach and expect orderliness, organization, and logic in written work.
6. Use all audio-visual aids available. Concepts are built through sensory experiences, but experience with word symbols alone is an ineffective way to broaden concepts. The concept of land erosion might be taught with words, i.e., "erosion is the wearing away of land by rain or the action of water." However, a single good picture

of badly eroded land might fix this concept and make it much more meaningful. A film showing the cutting of forests, plowing, and lack of cover grass, will broaden the concept even more.

7. Use purposeful study questions in advance of pupil reading. Questions given prior to reading can be most effective in structuring any reading situation. Eventually the student should get in the habit of asking the proper questions for himself, but this takes time and experience. In order to master this technique the child needs guidance and direction. Studies indicate that questions given prior to reading are the most effective use of the question method.[15] This is an excellent method of preparing the student and of giving him a motive or goal in his reading. Too often this technique is neglected or not used as a means of implementing critical reading.

8. Wide reading on fewer topics, rather than superficial reading on many topics, will permit students more practice in organizing, analyzing, seeing relationships, comparing sources, and determining whether information belongs or is related to the topic under discussion.

9. Teach interpretation of graphs, charts, tables, figures, wherever they occur in any subject area.

10. Explain and teach analogies and how the reader must always make sure the analogy applies.

11. Provide practice in recognizing bias, distortion, and various propaganda techniques. A recent study indicates that sixth grade children can be taught to detect some propaganda used in materials they read.[16] This does not mean they can become immune but that they can detect certain propaganda devices after periods of instruction aimed at helping them identify these techniques.

12. Help children develop a questioning attitude so that they will differentiate between fact and opinion, see cause and effect relationships, and use clues in evaluating the merit of a work. These clues might include the origin or context of the article (reputation of the

---

[15] J. N. Washburne, "The Use of Questions in Social Science Material," *Journal of Educational Psychology*, XX (1929), 321-59. E. Holmes, "Reading Guided by Questions versus Careful Reading and Rereading Without Questions," *School Review*, XXXIX (1931), 101-6.

[16] Robert R. Nardelli, "Some Aspects of Creative Reading," *Journal of Educational Research*, L (1957), 495-508.

How does a Jet work? Why does it fly? When children develop a questioning attitude, they are likely to read critically to get answers to the questions of *how* and *why*. *(Courtesy of Bexley Schools, Bexley, Ohio; photographer: Arthur Burt, Inc.)*

magazine or publisher); the writing or publication date (have significant advances taken place since publication?) and the reputation of the author (is he objective, is he selling a point of view?).

YOUR POINT OF VIEW?

Be sure to read the following statements critically before giving your analysis of them.

1. If we agree that we cannot talk in terms of the meaning of a passage, we must conclude that it is impossible either to evaluate or to teach critical reading.

2. A person with no training or background in physics or genetics could not read critically a series of conflicting reports on the effect of "atomic fallout."

3. A high school student could not arrive at a sound critical analysis of the effect of tariffs on American industrialization by critically reading only high school textbooks on American history.

4. Honest judges with equal ability in critical reading of statutes will agree on the constitutionality of a particular law. (Assuming, of course, that they have read the constitution critically.)

5. America's free public education system is the world's foremost example of "socialized education."

BIBLIOGRAPHY

Artley, A. Sterl. "Critical Reading in the Content Areas," *Elementary English*, XXXXI (February, 1959), 122-30.

Barbe, Walter B., and Williams, Thelma E. "Developing Creative Thinking in Gifted Children through the Reading Program," *Reading Teacher*, IX (April, 1956), 200-3.

Carver, Richard L., and Sheldon, William D. "Problems in the Development of Concepts through Reading," *Elementary School Journal*, LV (1954), 226-29.

Cole, Louella. *The Improvement of Reading*. New York: Farrar and Rinehart, Inc., 1938.

Cook, Luella B. "Language Factors Involved in Interpretation," *Reading Teacher*, XII (February, 1959), 152-57.

Crossen, Helen J. "Effect of Attitudes of the Reader upon Critical Reading Ability," *Journal of Educational Research*, XLII (December, 1948), 289-98.

Davis, Frederick B. "Fundamental Factors in Comprehension in Reading," *Psychometrika*, IX (September, 1944), 185-97.

Durrell, Donald D. "Development of Comprehension and Interpretation," *Reading in the Elementary School*. Forty-eighth Yearbook, Part II, National Society for the Study of Education. Chicago: University of Chicago Press, 1949.

Eller, William. "Fundamentals of Critical Reading," *The Reading Teachers' Reader*, ed. Oscar S. Causey. New York: The Ronald Press Co., 1958, 30-34.

Gray, William S. "New Approaches to the Study of Interpretation in Reading," *Journal of Educational Research,* LII (October, 1958), 65-67.

Greene, Harry A., and Petty, Walter T. *Developing Language Skills in the Elementary School.* Boston: Allyn and Bacon, Inc., 1959.

Hanna, Paul R. "Generalizations and Universal Values: Their Implications for the Social-Studies Program. *Social Studies in the Elementary School.* The Fifty-sixth Yearbook, Part II, National Society for the Study of Education. Chicago: University of Chicago Press, 1957, 27-47.

Harris, Albert J. *How to Increase Reading Ability* (3rd ed.). New York: Longmans, Green & Co., Inc., 1956.

Hillenbrand, Robert. "The Appreciation of Picturesque Language in the Intermediate Grades," *Elementary English,* XXXVI (May, 1959), 302-4.

Holmes, E. "Reading Guided by Questions versus Careful Reading and Rereading without Questions," *School Review,* XXXIX (1931), 101-6.

Macrorie, Ken. *The Perceptive Writer, Reader, and Speaker.* New York: Harcourt, Brace & Co., 1959.

McCullough, Constance. "Implications of Research on Children's Concepts," *Reading Teacher,* XIII (December, 1959), 100-7.

Nardelli, Robert R. "Some Aspects of Creative Reading," *Journal of Educational Research,* L (March, 1957), 495-508.

Nordberg, Robert B. "Levels of Communication in Reading," *Catholic Educational Review,* LIV (February, 1956), 92-100.

Petty, Walter T. "Critical Reading in the Primary Grades," *Elementary English,* XXXIII (May, 1956), 298-302.

Serra, Mary C. "A Study of Fourth Grade Children's Comprehension of Certain Verbal Abstractions," *Journal of Experimental Education,* XXII (December, 1953), 103-18.

Sochor, E. Elona. "The Nature of Critical Reading," *Elementary English,* XXXXI (January, 1959), 47-58.

Strang, Ruth, and Bracken, Dorothy Kendall. *Making Better Readers.* Boston: D. C. Heath & Co., 1957.

Stroud, J. B. *Psychology in Education.* New York: Longmans, Green and Co., Inc., 1957.

Triggs, Frances O. "Promoting Growth in Critical Reading," *The Reading Teacher,* XII (February, 1959), 158-64.

Walpole, Hugh R. "Promoting Development in Interpreting What Is Read in the Middle and Upper Grades," Supplementary Educational Monograps, University of Chicago. Chicago: University of Chicago Press, No. 61, 162-67.

Washburne, J. N. "The Use of Questions in Social Science Material," *Journal of Educational Psychology,* XX (1929), 321-59.
Williams, Gertrude. "Provisions for Critical Reading in Basic Readers," *Elementary English,* XXXVI (May, 1959), 323-31.
Wilson, Edna. "Promoting Growth in Interpreting Different Kinds of Material," *Promoting Growth Toward Maturity in Interpreting What Is Read,* ed. William S. Gray, Supplementary Educational Monographs, University of Chicago. Chicago: University of Chicago Press, 1951, No. 74.

chapter 10

EMOTIONS AND READING

> The school experience can play a major role in the total process with an emotionally disturbed child. It is an experience with great ego-building potentials since it is oriented to reality; it aims toward the development of skill and mastery; it can aid in the development of self. image and even of self esteem; it can offer a source of gratification at varying levels of ability, of aspiration, and of interests, and it can utilize, in successive stages of development and improvement in the child, varying amounts of group participation and group identification depending on the child's strengths and the needs at the time.
>
> Unfortunately it is also true that the school experience can be an ego-alien experience for the emotionally disturbed child unless certain factors in the school structure, in the teacher, and in the child himself are carefully evaluated.[1]

Whether or not the school and the teacher are aware of it, the school experiences that children have are a most important factor in determining the kinds of persons they will become. The school may take partial credit when children learn at a level approximating their capacity or when they exhibit social and emotional behavior that

[1] J. Cotter Hirschberg, "The Role of Education in the Treatment of Emotionally Disturbed Children Through Planned Ego Development," *American Journal of Orthopsychiatry,* XXIII (1953), 684-90.

society recognizes as acceptable and healthy. Yet few of us, as teachers, like to admit that the schools must also share the credit (or guilt) for pupil maladjustment. If reading disabilities are to be curbed, the school must seek out and attempt to mitigate its own contributions to pupil maladjustment.

Psychologists and psychiatrists as well as informed teachers know that maladjustments in the learning process (reading disabilities) do not stem from any one academic practice or malpractice as some popular writers seem to think.[2] Methodology alone is not responsible for producing the host of impaired readers and non-readers that plague our schools, homes, and guidance clinics. While methodology may often be a contributory factor, the human organism is extremely flexible and it is a proven fact that children can and do learn to read under the most adverse methodological procedures, provided that they are physically and emotionally ready to read.

GROWTH OF INTEREST IN EMOTIONS AS A FACTOR IN READING

In tracing the development of interest in the relationship between reading problems and emotional involvements several facts merit attention. First, the concept of a close relationship between the two was not accepted quite as readily by educators and teachers as were certain other concepts popular about the same time, such as readiness, individual testing, the role of phonics in reading instruction, and oral versus silent reading. Interest in these problems seemed to emerge quickly, once the concepts found their way into the literature on reading. On the other hand, educators tended to ignore the relationship between reading and the emotions, clinging to the theories of inadequate intelligence and special disabilities as means of explaining reading failures. Second, much of the data which tended to establish the relationship between reading disability and emotional causes came from clinics, clinicians, psychologists, and

---

[2] Rudolph Flesch, *Why Johnny Can't Read* (New York: Harper & Brothers, 1955). Flesch sees the modern schools' method of teaching phonics (or as he believes its lack of method) as the root of all reading difficulties.

psychiatrists.[3] Third, it is probably no exaggeration to state that at the present time most educators accept the premise that emotional problems can and do interact with the reading process and that in many reading disability cases there is some form of emotional involvement.

During the past decade a number of articles, books and monographs on reading have appeared whose purpose was to explore the relationship between emotional factors and the child's inability to learn to read. Various investigators and writers have not agreed on the incidence of emotional involvement connected with reading. Little would be gained by individually reviewing the findings of different researchers since their methods of selecting cases and the criteria used for determining maladjustment or emotional involvement would vary. In a summary of the research in this area, Smith stated that different investigators report from 42 per cent to 90 per cent of reading disability cases studied are accompanied by emotional disturbances.[4]

HOW EMOTIONS BECOME INVOLVED IN READING

It is apparent from the literature on emotions and reading that there are two major hypotheses which might account for the interaction between emotions and reading disability.

1. Where emotional behavior and reading problems are found together, the emotional involvement stems from failure, frustration, tension, and pressure connected with the reading problem.

Reading failure → Emotional reactions

Here it is implied that the child's emotions become involved in reading through success or failure. While competition may not be new to the child, the type of competition he encounters in the reading situation *is* new to him. Never before has so much been expected from

[3] See bibliography entries at end of chapter particularly: Axline, Baruch, Bell, Edelston, Ephron, Mehus, Odenwald and Shea, Preston, Robinson, Stover, Sylvester and Junst, Talbot.

[4] Nila B. Smith, "Research on Reading and the Emotions," *School and Society*, LXXXI (1955), 8.

him by his parents and his teacher. Reading ability is very highly prized in our society, and pressures on the child from parents, teacher, and peers all seem to focus on this one front. He has not sensed this type of pressure in his drawing and coloring activities, in rhythm activities, in listening to stories the teacher has read, or in other activities found in the curriculum.

The child's frustrations mount as a result of failure and also as a result of his inability to please the figures of authority—parents and teachers. His attitudes toward himself are influenced by attitudes around him. Feelings of inferiority and personal inadequacy result. When one's ego is threatened, tension and emotional conflict are inevitable. Under these circumstances, the child resorts to some behavior which, irrational as it may appear to adults, seems to the child to be a means of escape from an untenable position.

It is amazing how varied the responses of different children are to frustration and ego-threatening situations. The same classroom stimulus will not produce like responses among different children. The teacher's remark, "now let's open our reading workbooks—we should be on page thirty-nine," may elicit responses varying from elation to nausea among the various pupils in the class. The individual child's past experiences both at home and school, and the impact these experiences have had on the child's attitudes toward himself, toward the teacher, and toward parents and peers, will all determine the response which this stimulus evokes. One child may give the appearance of functional deafness—he didn't hear the request; one may request to leave the room; another child may respond with the ultimate of conformity, and open his book to page 39, even though he has never worked successfully on any of the preceding pages or any preceding workbooks.

2. Unresolved emotional problems, which originally need not have been related to reading, may prevent the child from applying his energies to the learning task. The non-reading behavior is simply a symptom of the emotional problem.

Unresolved emotional problem → Reading problem

When reading problems and emotional involvements are found together, there may also be other factors contributing to the reading problem (i.e., physical factors, educational procedures used, learned responses to frustration).

Several principles of teaching reading discussed earlier are related to emotional problems and reading. In Chapter 1 it was pointed out that learning to read is a very complicated process and that language functions are among the most sensitive indicators of maladjustment. Unrelenting pressure brought to bear on a child to make him read will not always achieve desirable results. Further, it was suggested that sometime in the future it is likely that children with emotional problems severe enough to prevent learning will receive treatment before being expected to harness their energies to learning tasks.

THE TEACHER'S ROLE IN DEALING WITH EMOTIONALLY INVOLVED READING PROBLEMS

What should the teacher do for children with reading problems who also show evidence that there is an emotional factor involved? Several factors make this question difficult to answer.

1. Some teachers, parents, school boards, and critics of education do not yet admit that in many cases non-learning and emotional problems are inextricably knit together. After several years of instruction in reading and special tutoring, Johnny, who has adequate intelligence, is still a non-reader. Some factor other than lack of intelligence or poor methodology must be contributing to Johnny's problem. However, if it is ruled out before the search is begun, emotional maladjustment will not be unearthed as the culprit.

The belief that the schools have a tremendous impact on ego-development or ego-starvation of pupils is gaining wider acceptance, and teachers are coming to realize that they are necessarily involved in the process of dealing with social and emotional maladjustments. Yet there are many critics of American education who think that the school's concern with the social and emotional development of children is a tender-minded, do-gooder escape mechanism thrown up as a rearguard action by confused teachers engaged in a retreat from teaching.

It must be admitted that some teachers who verbally embrace the principle that the school should be concerned with the pupil's emotional health are hazy as to *why*. To some teachers the reason may appear to be more closely allied to public relations than to learning.

These teachers may not be aware of the fact that the learning process is very sensitive to emotional and social disturbances and in the final analysis is affected by maladjustment in these areas. "Meeting the child's needs and interests" may have, through constant usage, been reduced to jargon, but it once was meaningful. "Educating the whole child" may share the same present-day reputation, but this too once had meaning. Both of these principles involved the recognition that all school experiences of children are related to learning. The school cannot meet the needs of children if it ignores psychological needs such as the need for success, self-realization, creativity, and an acceptable concept of self. Failure in school is the most important factor in thwarting the fulfillment of the child's needs.

2. The teacher's ego needs can contribute to the child's insecurity and pose threats to his adjustment and concept of self. The fact that some children fail to make progress commensurate with grade-level norms may become a threat to the teacher. This threat is often met with more pressure and sometimes with unconscious hostility.

3. Another important factor is the conviction on the part of teachers that they are not prepared to deal with emotional problems. This lack of preparation is undoubtedly the case with some teachers, some parents, some clinicians, and quite a few detention homes. Also, it is probably true that most of the maladjusted are not equipped to help themselves. There are some children who have emotional problems which teachers cannot hope to alleviate, just as there are some pupil maladjustments produced by the school which could have been prevented.

TEACHERS AS THERAPISTS

In recent years, however, there has been an awareness on the part of many clinicians in child-guidance clinics as well as remedial clinics that the school—or, more correctly, the teacher— is in a therapeutic relationship to children because of the very nature of the school and the activities which are carried on in the school. This is not to imply that teachers should consider themselves trained therapists when they are not, but rather that, try as they may, they cannot escape the fact that much of the activity in the classroom is ego-involved activity and how teachers handle everyday situations in the classroom has an impact on the mental health of pupils.

Asahel Woodruff, in his book *The Psychology of Teaching* states, "Every teacher is of necessity a psychologist in *function,* with or *without training.*"[5] (Emphasis added.) He does not say that teachers are psychologists, but rather implies that their daily tasks in the classroom require them to deal with, understand, and influence human behavior (learning). This they do with or without training in understanding or influencing behavior. Actually, the average teacher is not without training for this part of her job, and the better the teacher the more she understands her limitations. But with or without limitations, she must find ways to help children grow, to help children face frustration, to help children accept reality, and to help children drain off tension so they can apply energy to learning tasks instead of burning it up in behavior not related to learning.

The issue is that, if teachers see themselves as exclusively concerned with methodological procedures or techniques, they are likely to find that some of their pupils do not seem to profit from any of the procedures or techniques used.

> In dealing with reading problems it is easy to center attention upon technique. The science of remedial work in reading has expanded so rapidly in the production of objective measures for diagnosis, such as tests and scales, and of remedial techniques, that the use of these instruments has become a highly skilled art. Because of the excellence of many of the devices it has become tempting to the remedial expert to rely upon their efficiency, and to forget the complexity of the problems with which they deal. There is a tendency to overlook the fact that what is really being diagnosed and treated *is the whole personality of the person with the problem,* including the way that personality functions in the special area of reading.[6] (Emphasis added.)

When classroom procedures fail, certain pupils may be referred to a reading or child-guidance clinic for help. If, as a result, they receive the right combination of attention to their psychological needs and attention to techniques aimed at the mechanics of reading, all may turn out well. In many cases there are no such facilities available, at least not until the child's behavior becomes so deviant that something

[5] Asahel D. Woodruff, *The Psychology of Teaching* (3rd ed.; New York: Longmans, Green and Co., Inc., 1951), 8.

[6] John E. Bell, "Emotional Factors in the Treatment of Reading Difficulties," *Journal of Consulting Psychology,* IX (1945), 125-31.

has to be done. Can teachers themselves provide this right combination? Many teachers do practice a certain amount of therapy, and they rarely see it as something extraneous to the learning situation. It is simply part of the job of guiding the learning activities of children.

To illustrate, an elementary school arranged for a thorough diagnosis of a number of children with severe reading problems. One girl, Mary, in the third grade, was a non-reader. She had intelligence adequate for learning and was attractive but shy and retiring. When asked about friends, she had only one friend, Miss Blank (her teacher). In answer to other questions, "Whom do you like to play with? walk home with? visit?" Miss Blank was the only human being mentioned. At noon, this child and teacher were observed in the cafeteria. All the children in the third grade sat around one long table, the teacher at one end. Mary sat next to her and was most possessive. She put her hand in the teacher's, looked at her most of the time, talked to her (not shy here). In fact, before the meal was over, she had managed to slip her chair up very close to the teacher and place her head on the teacher's lap. The teacher stroked her head and shoulder all the while talking to others around her and keeping in touch with all that was going on around the large table. As the group left, Mary and the teacher left hand in hand.

Later, Mary's problem was discussed. Her teacher brought up the matter of the child's complete dependence on her and stated that she had to be very careful that Mary's possessiveness did not arouse antagonism among the other children. (There had been absolutely no resentment shown in the cafeteria although this type of behavior was a daily occurrence.) The teacher knew these facts: Mary lived with grandparents; her parents were divorced, and the father worked in another state. The child created fantasies of her father coming to see her; he never came. Several months earlier the mother had taken employment as a waitress in a large city several hundred miles away and had not been home to visit the daughter during this period. The grandparents fulfilled the child's physical needs, and she was fairly well dressed and clean. They completely failed to help the child in her emotional problem, which stemmed from feeling of rejection and attendant guilt feelings about her own contribution to parental rejection.

While all of this history was known to everyone in the small community, including Mary's two previous teachers, none had sensed the child's loneliness or great need for someone to tie to, until Miss Blank. The important point is that Miss Blank did not feel that she was doing something "nice" for Mary. She did not think of what she was doing as therapy. Her problem, as she saw it, was to protect Mary by concealing from the other children the fact that Mary was monopolizing the teacher. No change had yet occurred in Mary's reading behavior, but gradually she was able to bring some energy to bear on learning. Meeting the needs of children is therapy, and the more flexible and creative the reading teacher is in discerning the child's real needs, the more likely it is that she will alleviate present reading problems and forestall the appearance of others.

TEACHING AS THERAPY

Recently there have been a number of experiments and case studies which stress a therapeutic approach to dealing with reading problems. On this topic Smith writes: "A new frontier in reading remediation has opened—that of using psychotherapy as a part of the corrective program. Increasing numbers of reports on the combined use of therapy and reading instruction are appearing in educational literature."[7] Fisher suggests that some of the credit usually given to technique in remedial situations may actually belong to the therapeutic relationship established between tutor and pupil. Two groups of boys age 10-12, equated in I. Q., age, and reading age, were observed over a six-month period. The control group received only instruction in remedial reading, while the experimental group also received one hour per week of group therapy in which the boys were encouraged to talk about their problems, feelings, and experiences with an understanding tutor. This therapy group gained 3.25 months more in reading achievement than did the control group which received only remedial instruction. Fisher states:

---

[7] Nila B. Smith, "Therapy as Part of Remediation," *Reading Teacher*, IX (1955), 18.

> It has recently been suggested that in addition to the improvement of reading technique for the correction of reading disabilities, the psychotherapeutic relationship of the teacher, tutor or clinician was a major factor in the correction of the reading disability. *This suggests the possibility that all of the remedial methods may have had in common a psychotherapeutic relationship that arises when one person attempts to help another.*[8] (Emphasis added.)

R. G. Stauffer emphasizes that "therapists are in agreement that the treatment of symptoms is ineffective and undesirable. Remedial instruction, therefore, must give attention to the social and emotional status of the retarded reader and must provide instruction that effects functional adjustments psychologically as well as pedagogically."[9]

It has often been emphasized that no one technique or procedure is effective with every reading case. It is also true that the school or individual teacher is not equipped to deal with every case of maladjustment. The school is only one interacting institution which either gives or denies ego-fulfillment to the child, and it is not equipped to offset completely, or even to compensate for, poor social-emotional environments found in many homes. Several decades ago Arthur discussed the special training and abilities needed by tutors, clinicians, and teachers, who attempt to deal with reading-emotional problems. She pointed out that regardless of capability, hardly any tutor is equally effective in dealing with all types of children.[10]

As part of a project, each member of a group of experienced teachers worked individually over a period of months with a different child having a severe reading problem. These teachers met in group sessions to discuss the problems of the children they worked with and to share ideas. The emotional and social adjustment of the pupils

---

[8] Bernard Fisher, "Group Therapy with Retarded Readers," *Journal of Educational Psychology,* XLIV (1953), 354-60.

[9] R. G. Stauffer, "Basic Problems in Correcting Reading Difficulties," *Corrective Reading in Classroom and Clinic,* ed. Helen M. Robinson, University of Chicago, Supplementary Educational Monographs (Chicago: University of Chicago Press, 1956), No. 79, 118-26. Copyright 1956 by the University of Chicago.

[10] Grace Arthur, "Tutoring and Remedial Teaching as Educational Therapy," *Journal of Consulting Psychology,* IV (1940), 173-236.

came in for considerable discussion. A number of authorities were cited who emphasized that to work exclusively on reading with children whose behavior indicated emotional difficulties rarely resulted in appreciable gains in reading.[11] When the group was asked whether any of them attempted to use therapy, there was no response. Some wanted to know exactly what was involved in therapy.

Discussion developed the idea that therapy involved providing ego satisfactions, tension reduction, helping a child understand himself and tolerate his shortcomings, showing him that you do not treat him as a failure, and making him feel accepted. While admitting that they practiced these common-sense procedures, the teachers had not seen this as therapy. These experienced teachers had felt that therapy must take place in a clinic, be performed by a professional clinician, and be consciously planned.

The following quotation was read:

> What is therapy anyway? Is it anything that is good for a person—food, recreation, work, music and so on? Or does it have some more specific value, so that one can say this treatment is given to a patient to heal this disease, but would not be effective in treating that disease? Is intent the only criterion of therapy or must intent be backed up with reasonable evidence that this treatment may be effective? Must the person who administers the treatment be professional? Must the treatment be prescribed by a professionally skilled person? May it be administered by anyone sufficiently skilled to make it effective? Can we say that something is therapeutic even if it is not therapy?[12]

WHAT PRACTICES ARE THERAPEUTIC?

The group was surprised that the answers to these questions are not settled, that all therapy is not necessarily therapeutic, and that behavior can be therapeutic even though it has not been labeled

---

[11] Virginia Axline, "Nondirective Therapy for Poor Readers," *Journal of Consulting Psychology,* XI (1947), 61-69; Dorothy W. Baruch, "Therapeutic Processes As a Part of the Education Process," *Journal of Consulting Psychology,* IV (1940), 165-72; Henry S. Maas, "Applying Group Therapy to Classroom Practice," *Mental Health,* XXXV (1951), 250-59.

[12] George S. Stevenson, "Therapy-Therapeutic-Therapist," *Mental Hygiene,* XXXV (1951), 529-31.

therapy. The teachers were then asked to carefully write up some recent incident which had happened either in their classroom or during their work with the child being tutored. The only requirement was that the incident be one which they now judged as having been "therapeutic." These teachers had little difficulty in fulfilling this assignment, although one or two who gave excellent examples seemed pleasantly surprised with the idea that they had actually been involved in a relationship with a child which might merit the designation therapy.

Study 1. Examples given by teachers ran from the simple one of coping with disappointment stemming from a promise not immediately fulfilled to extremely complicated and threatening home and family deprivations. The following examples will no doubt remind experienced teachers of many similar incidents to which they were a party, which at the time may not have been specifically thought of as therapy. Mrs. L. S., who worked with an eight-year-old girl, reported the following:

> It was our third meeting. Kathy had been promised a new puppy that afternoon. For the oral reading a story was selected about two dogs playing a game of tag. After reading, we made a list of names that would be nice for a new baby puppy and discussed why some names would be better than others. Kathy went home happily, holding the paper with the list of names.
>
> The next day Kathy was disappointed; the puppy had not been delivered. She read from the filmstrip and from the chalkboard, but showed no desire to read from a book or to finish the story about the dogs. The next day I managed to have some nice pictures of puppies at play in the classroom when Kathy arrived. The first look at her face told me she had gotten the puppy and was ready for me to ask her about him. "Oh, so the puppy came," I said, to which she answered, jubilantly, "Yes, Mrs. S. I wish you could see him, he's a boy; he jumps, and runs, and does everything." "Wonderful," I exclaimed. "Now tell me what did you name him?" "Tiny," was the quick reply. "He was so little, and so *cute*. 'Tiny' seemed to fit best and my little brother John can say that real easy. Do you know what we did, Mrs. S? We put my doll clothes on Tiny and he looked so cute." After this we both had a good laugh and when asked what she would like to read today, she immediately answered, "I want to read the story about that other dog today." She did read it very nicely.

This is a simple and undramatic incident which indicates this teacher's recognition that even though she was providing special instruction for a child, reading cannot be separated from the child's total experience and needs. Second, this teacher recognized that the child needs to identify with an understanding adult. Third, this child, while very co-operative, did not have an overwhelming desire to read. However, the child was very deeply ego-involved in some things, in this case the acquisition of a puppy. This teacher made a successful effort to harness the child's ego to the reading task, and the result was a pleasant and profitable learning experience.

Study 2. The following is an example of a teacher's insight into a child's problem and how her awareness of his needs helped her in helping him.

> Phillip is a ten year old boy who apparently does not project himself very much. Until about ten days ago he had shown no indication of interests which one would expect of the average ten-year-old. Upon questioning him concerning such, his answer usually was, "I don't know," or "I guess," or "It's all right."
>
> When we started using the word games Phonics Rummy and Quizmo as an aid in helping Phillip with certain consonant blends, vowel sounds and pronunciation, he became so intent on playing the game he lost sight of the fact that the games were actually techniques which were to help with his reading difficulties. The games have helped reduce his difficulty in sounding unknown words.
>
> In Phonics Rummy Phillip won despite the fact that I was not particularly trying to help him win. He also won the Scramble game but not by such a wide margin. At the beginning of several sessions Phillip either had the Phonics Rummy game in his hand or was searching for it. Since he seemed to enjoy the games so much, we spent the first few minutes of each session playing Phonics Rummy. One morning during the course of the game Phillip said, "My sister makes all A's in school. She likes school." I wanted to know then if he didn't like school, to which he replied, "a little." Then I asked him what he liked best in school. His answer was, "Drawing." I then told him I would like for him to draw a picture for me because I was certain that he could draw beautifully. Phillip's face lighted up. (This was something for him as he seldom showed any emotion.) I told him how nice I thought his drawing was and suggested that he might be interested in taking art some day. He said he might.

I feel that Phillip needs to experience a feeling of success and achievement in some area. This is evident by the fact that he plays the games so intensely. The fact that he wins the Phonics Rummy game by a greater margin than the other games accounts for the fact that he prefers it. Winning the Phonics Rummy gives him a greater feeling of success. I think he feels inadequate because his sister does better scholastically than he.

I feel that not only does Phillip need to experience success in some phase of his school activity but he also needs to be helped to gain insight into his own problem. It is not healthy that Phillip needs to be best or that he is satisfied only when he is the winner.

However, it is only during the time that he is playing a game in which he is the winner that he has been able to talk even a little about that which might be worrying him.

Here we find a child frustrated by his relative position on the success-failure continuum. He is cautious about getting involved in competitive activities, since his own appraisal of his abilities tells him that he will fail and that he is inferior. Reading, along with other academic tasks, is one area in which he has much concrete evidence to support his concept of self as inferior. His older sister is the symbol of success to the parents and his teachers. Her superiority is known to him, along with the fact that he is occasionally compared with her. The course he follows is withdrawal whenever this response is possible; he can forestall failure by not getting involved. So far, his pattern of behavior does not include overt hostility. He is amazed to find an adult who is sincerely interested in him. Yet the prognosis is good, for he shows emotion when he is praised for his drawing. He responds to acceptance, yet at the same time he shows his tremendous need to succeed to defeat others.

This boy's teacher understood his needs and accepted his behavior. Her conclusion that "it is not healthy that Phillip needs to be best" is not an indictment of him but rather a road-marker for herself as she works with him in the future. Although she was engaged in a teaching-learning situation, what took place was therapeutic in nature, whether or not it was seen by her as therapy.

Study 3. The following is a report of an incident which occurred in the reporting teacher's regular sixth grade classroom.

I noticed that one of my pupils, a very attractive, clean, quiet, and courteous child was becoming an isolate. I noticed that he tried time and again to be friends with some of the other pupils in the room and they tried in many ways to discourage his friendship. I was unable to detect anything in his behavior that would merit the type of treatment that he was receiving. He seemed very listless and his work was not what I felt he could do.

I went to his cumulative folder and looked for evidence that could indicate trouble. I could find nothing there.

I inquired at various places and finally pieced together this data: The boy's mother left the family, divorced the father, and remarried. The father was a skilled laborer, very dependable, having worked for the same firm many years. His work necessitated his being away from home on occasion. At the moment he was scheduled on a job which would keep him away from home for three weeks. He hired a woman to cook, work, etc., for this boy and a younger brother. Sometimes the boys stayed alone in the house nights. It made me sort of sick to think of two little boys alone in a big house. At this point I scheduled an interview with the father.

When the father came back after the three weeks, he came to my room. I was favorably impressed with him. He was a person that was easy to talk to and seemed quite responsible. I'm afraid I sort of let him have both barrels. I told him that the boy was having quite a problem and that I thought a lot depended upon him. I told him that I felt the boy needed his love and companionship at that time if he ever needed it and to try to take him with him fishing and the like. I told him that I would be in my room by eight every day and if the boy wanted to come early to visit with me to allow him to do so. The father began to co-operate very well. When he was home, he had to leave for work early but he would try to eat breakfast with the boy. The boy in my room would come in early and just visit or I would let him help me do odd jobs around the room. This continued regularly for about three months. He was allowed to bring many relics that the father brought home from the Pacific Area. This included native combs, models of outrigger canoes, etc. The other children in the class were very interested in these. Gradually I found them accepting him more and more. The father was quite an artist and I suggested that he could help the boy with his notebook on the South Pacific. The boy's work improved and I found that he gradually was spending more time out on the playground playing with the other youngsters. He apologized for not coming in and I assured him that I was glad he was having fun outdoors and that I was pretty well caught up on things that had to be done in the room before school.

By Easter he was accepted by the group. The father remarried and the boy told me about his new mother. Although he was just a little uncertain as to how he felt toward her, his actions indicated that he was pretty happy and seemed contented.

On the achievement tests given in the spring I found that he had made two to three years growth in all subjects. That brought him nearly up to normal sixth grade work. I think that the testing of the year before was not valid because of the emotional strain he was under.

One fortunate circumstance in this case was that the father could "take both barrels" without resentment. Another was that the boy had not yet developed hostile responses to the rejection he experienced from his peers.

Study 4. The concluding example illustrates an incident which is highly creative on the part of the child, a ten-year-old boy who was a very poor reader. The teacher was alert to the ego-strengthening potential in this situation and let the child enjoy success in peripheral activities which in turn helped him face his reading weakness somewhat more realistically because he had this success to bolster him.

During our fifth and sixth reading lessons Jack read *Why Cowboys Sing, in Texas.* I had suggested this book because Jack said he liked to sing. During our next lesson we worked with the tape recorder. We had used the recorder once before, and Jack had recorded a song that I had taught him. When he finished reading, he wanted to record the song again. When he finished, he said he would like to record a song he made up about Slim Jim Bean.

We decided to make a written copy of the song. Jack worked the recorder while I wrote. He can't write or spell very well. When I finished copying the song, Jack said he would like to have a copy of the song to take home to show his parents what he was doing.

We talked about music and Jack said that someday he would like to major in music. I asked him if he played any musical instrument and he said that he played the trumpet. He said his parents were very proud of him for his music accomplishments.

I asked Jack if he was able to do anything else, like making up stories. He said, "Sometimes I like to make up poems." I told him I was very pleased with his song, because it was his own idea; also it proved he could remember and enjoy what he had read. This quality was, I told him, what made a person a good reader.

It should be kept in mind that all of these examples were supplied by teachers out of their personal experience. However, most of the examples come from situations where the teacher worked with one child for a given period of time, an advantage which made it possible for her to observe closely and to give the child the attention and help needed. The point that they were able to perceive needs, plan activities to meet needs, and understand the therapeutic impact of their relationships with the pupil, indicates that when the conditions under which teachers' work permit it, they are capable of meeting the emotional needs of children.

Most of the therapy taking place in the classroom is neither flashy, dramatic, nor systematically planned. A teacher perceives symptoms of social-emotional problems or needs and then takes steps to make the child feel accepted or a little more sure of himself and his place in the group. Various symptoms are known to any adult, but teachers, by the nature of their role, should be more sensitive in detecting loneliness, shyness, feelings of inferiority, lack of belonging, need for success, and lack of confidence in both social and academic situations.

BIBLIOTHERAPY

Another type of therapy available to classroom teachers is found in reading materials themselves. Reading provides vicarious experiences, and it is through experience that children work out their problems. Whether these solutions are inadequate, unrealistic. or desirable depends on the experiences and the person's reaction to them. Russell and Shrodes state: "*Bibliotherapy* may be defined as a process of dynamic interaction between the personality of the reader and literature—interaction which may be utilized for personality assessment, adjustment and growth."[13]

In order to see how literature affects individuals, we might start with a discussion of the pre-school child. Children are enthralled by stories read to them. If you are a parent, you probably recall certain favorite stories which never seemed to lose their appeal for your

---

[13] D. H. Russell and C. Shrodes, "Contributions of Research in Bibliotherapy to the Language Arts Program," *School Review*, LVIII (1950), 335-42.

child, regardless of how often the stories were heard. In fact, long after you felt that the child could not possibly be interested in hearing that story again, he would insist on hearing it. Maybe on some occasion you attempted to skip a page or two only to have him stop you and point out the omission. Perhaps you noticed that each time you went through a certain passage the child would ask the same question or make the same statement.

On the other hand, there would be certain stories which, after having heard once, the child never selected again. Some stories you might start only to have him select another one. It is doubtful that you attempted to determine the reasons for these choices. It was common sense to conclude that he liked some stories better than others. Also, at this age you could expect no help if you asked him why he liked this story. It would be hard to deny that something other than the literary tastes of two- or three-year-olds enters into these choices. The following is an excerpt from a case history, which, although a very small sample of behavior, is quite suggestive of a child's needs in relation to literature.

> A boy (age approximately 3 years), both parents living and together, social-economic status high. Child read to quite a good deal, has many children's books. The mother relates the following: "He likes for me to read to him before he goes to bed and I do just about every night. His favorite story just now is the *Three Little Kittens*. He likes that to be the last story, but he will not go to bed until he has been assured several times that 'the naughty kittens are okay now.' "
>
> "Did they find their mittens?" he asks.
>
> "Yes, they found their mittens."
>
> "Kittens okay now?"
>
> "Yes, kittens are all right now."
>
> The mother states that the boy dislikes the poem "Dapple Grey." She thinks it is because the woman in the poem whipped the pony. The child has never been subjected to any corporal punishment with the exception of an occasional light slap on the hand accompanied by "no-no!"
>
> A tenable hypothesis is that the child identified with the three little kittens whose behavior displeased their mother. The kittens were in fact rejected for their behavior, but they were able to reinstate themselves in their mother's affection and they were fed pie, a most demonstrative form of affection and reward. Having identified with the kittens, reassurance that all was well with them was necessary before the child felt entirely secure. Thus, the insistence on the happy ending. Even the

wisest parent is sometimes unaware of the innumerable times each day a child of two or three years engages in behavior which results in reproof, scolding, and disapproval. The child, like the kittens, has much to learn about property and propriety, and while he cannot understand the terms which we have used to describe the situation, he does grasp the dynamics of the authority-child, affection-rejection situation.

The aim of the discussion above is to point up the fact that children use stories and literature as a means of finding parallels to their own problems and needs even before they can read themselves. The possibility of using bibliotherapy, of course, increases with age, understanding, and the acquisition of mental age and insight in dealing with concepts.

In an analysis of the bibliotherapeutic value of a series of books by Clara Ingalls Wilder, it is suggested that this author's writings help children with the solution to problems in such areas as gaining maturity, fears and misunderstandings, and physical, intellectual, and moral achievement, as well as dealing with the growing-up process which reflects the child's need for material and emotional security. Wenzel states: "There are many people who know a great deal about books and many others who are thoroughly familiar with children. It is only in the last few years, however, that attempts have been made to bring books and children together."[14] It is encouraging that an increasing number of teachers are becoming interested in the value of books and literature as a means of helping children help themselves in dealing with their personal problems.

THE USE OF BIBLIOTHERAPY

There are many suggested helps in the literature for teachers desiring to use bibliotherapy in their classroom. Russell discusses procedures appropriate for use in guidance programs and lists books dealing with topics such as adoption and foster homes, belonging to the group, family relations, working with others, and the like.[15]

---

[14] Evelyn Wenzel, "Little House," "Books of Laura Ingalls Wilder," *Elementary English*, XXIX (1952), 65-74.

[15] David H. Russell, "Adventuring in Literature with Children," *Association for Childhood Education*, Washington, D. C., Leaflet No. 5.

Shrodes stresses the value of using literature as a means of providing vicarious experiences, stating: "Bibliotherapy is made possible by the shock of recognition the reader experiences when he beholds himself, or those close to him, in a story or some other piece of literature."[16]

Bibliotherapy, while particularly well-suited for children showing symptoms of maladjustment, should also be considered as a method of presenting challenging ideas, promoting growth in concepts, and developing insight into one's own behavior, for all children, whether maladjusted or not. Reading literature or viewing drama provides many psychological outlets. Any adult who can recall his own growing-up process can probably also recall some emotional experiences stemming from reading or seeing plays or movies. Reading lends itself to practically all of the mechanisms of adjustment: compensation for weaknesses and failures; identification with heroes, and, in the same process, the identification of qualities and behaviors which the society respects and rewards; a haven for withdrawal; a substitute for overt aggression.

One of the virtues of using reading as a form of therapy is that the reader remains in control of the degree to which he becomes involved in identifications. His discoveries of self will usually not be traumatic. He can gain insight into his own problems (and behaviors) at a pace which he can tolerate. Therapeutic values may be inherent in reading materials anywhere on the literary continuum from the *Three Little Kittens* to Dostoevsky's *Notes from the Underground.*

The teacher's task is to perceive the child's needs, bring the child and the right book together,[17] draw out meanings from the book by questioning, and help the child develop confidence and self-assurance as insight permits him to see himself and his problems mirrored in what he reads.

YOUR POINT OF VIEW?

1. Emotional factors are no more important in the learning of reading than in any learning situation.

---

[16] Caroline Shrodes, "Bibliotherapy," *Reading Teacher*, IX, (1955), 24-29.

[17] Nancy Larrick, *A Teacher's Guide to Children's Books* (Columbus: Charles E. Merrill Books, Inc., 1960).

2. Inadequate reading ability, or failure to learn to read well enough to meet the demands of the school curriculum, is a factor in producing anti-social behavior and delinquency.

3. Teachers should not become involved in trying to alleviate pupils' emotional problems because the teacher as a rule is not trained to do this.

4. In most remedial reading situations the method of approach is less important in changing reading behavior than is the type of relationship established between teacher and child.

5. Educators have been derelict in interpreting to the general public the relationship between emotional factors and learning to read.

BIBLIOGRAPHY

Alpert, Agusta. "Education as Therapy," *Psychoanalytic Quarterly,* X (1941), 468-74.

Arthur, Grace. "Tutoring and Remedial Teaching as Educational Therapy," *Journal of Consulting Psychology,* IV (1940), 173-76.

Axline, Virginia. "Nondirective Therapy for Poor Readers," *Journal of Consulting Psychology,* XI (1947), 61-69.

Baruch, Dorothy W. "Therapeutic Processes as Part of the Education Process," *Journal of Consulting Psychology,* IV (1940), 165-72.

———. "Incorporation of Therapeutic Procedures as Part of the Educative Process," *American Journal of Orthopsychiatry,* XII (1942), 659-65.

Bell, John E. "Emotional Factors in the Treatment of Reading Difficulties," *Journal of Consulting Psychology,* IX (1945), 125-31.

Bills, Robert E. "Nondirective Play Therapy with Retarded Readers," *Journal of Consulting Psychology,* XIV (1950), 140.

Bixler, Ray H. "Treatment of a Reading Problem through Nondirective Play Therapy," *Journal of Consulting Psychology,* IX (1945), 105-18.

Blanchard, Phyllis. "Reading Disabilities in Relation to Maladjustment," *Mental Hygiene,* XII (1928), 772-88.

———. "Reading Disabilities in Relation to Difficulties of Personality and Emotional Development," *Mental Hygiene,* XX (1936), 384-413.

———. "Attitudes and Educational Disabilities," *Mental Hygiene,* XIII (1929), 550.

Clothier, Florence. "The Treatment of the Rejected Child," *Nervous Child,* III (1943-44), 89-110.

Edelston, H. "Educational Failure with High Intelligence Quotient: A Clinical Study," *Journal of Genetic Psychology* (1950), 77, 85, and 116.

Ephron, Beulah Kanter. *Emotional Difficulties in Reading*. New York: Julian Press, Inc., 1953.

Evoy, John J. "Mental Hygiene and the Teacher," *Education*, LXXVIII (February, 1958) 341-45.

Fendrick, Paul, and Bond, Guy L. "Delinquency and Reading," *Pedagogical Seminary and Journal of Genetic Psychology* XLVIII (1936), 236-43.

Fisher, Bernard. "Group Therapy with Retarded Readers," *Journal of Educational Psychology*, XLIV (1953), 354-60.

Fleege, Urban H. "The Child's Emotional Health and the Teacher," *Catholic Educational Review*, LV (May, 1957), 312-20.

Gates, Arthur I. "Failure in Reading and Social Maladjustment," *NEA Journal*, XXV (1936), 205-6.

———. "The Role of Personality Maladjustment in Reading Disability," *Journal of Genetic Psychology*, LIX (1941), 77-83.

Harris, Albert J., and Roswell, Florence G. "Clinical Diagnosis of Reading Disability," *Journal of Psychology*, XXXVI (1953), 323-40.

Hirschberg, J. Cotter. "The Education of Emotionally Disturbed Children," *American Journal of Orthopsychiatry*, XXIII (1953), 684-90.

Kanner, Leo. "The Role of the School in the Treatment of Rejected Children," *Nervous Child*, III (1943-44), 236-48.

Kolesnik, Walter B. "Mental Health and Mental Discipline," *Catholic Educational Review*, LVIII (February, 1960), 73-77.

Lambert, Philip. "The Principal and the Problem Child," *Elementary School Journal*, LX (November, 1959), 75-83.

Larrick, Nancy. *A Teacher's Guide to Children's Books*. Columbus: Charles E. Merrill Books, Inc., 1960.

Louttit, C. M. "Emotional Factors in Reading Disabilities: Diagnostic Problems," *Elementary School Journal*, LVI (October, 1955), 68-72.

Maas, Henry S. "Applying Group Therapy to Classroom Practice," *Mental Hygiene*, XXXV (1951), 250-59.

McKenzie, Marion. "Orientation in Clinical Approach through Remedial Reading Instruction," *American Journal of Orthopsychiatry*, XII (1942), 325-34.

McGann, Mary. "Dramatic Dialogues for Simultaneous Treatment of Reading and Personality Problems," *Journal of Educational Psychology*, XXXVIII (1947), 96-104.

Mehus, Hilda. "Learning and Therapy," *American Journal of Orthopsychiatry*, XXIII (1953), 416-21.

Missildine, W. H. "The Emotional Background of Thirty Children with Reading Disabilities with Emphasis on Its Coercive Elements," *Nervous Child,* V (1946), 263-72.

Odenwald, Robert F., and Shea, Joseph A. "Emotional Problems of Maladjustment in Children with Reading Difficulties," *American Journal of Psychiatry,* CVII (1951), 890-93.

Persons, Gladys L., and Grumbly, Mary H. "Group Guidance in the Program of a Reading Laboratory," *Journal of Educational Psychology,* XLI (1950), 405-16.

Preston, Mary I. "Reading Failure and the Child's Security," *American Journal of Orthopsychiatry,* X (1940), 234-52.

Robinson, H. M. "Treatment of Severe Cases of Reading Disability," *Journal of Educational Research,* (March, 1939), 531-35.

Ryan, W. Carson. "The Emerging Concept of Mental Health in Education," *Review of Educational Research,* XXVI (December, 1956), 417-28.

Sister Mary Xavier, O.S.U. "Fostering Security of Youth through Guidance Programs," *Catholic Educational Review,* LVIII, (January, 1960), 34-43.

Smith, David Wayne. "Schools and the Emotionally Disturbed," *Education,* LXXX (December, 1959), 195-200.

Smith, Nila B. "Research on Reading and the Emotions," *School and Society,* LXXXI (1955), 8-10.

———. "Therapy As a Part of Remediation," *Reading Teacher,* IX, (1955), 18-23.

Spache, George D. "Personality Characteristics of Retarded Readers As Measured by the Picture-Frustration Study," *Educational Psychology Measurement,* XIV (1954), 186-92.

———. "Personality Patterns of Retarded Readers," *Journal of Educational Research,* L (February, 1957), 461-69.

Stauffer, R. G. "Basic Problems in Correcting Reading Difficulties," *Corrective Reading in Classroom and Clinic,* No. 79 (1953), 118-26.

Staver, Nancy. "The Child's Learning Difficulty As Related to the Emotional Problem of the Mother," *American Journal of Orthopsychiatry,* XXVIII (1953).

Stevenson, George S. "Therapy—Therapeutic—Therapist," *Mental Hygiene,* XXXV (1951), 529-31.

Sylvester, E., and Kunst, M. S. "Psychodynamic Aspects of the Reading Problem," *American Journal of Orthopsychiatry,* XIII (1943), 69-76.

Talbot, Mira, and Henson, Isabelle. "Pupils Psychologically Absent from School," *American Journal of Orthopsychiatry,* XXIV (1954), 381-90.

Tulchin, S. H. "Emotional Factors in Reading Disabilities in School Children," *Journal of Educational Psychology,* XXVI (1936), 443-54.

Vorhaus, P. G. "Non-Reading As an Expression of Resistance," *Rorschach Research Exchange,* X (1946), 60-69.

———. "Rorschach Configurations Associated with Reading Disability," *Journal of Projective Techniques,* XVI (1952), 3-19.

Zachry, Caroline B. "The Psychotherapist and the School," *Nervous Child,* III (1943-44), 249-57.

Zolkos, Helena H. "What Research Says about Emotional Factors in Retardation in Reading," *Elementary School Journal,* LI (1951), 512-18.

chapter 11

SEX DIFFERENCES IN LEARNING TO READ

Even though there are many studies which purport to throw light on the question of whether boys and girls differ in their ability to master the process of reading, this issue has remained somewhat clouded. One of the complicating factors is that the culture, and the school as part of the culture, may have unconsciously assumed that there is no difference between the sexes. This preconception could stem from the following factors:

1. Standardized achievement tests are built and used on the basis that the "norms" are equally adequate for both sexes. Reading readiness tests use the same problems and the same norms for both sexes. This is also true of reading tests and achievement tests used throughout the grades.
2. American schools in their actual practice have rejected the idea of any sex difference in learning to read, since both boys and girls enter school at the same chronological age.
3. Since the American schools recognize no sex differences, it is a simple matter to assume that there are none.

It is often alleged that the studies on sex differences in reading ability are not in agreement in their reported findings. In other words, the data are said to be inconclusive on this subject. In part, the inconclusiveness of the data stems from the fact that studies which are not actually comparable are sometimes treated as if they were.

Whether two studies are comparable depends on the answers to the following questions:

1. Do the studies deal with the same age group?
2. Are the sexes equated on M.A., I.Q., past experiences, etc.?
3. When grade level is the criterion, is C.A. equated within the grade level?
4. Are the measuring instruments comparable?
5. Are the statistical procedures in both studies comparable?

Assume that Study A, testing six- and seven-year-olds, finds girls superior to boys in reading, and Study B, testing ten-and eleven-year-olds, finds no statistical difference between the sexes. These studies should not be thought of as comparable, and contrary findings should not be viewed as canceling each other. The point here is that, if the issue is to discover sex differences in learning to read, we should be most interested in the early elementary age levels.

Assume that one study tested four facets of achievement customarily measured at a given grade level. Girls were superior on X subtest, and boys were superior on Y subtest, while no statistically significant differences were found on subtests W and Z. Now, if subtests W-X-Y-Z are lumped together under the heading Achievement, the conclusion may emerge that there is no sex difference. However, if X is considered alone, girls were found superior; if Y is considered alone, boys were found superior. The question is whether each of the subtests W-X-Y-Z is equally related to learning reading. Unfortunately, many studies are based on the cancellation process, and conclusions that there are no sex differences is often advanced in situations similar to the illustration above.

Another problem which clouds the issue is whether disparities reported in different studies are actually statistically significant—that is, are the differences real, or does the difference stem merely from chance factors? Four methodological practices bear on this problem: (1) Some experimenters have reported differences but have not tested their results for significance; (2) different studies employ different statistical procedures for arriving at conclusions of statistical significance; (3) different experimenters use different criteria for establishing statistical significance;[1] (4) conclusions advanced by experimenters are not always completely supported by their data.

Despite the fact that our schools operate from a premise of no sex differences in reading and that standardized readiness and reading tests also seem to embrace this hypothesis, many teachers and educators do feel that there are real differences between boys as a group and girls as a group in the way they respond to the learning situation labeled "learning to read."

The more one delves into the literature on reading (and nonreading), the harder it becomes to believe that there are no differences between the sexes in mastering the beginning stages of reading. It would be extremely difficult, if not impossible, to find a sizeable group of experienced teachers in the primary grades who, on the basis of their experience, could say that boys as a group and girls as a group are equally inept at mastering the reading process during the first few years of formal instruction.

The purpose of this discussion is to focus attention on sex differences in learning to read. The period dealt with is arbitrarily limited to the elementary years, with emphasis on the primary grades.

DATA RELATED TO SEX DIFFERENCES IN LEARNING READING

As studies are reviewed the cautions mentioned above must be kept in mind. The problem is not a simple process of counting so many studies reporting differences and so many reporting no differences. The effect of a study reporting differences between seven-year-old boys and girls is not cancelled or refuted by a study reporting no differences between high school boys and girls.

The sources of data on this topic fall into three main categories:

1. Data from school situations where the two sexes are compared on reading achievement. *Reading achievement* may include many different subheadings.

---

[1] One experimenter may insist that a real difference is established only if he could expect to find a difference, as large as he found, once in one hundred times. Another might accept five chances out of one hundred as significant.

2. Data reported from clinical sources, child-guidance clinics, and reading laboratories and clinics.

3. Summaries of the research in this area. Usually these summaries attempt to "compare" and to evaluate findings to some degree.

Representative studies from each of the categories listed above will be cited, starting with data from school situations. The question we are dealing with is, do boys as a group differ from girls as a group in their response to a particular situation called "learning the fundamentals of reading"?

Ayres[2] was one of the first to call attention to sex differences in school achievement. His book *Laggards in Our Schools* does not deal with differences in reading per se. However, he pointed out that 12.8 per cent more boys than girls repeated grades; that 17.2 per cent more girls than boys completed "common school" (eighth grade); and that there was 13 per cent more retardation among boys.

St. John[3] reported no significant difference in the measured intelligence of approximately one thousand pupils in grades one through four, but stated that girls very distinctly excel boys in reading at grade levels one through four. The study covered a four-year period and reported that boys showed 7 per cent more repeating of grades or non-promotions than did girls.

Heilman, using 482 girls and 464 boys (ten-year-olds) as subjects, measured a number of facets of reading and reported that the total reading scores favored girls. The difference was not statistically significant (ninety-two chances in one hundred that the true difference between boys and girls was above zero). On language usage girls were superior, but not significantly so while on spelling girls were significantly superior.[4]

Wilson, *et al.*,[5] reports a study covering three years at Horace Mann School. Boys and girls in first grade showed no differences on mental

---

[2] Leonard Ayres, *Laggards in Our Schools* (New York: Russell Sage Foundation, 1909).

[3] Charles W. St. John, "The Maladjustment of Boys in Certain Elementary Grades," *Educ. Adm. and Super.*, XVIII (1932), 659-72.

[4] J. D. Heilman, "Sex Differences in Intellectual Abilities," *Journal of Educational Psychology*, XXIV (1933), 47-62.

[5] Frank T. Wilson, Agnes Burke, and C. W. Flemming, "Sex Differences in Beginning Reading in a Progressive School," *Journal of Educational Research*, XXXII (1939), 570-82.

tests, but the authors state "... the difference between girls and boys in paragraph reading in this grade was statistically reliable." In reading at second grade level "the average of chances was 88 in 100 that the girls would be superior." At third grade level, girls surpassed the boys but not significantly. It should be pointed out that the intelligence level of the pupils in this study was considerably above the mean for all children their age.

Alden, *et al.*,[6] reports data from children in grades two through six who were tested with the Durrell Sullivan Reading Capacity Test.[7] Over six thousand children were tested and the number of boys who were one or more years retarded in reading was double that of girls in each of the first five grades. Table 6 gives the data on these sex differences.

TABLE 6

SEX DIFFERENCES BETWEEN BOYS AND GIRLS IN READING RETARDATION MEASURING ONE YEAR OR MORE RETARDATION

Grade	Per cent Boys Retarded	Per cent Girls Retarded
2	9.7	4.2
3	14.7	7.1
4	23.6	12.0
5	25.5	11.6
6	13.7	9.9

One of the most significant studies on sex differences was reported by Stroud and Lindquist in 1942.[8] Over three hundred schools with 50,000 pupils were the source of data. The data compiled covered a

[6] Clara Alden, Helen B. Sullivan, and Donald Durrell, "The Frequency of Special Reading Disabilities," *Education*, LXII (1941-42), 32-6. By permission of the Bobbs-Merrill Co. Inc., Indianapolis, Indiana.

[7] *Durrell Sullivan Reading Capacity Test* (Tarrytown-on-Hudson, New York: World Book Company).

[8] J. B. Stroud, and E. F. Lindquist, "Sex Differences in Achievement in the Elementary and Secondary Schools," *Journal of Educational Psychology*, XXXIII (1942), 657-67.

number of years of testing in the Iowa schools, using the Iowa Every-Pupil Basic Skills Test. In this program, grades three through eight are tested on reading comprehension, vocabulary, word study skills, basic language skills, and arithmetic skills. The authors state, "Girls have maintained a consistent, and on the whole, significant superiority over boys in the subjects tested, save in arithmetic, where small insignificant differences favor boys." Table 7 shows the mean difference in reading comprehension scores between boys and girls for grades three through eight. It should be noted that the largest differences occur at grades three and four and decline significantly at grade six.

TABLE 7

SEX DIFFERENCES IN READING COMPREHENSION AS MEASURED BY THE IOWA EVERY-PUPIL TEST OF BASIC SKILLS

Grade	Mean Differences (all favoring girls)	Significance Ratios
3	2.12	2.57
4	2.75	3.38
5	1.29	1.77
6	.30	.39
7	.10	.14
8	.47	.50

Jackson wished to ascertain whether advanced readers and retarded readers could be differentiated on the basis of psychological, social, or environmental factors. He selected 300 advanced readers and 300 retarded readers in grades two through six. The criterion for selection was that pupils fall in either the upper quarter or the lower quarter of their grade in reading ability. The significant fact is that Jackson found a disproportionate number of girls (59 per cent) among the advanced readers and a disproportionate number of boys (63.3 per cent) among the retarded readers. He states, "The data reveal a statistically significant difference between the sexes in relation to reading ability."[9]

[9] Joseph Jackson, "A Survey of Psychological, Social, and Environmental Differences Between Advanced and Retarded Readers," *Journal of Genetic Psychology*, LXV (1944), 113-31.

Pauley[10] is less reticent than most educators when considering whether real differences exist between boys and girls in school achievement and reading. He states that "there is a need for different legal entering ages (beginning school) for boys and girls." This position is warranted, he believes, on the basis of studies carried out over a period of ten years in the Tulsa schools. "Many children are not ready for the traditional first grade of public school when they are chronologically approaching six years of age; *particularly is this true of boys. Boys usually develop in nearly all respects more slowly than girls.*" (Emphasis added.) Pauley also cites data for over 1500 second grade pupils which show the mean chronological age of boys to be two months higher than that of girls, while in reading achievement the mean for the boys, as a group, is two months below that of the girls.

Hughes,[11] using the total comprehension scores from the Chicago Reading Tests, measured reading achievement of boys and girls in grades three through eight. She found that the greatest difference was at grade three, where the girls achieved more than a half school year above the boys. This difference favoring girls was significant at the 1 per cent level. At grade four the difference favoring girls was significant at only the 5 per cent level, while in grades five through eight girls made higher reading scores than did boys, but the differences were not statistically significant.

Nila, during the first weeks of school, tested three hundred first graders on a number of individual and group readiness tests. She reports that on the basis of these test scores the boys as a group and the girls as a group were equally ready to read. These pupils were tested at the end of the school year for reading achievement. Seventy-two were designated as reading failures; forty-five, or 63 per cent of the failures, were boys, and 37 per cent were girls.[12]

---

[10] Frank R. Pauley, "Sex Differences and Legal School Entrance Age," *Journal of Educational Research,* XXXV (1951), 1-9.

[11] Mildred C. Hughes, "Sex Differences in Reading Achievement in the Elementary Grades," *Clinical Studies in Reading II* (Chicago: University of Chicago Press, 1953), Supplementary Educational Monographs No. 77, 102-6.

[12] Sister Mary Nila, "Foundations of a Successful Reading Program," *Education,* LXXIII (1953), 543-55.

Prescott tested over 7,000 boys and 7,000 girls, beginning first grade, on the Metropolitan Readiness Test to determine whether this test showed sex differences. He reports that when chronological age is equated the performance of girls is superior to that of boys (difference favoring girls significant at the 5 per cent level).[13] Carroll also found sex differences in reading readiness at first grade level. These differences were in favor of girls, and were large enough to be statistically significant.[14]

Fabian reports data for 200 second grade pupils tested at the end of the school year on the Metropolitan Achievement Test, Primary II. Thirty-eight pupils were found to be more than a half year retarded in reading. When the pupils with low I.Q. and those with a history of interrupted schooling were removed from this group, there remained twenty cases designated as reading retardation cases. Nineteen of the twenty were boys.[15]

This is not an exhaustive treatment of the literature on sex differences in learning to read, but it is believed that the studies cited give a representative picture of the evidence on this topic. No data on junior high school, high school, or college reading habits are included because the data from these studies cannot help us with our original question, "Are there sex differences in learning the fundamentals of reading?" Other studies deal with sex differences in intelligence, achievement, and personality. No attempt was made here to review those studies or any which deal with sex differences in reading above the elementary grades.

In brief, the data cited above support the following conclusions:

1. Boys as a group are surpassed by girls as a group in reading achievement in grades one, two, and three.

2. The superiority in the reading ability of girls tends to diminish during the intermediate grades.

---

[13] George A. Prescott, "Sex Differences in Metropolitan Readiness Test Results," *Journal of Educational Research,* XLVIII (1955), 605-10.

[14] Marjorie W. Carroll, "Sex Differences in Reading Readiness at the First Grade Level," *Elementary English,* XXV (1948), 370-75.

[15] A. A. Fabian, "Reading Disability: An Index of Pathology," *American Journal of Orthopsychiatry,* XXV (1955), 319-29.

The second source of data on sex differences in reading is found in reports from clinical sources, such as child-guidance clinics and remedial reading clinics. Rarely do the data from these sources deal primarily with sex differences. As a rule, the titles of reported research do not indicate that sex differences are discussed, but, almost without exception, these studies reveal a disproportionate number of referrals of boys as compared with girls and, also, an even more disproportionate percentage of seriously retarded readers among boys. The range of percentages is from approximately 65 per cent boys and 35 per cent girls to 90 per cent boys and 10 per cent girls. Monroe reported an exhaustive study of over 400 children who had been referred to the Chicago Institute for Juvenile Research for various problems, including impaired reading. One group of 155 children was referred specifically for reading problems; in this group 86 per cent were boys and 14 per cent were girls.[16]

Blanchard,[17] in discussing seventy-three consecutive cases seen at the Philadelphia Child Guidance Clinic, in which reading was given as one reason for referral or where a reading problem was found to exist, reports that sixty-three of these cases were boys, and ten cases were girls.

Young, investigating forty-one cases diagnosed as retarded in reading and referred to the Psycho-Educational Clinic, Harvard University, reports that thirty-seven of the cases were boys and four cases were girls. He further reports that over a period of years this same ratio held for all children referred who were retarded in reading but had at least average intelligence.[18]

Preston[19] studied the effects of security-insecurity in the home, the school, and the social situation of retarded readers. In a sample of 100 reading failures possessing normal intelligence and no physical defects, there were seventy-two boys and twenty-eight girls.

---

[16] Marion Monroe, *Children Who Cannot Read* (Chicago: University of Chicago Press, 1932).

[17] Phyllis Blanchard, "Reading Disabilities in Relation to Difficulties of Personality and Emotional Development," *Mental Hygiene*, XX (1936), 384-413.

[18] Robert A. Young, "Case Studies in Reading Disability," *American Journal of Orthopsychiatry*, VIII (1938), 230-54.

[19] Mary J. Preston, "Reading Failure and the Child's Security," *American Journal of Orthopsychiatry* (1940), 239-52.

Missildine, studying the emotional adjustment of thirty retarded readers picked at random from clinic files, reported twenty-five of the thirty were boys. All but two of the children in this study were below ten years of age.[20]

McCollum, discussing forty severe reading disability cases referred to a reading clinic during one year, reports that 78 per cent were boys.[21] Axline reported a study of thirty-seven second graders selected on the basis of reading retardation or non-reading. Twenty-eight, or 76 per cent of the retarded readers, were boys.[22] Vorhaus described 225 reading disability cases seen at the New York University Reading Institute. One hundred and seventy-eight, or 80 per cent of these cases, were boys. All cases were reported as having average or better intelligence.[23] Johnson cites data gathered at Temple University Reading Clinic. Of thirty-four full-time tutored cases analyzed, 67 per cent of the cases were boys. The author states, "Among cases of extreme reading retardation, as many as two-thirds might be expected to be boys."[24]

Fabian reports on a group of 279 children given diagnostic tests at the Brooklyn Juvenile Guidance Center. Ninety-nine of these children were at least eight years of age, had I.Q.'s of eighty or above, and showed reading achievement at least 25 per cent below expectation based on mental age. Of these ninety-nine children, sixty-seven were boys, and thirty-two were girls.[25]

Many other clinical and remedial studies, particularly those of a "case study" nature, also report a preponderance of boys as remedial

---

[20] W. H. Missildine, "The Emotional Background of Thirty Children with Reading Disabilities with Emphasis on Its Coercive Elements," *Nervous Child*, V (1946), 263-72.

[21] Mary E. McCollum and Mary J. Shapiro, "An Approach to the Remediation of Severe Reading Disabilities," *Education*, LXVII (1947), 488-93.

[22] Virginia Axline, "Nondirective Therapy for Poor Readers," *Journal of Consulting Psychology*, XI (1947), 61-69.

[23] Pauline G. Vorhaus, "Rorschach Configurations Associated with Reading Disability," *Journal of Professional Teaching*, XVI (1952), 3-19.

[24] Marjorie S. Johnson, "A Study of Diagnostic and Remedial Procedures in a Reading Clinic Laboratory School," *Journal of Educational Research*, XLVIII (1955), 572.

[25] A. A. Fabian, "Reading Disability: An Index of Pathology," *American Journal of Orthopsychiatry*, XXV (1955), 319-29.

reading cases. However, these reports are not cited here because the number of cases they discuss is too small for evaluation. Table 8 summarizes the above data on sex differences in reading retardation from a number of studies, all of which reported on thirty or more cases.

TABLE 8

DATA SHOWING AUTHOR, YEAR OF PUBLICATION, NUMBER, AND PER CENT OF BOYS AND GIRLS REPORTED AS REMEDIAL READING CASES

Study	Year Published	Number of cases		Per Cent	
		Boys	Girls	Boys	Girls
Blanchard	1936	63	10	86	14
Young	1938	37	4	90	10
Preston	1940	72	28	72	28
Missildine	1946	25	5	83	17
McCollum Shapiro	1947	31	9	76	24
Axline	1947	28	9	76	24
Vorhaus	1952	178	47	80	20
Johnson	1955	23	11	67	33
Fry	1959	163	39	81	19

The third source of data on sex differences in learning to read is summaries of the literature. For several reasons these summaries are the least helpful of the three sources to the individual seeking information on differences in reading. First, the summaries deal with sex differences reported in the literature on all facets of human development, such as mental growth, physical growth, dexterity, personality, memory, school achievement, and the like. Second, the reviewers are not always careful to distinguish between the age groups studied. They sometimes tend to equate studies at radically different educational levels, thus possibly obscuring significant trends. Third, by the very nature of their task they are forced to interpret a vast amount of material, and in the process of abstracting and quoting they may follow and perpetuate an unconscious bias found in the literature. Fourth, summaries on sex differences are, as a rule, less concerned with children's learning reading skills than with other facets of development or achievement.

Allen's[26] summary of literature on sex differences emphasized research on motor development and social-personal behavior. His bibliography contained well over a hundred entries. Nevertheless, he had no section or comment devoted to differences in reading.

Johnson and Terman, discussing the literature on psychological sex differences, deal with two aspects of personality—social attitudes and emotionality. One statement which might be related to the data from child-guidance clinics and reading clinics is "that there is a significant difference between boys and girls in aggressiveness—there being more aggression among boys."[27]

Freeman and Miles summarizing sex differences in the *Encyclopedia of Educational Research* devote little attention to reading, but do state, "Girls usually excel in oral and silent reading, language usage, spelling, and handwriting."[28]

Terman and Tyler[29] treat reading in more detail than do the above-mentioned sources. Under the heading "Sex Differences in Ability" the authors list a number of generalizations which include the following points:

1. Intelligence tests in use today are not adequate for establishing differences in intelligence between the sexes.
2. Girls tend to excel on verbal tests; boys excel on quantitative or spatial tests.
3. School marks on achievement favor girls. Achievement tests on language materials show girls superior, while achievement tests in science and mathematics show boys superior.
4. Most ability differences do not show up at the pre-school period.

---

[26] C. W. Allen, "Recent Research on Sex Differences," *Psychology Bulletin*, XXXII (1935), 343-54.

[27] Winifred B. Johnson and Lewis M. Terman, "Some Highlights in the Literature of Psychological Sex Differences Published Since 1920," *Journal of Psychology*, IX (1940), 327-36.

[28] Frank Freeman and Catherine Miles, *Encyclopedia of Educational Research*, ed. Walter S. Monroe (Rev. ed.; New York: The Macmillan Co., 1952), 1205.

[29] Lewis M. Terman and Leona E. Tyler, "Psychological Sex Differences," *Manual of Child Psychology*, ed. L. Carmichael (2nd ed.; New York: John Wiley & Sons, Inc., 1954), Chap. 17.

The authors are willing to concede female superiority in "verbal fluency," but state: ". . . Most of the reading investigations reporting female superiority have been based on speed of reading tests. . . ." While this statement might be defensible if one were concerned only with data from upper grades, high school, and college subjects, it appears to be an overstatement if the early elementary grades are under consideration. This latter view is supported by the authors when they state, "School surveys using reading tests, if they show any significant differences, usually show higher scores for girls."[30]

The evidence seems to indicate that there are differences between boys as a group and girls as a group in learning the fundamental skills of reading in the primary grades, but it is not clear what causes these differences. A number of hypotheses have appeared in the literature which attempt to explain the data discussed in this chapter. Some of the more frequently mentioned hypotheses are listed and discussed below. The aim is not to attempt to prove or disprove these various points of view, but rather to present them for critical consideration.

1. *Boys and girls at certain ages differ in "intelligence."* This issue will probably have to go unresolved at the present because, as Terman points out, contemporary tests of intelligence are not constructed so as to point up differences. And if boys surpass girls on some items and girls surpass boys on other items, who is to say which items are the more valid indicators of general mental ability.[31]

2. *Boys and girls mature at different rates and some phases of growth are closely related to reading.* Since the data are conclusive that girls develop more rapidly than boys, this hypotheses is sometimes seen as the key to the problem under discussion. In skeletal development, girls as a group, are superior to boys throughout the pre-school period, and by the age of six years they are at least a full year in advance of boys. Since boys are less physiologically mature, eye muscles and visual acuity may not be equal to the task of beginning reading, and their attention span may not be developed enough to allow for lengthy concentration on teacher guidance. Maturation cannot be hastened through stress or training. The results of a large

[30] *Ibid.*, 1070.

[31] L. N. Terman, L. E. Tyler, *op. cit.*, 1068.

number of different experiments in language development present, practically without exception, data showing girls to be statistically superior in language usage and facility throughout the pre-school and primary periods.[32]

A long-term study carried out at the University of Michigan compares the chronological age at which boys and girls begin to read and the "rate of progress" made after each has mastered a certain level of reading ability. The authors report a significant difference favoring girls in the age of learning to read. However, once children achieved a reading age of eighty-four months on the Gates Primary Reading Test, no difference between boys' and girls' rate of advancement was found.[33]

The champions of the organismic age concept attempt to show a relationship between rate of development in many phases of growth, both physical and mental, and reading ability. Organismic age is the average of age scores on height, weight, mental age, dentition, grip, and the like. Thus, organismic age is weighted quite heavily with physical growth factors. For an explanation of the organismic age concept see Olson,[34] and Olson and Hughes. [35, 36] For a critical analysis of this concept see Blommers, *et al.*,[37] and Tyler.[38]

---

[32] Dorothea McCarthy, "Language Development in Children," *Manual of Child Psychology*, ed. Leonard Carmichael (New York: John Wiley & Sons, Inc.).

[33] Irving H. Anderson, Byron O. Hughes, and W. Robert Dixon, "Age of Learning to Read and Its Relation to Sex, Intelligence, and Reading Achievement in Sixth Grade," *Journal of Educational Research*, XLIX (1956), 447-53.

———. "The Rate of Reading Development and Its Relation to Age of Learning to Read, Sex, and Intelligence," *Journal of Educational Research*, L (1957), 481-94.

[34] W. C. Olson, "How Children Grow," *NEA Journal*, XXVI (1947), 436-37.

[35] W. C. Olson and B. O. Hughes, "The Concept of Organismic Age," *Journal of Educational Research*, XXV (1942).

[36] W. C. Olson and B. O. Hughes, "Growth of the Child as a Whole," *Child Behavior and Development*, ed. Roger G. Barker, *et al.* (New York: McGraw Hill Book Co., Inc., 1943), Chap. 12.

[37] P. Blommers, *et al.*, "The Organismic Age Concept," *Journal of Educational Psychology*, XLVI (1955), 142-50.

[38] F. T. Tyler, "Concepts of Organismic Growth: A Critique," *Journal of Educational Psychology*, XLIV (1953), 321-42.

3. *The school environment and curriculum at the primary level are more frustrating to boys than to girls.* This hypothesis is very closely related to the preceding one. For instance, if boys and girls mature at different rates it is logical to suppose that participating in the same classroom activity is not the same experience for each group. One group is more mature than the other, but each group is equally expected to do close work, make fine discriminations, sit quietly for extended periods of time, pay attention, co-operate, finish tasks, and inhibit aggression. Many educators think that these are the factors which frustrate boys as a group more than girls.

A study of over seven-hundred children in grades one through five who, due to academic retardation, were selected for special classes, showed boys outnumbering girls by a ratio of more than two to one. Yet the mental age of the boys was slightly, but not significantly, higher than that of the girls. It was concluded that boys were more interested in concrete things and in problem-solving in areas other than those which are purely linguistic. In other words, boys were more interested in unacademic things, as measured by the actual school curriculum, and were penalized for this. Noting that there was more instability among the boys, the author asked, "Is the instability of retarded boys an essential trait or one produced by a school environment that is not altogether fitting?"[39]

During the primary and early elementary years the emotional, personality, and behavioral problems which schools refer to various agencies include a disproportionate number of boys as compared with girls. Since boys are the poorer achievers, it follows that in our culture the school, the teacher, and the home (automatically but perhaps unconsciously) put more pressure on boys at this age level. Frustration results and is reflected in poor or inadequate responses in any stress situation, such as learning a very complicated symbol system. The disproportionate number of boys found as referrals to guidance clinics and reading clinics may be related to this cultural tendency.

Robinson is convinced that research supports a hypothesis of a sex difference in reading achievement during the first few years of formal

---

[39] Ethel Cornell, "Why Are More Boys Than Girls Retarded in School?" *Elementary School Journal*, XXIX (1928), 213-26.

schooling, but she states: "At present it is not clear whether just being a girl gives a young child a better chance for early reading success or whether something inherent in the school situation or the social setting militates against the progress of boys."[40] After pointing out that boys as a group produce more remedial reading problems, get lower school marks, have a higher incidence of non-promotion, and produce more "behavior problems" than do girls as a group, Smith and Jenson conclude, "all these findings emphasize the fact that the school functions less effectively for boys than for girls.[41]

4. *Basal reader materials are less motivating and satisfying to boys than to girls.* This idea is an extension of the preceding hypothesis, three, since the reading materials are naturally part of the curriculum. The rationale behind this hypothesis is that the rather sterile, repetitious "look, oh, look; see baby play" vocabulary and the rigid conformist mood, tone, and atmosphere contained in and conveyed by the pre-primers, primers, and early readers are considerably less challenging to boys than to girls. It is often alleged that the "content" is a far cry from what the culture has taught to and expects from boys. Therefore, beginning reading, which should be an exciting, challenging new adventure, is actually a dull, regressive sort of experience unless the teacher can project a great deal into the material.

It is highly doubtful that available data would substantiate this hypothesis, since there are not several radically different types of basal readers available for use in comparative studies. It should also be obvious that the lack of data does not disprove the hypothesis.

5. *Most primary teachers are women.* Allen states: "Social environments for males and females are not and never have been the same or equal," and points out that from this fact may stem differences in interests, values, and achievement.[42] Bell holds that the difference in reading success between boys and girls is related to their emotional relationships with their teachers. It is his opinion that it is easier for

---

[40] Helen M. Robinson, "Factors Which Affect Success in Reading," *Elementary School Journal,* LV (1955), 266.

[41] C. A. Smith and M .R. Jenson, "Educational, Psychological and Physiological Factors in Reading Readiness," *Elementary School Journal,* XXXVI (1936), 689.

[42] Allen, *op. cit.,* 343.

girls to identify with women teachers, and that boys are not provided with enough opportunities for the expression of aggression.[43] The various studies all agree that boys show more aggression and aggressive tendencies than do girls. Of course, the school frowns on aggressive behavior and no doubt influences some teachers to react toward boys in a manner different from that manifested toward girls who, as a group, may have a reputation for being docile, quiet, and co-operative. Terman[44] states that there is ample indication that some sort of "halo" effect operates in the classroom to give girls higher teacher ratings or grades than would be merited on the basis of objective achievement test results. St. John does not question the fact that in grades one through four girls "distinctly" excel boys in reading and general school achievement, but he states: "They (girls) excel *less* when achievement is measured by standard tests than when it is measured by *teacher marks*."[45] (Emphasis added.)

6. *Boys are less motivated to learn to read.* This hypothesis is closely related to certain others that have previously been mentioned, but it is advanced often enough in the literature on reading to be considered independently. Nila is of the opinion that girls are more likely to work up to the capacity of their abilities than are boys. She states: "The writer believes that the reason boys and girls who are equally ready to read do not make the same progress lies in the factor of motivation."[46] Wilson, *et al.*, states: "It would seem probable that the reasons for more rapid progress by girls are related to learning interests and dispositions, rather than to more subtle sex differences such as mental qualities or characteristics of femininity."[47]

SUGGESTIONS FOR ALLEVIATION OF THE PROBLEM

Coping with the problem of sex differences is a difficult problem, since, as stated previously, our schools tend to operate from the premise that in the early grades there are no significant sex difference in

[43] John E. Bell, "Emotional Factors in the Treatment of Reading Difficulties," *Journal of Consulting Psychology*, IX (1945), 125-31.

[44] Terman and Tyler, *op. cit.*, 1088.

[45] C. W. St. John, *op. cit.*

[46] Sister Mary Nila, *op. cit.*, 548.

[47] Frank T. Wilson, Agnes Burke, C. W. Flemming, *op. cit.*, 581.

learning to read. Although evidence from primary classrooms does not support this premise, established use is often accepted as the best of evidence that that practice is correct. Any of the factors mentioned above may be present in the case of an impaired reader without justifying the conclusion that the factors in question cause the impaired reading. On the other hand, rejecting all hypotheses would not reduce the ratio of failure among boys as compared with those among girls. Since reading is such an important achievement in our culture, educators should not think of sex differences in learning to read as just another statistic. If there is anything the school can do to prevent the present number of failures in learning to read, it should be done. The following suggestions attempt to focus on school practices which might alleviate this problem.

1. *Staggered school entrance* based on the demonstration of a maturity level (social, emotional, intellectual) which would assume readiness for reading tasks. A genuine pre-school or readiness program, with children moving into grade one at any time during the academic year, would likely be an outgrowth of following this practice. This proposal has several advantages: (1) De-emphasizing chronological age as the criterion for school entrance; (2) The initial number of pupils that first grade teachers have to deal with would be smaller, giving the teacher a chance to know each child better. As other pupils come in, she could spend more time getting to know them; (3) This practice would destroy the myth that all pupils in a given classroom should be doing the same tasks. The great disadvantage of the proposal is that it is too wide of a departure from present practice to be acceptable to schools and parents. The ungraded primary holds more promise at the moment.

2. *The ungraded primary,* functioning ideally, would encompass all the advantages listed above, since the child moves through the curriculum at his own rate. The concept of promotion is discarded for the primary grades, as is an arbitrary achievement schedule. Thus, the ungraded primary could permit the less mature, the less ready, to have a longer period of time to adjust to reading tasks without risking the stigma of failure. This plan is not a panacea, and the administrative framework alone will accomplish nothing. It is the philosophy and the practice in the classroom which give the plan value.[48]

---

[48] The ungraded primary plan is discussed in Chapter 4.

3. *An educational program for adults* which would explain the fact that children of a given chronological age are all not equally ready for the same tasks. In fact, before an ungraded primary plan could possibly be successful, parents and teachers would have to understand and accept this truth. Further, the fact should be accepted that a child's growth is not uniform and that there will be plateaus as well as normal and rapid growth periods.

4. *Less pressure* on children in learning to read would be a natural outcome if the preceding suggestion were acted upon in our schools and communities. This would have a salutary effect in reducing reading problems, particularly among those children who react adversely to pressure. Certainly, it is evident to observant teachers and clinicians that extreme pressure brought to bear in learning as complicated a symbolic process as reading often inhibits learning. Since boys as a group appear to suffer most from school and home pressures during the primary years, they would gain the most from a lessening of school and social pressures.

5. *More emphasis on psychological assessment* than we now have in the primary grades is essential if all children are to be taught effectively in the classroom. Five times as many boys as girls are referred to clinics after academic or behavioral problems are noted by the school. It seems likely that boys as a group would profit considerably from earlier diagnosis and guidance.

6. *Research on reading interests* of boys and girls, together with research on the nature and the content of required reading materials in the schools, might suggest changes which would be favorable to boys. This research would have to go far beyond the questionnaire method and would actually involve the use of quite varied materials.

YOUR POINT OF VIEW?

1. The teacher is not a causal factor in the disproportionate number of reading failures among boys as compared with girls.

2. The reading materials used in beginning reading are not more appropriate or interesting for girls than for boys.

3. Using the same chronological age as the basis for starting school is equally fair for boys as a group and girls as a group.

4. The elementary school curriculum and total environment is more frustrating for boys than for girls in our culture.

5. The school is an important contributing factor in the production of maladjustment and anti-social behavior.

6. Since research data tend to indicate that sex differences in reading are not significant at the end of the elementary school period, sex differences in learning to read are of little educational importance.

BIBLIOGRAPHY

Alden, Clara, Sullivan, Helen B., and Durrell, Donald. "The Frequency of Special Reading Disabilities," *Education,* LXII (1942), 32-36.

Allen, C. N. "Recent Research on Sex Differences," *Psychological Bulletin,* XXXII (1935), 343-54.

Anderson, Irving H., Hughes, Byron O., and Dixon, Robert W. "Age of Learning to Read and Its Relation to Sex, Intelligence, and Reading Achievement in Sixth Grade," *Journal of Educational Research,* XLIX (February, 1956), 447-53.

———. "The Rate of Reading Development and Its Relation to Age of Learning to Read, Sex, and Intelligence," *Journal of Educational Research* (March, 1957), 481-94.

Axline, Virginia. "Nondirective Therapy for Poor Readers," *Journal of Consulting Psychology,* XI (1947), 61-69.

Ayres, Leonard. *Laggards in Our Schools.* New York: Russell Sage Foundation, 1909.

Bell, John E. "Emotional Factors in the Treatment of Reading Difficulties," *Journal of Consulting Psychology,* IX (1945), 125-31.

Blanchard, Phyllis. "Reading Difficulties in Relation to Difficulties of Personality and Emotional Development," *Mental Hygiene,* XX (1936), 384-413.

Blommers, P., Knief, L., and Stroud, J. B. "The Organismic Age Concept," *Journal of Educational Psychology,* XLVI (1955), 142-50.

Carroll, Marjorie W. "Sex Differences in Reading Readiness at the First Grade Level," *Elementary English,* XXV (October, 1948), 370-75.

Cornell, Ethel. "Why Are More Boys than Girls Retarded in School?" *Elementary School Journal,* XXIX, 213-26.

Fabian, A. A. "Reading Disability: An Index of Pathology," *American Journal of Orthopsychiatry,* XXV (April, 1955), 319-29.

Freeman, Frank, and Miles, Catherine, *Encyclopedia of Educational Research,* ed. Walter S. Monroe. New York: The Macmillan Co., 1952, 1205.

Heilman, J. D. "Sex Differences in Intellectual Abilities," *Journal of Educational Psychology,* XXIV (1933), 47-62.

Hughes, Mildred C. "Sex Differences in Reading Achievement in the Elementary Grades, *Clinical Studies in Reading II,* Supplementary Educational Monographs, Chicago: University of Chicago Press, No. 77, 102-6.

Jackson, Joseph. "A Survey of Psychological, Social, and Environmental Differences between Advanced and Retarded Readers," *Journal of Genetic Psychology,* LXV (1944), 113-31.

Johnson, Winifred B., and Terman, Lewis M. "Some Highlights in the Literature of Psychological Sex Differences Published Since 1920," *Journal of Psychology* (1940), 327-36.

McCollum, Mary E., and Shapiro, Mary J. "An Approach to the Remediation of Severe Reading Disabilities," *Education,* LXVII (March, 1947), 488-93.

Missildine, W. H. "The Emotional Background of Thirty Children with Reading Disabilities with Emphasis on Its Coercive Elements," *Nervous Child* (July, 1946), 263-72.

Monroe, Marion. *Children Who Cannot Read.* Chicago: University of Chicago Press, 1932.

Nila, Sister Mary. "Foundations of a Successful Reading Program, *Education,* LXXIII (May, 1953), 543-55.

Olson, W. C. "How Children Grow," *NEA Journal,* XXVI (September, 1947), 436-37.

Olson, W. C., and Hughes, B. O. "The Concept of Organismic Age," *Journal of Educational Research,* XXV (March, 1942).

Pauley, Frank R. "Sex Differences and Legal School Entrance Age," *Journal of Educational Research,* XXXV (1951), 1-9.

Prescott, George A. "Sex Differences in Metropolitan Readiness Test Results," *Journal of Educational Research,* XLVIII (April, 1955), 605-10.

Preston, Mary J. "Reading Failure and the Child's Security," *American Journal of Orthopsychiatry,* X (1940), 239-52.

Robinson, Helen M. "Factors which Affect Success in Reading," *Elementary School Journal,* LV (January, 1955), 266.

Smith, C. A., and Jenson, M. R. "Educational, Psychological and Physiological Factors in Reading Readiness," *Elementary School Journal,* XXXVI (April, 1936), 689.

St. John, Charles W. "The Maladjustment of Boys in Certain Elementary Grades," *Educ. Adm. and Super.*, XVIII (1932), 659-72.

Stroud, J. B., and Lindquist, E. F. "Sex Differences in Achievement in the Elementary and Secondary Schools, *Journal of Educational Psychology,* XXXIII (1942), 657-67.

Terman, Lewis M., and Tyler, Leona E. "Psychological Sex Differences," *Manual of Child Psychology* (2nd ed.), L. Carmichael (ed.). New York: John Wiley & Sons, Inc., 1954. Chap. 17.

Tyler, F. T. "Concepts of Organismic Growth: A Critique," *Journal of Educational Psychology,* XLIV (1953), 321-42.

Vorhaus, Pauline G. "Rorschach Configurations Associated with Reading Disability," *Projective Techniques,* XVI (1952), 3-19.

Wilson, Frank T., Burke, Agnes, and Flemming, C. W. "Sex Differences in Beginning Reading in a Progressive School," *Journal of Educational Research,* XXXII (April, 1939), 570-82.

Young, Robert A. "Case Studies in Reading Disability," *American Journal of Orthopsychiatry,* VIII (1938), 230-54.

chapter 12

REMEDIAL READING

The failure of large numbers of children to learn how to read to the maximum of their ability is a major educational problem. Evidence that such a problem exists is found in the large amount of time and energy devoted to the educational practice called remedial reading. The practitioners of remedial reading can hardly fill the demand for their services. There are numerous college courses, workshops, conferences, in-service programs, and laboratories devoted to remedial reading.

REMEDIAL READING DEFINED

Remedial reading is usually associated with instruction which attempts to remedy a condition which it is believed can be remedied, i.e., a child reading considerably below his ability level. Confusion is sometimes introduced by the fact that children reading far below their capacity are referred to as remedial readers. It is a matter of record that many remedial *readers* can be found in schools where there is no provision for remedial *instruction*. Remedial reading implies instruction aimed at bringing a child's achievement closer to his actual ability and does not relate to grade level or chronological age norms. For instance, we might have two third grade pupils of the same age reading at a high first grade level, as illustrated below:

Child A	C. A. 8-4	M. A. 9-2	I. Q 110	Reads 1^2
Child B	C. A. 8-4	M. A. 7-0	I. Q. 84	Reads 1^2

Although both pupils are in the same grade and are reading at the same level, only pupil A should be thought of as a remedial reader. He has above-average intelligence, but he is learning at a rate far below his capacity. Child B, although in the third grade, is achieving as well as could be expected on the basis of his ability, and, according to the preceding definition, would not be a logical candidate for remedial reading. He is now learning about as rapidly and as thoroughly as can be expected. Should we decide to give him remedial instruction aimed at bringing him up to his grade level (or chronological age level), we would be implying that methodology or technique in instruction can actually compensate for a lack of ability as far as academic achievement is concerned. Since we do not believe this, it would be irrational to attempt to practice it. However, it is important to realize that when we take this position we assume that our assessment of his ability is accurate. Pupil A, who is reading slowly in view of his ability, might profit from a change in technique and from individual instruction in certain mechanics of reading. These practices might help him to move forward at a rate commensurate with his ability. This in essence is the philosophy behind remedial instruction.

It has been pointed out previously that reading ability is held in very high esteem in our culture and that children are expected to achieve up to an arbitrary grade-level standard. The fact that at least a third of all pupils in a given grade fall below this standard is well known to educators. Schools which are geared to mass education, a rigid grade level structure, and promotion without regard to mastery of skills, will continue to produce remedial readers.

Remedial reading, as it is usually understood, puts the onus of failure on the child who needs the remedy. Some authorities have suggested that the term should be *remedial teaching* so as to intimate that the teaching, not the pupil, is at fault. Neither position is always fair to either pupil or teacher when all factors in reading failures are considered.

It is easy for a teacher to blame the child who develops habits of laziness, inattention, disinterest, withdrawal, or aggression. It is just as easy for parents and critics of schools to blame schools and teaching methods or for teachers to blame parents and home environments. Fixing blame, unless the blame is clear-cut, is dangerous.

DEGREE OF IMPAIRMENT AS CRITERION FOR REMEDIAL INSTRUCTION

There is general agreement in the literature on remedial instruction that before the child can qualify for remedial reading the gulf between his ability and his achievement should measure at least a year. It should not be inferred that such a discrepancy will, as a general rule, result in a child's receiving special help in reading. Usually there are long histories of failure and frustration. Work in the area of remedial reading is often accompanied by a recognition of the dual tragedy of much unnecessary suffering experienced by children who fail and much educational energy expended in remedial rather than preventive efforts. In general, when our schools observe the maladjustment stemming from failure to learn, and when this maladjustment is expressed in behavior which the school does not condone, a remedy is advocated. All too often remedial reading is a form of educational penance in which schools and teachers practice the principles they believe in, but which they either failed to follow or found it impossible to follow, in the regular process of teaching reading.

COMMON MISCONCEPTIONS ABOUT REMEDIAL READING

Despite the widespread use of the term remedial reading, there is some degree of confusion regarding what it is, what practices it embodies, and who its practitioners are. Vague concepts often give rise to misconceptions. Some of these are discussed below.

The most widely held misconception is that remedial reading instruction is based on a set of principles which differ appreciably from those principles which are the basis for the school's regular developmental reading instruction. It is easy to see how such a misconception might develop. Virtually every college or university which prepares teachers for the elementary schools has one or more courses entitled "Remedial Reading," "Practices in Remedial Reading," or "Methods and Techniques in Remedial Reading." Many textbooks bear similar titles. Remedial reading clinics are found on almost every university campus. Schools hire "Remedial Reading Teachers." Workshops devoted to remedial reading are commonplace. With this much evidence it is easy to conclude that remedial reading is a subject matter different from the teaching of reading. It is sometimes difficult to convince teachers that all of the principles and most of the practices which are characteristic of remedial reading are also applicable to developmental reading.

An illustration of this point is found in the behavior and the attitudes of two groups of teachers enrolled in different sections of a course entitled "Remedial Techniques in Reading." In the first section the instructor stated that there were not two distinct approaches, one regular and the other remedial, to teaching reading. Some teachers seemed skeptical and were quite reluctant to accept this point of view. In the second class a different approach was tried. Each student was handed a sheet of paper and was asked to list all of the principles of teaching which she identified with remedial reading. The major points mentioned included:

1. Go back to the child's present reading level.
2. Do not expect the child to read material which forces him to experience failure, i.e., he must have developed readiness for the task.
3. Help the child build self-confidence—use abundant praise. Undue pressure in the learning situation may interfere with learning.
4. Use a variety of approaches.
5. Base instruction on a thorough diagnosis.
6. Build interest in reading—have a large stock of supplementary reading materials.

As each point was mentioned, the group noted that it applied equally well to any good classroom program. It was conceded that no principles had been listed which applied exclusively to remedial reading.

A second misconception centers around the practices and the procedures believed to be reserved to remedial reading instruction. Remedial reading is sometimes thought of as consisting of a bag of tricks which includes, among other items, a vast number of games and motivators. When experienced teachers attempt to list methods and procedures which might be identified as "remedial," it is obvious that these methods and procedures are equally justifiable for use during the months in which the pupil is becoming a remedial reader. It might be conceded that in remedial teaching there is more emphasis on devising unique ways of approaching a particular learning task. This emphasis is justified because the remedial reader usually needs more motivation for reading than does the successful reader. It should be pointed out that games and motivators are used to arouse the pupil's interest and to hold his attention in the hope that this attention and energy can be directed toward reading. These "crutches" must be replaced with more effective and less time-consuming procedures as soon as the child can make the transition. Therefore, to make the use of motivators the identifying badge of remedial reading is misleading.

Experienced teachers often think of remedial reading as being composed of a number of highly specialized techniques which only the initiated can practice. For example, a group of teachers, as part of a course in remedial reading, were to tutor a child whose reading achievement was considerably below his ability. There was a file available for each child which contained intelligence test results, parent interviews, and a summary of the child's reading level and reading weaknesses. Later, several of these experienced teachers admitted that they "felt completely lost" during the first few sessions because they were not sure that they knew enough about remedial reading to work with the case. In a discussion, they admitted having had children in their regular classes with problems at least as serious as those found in the assigned case. They also indicated that they expected something special or extraordinary to be imparted to them in the area of remedial reading before they could work with an impaired reader. Once this notion had been dispelled, they taught successfully and with much creativity and insight.

A third misconception is that remedial reading is something that must be done outside of the regular classroom. It is true that in some school systems the remedial program develops as a sort of appendage to the regular structure, but remedial reading must of necessity be conducted in the classrooms of those schools which have no such special provision. There are inevitably pupils in these classrooms who must be considered remedial readers.

DIFFERENCES BETWEEN REMEDIAL AND REGULAR READING INSTRUCTION

The position has been taken that there should be little if any difference between the principles or the practices followed in remedial reading and the everyday instructional activities of a conscientious, creative classroom teacher. Nevertheless, when remedial programs supplement the regular reading instruction there are probably some real differences between the two. The chief cause of the differences has already been implied: in remedial reading we conscientiously adhere to the principles that we often only verbalize in the regular classroom instruction. Thus, when differences exist they probably stem from two sources:

1. *The attitudes and philosophy of administrators and teachers*

a) In the remedial program, as a rule, there is no immediate conscious endeavor to get the child up to "grade level" or some other arbitrary standard. He will read materials which he can read with some degree of success regardless of his grade placement.

b) The teaching-learning atmosphere will probably be more permissive. The child will not be labeled a failure, and he will be accepted as a person. Even though the objective is to read, pressure on the child to read will be lessened. As a result, he will be less threatened by the reading situation.

c) In the remedial program more attention might be focused on the reasons for failure, thus revealing certain other factors which may have to be dealt with concurrently with the actual reading problem. Considerable emphasis will be placed on how to interest the child in reading; as a result, senseless drill is likely to be held to a minimum.

d) There will be conferences with parents, if it appears that the child is under pressure and tension at home.

e) A great variety of reading materials will be available and children will be permitted to choose what they wish to read. They will be encouraged to read books they *can* read, not necessarily books at their grade level.

f) The teacher will know a great deal about the child and she will know exactly his reading achievement as well as his instructional needs.

g) There will be time for individual instruction as needed, and each child in the group will require such instruction.

h) In the remedial program, there may be more emphasis on the use of "motivators"—in the regular classroom only a few pupils need this type of instruction in order to learn.

i) In remedial reading, the psychological needs of the child are considered to be very important. He is encouraged to set goals he can achieve and is praised for any accomplishment.

j) In remedial reading, children never feel as if they are in reading competition with others. They may compete with their own previous performance, but they do not have to measure up to some arbitrary standard.

These attitudes and goals undoubtedly differentiate between remedial and regular instruction, yet the regular classroom teacher probably subscribes to all of them. They are universally advocated as sound classroom procedure. How, then, do these factors become more characteristic of remedial reading than of the regular classroom instruction? The answer is found in the second source of difference between regular and remedial instruction.

2. *The conditions under which teachers function*

These conditions have been briefly discussed in Chapter I under the heading "School Practices Affecting Instruction." Included were: too many pupils per teacher to permit individual instruction; universal promotion in a grade-level system; non-teaching activities of teachers; the schools' and the communities' disinclination to wait for readiness; school entrance based on C. A.; and others. Some teachers in the first grade have admitted to attempting to teach as many as forty children how to read. Fortunately, this would never happen in a remedial class. In the remedial class there is time for diagnosis, time for building a program to fit individual needs as disclosed by the diagnosis, and time to give individual attention where it is needed.

Supplementary materials are available and competitive pressures are removed from the learning task. These steps are taken because educators know that this is the way to get the job done, and they see to it that it is done this way. They also say that these are the principles and the practices to follow in the teaching of reading prior to the child's becoming a severely handicapped learner, but they somehow do not insist that conditions prevail which will permit these principles and practices to be followed.

It is a sad commentary on American education that sound principles of teaching a skill as important as reading can be followed only after so many children have suffered so much due to the inadequacy of the instruction. Teachers regret this terrible waste and the attendant risks of producing maladjustment and anti-social behavior. They have guilt feelings because teaching as a profession has not as yet evolved the procedures which would prevent teaching under conditions that threaten the mental health of their pupils.

CAUSES OF READING IMPAIRMENT

A survey of the literature on reading reveals a number of factors reported as possible causes of reading problems.[1] Those which seem to be universally agreed upon are:

1. Physical handicaps
2. Intellectual capacity
3. Educational factors
4. Emotional involvement
5. Home environment

These topics are discussed in other chapters of this book. However, it should be noted that each of the topics covers an extensive range of causal factors, as illustrated below under the major headings of physical and educational factors.

---

[1] Glenn M. Blair, *Diagnostic and Remedial Teaching* (New York: The Macmillan Co., 1956), Chap. 3. Guy L. Bond and Miles A. Tinker, *Reading Difficulties: Diagnosis and Correction* (New York: Appleton-Century-Crofts, Inc., 1957), Chaps. 4-6. Albert J. Harris, *How to Increase Reading Ability* (3rd ed.; New York: Longmans, Green & Co., 1956), Chaps. 9-10. Margaret G. McKim, *Guiding Growth in Reading* (New York: The Macmillan Co., 1955), Chap. 14.

1. Physical handicaps:
   a) Impaired vision.
   b) Hearing loss, or a lack of facility in auditory discrimination.
   c) Low vitality, lack of energy to apply to the learning task.
   d) Inadequate attention span.
   e) Absence from school due to illness at crucial instructional periods.
2. Educational factors:
   a) The child, having moved from school to school, has encountered different methods of teaching which may have produced confusion.
   b) Lack of individual instruction when needed.
   c) Failure of the school to detect reading weaknesses.
   d) Universal promotion not related to the mastery of basic skills.
   e) Inadequacy of the instruction stemming from poor teacher preparation.
   f) Lack of an adequate supply of interesting reading materials at the pupil's reading level.

In a majority of the reading problems it is unlikely that severe impairment can be traced to one and only one factor. If it is true that there are innumerable factors which affect learning to read, it is logical to surmise that these factors can work together in hundreds of different combinations. This makes diagnosis, particularly from the psychological standpoint, extremely difficult and complicated. Figure 34 attempts to illustrate the complexity of factors which may influence the development of good reading habits. While any one of these is sufficient to cause trouble in learning to read, it is unlikely that any one operates alone for any great length of time. Unresolved problems seem to hasten the growth of other problems.

When faced by a complex problem, most people prefer simple explanations and simple remedies. This is true of the complex problem of explaining how and why such a large number of school children with adequate intellectual endowment become seriously impaired readers. Earlier it was pointed out that at different times simple explanations and remedies for this problem enjoyed widespread acceptance. Inadequate intelligence, special disabilities, and the schools' discontinuing the synthetic method of teaching phonics

FIGURE 34

SOME FACTORS INFLUENCING THE ACQUISITION OF READING ABILITY.

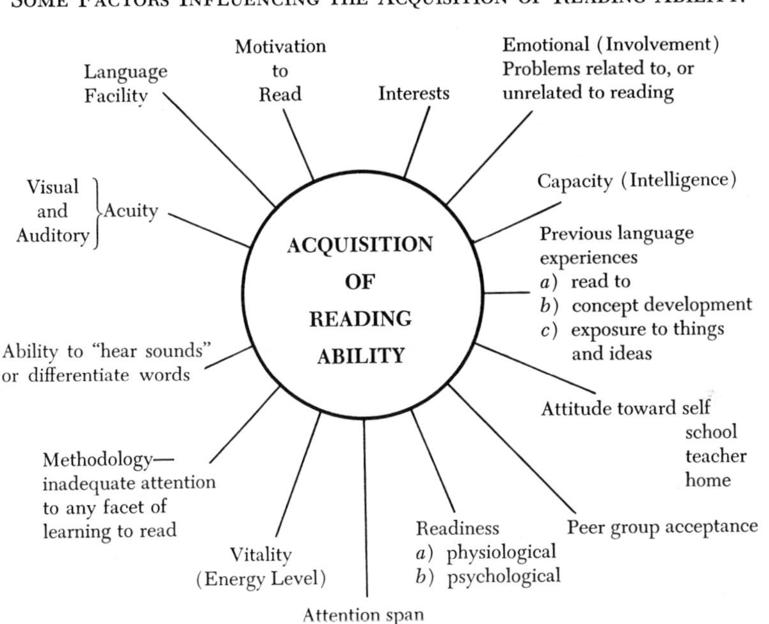

have at one time or another been advanced as the chief cause of reading problems. Certain of these theories have been downgraded as explanations of reading failures. Nevertheless, there is still the tendency to advance hypotheses which in the final analysis may be oversimplifications in that they neglect to take into consideration the interaction of various factors.

EXPERIENCE DETERMINES POINT OF VIEW TOWARD CAUSES

Educators and clinicians who deal extensively with reading problems undoubtedly have vastly different experiences with readers. There are significant differences in the role of each group and in the work climate in which each group operates. The community expects different types of behavior from educators and clinicians. Therefore, it should not be considered unusual when divergent views emerge relative to the cause and cure of reading problems. It should be kept in mind, however, that one's original premises relating to the cause of reading problems will influence the procedures advocated for working with impaired readers.

When blind men feel different parts of an elephant, each man forms a disparate hypothesis on the nature and structure of elephants, even though all the men had a common experience labeled "elephant feeling." This is demonstrated by the story of the five blind men, each of whom felt only a part of the elephant, such as the trunk, tail, leg, ear, and side. They variously described an elephant as being like a snake, a rope, a tree, a fan, and a wall. The reasons for their varied conclusions are quite evident to the person who entertains the total picture of an elephant. It is also quite obvious that, on the basis of their individual experiences, their deductions were quite plausible, despite the fact that not one of them emerged with a good concept of an elephant.

All people who work with impaired or disabled readers do not work from the same side of the elephant. Educators differ among themselves regarding the origin and the cure of reading problems, as do psychologists, clinicians, and therapists. This divergence of opinion may have arisen from differences in training which lead to dissimilarity in the relative emphasis placed on learning factors.

Most educators have reasoned that when a child has been exposed to reading instruction which has not "taken," it is obvious that the instruction was not adequate for this particular child. The proper approach to such failure was to vary the method of teaching and to introduce new techniques which might prove effective. Experiments were designed to test or establish this premise. Groups of retarded readers were subjected to specific types of instruction for varying periods of time. Strangely enough, almost any technique advocated and reported had a degree of efficacy with some cases. The data for a group of retarded readers are given on reading tests in the form of pre-test and end-test means, and the group gain reported is often significant. In most cases, the data show that some individuals made no gain or even appeared to decline in reading ability, as measured by the tests used. The important conclusion of such studies, however, is that the group made a mean gain of so many months' reading when compared with a control group of retarded readers who were not exposed to these particular methods and techniques. The methods used to effect these changes gain widespread appeal among teachers having in their classes children who have failed in reading.

In our society the educator's duties include responsibility for methodology and for techniques of teaching. It is only natural that educators have tended to concentrate on experimentation in the area of method. Figure 35 attempts to illustrate the behavior most likely to result when one starts from the premise that methodology is the key to all reading problems.

FIGURE 35

Illustration of How the Attitude Is Reinforced That Failure in Reading Can Be Remedied by Change in Method

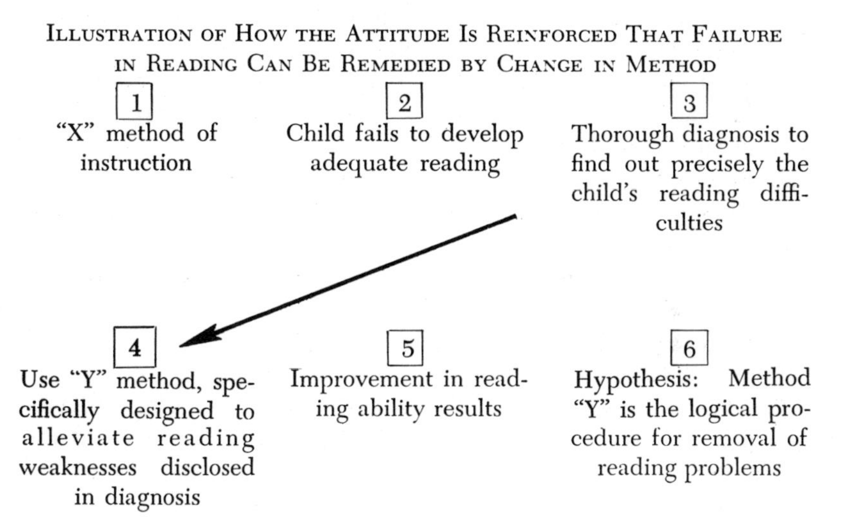

If all children who failed to learn to read did learn to read as a result of varying techniques and methodology, the only necessary premise would be the one discussed above. Unfortunately, this is not the case. We know that some children have had several different teachers who used different approaches to teaching reading, but the children still failed to learn to read. Neither pressure, punishment, nor variation in procedures proved effective with these children. Quite often they developed behavorial problems and showed evidence of maladjustment. If the behavior problems were of the overt aggressive type, the child was probably referred to a child-guidance clinic, a reading laboratory, or psychiatric help if it were obtainable. Referrals undoubtedly included children with high intelligence who had not, over a period of years, profited from instruction.

The psychologist-clinician finds that most cases of referral for reading failures are not, at the time of referral, simple uncomplicated learning problems amenable to solution by methodology alone. The evidence already at hand makes it obvious that more work on the reading problems alone will probably not be any more effective than it has been in the classroom. The clinician may tend to see all reading problems in the light of his own experiences. His role, and the type of cases he is likely to see, may lead him to the premise that impaired reading ability and emotional problems are inseparable. Usually, prior to or along with any work on reading, some form of therapy is introduced. Regardless of the therapeutic approach, the goals of this therapy are likely to include:

1. Reduction of the tension connected with reading.
2. Change of the child's attitude toward self (ego-rehabilitation, self-confidence, etc.).
3. Change of the child's attitudes toward authority (school and parents).
4. Building a tolerance for interest in reading.

Figure 36 is an attempt to illustrate this concept.

The best informed opinion today seems to be that reading behavior is a part of one's total development. The reading process and the reader interact at all times. While one may be primarily interested in a child's reading behavior, this behavior is but one facet of the individual's total growth process. It is generally conceded that both conscious and unconscious motivations are involved in reading difficulties.

Reading difficulties stem from many causes; but, no matter what the cause, any child having difficulty with reading needs special help. Perhaps the child is socially immature or lacks experience. He may not have mastered a vocabulary sufficient to express his own ideas

FIGURE 36

(Methodology and techniques cannot always remove reading failures and concomitant behavior problems. Some reading problems have their roots outside the reading situation and a frontal attack on reading will not solve the problem.)

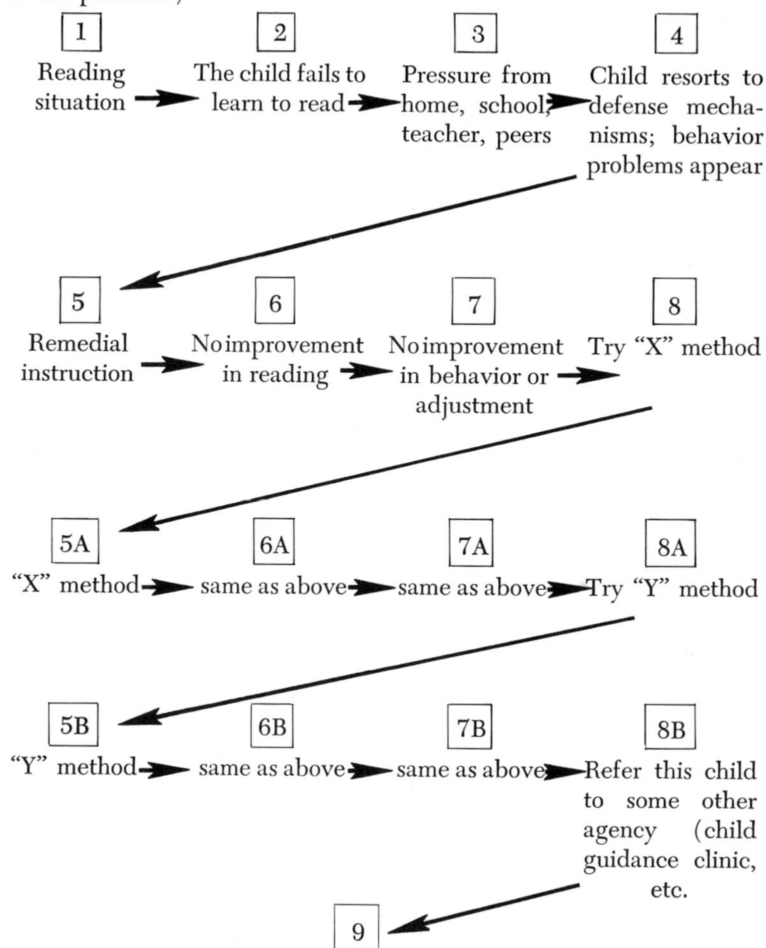

Hypothesis: Some emotional problem (possibly originally not related to reading) is still unresolved. The problem must be attacked and alleviated before the child can bring energies to bear on the learning task.

or to understand the ideas of others. Perhaps he comes from an underprivileged family and poverty has affected his health, leaving him undernourished or undersized. Perhaps his mind is undernourished, too, because his parents read very little or speak English imperfectly. He may lack security because his father keeps moving from job to job, thus interrupting his school work. It may be that his parents neglect him or favor a brighter child in the family. Or he may lack emotional maturity and cannot concentrate on a difficult abstract skill such as reading because he is anxious, unhappy, hostile, or depressed.[2]

ADMINISTRATIVE PROCEDURES

Many schools and communities have inaugurated reading programs designed to help those children who have failed or who are not progressing at a rate commensurate with their ability. The administration and operation of programs differ, sometimes because of the belief that one administrative setup has certain inherent superiorities over all others, and in other cases because at the moment other approaches are not possible because of financial or other limiting factors. One of the most common or widely followed procedures is remedial reading carried on by the regular classroom teachers.[3] Most teachers group pupils on the basis of their reading ability. Whether or not this practice qualifies as remedial is determined by what goes on in the classroom. While grouping may be the first step toward providing remedial instruction, it is obvious that provision must be made for some individual instruction, or else the grouping will result in structure without substance. In a school which has no other method of dealing with impaired readers, the only remedial

---

[2] Lillian Gray and Dora Reese, *Teaching Children to Read* (New York: The Ronald Press, 1957), 343-44.

[3] Emmett A. Betts, "The Appraisal of Current Practices in Reading," *Journal of Educational Research,* LXI (1945). Helen E. Donnelly, "The Remedial Reading Classroom," *Education,* LIX (1938), 31-36. Sigmund Fogler, "An Experiment in a Planned Program of Remedial Reading," *Elementary School Journal,* LIV (1954), 212-24. Sister M. Jeromine, "Classroom Use of Clinical Principles and Techniques in Remedial Reading," *Catholic Education Review,* LII (1954), 289-305.

teaching which will be done will be provided by the regular classroom teachers. However, the fact that reading problems are not dealt with in a special setting is not prima facie evidence that they are being dealt with in the classroom.

A second approach is the use of a reading specialist or a remedial reading teacher. In some instances, such a teacher's duties consist exclusively of remedial work; she teaches no regular classes.[4] In other situations, one or more teachers may divide their time between a regular assignment and remedial teaching. An interesting variation of this is the practice of the Dearborn schools, as reported by Jackson. Elementary teachers spend five weeks in the Dearborn Reading Center working with cases and building materials. They then return to their regular classrooms with new insights in reading problems.[5]

Another issue is whether to work with impaired readers as individuals or in small groups. Often the reading problems involved dictate the answer to this question. Group instruction probably should be used wherever it is feasible. This is done not only for the sake of economy, but also because grouping provides a social setting for the instruction. Small groups of five or six are sometimes superior to a group of two children. Two pupils often get involved in competing for the attention of the tutor. If one of the two is, or feels, inferior to the other in reading, the problem is accentuated by the direct comparison. Children will feel less singled out and possibly less threatened in a slightly larger group situation. Small group instruction in no way precludes individual work and individual help within the group. In any case, the size of the group should be adjusted to the instructional problems to be solved.

There are certain other administrative practices which do not fit the traditional framework of classroom instruction. One of these is the use of part of the summer period as a make-up term. This practice, while not widespread, has in recent years found its way into a

---

[4] L. Edwards and E. W. Dolch, "Introducing a Remedial Program," *Elementary English,* XXXII (1955), 36-43. Sigmund Fogler, "An Experiment in a Planned Program of Remedial Reading," *Elementary School Journal,* XLVI (1945), 444-50. M. E. McCollum and M. J. Shapiro, "An Approach to the Remediation of Severe Reading Disabilities," *Education,* LXVII (1947), 488-93.

[5] Joseph Jackson, "A Reading Center Approach Within the Classroom," *Journal of Educational Psychology,* XLVII (1956), 213-22.

number of schools. In some instances, instruction is provided during the summer for children reading far below their ability level. This instruction might be for one or two hours per day, in small groups, one or more teachers from the school being hired for a specified number of weeks. In other cases such instruction is provided on a tuition basis. The latter practice can raise serious problems unless it is possible to enroll children who need instruction but who are unable to participate for financial reasons.

Summer programs are usually voluntary on the part of the student, but some schools use the subtle pressure of tentative non-promotion or of probationary promotion as a means of motivating the poor readers and the under-achievers to participate in the summer program.

GENERAL ADMINISTRATIVE CONSIDERATIONS

Regardless of what administrative procedure is followed, the resultant program can be successful. On the other hand, following any particular method will not in itself assure a successful program. Any administrative plan or organization is at best only the bare framework upon which a program can be built. The principles and practices which are followed determine the degree of success any remedial program will enjoy. Thus, the administrative details may vary without hindering a program as long as teachers follow sound practices. There are a number of general considerations which are very important in determining the success or failure of a special reading program. Some of these are listed below.[6]

1. *In inaugurating a new program the administrator should be certain to involve the teaching staff, since the teachers are ultimately responsible for making the program work.* A new program or a program change should evolve out of a co-operative effort of both administrators and teachers. Both have areas of responsibility, of training, and of competency, which will help them in foreseeing and solving the problems which are sure to arise.[7]

---

[6] See Arthur Traxler, "Current Organization and Procedures in Remedial Reading," *J. Exp. Educ.*, XX (1952), 305-12.

[7] Janet D. Harris, "The Specialized Remedial-Reading Program versus the Remedial-Reading Program in the Classroom," *Elementary School Journal* (1945), 160-66.

2. *As new personnel come into the school, they must be thoroughly briefed on all phases of the program—its goals, how referrals are made, and each teacher's role and responsibility in the total effort.*

3. *All teachers should be conversant with both the goals and the limitations of the program.* It would be psychologically bad for teachers to expect more from the program than it is designed to deliver. For instance, remedial instruction outside of the classroom cannot be expected to relieve the regular classroom of pupil variability. Neither should such a program be permitted to become a dumping ground for all reading cases which merit some individual attention.

4. *The remedial instruction must not be an ego threat to the pupil.* It might be construed as a punishment if it is tacked on the end of the school day or if it takes the place of play, recess periods, or any other activity which the child values.

5. *The instruction should have regular curriculum status and should be integrated with all school goals in the teaching of reading.* If the remedial instruction is done outside of the classroom and is not integrated with the regular classroom instruction, the child may possibly be exposed to poor educational practices. In one situation he is expected and encouraged to read materials considerably below his grade level, while in the other situation he may be expected to cope with workbook exercises and textbooks at his grade level even though these materials are too difficult for him. Methods of approaching the same goal, such as phonic analysis or sight word study, may vary considerably or even be contradictory. One reading situation may be permissive, and the other may be rigidly structured.

6. *Releasing a teacher for remedial work at the expense of increasing the class size of other teachers may result in unconscious resentments against the program.* If teachers feel that they are forced to work under more difficult conditions, they may feel justified in attempting to shift any and all problem cases to the remedial reading teacher.

7. *If a special program is inaugurated, it is important to "take parents along."* An interview may help explain what the school is attempting to do—and that it is being done for the child's good.

8. *The basic criterion as to whether there* is *a program is whether the teacher or teachers have time to prepare lessons and materials.* If this important factor is missing, one can conclude that at the most there is only a "paper program."

9. *Where a special program or out-of-class teaching exists, there should be a clearly understood method of referral.* Most schools have a testing program, and test results coupled with teacher judgment are probably the most widely practiced referral procedure. Where reading, intelligence, and academic achievement scores are available, all should be used as criteria for referral.

SPECIAL PROBLEMS

NEED FOR PREVENTION

In addition to these administrative considerations, there are several special problems which are extremely important and which are both administrative and procedural in nature. The first of these is the recognition and referral of first stage remedial cases, or emphasis on prevention rather than cure. The longer reading failures go uncorrected, the more complicated and severe they are likely to become. As a rule, reading problems become interwoven with social, emotional, and behavioral problems.

Preston, in a study of forty cases of reading failure referred by school authorities, states, "Obviously, in most of those cases the school authorities—teachers and principals—had been tragically ignorant of the real difficulties that the pupils were experiencing."[8] Seven cases had been referred as problems of low intelligence, yet they tested in the normal range. Only two of seven alleged visual-auditory deficiencies were substantiated. These data suggest that children who are reading failures often develop symptoms which are then advanced as the *cause* of the reading problem. In a study of fifty children who had been tutored at a university reading clinic, Bond concluded that preventive measures would sharply reduce the incidence of reading retardation. Stating that in many instances school practices had not been appropriate for a particular child's needs, he suggested that the school administration, the classroom teacher, and the community social agencies work together on preventing reading problems.[9]

---

[8] Mary I. Preston, "The School Looks at the Nonreader," *Elementary School Journal,* XL (1940), 450-58.

[9] George W. Bond, "Meeting the Needs of Children with Reading Disabilities," *Educ. Adm. and Super.,* XXXVIII (1952), 33-34.

Ordinarily, children are not referred to a reading or child-guidance clinic until some time after the problem has developed.[10] Also, it is undoubtedly true that many schools which attempt to provide some formal program of help for retarded readers fail to get the children and the special help together until poor habits and poor attitudes have had a chance to become solidified. A group of first grade children, who were markedly retarded in reading at the end of approximately six months of school, were given three weeks of individual instruction. Their improvement in reading was pronounced by the end of the school year.[11] Gates and Bond point out that 17 per cent of the pupils who finish the first grade are unable to read first grade material, and that the percentage of pupils unable to cope with grade-level materials increases in succeeding grades. This statement emphasizes the importance of individual help early in the process of experiencing difficulty.[12]

An analogy might be drawn between working with reading problems and the prevention and cure of tuberculosis. If the medical profession and our society had continued to attempt to cope with tuberculosis the way we still try to deal with reading problems, today we would undoubtedly be a nation of consumptives. Fortunately, medical practice and concern shifted from emphasis on "cure" to emphasis on prevention. Slum clearance, diet, sunlight, mobile X-ray units, health education, and stress on early detection—all practices evolving from sound principles—have, to a considerable extent, controlled this malady. Even if American education achieves a mushrooming of good reading sanatoriums aimed only at cure, we will never be able to cope with our reading problems because our educational system is geared to mass production. Unfortunately, it becomes very apparent that remedial reading is not thought of as concerned with prevention of reading problems but rather with their cure.

Perhaps one reason why teachers and schools do not get to reading cases earlier is the belief that these problems will disappear with

---

[10] Albert J. Harris and Florence C. Roswell, "Clinical Diagnosis of Reading Disability," *Journal of Psychology,* XXXVI (1953), 323-40.

[11] Arthur I. Gates and Guy L. Bond, "Reading Readiness: A Study of Factors Determining Success and Failure in Beginning Reading," *Teachers College Record,* No. 37 (1936), 659-85.

[12] Arthur I. Gates and Guy L. Bond, "Failure in Reading and Social Maladjustment," *NEA Journal,* XXV (1936), 205-6.

passing time. Some problems perhaps do solve themselves. Others, when ignored, become stubborn, severe, complicated problems. Tulchin cautions, "The optimistic faith of some teachers that the disability will be outgrown is fraught with real danger."[13] When children with adequate ability fail to learn to read when exposed to the usual classroom procedures, they need help quickly. The school's failure to put emphasis on early detection and immediate help for children failing in reading is undoubtedly a factor in producing some reading difficulties which, once the process of cure is undertaken, are slow to improve.

NEED FOR A VARIETY OF MATERIALS

Supplying a variety of materials is a second special administrative and instructional problem. According to Whipple, one of the first steps necessary to improve reading instruction in most schools is to secure a wide variety of supplementary reading material. She states, "Teachers have indicated that they need much more reading material in order to satisfy pupils' needs, especially supplementary material and less difficult reading material for retarded pupils."[14] There are some obvious reasons why a great variety of materials are needed when working with seriously impaired readers. Each reading failure case in the elementary grades has failed while using the conventional classroom materials, composed of basal readers, workbook-type materials, and textbooks in the various curricular areas. Thus, in many instances, they develop an aversion for these materials.

Since these children are reading at a level below their grade placement, their experience level is often far in advance of their reading level. The content of basal reader materials which can be read successfully may be quite elementary. Poor readers of average or superior intellect have a special need for materials which are easy to read, from the standpoint of mechanics, and yet have a high interest potential. As a general rule, a seriously impaired reader does not volunteer a multitude of topics he is interested in exploring through

---

[13] Simon H. Tulchin, "Emotional Factors in Reading Disabilities in School Children," *Journal of Educational Psychology*, XXVI (1936), 446.

[14] Gertrude Whipple, "Desirable Materials, Facilities and Resources for Reading," *Reading in the Elementary School*, 48th Yearbook, N.S.S.E., Part II, 147-71.

reading. Anyone who has worked at length with such cases will recall those youngsters who maintained that they wanted to read only stories about horses, jets, fairy tales, cowboys, space travel, or some other specific topic. Such an interest is the most important lever available to the teacher, provided that she has accessible materials on the topic at the child's reading level.

The more reading ability the child has, the easier it is to find supplementary material on any given subject. During recent years, more and more supplementary materials at the easier levels have been published. Teachers should be familiar with a number of books and series of books which are available and of particular interest to poor readers. In addition, teachers should be conversant with guides, reviews, and bibliographies which can be used as resources for finding new materials as they are published. A representative list of reading materials and of sources of information about materials is found at the end of this chapter.

PARENTAL REACTIONS TO READING PROBLEMS

Parents' reaction to poor reading is a third special problem. A parent who has worked with a child daily and week ends, who has drilled him on sight words, such as *them-then; when-where; these-those; but-buy;* etc., only to have the child miss these same words day after day usually displays some hostility, either overt or unconscious, toward the child. Parental reactions can take many forms, but some variation of one of the following is very common. Shifting all blame to the child, the parents come to believe that he is lazy, obstinate, and deliberately trying to exasperate adults, or that he is just dull. Even when parents entertain the latter hypothesis they usually continue to drill, pressure, or shame the child, evidently supposing that he can somehow be sharpened by this procedure.

Another reaction is to posit that the reading failure stems from some special defect other than lack of intelligence, such as poor vision. This assumption is a form of rationalization; the physical factor in question is not the real cause. The disability hypothesis is not destroyed by hearing or visual examinations which result in negative findings, because it can be reasoned that the diagnosis may be in error.

A third solution is to shift the blame outside the child-home orbit, and then the most obvious recipient is the school. In a case where the reading problem has existed for several years, the present teacher is often excused, but some previous teacher, usually the first, is seen as the source of the trouble. This analysis, of course, can be correct. However, in many cases it is not. Many parents vacillate between the three positions, emphasizing different ones at different times.

Rarely are parents able to see how the home and patterns of over-protection, psychological rejection, excessively high standards, perfectionism, or unfilled psychological needs stemming from the family configuration, are related to reading failures. There is no doubt among clinicians who work with remedial cases that an emotionally unstable home environment is a factor in many such cases.[15] Self-confidence or the lack of it is conditioned by home, as well as school, experiences. Initiative, self-direction, and social adequacy are determined by attitudes found in the home. Preston reports that, on the whole, parents have little insight into how their own expectations and responses to children's failures are related to reading difficulties.[16]

If the reading problem is to a large degree a symptom of maladjustment in the home, then working with reading alone is not going to the root of the problem. In cases where a child is referred to an outside agency, such as a child-guidance clinic or reading laboratory, parents are often counselled and worked with prior to, or concurrently with, reading instruction for the child. This, of course, is one of the most difficult problems facing the schools. At the present time, schools lack the authority and the facilities for dealing with home conditions which are closely related to school learning situations. Thus, the school is often handicapped in that it is forced to deal only with a symptom—poor reading—rather than with the basic cause of the poor reading. Parents are not likely to be aware of the fact that their attitudes and behavior are related to their child's poor reading, and attempts on the part of the school to probe this very sensitive area are likely to arouse strong resentment and hostility.

(Bibliographical references follow Chapter 13.)

[15] Helen S. Grayum, "How Parents' Attitudes Affect Children's Reading," *Reading Teacher*, VII (1954), 195-99.

[16] M. S. Preston, "The Reaction of Parents to Reading Failure," *Child Development*, X (1939), 173-79.

BOOKS OF HIGH INTEREST LEVEL AND EASY OR MODERATE DIFFICULTY LEVEL

Cowboy Sam Series. Eight titles, easy reading primer through primary grade level, illustrations. Subject matter: Indians, rodeos, rustlers, and other cowboy adventures. Beckley-Cardy Co., Chicago.

The American Adventure Series. More than a dozen books chiefly biography and adventure, dealing with the lives and exploits of such figures as Daniel Boone, John Paul Jones, Kit Carson, Chief Black Hawk, etc. Third grade level and above. Wheeler Publishing Co., Chicago.

Little Wonder Books. Approximately 90 titles, levels 1-6 grades; transportation, inventions, occupations, exploration, etc. Charles E. Merrill Books, Columbus, Ohio.

Allabout Books. Intermediate grades; weather, whales, chemistry, stars, dinosaurs, volcanoes, etc. Excellent drawings, indexed. Random House, New York.

Pleasure Reading Series. Eight books. Greek stories, Aesop's stories, Bible stories, Andersen stories, etc. Controlled vocabulary, illustrated. The Garrard Press, Champaign, Illinois.

The Every Reader Library and *Junior Every Readers.* Intermediate grades, simplified classics. *A Tale of Two Cities, Sherlock Holmes, Ivanhoe, The Trojan War,* Greek and Roman myths, etc. Webster Publishing Co., St. Louis.

Childhood of Famous Americans Series. Can be handled with third grade reading ability; more than 50 titles. Biographies of American presidents, writers, inventors, scientists, including George Washington Carver, Alexander Bell, Luther Burbank, Jane Addams, Clara Barton, Lou Gehrig, etc. Bobbs-Merrill Co., Inc., New York.

Landmark Books. Biography, history, exploration; nearly a hundred titles on a great variety of topics from the voyages of the Vikings to the story of the F.B.I.; upper intermediate grades. Interest level ranges much higher. Random House, New York.

Real Books. Supplementary reading on a vast variety of topics. Real Books about stars, space travel, baseball, camping, pirates, explorers, inventors, famous Americans, etc. Intermediate grade level, indexed, illustrated. Garden City Books, Garden City, New York.

The Basic Vocabulary Series. Ten titles. Folk stories, animal stories, circus stories, "why" stories, etc. Books composed of basic words, plus 95 of the most common nouns and a controlled vocabulary of not more than one new word per page. The Garrard Press, Champaign, Illinois.

Signature Books. Biographies of "names that made history." Dozens of books about American presidents, world-famous authors, inventors, explorers, scientists, etc. Intermediate grade level, interest level of teens and adult. Grosset and Dunlap, New York.

The Reading Laboratory. Four sets of material; short complete stories, ranging in difficulty from primary level through high school. Questions and answer keys provided and teacher's handbook available as well as individual student record books. Science Research Associates, Inc., Chicago, Illinois.

SOURCES OF INFORMATION ABOUT MATERIALS FOR RETARDED READERS

I. READING TEXTBOOKS

Glenn M. Blair, *Diagnostic and Remedial Teaching* (New York: The Macmillan Co., 1956), Chap. 8.

Gertrude Hildreth, *Teaching Reading* (New York: Henry Holt & Co., 1958), Chap. 22.

Guy L. Bond and Miles A. Tinker, *Reading Difficulties: Their Diagnosis and Correction* (New York: Appleton-Century-Crofts, 1957), 472-76.

Ruth Strang and Dorothy K. Bracken, *Making Better Readers* (Boston: D. C. Heath & Co., 1957), 348-55.

Albert J. Harris, *How to Increase Reading Ability* (3rd ed.; New York: Longmans, Green & Co., 1956), 592-622.

II. BIBLIOGRAPHIES AND PERIODICALS SUPPLYING BOOK REVIEWS

A. The Association for Childhood Education (Washington, D. C.)
   1. *Childhood Education.* This periodical has an excellent book review section in addition to many articles of professional interest.
   2. *Bibliography of Books for Children.* Revised annually.
   3. *Children's Books for $1.25 or Less.* 1957, a bi-annual publication.

B. American Library Association (Chicago)
   1. *The Booklist: A Guide to New Books.* A journal published bimonthly; contains a section describing current publication of children's books.
   2. *Annual List of Children's Literature*

C. *Good Books for Poor Readers.* George Spache, author and publisher. Reading Laboratory and Clinic, University of Florida, Gainesville, Florida.

D. National Council of Teachers of English (Champaign, Illinois)

   1. *Elementary English.* Published monthly except summer months. Contains excellent section "Books for Children," edited by May Hill Arbuthnot.
   2. *The English Journal* (high school). Published monthly except summer months. Contains reviews of fiction, drama, and poetry.

E. State Department of Education of the various states often compiles a graded list of supplementary reading materials. Some also have a separate division of books for retarded readers.

chapter 13

WORKING WITH REMEDIAL READERS

CHARACTERISTICS OF A SOUND REMEDIAL PROGRAM

Previous discussion has presented the fact that remedial and regular instruction are *not* two entirely different approaches. Admittedly, teaching a severely retarded reader may be complicated by his previous failure experiences and his reactions to them. For this reason the process of learning is more complex for remedial readers than for normal readers. The following discussion of sound practices in remedial reading does not imply that there is one best way to deal with slow learning readers. There are a number of practices which should be common to most programs, because they can be accommodated within any framework designed for working with remedial readers. The topics discussed below are important because they relate to the teacher's daily contact with children, and influence the degree of success her program will enjoy.

THOROUGH DIAGNOSIS—THE FIRST STEP

In diagnosing the reading problems of children in a given class, a teacher must determine each child's full academic potential, as well

FIGURE 37

PERSONAL ADJUSTMENT INVENTORY FOR RETARDED READERS

Name: ____________________
Address: ____________________
Age: ____________
Grade: ____________

Father: Living ( ) Deceased ( ) Occupation: ____________
Mother: Living ( ) Deceased ( ) Occupation: ____________

	Above Average			Average			Below Average		
Feeling of security	( )	( )	( )	( )	( )	( )	( )	( )	( )
Acceptance by peer group	( )	( )	( )	( )	( )	( )	( )	( )	( )
Attitude toward school	( )	( )	( )	( )	( )	( )	( )	( )	( )
Degree of self-confidence	( )	( )	( )	( )	( )	( )	( )	( )	( )
Reaction to frustration	( )	( )	( )	( )	( )	( )	( )	( )	( )
Language facility	( )	( )	( )	( )	( )	( )	( )	( )	( )
Ability to follow directions	( )	( )	( )	( )	( )	( )	( )	( )	( )
Independent work habits	( )	( )	( )	( )	( )	( )	( )	( )	( )
Concentration span	( )	( )	( )	( )	( )	( )	( )	( )	( )
Background and experiences which relate to reading	( )	( )	( )	( )	( )	( )	( )	( )	( )
Parents' attitude toward child's reading	( )	( )	( )	( )	( )	( )	( )	( )	( )
Parents' acceptance of child	( )	( )	( )	( )	( )	( )	( )	( )	( )
Estimate of home:									
(Socio-economic status)	( )	( )	( )	( )	( )	( )	( )	( )	( )
(Emotional climate)	( )	( )	( )	( )	( )	( )	( )	( )	( )

Observed behavior which is related to judgments on above items:

____
____
____
____

as his present reading skills, weaknesses, and habits. (A diagnosis of reading behavior alone is illustrated by the check list of reading problems in Figure 16, Chapter 5.) When the etiology of a reading failure is not a simple one, a teacher needs a comprehensive set of data in order to work intelligently with the child. The diagnosis should extend to not only the reading but also to the reader himself, and should be concerned with all educational, emotional, and environmental factors. Knowing her pupils' psychological needs and observing their social behavior can help a teacher detect many signs of maladjustment which are, or may become, related to reading behavior. Figure 37 is a personal inventory containing items which focus the teacher's attention on social-emotional behavior and which may reveal the presence of unresolved problems.

If the school makes psychological assessments of pupils, a teacher should refer problem children as soon as possible after she detects behavior patterns which indicate poor adjustment. Even when there are no clinical facilities available, a teacher aware of the fact that a particular child is under strain and tension may permit her relationships with this child to be more therapeutic than usual. The experienced teacher knows she must discover why non-learning or poor learning takes place. If the answer is simply poor teaching, rather than emotional reactions that have become attached to the reading problem, then remedial reading instruction is much different and much easier.[1] Therefore, one of the objectives of remedial reading instruction is that the program must take into account both the individual's reading problems and why he has failed in his overall school efforts. In many cases it would be useless, if not unwise, to proceed without concern for the reasons why an individual has developed as he has.

The assessment of reading ability has been discussed in Chapter 5. The discussion of standardized and informal reading tests found there is equally applicable to remedial reading and will not be repeated here; however, one caution should be reviewed. Although standardized tests may differ in merit, the best available test is almost useless without a careful evaluation of its conclusions in the light of the testee's individual characteristics. When emphasis is placed more on administering tests than on their instructional implications, it is easy to acquire the feeling that testing is an automatically desirable academic rite.

---

[1] S. H. Tulchin, "Emotional Factors in Reading Disabilities of Children," *Journal of Educational Psychology*, XXVI.

A group test, which yields a score that in turn is translated into grade-level or age norms, may not tell much about why a child reads poorly. Most standardized tests which are administered individually at the various grade levels are composed of relatively short reading passages. These tests tend to overestimate readers, placing their reading ability level somewhat higher than the level they can actually handle in sustained reading. Margaret McKim points out that reading tests are designed to measure the same skills that a child is using in his daily reading activities.[2] Therefore, it should be kept in mind that teachers have a number of procedures available in the classroom for discovering a child's strengths and needs in reading. These include:

Standardized group and individual tests and informal teacher-made tests (see Chapter 5).

Basal reader material. Reading orally for a few minutes from any graded basal reader series will disclose whether a child can read successfully the material he is attempting.

Various word lists for sight recognition tests.

Worktype assignments such as workbook exercises for evaluating particular skills.

Group participation situations in the classroom, which are the culmination of a reading assignment.

Classroom achievements in spelling, writing, and unit work.

Cumulative records which show the child's achievements and how he handled tasks over a period of time. These point up both the progress made and the skills yet to be mastered.

Diagnosis Is Continuous. The alert teacher guards against thinking of a standardized test or any testing situation as if it were terminal. No child reveals all there is to know about his reading in any one given sample of his reading behavior. When diagnosis is continuous, "patterns of errors" become more apparent. An isolated observation may in itself be valid, but it is the sum of many observations and their relationship to each other which gives a total picture of the remedial reader. Something is learned each time a child reads aloud to the

[2] Margaret McKim, *Guiding Growth in Reading* (New York: The Macmillan Co., 1955), 472.

teacher, each time he attempts seat work or exercises. Group discussion may reveal clues like vocabulary weakness or misconceptions about words. Diagnosis must be seen as part of the whole remedial process, not just the prelude to remedial instruction.

Keeping a record of each remedial session is an important and closely related part of continuous diagnosis and the use of varied techniques. A record of what was done and the apparent success or usefulness of each procedure can serve as a guide to future preparations. Out of such a record will emerge a series of immediate goals.

STRESS EVIDENCE OF PROGRESS

A thorough diagnosis will reveal certain mechanics of reading in which the child is weak. It is a good policy to work on some phase of reading which will yield objective evidence of progress. Lack of confidence and aversion to reading must be overcome and one of the best ways to do this is to dramatize progress. If the lack of a particular skill is an obstacle to further progress in reading, working on that specific skill is a highly justifiable procedure. If a remedial teacher discovers a key weakness and diminishes it, certain other weaknesses may recede with it. For example, the lack of an adequate sight vocabulary is a common weakness of remedial readers. A child with an inadequate sight vocabulary is likely to develop a number of other reading weaknesses which are related to this deficiency. (See Figure 38.) Therefore, any appreciable success in extending a child's stock of sight words may be instrumental in reducing other weaknesses.

It is often said that a superior reader can omit a number of words and still salvage meaning from what he is reading. To do this he must omit only those words which are expendable. The following sentence serves as an example:

> Many writers have on occasion demonstrated that you can omit or strike out as high as one fifth or one sixth of the running words in a paragraph or on a page and still not distort or destroy the author's intended meaning.

In the following version, 40 per cent of the words are removed without any appreciable distortion of meaning:

> _______ writers have _______ demonstrated _______ you can omit _______ _______ _______ as high as one fifth or _______ sixth of

the _______ words _______ _______ _______ _______ on a page and _______ not distort _______ _______ the _______ intended meaning.

On the other hand, one or two substitutions may completely destroy the intended meaning. Assume the reader substitutes *hit* for *omit* and *runners* for *running* in the illustrative sentence above. We now have:

> Many writers have on occasion demonstrated that you can hit or strike out as high as one fifth or one sixth of the runners . . .

With this much of an erroneous start the reader will probably conclude he is reading about baseball. To salvage the meaning, he must change following words. Eventually he will have to begin again, thus introducing another reading fault—repetition. Moving his eyes back over words may cause him to make reversals (*was* for *saw; on* for *no; won* for *now; pot* for *top.*) He may change, omit or transpose letters in his search for familiar words, leading to miscalling smaller words such as *sack, lacks; them, then; thin, than.* He may lose his place, skip lines, or reread passages, exhibiting the numerous habitual responses of the slow reader.

This illustration has dealt exclusively with the errors which fall under the general heading, mechanics of reading. It is apparent that all the weaknesses cited can also handicap the reader's comprehension. Figure 38 attempts to show the relationship between inadequate sight vocabulary and other reading defects.

FIGURE 38

(How low sight vocabulary becomes a contributing factor in other poor reading habits or mechanical weaknesses—which in turn are related to comprehension.)

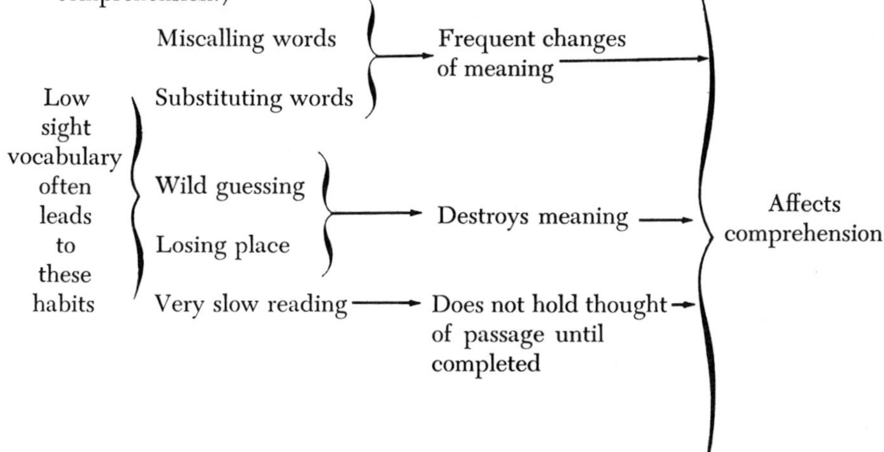

Two or more children with approximately the same level of achievement can work together in a learning situation. Mastering common service words as sight words is an important accomplishment. The child manipulating the pointer is at the moment the "teacher." If he is challenged and cannot say the word, the challenger takes over the pointer. *(Courtesy of Eastern Illinois University)*

HELP CHILD GAIN INSIGHT

The attitudes toward self and reading which a child has formed while failing in reading are often inhibiting factors in remedial situations. Most remedial readers have been conditioned to suspect and dislike reading. If instruction is to be successful, the child must go through another conditioning process in which he finds reading pleasant and rewarding. Since his previous reading situations produced tension and threatened the child, a climate which he can tolerate must be developed.

Establishing rapport is primarily the responsibility of the teacher. In many cases the child conceals his real attitude toward reading, authority, and books. A teacher may think she is working with a docile, co-operative child. but she may be working with one who has learned it is best to conceal resentment and hostility and to feign interest. Such a child is probably burning up energy which might well be channeled into the learning situation. His reading progress depends on the child perceiving and accepting the fact that he actually can succeed at reading, which in turn may depend on his gaining insight into the causes which have contributed to his poor reading. A remedial program should help the child gain such insights. This insight provides him with direction and motivation, and helps him obtain a degree of objectivity in regard to himself and his capabilities.

Once he has gained insight, the child should be helped to set his own goals. Attainment of this objective can be the basis for a healthy teacher-pupil relationship. If the child is resentful of authority, his setting his own goals will have therapeutic value, especially if, with guidance, he can make these goals realistic.

Realistic goal-setting and insight into the causes of his reading problems should help the child overcome whatever poor work habits he may have developed. Many children have experienced difficulty in completing workbook assignments. They have learned to omit questions or problems which they do not understand because their asking for help calls attention to their inadequacy. They may develop the habits of guessing when in doubt, wasting time, or seeking ways of evading doing tasks which are distasteful. It may be a long road back to good work habits, but traveling this road is an important function of remedial instruction.

DEVELOPING AND MAINTAINING INTEREST IN READING

Building rapport between teacher and pupil helps the child tolerate the reading situation, but success in reading provides the drive which will keep him at the task. Following a change in attitude toward reading, the next logical step is to help create within the child a desire to want to read. This can best be accomplished if the child's reading materials parallel his interests. Remedial readers, as a rule, do not respond helpfully to questions such as "What are you interested in?," or "What do you want to read today?" The answer is likely to be "nothing," said more or less politely. A number of techniques can be used either to discover or to arouse a remedial reader's interest:

1. Books with colorful jackets, or books opened to interesting pictures, may be left where they will be noticed. The teacher can observe the child's reactions to see which books he rejects and which ones hold his attention. The teacher might discuss or read from one that captured the pupil's attention in order to whet his appetite for reading.
2. Thorough preparation of lesson plans is of great importance; the problems of motivation, interest, attitudes, work habits, and attention span are more acute with a remedial reader. Lesson plans should always include alternate tasks, in case a particular task fails to motivate the remedial reader or hold his interest.
3. The child can be asked to participate in a sentence completion task wherein he supplies information:
   a) "When I grow up, if I am able to do the type of work I like to do best, I will be a _______."
   b) "The person I would like best to meet and talk with is _______."
   c) "If I could travel anywhere in the world, the place I would like most to visit is _______."

These and other items can be used to discover areas of the child's interest such as science, exploration, athletics, aviation, or medicine.

4. One teacher used this technique successfully: a child found her reading a book when he arrived for his session of individual instruction. The book was at his reading level, and was one she believed he would enjoy. The boy, noting that it was not an adult book, looked at the picture and read the text beneath it. "I can read that," he said. The teacher replied, "Good, someday you can read this book, but today we are going to review sight words, work on prefixes, read a story . . ." The boy then interrupted with, "I'd like to read that story." The fact that the teacher was reading and enjoying the book, plus the fact that the boy had demonstrated to himself he could read it, were factors in producing his reaction. The teacher was wise to not immediately suggest that the boy read the book. His own decision to do so made his reading "ego-involved," and he eventually asked to read other books in the series.

5. Another approach, that proved successful in working with a child who seemingly could not get interested in any reading matter, was a tape recorder and microphone "left" on the table. The child walked in and immediately inquired "What's that?" "Oh, that's a tape recorder—someone else was using it today." "Can I use it—can I record something?" "Sure, you can use it sometime." "How about today?" "Well, I don't know—if you can find something you want to read, I guess we can record it today." The boy went at once to the shelf containing books at his reading level, looked at two books, put them back, and selected a third. It was a book about flying and airplanes which the teacher had unsuccessfully tried to get the child to choose and take home at a previous session. The novelty of recording interfered with reading for a few minutes, but then served as a highly motivational device for many succeeding sessions. Eventually the child was able to listen to the playback, correct his own errors, and point out the types of improvement he should work for.

This suggestion will not prove effective with every child. In one case, that of a boy of ten reading at the first grade level, the recorder was tried unsuccessfully. The slow, halty, error-ridden reading on the playback was too much for him. He volunteered that he did not want to use the recorder any more.

TYPES OF REMEDIAL READING CASES

It is quite likely that the individual differences among remedial cases being taught at a given level are much greater than those among normal readers who are being taught at that level. The immediate reading problems of remedial readers are often quite varied. Page two of the Durrell Analysis-of-Reading-Difficulty Test[3] lists ninety-eight different problems the test administrator is alerted to look for in administering this test. These problems fall under fourteen different headings, and cover skills in the mechanics of reading and the habits which make for facile or poor reading. Such a check list indicates the tremendous differences among children who are experiencing difficulty in reading. What it does not show is that equivalent failure, as measured by achievement tests, does not evoke equivalent behavior.

In teaching remedial reading, there is no one procedure which can be recommended as having universal efficacy in dealing with different cases, nor is there one procedure which is necessarily best for eliminating what might appear to be the same problem found in different cases. Because of the vast differences found among remedial readers, it is important for the teacher to look for some means of identifying or classifying these cases. It would be extremely helpful if such a classification could be done on the basis of some specific characteristic or criterion, if that characteristic is of fundamental importance in dealing with the child.

In the discussion which follows, an attempt is made to identify several types of remedial reading cases on the basis of one important criterion which then becomes the key to how the remedial instruction should be approached. Identifying these types does not imply that all cases which fall under a given type are alike, or that specific teaching techniques and methods should be associated with a particular type of case. However, it is undoubtedly true that cases falling logically into one or another of these types are more alike than would be cases taken at random from the total population of remedial cases.

---

[3] Published by World Book Co. (Tarrytown-on-Hudson, New York: 1937).

FIRST TYPE

Type I embraces those cases where the reading problem is fairly uncomplicated as far as the pupil-learning situation is concerned. The criterion for placing a case under Type I is that the child has failed to master important steps or skills in the reading process and systematic work on those weaknesses is the most logical approach to the removal of the reading difficulty. The root of the child's problem may have been non-readiness to read, poor educational practices, or absence from school at critical periods. However, antecedent conditions or experiences are not the important factors when dealing with these cases because, by definition of Type I, these antecedent conditions have little relationship to what we do now.

Don was a second grader of average intelligence, seven years and eight months old. The family lived on a farm; Don attended a rural school and was doing poorly in reading. At a parent-teacher conference his teacher stated that he was not reading up to his ability and that she would not be able to give him the individual help he needed. His mother had neither the training nor the time to help Don, but she did make arrangements to have him receive individual instruction outside the school three evenings a week. Some of the more important conclusions abstracted from the diagnosis were that Don was weak in sight word recognition, often ignored or failed to profit from punctuation, substituted, added, and omitted words, and, as a consequence read very slowly. His reading level was primer level, although he could slowly work his way through material in a first reader. Don was not defensive about his poor reading. Neither his teacher nor the home had caused him to feel like a failure and he did not feel that he was letting his parents down. He quite frankly admitted that he needed help in reading and was able to work effectively on reading problems from the very first individual meeting. In a few weeks Don could actually see that he was improving. He kept 48 consecutive appointments over a sixteen-week period. His teacher wisely used a variety of approaches, and attacked several different problems in each hour session. Thus, fatigue and loss of interest were avoided. This, coupled with much praise, helped Don to build self-confidence in his ability as a reader.

SECOND TYPE

Type II cases are similar to those of Type I in that a frontal attack on reading is the logical approach; but they differ in that the antecedent conditions or experiences which produced the reading problem should be considered when attempting remedial work. In these cases, to ignore these antecedent conditions in working with the problem may be wasteful or even harmful. The following example does not attempt to answer the question why two boys in the same classroom, diagnosed as having the same problem, learned differently, but rather to point out that two children reading at the same level and having much the same reading weakness may have acquired it under different circumstances; therefore, each one needs different remedial help.

Two fourth grade boys who had failed to make adequate progress in reading after a relatively successful beginning were diagnosed as being handicapped by very poor phonic analysis skill. Their patterns of reading were very similar. The first boy attempted to sound words as a whole. He would not follow through on a word nor divide unknown words with syllables. When he came to an unknown word, he would size it up as a unit and make a hurried guess. When he guessed wrong, he remained loyal to his response and, if necessary, would change, add, or omit words which followed, in order to salvage meaning from the passage. It was surprising to discover that he could correctly sound syllables if words were divided for him.

In the early stages of reading, he had been put under pressure by his parents not to hesitate or stall in pronouncing words, particularly words he had previously pronounced correctly. As a result, he learned the habit of "saying something" instead of relying on the slower method of analyzing the sound components of the word. Many of his rapid responses were correct and the habit became reinforced. As the material he read became more difficult, his percentage of correct guesses declined, but the habit continued. Other poor reading habits were natural outgrowths of his attempts to *make* meaning from his reading.

The other fourth grader knew a considerable number of sight words, but, in contrast to the first boy, he was completely incapable of sounding syllables or letters in combination, even in words he knew by sight. Also, recognizing meaning did not seem to be an objective of his reading. He also miscalled, substituted, and omitted words, but not in an effort to invent meaning. He did well in spelling on weekly tests, but, a short time after each test, he could not spell a fourth of the words he had previously spelled correctly. Spelling was a rote memory process.

The first boy overcame his word-attack problem in approximately twelve hourly sessions of instruction, much of it on syllabication. The second boy required a number of months to help him overcome his difficulty. He needed hours of drill on distinguishing speech sounds in words, including extensive work on such elementary phonic skills as initial consonants and consonant blends. Progress in mastering vowel sounds was slow, and it was necessary to give him constant praise for even the smallest accomplishments. At the time of diagnosis, both boys showed much the same reading behavior, with a crucial weakness in phonic analysis. However, the way in which each boy's problem had developed called for different approaches or solutions.

THIRD TYPE

Type III includes those reading cases where the child's reaction to his failure in reading is a significant factor. It would be quite helpful if most reading cases in our schools fell under Type I, but we would be ignoring a great deal of research data, and going contrary to the experience of most elementary teachers, if we believed this to be the case. Under Type III we are assuming that no matter how obvious the reading problem may be, it is difficult to come directly to grips with it through instructional techniques alone. We must deal with the child's reaction or attitude toward himself and toward reading. In other words, he is not emotionally ready to face the reality of his reading problem. As a rule, a program of therapy must be inaugurated in conjunction with any work on reading.

The objective is to produce a reading situation which is uncomplicated and which will lend itself to a successful attack on the reading problem. In short, cases which fall in Type III must have tensions reduced and attitudes changed in such a manner and to such an extent that the case logically becomes a candidate for inclusion in

Type I. All pressure, judgments, and threats of failure or inadequacy must be removed before the child can make progress in reading. The real difference between Type I and Type III cases is that in the former we can safely work on the reading problem, but in Type III this may be useless or harmful until the intermediate step, reducing tension and changing attitudes, has taken place.

An illustrative case of Type III is that of Robert, a third grade child of above-average intelligence, who had difficulty reading at primer level. At home, he had been drilled on reading by both parents, neither of whom had the patience that was needed to help Robert overcome his difficulty. His self-confidence had been destroyed, and, as pressure in the reading situation mounted, his effectiveness as a reader decreased. He was an extremely frustrated child, and was showing definite signs of withdrawal in the reading situation. His teacher was annoyed at some of the odd mistakes he made when reading or attempting to work independently in a workbook. The first step in helping Robert deal with his problem was a series of conferences with his parents. It was agreed that they would give up all their efforts to teach him reading themselves. This was not an easy decision for the parents to make, since they naturally did not see the relationship between their behavior and his reading problem. The next few months Robert showed very little measurable growth in reading ability. However, in this situation, Robert was accepted by his teacher in spite of his reading failure. As the pressures at home diminished, he was gradually able to bring his energy to bear on the reading task and he did begin to learn.

FOURTH TYPE

Type IV is very similar to, and possibly just an extension of, Type III. Here, pupils have severe reading problems and may even be nonreaders. The majority of these cases show an unresolved emotional problem, the origin of which may be quite unrelated to the reading situation itself. These cases are apparently much more complicated than Type III. Here, the unresolved emotional problems are such strong barriers to learning that the child is at the moment uneducable (as far as learning to read is concerned). And yet, the lack of reading ability is only a symptom of some larger problem. Results cannot be expected from working with the symptoms alone. In most instances of this nature, it is necessary to inaugurate a program of therapy prior to attempting to work directly with the reading problem. A brief description of such a case follows:

Edward was a second-grader, seven and one-half years old, whose father was successful in business; both parents were well-educated. He had a younger sister four and a half years old. Even though Edward was beginning the second grade, he was virtually a non-reader. His mother was quite concerned about his lack of academic success. Diagnosis showed that Edward was a very bright boy (a Stanford-Binet I.Q. of 140) but on a reading test he knew practically no words. The examiner reported that he was very polite and co-operative and did everything that he was requested to do.

Edward's apparent willingness to work held out high hopes that, through individual help, he would learn to read. Here are brief descriptive passages abstracted from his tutor's daily reports (emphasis has been added):

> *Second meeting:* Edward stares hard at the words for a long time and *gives the appearance* of trying very hard.
>
> *Third meeting:* We took a trip to the museum and Edward dictated a story about what he saw and did. He enjoyed the trip very much. *He seemed panicky when I suggested he read our story about the trip.*
>
> *Fourth meeting:* An unsuccessful attempt was made to teach Edward words by the kinesthetic method. He writes the words mechanically and does not *remember* the pronunciation *immediately* after he has finished tracing a word.
>
> *Fifth meeting:* Edward appears to be testing the limits. Sometimes he is co-operative and appears to be trying his best; at others he appears to be trying to see what the tutor's reaction will be to things he says and does *which he probably considers bad and unacceptable.*
>
> *Seventh meeting:* I definitely have the feeling that Edward is *trying not to learn to read* and at the same time leaves the impression that he is trying very hard.

At this point it became obvious that continued work on reading alone would not be advisable or profitable. This conclusion should have been arrived at sooner; however, too much emphasis was attached to high intelligence and seeming willingness to work co-operatively. From this time on, as each session was devoted more to therapy than to instruction, these facts emerged. Edward had strong feelings of hostility toward his younger sister and also toward his mother. He felt his sister was favored in the home, "[he] was punished more," "she could get by with more," "[he] was picked on," all symptoms of a feeling on his part of psychological rejection at home.

It was hypothesized that Edward was using non-reading as a means of getting revenge on his mother. He was asked who would be made most happy if he became a good reader. Without hesitation he replied, "My mother." Edward and the teacher discussed why a baby sister "could get by with more" than an older brother, how people sometimes got mad at their parents even though they loved them, and how almost everyone tried to "get even." Finally the teacher said to Edward, "I know you can learn to read whenever you want to, but you don't have to learn to read here if you don't want to; however, we would be happy if you did decide to learn to read." Edward could accept this because he had developed guilt feelings, but he had not been able, by himself, to find a way out. Being told "you will learn to read when you want to" and not being judged for his behavior gave him a chance to work out a solution. He seemed to make very little progress in reading in the tutoring sessions, but at school his behavior changed quite drastically. He ceased being passive and retiring in the group and his reading improved greatly. His need for non-reading was disappearing.

In this attempt to identify types of remedial cases, the aim has been to provide a framework for leading teachers to a better understanding of reading problem cases. The aim has also been to suggest that different approaches are indicated in attempting to deal successfully with different types of readers, even though their reading problems may appear on the surface to be very similar. Teachers should guard against the several pitfalls in this process of classifying.

1. The boundaries between types should not be considered as rigid.

2. The correct diagnosis of a child as one problem type or another is not a permanent classification analogous to blood type or fingerprints. As children have new experiences, their needs, attitude toward self, others, and toward learning will change.

3. A teacher working with children may develop an unconscious bias which supports one particular hypothesis. This will, of course,

interfere with accurate diagnosis, and an accurate diagnosis is the basis for all good remedial instruction.

TECHNIQUES AND PROCEDURES

Several children who had been referred to a reading laboratory for diagnosis and remedial instruction are discussed here. The objective is to illustrate both the different problems and the teaching procedures used in an attempt to alleviate these problems. The diagnosis of the first case is discussed in detail and several lesson plans are presented. The other cases are treated in less detail.

STUDY 1: WILLIAM

William was a nine-year-old boy with above average intelligence who had been referred because of very poor reading ability. For some time he had made no noticeable progress in reading and had been held in the third grade for a second year. The initial testing in reading included a standardized reading test, a recognition test of sight words in isolation, and an informal reading test using materials from basic readers. On the standardized test he failed the second grade level (a passage of fifty-one running words), because he was unable to recognize the words *began, rain, wanted,* and *know,* miscalled the words *by, little, took,* and *take,* added the word *it,* and omitted one word. The major weaknesses revealed by the diagnosis included:

1. Very slow and labored reading—many hesitations
2. Words omitted
3. Miscalling of many easy words, with occasional self-correction
4. Lip movements in silent reading
5. Poor or inadequate phrasing
6. Missing one fourth of the 220 words on the Dolch Sight-Word Test[4]
7. Repetitions
8. Poor posture—pointing at words

---

[4] Edward W. Dolch, *The Basic Sight Word Test* (Champaign, Illinois: Garrard Press).

TABLE 9

Diagnosis of Reading Problem Case Showing Tests Used and Types of Errors Found
(Boy, Age 9: I.Q. 110; Third Grade; Reading Level 1^1-1^2)

Test Used	Grade Level	Errors and Weaknesses Noted: Sight Words Not Known	Words Miscalled	Repetitions	Words Omitted or Added	Rate
Durrell Analysis of Reading Difficulty	1st	Could not pronounce: *drink* (21 running words in passage)	*chair* called *couch*	2 repetitions in 21 running words	*is* (omitted)	21 running words 32 secs.
	2nd	Could not pronounce: *began, rain, wanted, know* (51 running words)	*big* called *little; took* called *take*	3 repetitions	*it*—added; *away*—omitted	51 running words 80 secs. (scored middle first grade on rate)
Informal Reading Test	First Grade Reader	missed 6 words in 103 running words: *once, only, they, under, could*	*must* called *much; cross* called *across; then* called *when; raised* called *rushed; think* called *like; point* called *plant*	5 repetitions	omitted: *far, any, my*	Very slow
Dolch Basic Sight Word Test	1st to 3rd	missed 1 out of 4 words—miscalled and then corrected a number of words	examples of words missed: *by, drink, any, kind, just, both, found, grow, first, away, cold, best, light, gave, hurt, red, try, only, there, woman, chose*			Very slow

Table 9 summarizes the child's reading behavior and illustrates a one-page form which might be utilized to record the results of diagnostic testing.

Results of any diagnosis, shown in a concrete manner, would alert a teacher to specific problems which need attention. Poor habits and the absence of needed skills become more obvious when precise errors are noted. As one studies this table, he sees that a small stock of sight words and lack of ability to sound words are major obstacles to reading progress. However, there is evidence that the boy did pay attention to initial consonants, but did not "follow through" the entire word. For example, he called chair *co*uch; took, *ta*ke; raised, *ru*shed; must, *mu*ch. He also appeared to have considerable trouble with the initial blends *th, wh, ch,* and others. His very slow rate suggested that he may not have developed instantaneous recognition of small service words, although, after study, he may have named them correctly.

The Remedial Program for William. One of the first entries made by the tutor included the following:

> William's interest span is quite short, and motivating him for an hour is a problem. However, he is not a behavior problem and is very co-operative. He likes to talk and does talk quite fluently. His comprehension of what he reads is extremely good. This is surprising in view of his many poor reading habits and very slow reading. In addition to working on sight words and word analysis the boy's attitude toward reading must be changed. Work on these objectives can go on simultaneously.

Illustrative Lessons Used with William. A few sample lessons taken from the tutor's files are cited along with illustrations of actual materials used.

> (Lesson 3)
>
> We talked for a few minutes about things Bill has been doing at school. I told him he has an interesting way of expressing himself—I think he would have enjoyed talking for the full hour, but when I suggested we go to work he was quite co-operative and worked very well this period.
>
> 1. We worked with a film strip, *Vowel Sounds Help You*[5] (10 minutes).

[5] "Vowel Sounds Help You," "Your Eyes and Ears Are Good Helpers," "Test Yourself on Sounds," "The Vowel," "Backbone of a Syllable," are some filmstrips on phonics available from The Society for Visual Education, Inc., Chicago, Illinois.

"Hearing Sounds in Words," "Letters Which Work Together," "Long Vowel Sounds," and others are available from Popular Science Publishing Co., Audio Visual Division, New York.

2. [We] worked on "hearing vowel sounds." I would drop the initial consonant from three-letter words and sound the remaining two letters. Bill was to:

a) tell which vowel was sounded.

b) say the letters which made the sound heard (i.e., um, et, at, im, en, un, ug, ap, ip, etc.)

c) give a word which used this sound (i.e., hum, met, hat, him, pen, sun, rug, cap, sip, etc.) (5 minutes).

3. We read from *Young Reader's Animal Stories*[6] (12 minutes).

a) [We had] blackboard work on the words Bill missed during his reading (3-4 minutes).

During the reading I praised Bill for things he did well and tried to point out concretely how he was making progress in his reading. [I] also pointed out things we had to work on. He could supply some of these goals himself, which indicates he is gaining insight into reading problems.

4. [We] worked on syllabication (5 minutes). Stimulus words were presented in one column and the words were to be broken into syllables in an adjoining column (See Figure 39).

FIGURE 39

Divide each word into syllables. See sample on first line.

locomotive	lo-co-mo-tive	vacation	va-ca-tion
window		together	
yesterday		picture	
afternoon		valentine	
nothing		tomorrow	
pencil		halloween	
children		hundred	
another		grandmother	
stockings		arithmetic	

[6] David Thomas, *Young Reader's Animal Stories* (New York: Grosset & Dunlap, Inc., 1950).

5. Billy read silently to get the answers to five questions given him prior to the reading. ([We] finished out the hour with discussion.)

(Lesson 5)

1. [We] worked (5 minutes) on attacking longer words—names of famous people, cities, states, and compound words (Figure 40).

FIGURE 40

Fold the paper on the dotted line. Pronounce the words in Column A. If you need help, see Column B where words are broken into syllables.

COLUMN A	COLUMN B
Steinmetz	Stein metz
blacksmith	black smith
George Washington	George Wash ing ton
Andrew Jackson	An drew Jack son
themselves	them selves
fisherman	fish er man
wonderful	won der ful
Benjamin Franklin	Ben ja min Frank lin
Canada	Can a da
President Cleveland	Pres i dent Cleve land
holiday	hol i day
fireplace	fire place
fairyland	fair y land

2. [We] used the tape recorder as Bill read from the book *Let's Look Around.* When we played the story back I noticed that Bill could fill

in the words quite easily where he paused or was helped during the recording (20 minutes).

3. I read to Bill in the area of science. Afterward I asked him several questions over the material and he demonstrated good comprehension (10 minutes).

4. [We] worked on initial blends *br, fl, pl, tr, dr,* [and] used [a] separate card for each blend. [We] used cards containing easier words utilizing each initial blend (8 minutes) (See Figure 41).

FIGURE 41

ILLUSTRATION OF CARDS PREPARED TO FACILITATE DRILL ON INITIAL CONSONANT BLENDS

Card 1	Card 4	Card 8	Card 10	Card 3
brag	flag	plan	trip	drop
braid	flood	play	track	drink
brick	fled	plain	trap	dress
broke	flat	plant	train	drug
broom	flock	plug	tree	dream
bread	flash	plenty	trim	drive
brave	flame	plot	trust	draw
brain	flee	plum	tribe	drank
break	fleet	planned	trade	dry

5. Bill finished out the hour reading silently from *Let's Look Around.*

(Lesson 8)

1. [We] played "word-war" [with] 50 cards.[7]

[7] A competitive game which permits drill on sight words. This game calls for two players, teacher and child, and an even number of cards. On one side each card bears a word which the child is in the process of learning. The back of the cards are blank. Cards are shuffled like dominoes in the middle of the table and each player draws 10 cards at a time. Players alternate in "leading" a card, which is then played on by opponent. However, the pupil *always* attempts to call or name both cards. If successful, he takes both cards for his "army stack." If he fails on either, both cards go to opponent's army. The largest army at the end of the game wins. This game is extremely successful, since the tutor can control the game by the way he plays his "difficult" and "easy" cards, and also by the words he includes in the game.

2. Bill related a story which I took down verbatum.
3. Bill read silently from *Cowboy Sam and the Fair.*[8]

While Bill read, I typed the story he had just dictated.

4. [We had a] brief discussion of material read silently.
5. [We] worked on a special "sounding page," whose aim is to help Bill "go on through a word" when he is attempting to sound words. Longer phonetic words are in a column on the left. To the right are the same words with one syllable added on each new line. The column on the right is covered with a card until a word on the left is missed, then the pupil looks at the word in its syllabic units. Of all the techniques for teaching sounding, this was the most successful with Bill (See Figure 42).

FIGURE 42

Pronounce the words in Column A. When you meet a word you cannot pronounce, go to Column B for help.

A	B	A	B
	No		Wash
November	Novem	Washington	Washing
	November		Washington
	in		sen
inventor	inven	senator	sena
	inventor		senator
	el		hol
elephant	ele	holiday	holi
	elephant		holiday
	lo		Wis
locomotive	loco	Wisconsin	Wiscon
	locomotive		Wisconsin
	re		im
remember	remem	important	import
	remember		important
			con
		continent	contin
			continent

[8] Edna W. Chandler, *Cowboy Sam and the Fair* (Chicago: Beckley-Cardy Co., 1953).

6. Bill read [the] typed story he had dictated earlier. We then worked on the words he missed.
7. Bill selected the book *Riding the Pony Express*[9] to take home.

From the sample lessons cited, note that a good balance was maintained between sustained reading and drill on mechanics. The reading program was designed to include a variety of interesting activities. ("William's interest span is quite short and motivating him for an hour is a problem.")

STUDY 2: MARTHA

Martha was a ten-year-old girl in the fifth grade. She was a good student, had never repeated a grade, and was very personable and apparently well liked by other children. She volunteered that she liked the subjects health, spelling, physical education, and music. She disliked science, reading, and social studies. Martha had developed a few bad reading habits which prevented her reading from being pleasurable. She had been referred to the reading laboratory, at least in part, because she did not like to read and, as a result, read very little. Without going into detail, the relevant findings disclosed by the diagnosis could be summarized as follows:

1. Martha ignored or failed to profit from punctuation.
2. She miscalled many words which she actually *could* get correctly.
3. She was not concerned by the fact that her frequent substitutions of words and ignoring of punctuation destroyed meaning.

In one brief reading session Martha made the following errors and did not correct any of them on her own initiative.

leading	(called)	leaning	lessons	(called)	classes
pleasant	"	present	grin	"	gleam
searching	"	seeking	quickly	"	quietly
long	"	large	echoed	"	shouted
called	"	said	beamed	"	because
problem	"	program	admiringly	"	approval
shaping	"	shaking	Hale (proper name)		Hall

---

[9] Clyde R. Bulla, *Riding the Pony Express* (New York: Thomas Y. Crowell Co., 1948).

A large majority of the errors indicate no effort at maintaining the sense of the passage. Context was simply ignored. Following the reading, Martha was asked to identify the words she missed, and she was able to do so in 80 per cent of the cases.

Martha did admit being interested in fairy tales and myths. Fortunately this was an area in which material at a reading level which held her interest was plentiful. It was pointed out from the very beginning that a change in two or three reading habits would make a noticeable improvement in her reading ("use punctuation"; "do not guess at or substitute words"; "be sure what you read makes sense").

Following are some of the procedures used in working with Martha.

1. If she ignored or missed punctuation, her teacher would read the same paragraph, asking Martha to listen. This served as a good model which Martha could hear as she followed the passage with her eyes.

2. A tape recorder was used for a few minutes each session. Martha was asked to criticize her own reading as she listened to the playback. She was able to point out errors, thus demonstrating that she understood the problem and that she was capable of a better performance.

3. It was agreed that when Martha miscalled a word and went on, her attention was to be called to the error. This emphasized reading for meaning, and gradually Martha was able to catch some of her errors without being prompted.

4. A limited amount of drill was provided each day on words that look alike, start alike, or sound alike. Martha was to pronounce each word, and, when asked, use it in a sentence. This type of drill emphasized that minute differences in words must be noticed, and that paying heed to the initial letter or blend is not enough to assure reading accuracy if the reader guesses from that point on (see figure 43).

5. As Martha paid more attention to the total word and made fewer errors and substitutions, her reading became more "meaning-centered." Reading became more interesting and challenging, and she was gradually guided into reading materials other than fairy tales and fables.

FIGURE 43

Below are columns of three words which look alike or sound alike. Pronounce each word carefully.

tired	tried	trial	farther	father	further
cease	crease	crash	crayon	canyon	canteen
mouth	month	moth	quiet	quite	guilt
flash	flush	flesh	with	which	width
board	broad	broth	except	accept	expect
adopt	adapt	adept	reflect	respect	relate
dairy	diary	daily	whether	weather	whither
seize	seige	size	thing	think	thank
desert	disturb	dessert	vary	very	every
easiest	earliest	earnest	advice	advise	adverse
brother	broth	bother	crash	cash	clash

6. Thought questions were prepared on sustained reading materials, and these questions were given to Martha prior to having her read the passage.

7. Two-part plays and poems were occasionally used, the teacher reading one part, Martha the other. This type of exercise helped stress accurate reading, attention to punctuation, and reading for meaning.

Martha may have had more reading ability than many remedial cases in that she knew many sight words and could sound out words. Nevertheless, she had reached the stage where she apparently could not resolve her reading problem by herself. In reality she had quite a serious reading problem, since her attitude toward reading made it a distasteful chore and a meaningless ritual. Fortunately, with guidance and individual help, she was able to overcome her poor reading habits. When her reading became meaningful it also became pleasant and rewarding.

STUDY 3: JERRY

Jerry was a nine-year-old fourth-grader and an only child. His father was successful in business and his mother was active in community and social affairs, but not to the point of neglecting her role as a homemaker. Following an interview with Jerry's mother, an experienced clinician characterized her as "not being rejecting, but somewhat cold and reserved." The mother made the following comments about Jerry's reading: "Jerry is concerned with his reading ability; in fact, he has been, even from the first grade. He seems nervous when he reads and he doesn't like to try reading situations. He lacks confidence and will not attack new words or words he doesn't know. He is very poor in spelling, too."

The examiner made the following comments about Jerry: "Jerry is a very bright boy; he loves to talk and he has had many experiences about which he talks quite intelligently. However, he talks most about his father, whom he reveres. In his reading Jerry shows signs of insecurity, reading with more volume than necessary, seems to go to pieces when attempting to read material that is difficult for him—will bite his nails during such a reading session."

Jerry's behavior in reading is summarized in the following findings from the diagnostic tests:

1. Moves lips excessively in silent reading.
2. Reads slowly and seems threatened by this habit—tries to speed up and then miscalls words he knows, then he reads very choppy, missing punctuation, losing place, says "just a minute"—rereads, etc.
3. Missed only 14 of 220 words on Dolch Sight Word Test and corrected all but four of these errors on second trial. Yet, in sustained reading situations, Jerry miscalls a number of these same words.
4. Repeats words and groups of words even when he knows all the words involved. This was a habit Jerry developed as a means of giving himself time to probe ahead into the remainder of the sentence; also this sometimes occurred when he was deliberately attempting to speed up his reading.
5. Phrasing is inadequate.
6. Occasionally ignores punctuation.
7. Not consistent in word attack or sounding.

Following are some conclusions which grew out of the testing and interview with the mother.

1. The parents had high aspirations for Jerry.
2. Jerry was very much aware that his father was successful and he seemed to be attempting to measure up to his father.
3. Father and son got along fine, but the father apparently did not have enough time to spend with Jerry—at least not enough to meet Jerry's needs at the moment.
4. Jerry needed a tremendous amount of reassurance because he sensed he was not measuring up to his parent's academic standards and expectations.
5. Unconsciously, his parents had, and were, putting pressure on him to improve in his reading. Feeling that his relationship with his parents (love, respect, affection) was dependent on his performance in reading, he put pressure on himself to succeed.

Many of the procedures mentioned previously were used with Jerry. No opportunity was missed by the teacher to praise Jerry for his improvement in reading and his excellent attitude in the reading situation. His reading problems were played down. Speed of reading, which seemed to be very important to Jerry, was ignored during sustained reading. Eventually he stopped pushing for speed, and his mechanical errors declined in frequency. Speed was touched on indirectly in an exercise designed to help Jerry read in phrases or thought units. Jerry would read a series of phrases and the teacher would record the time and the number of errors. Then, later in the hour or at the next session, Jerry would attempt to improve his scores. Before long he wanted to manipulate the stop watch himself, mostly to prove beyond doubt that his improved scores were on the level. Columns of phrases are illustrated in Figure 44.

Jerry enjoyed role-playing. He pretended that he was a radio announcer when using the tape recorder. He became very ego-involved in this procedure, and the purely mechancial defects of his reading (repetitions, substituting smaller words, phrasing, and ignoring punctuation) were often present to a smaller degree than at other times. Since he played back these recorded sessions, it was easy to demonstrate improvement in his reading. He enjoyed working with jigsaw maps of the United States and of countries making up other continents. He would sound out the name of the state or country as he

FIGURE 44

near an old well	would swing very high
still on the ground	liked to count
mud on the fence	caught in the act
forgot to get up	then and there
saw the other neighbors	right in the middle
by the side	beat the drum
winked his eye	wanting to fly
gave him some	into the garden
plenty of cakes	funny little man
under the tree	book on the table
see the surprise	left them behind
when he looked	came over the hill
just what is	was very fine
eggs for breakfast	light as a feather
fishing near by	how much money
waved from the door	bother the robber
where the corn grew	a ride in the forest
must be something	tied in a knot

placed it and, when asked, would attempt to spell the names by syllables. Occasionally the teacher would print a state name on paper or the blackboard and they would sound it together.

CONCLUSION

Earlier chapters have emphasized the importance of a good start in reading while at the same time stressing that reading is a developmental process. Since reading is a developmental process, it is inevitable that barriers to successful reading will be found at all levels of instruction. This problem is accentuated by the fact that our schools operate on a grade level structure which permits pupils to move upward through the grades without having mastered the skills which are prerequisite for dealing with the planned curriculum. As a result, the reading abilities of some pupils and the curricular aims and the materials used to achieve them are not always synchronized.

There are an unlimited number of factors which can contribute to poor reading. Rarely, however, does one factor stand alone as the sole cause. The interaction of various factors makes it difficult to accurately evaluate causation of impairment in reading ability. This in turn makes it imperative that all available data be used in discovering causes, as well as any tentative prognosis as to what programs will lead to cure. Thorough and continuing diagnosis is essential in working with seriously impaired readers. The experience of failure in reading produces a complex teaching-learning situation. The longer the process of failure has operated, the more complex the problem is likely to be.

There is no dichotomy between remedial and regular classroom teaching, at least as far as principles and instructional practices are concerned. The most perceptible difference is that remedial programs are more likely to permit teachers to follow sound principles of teaching. Remedial reading has not been treated as a separate type of instruction, since it is believed that most regular classroom teachers will also be called upon to function as remedial teachers. This is true because they will most certainly have remedial readers in their classes. No particular administrative pattern for remedial programs has been singled out as superior. Factors in the local school system undoubtedly determine which of several approaches would be most productive. The mechanical details of operation are not the essence of a program; what each individual child does *is* the program.

Motivating the reader is the key to the success of any remedial program. After years of instruction, failure and drill, impaired readers are likely to resist all reading situations. It would be difficult to list all the factors which might conceivably be useful in motivating poor readers. Those factors, which have been discussed in some detail, include the necessity of having a variety of reading materials at the difficulty level the reader can handle; working on factors which will make the most difference in the child's reading, and which help to emphasize progress; helping the child to develop insight into his reading and allied problems; seeing that reading is always purposeful; helping the child regain self confidence and accept the fact that he can learn to read. All of these are instrumental in reducing tension in the reading situation.

A good remedial program must consist of the proper blend of instruction and a degree of rapport between teacher and child which can lead to the child's acceptance of himself as a person and as a reader. If this is interpreted as therapy, then good teachers are therapists. Reading is a major part of an individual's total educational development.

YOUR POINT OF VIEW?

1. When a school system makes provisions for remedial reading instruction, it is likely that this instruction will follow sounder principles of teaching than does the regular instructional program.

2. Because of the nature of the teaching tasks in all elementary grades, teachers are inevitably remedial reading teachers if they teach all children in their respective classrooms.

3. The effectiveness of remedial instruction in reading is largely determined by the degree to which it meets the child's psychological needs.

4. Assume that you are assigned the task of materially reducing the number of remedial readers normally found in a given school system. Would your recommendations deal primarily with teaching methods, school practices other than methodology, or both? Would you also have to deal with parents' attitudes?

5. Points *A* and *B* are advanced as facts. If the reader accepts them as facts, the problem is to deal with the premise which follows.

A. Classroom data indicates beyond doubt that individual differences of considerable magnitude in reading ability will occur among children of comparable capacity or ability.

B. Equal amounts of expert instruction given to all of these children will actually result in extending the range of differences in reading ability.

Premise: "The degree of emphasis placed on remedial reading in the past fifteen years indicates a lack of willingness to accept the premise of individual differences in learning to read and applies special instruction where it will have the least impact on achievement."

BIBLIOGRAPHY

Austin, Mary C. "Retarded Readers Speak," *Reading Teacher*, XII (October, 1958), 24-28.

Betts, Emmett A. "Factors in Reading Disabilities," *Education*, LXXII (May, 1952), 624-37.

Blair, Glenn Myers. *Diagnostic and Remedial Teaching* (2nd ed.). New York: The Macmillan Co., 1956.

Bland, Phyllis. "Helping Bright Students Who Read Poorly," *Reading Teacher,* IX (April, 1956), 209-14.

Bliesmer, E. P. "Some Notes on Helping Children with Reading Difficulties," *Education,* LXXVII (May, 1957), 551-54.

Bond, Guy L., and Tinker, Miles A. *Reading Difficulties: Their Diagnosis and Correction.* New York: Appleton-Century-Crofts, Inc., 1957.

Chall, Jeanne S. "Reading Disability and the Role of the Teacher," *Elementary English,* XXXV (May, 1958), 297-98.

Dolch, E. W. "So You Are Going to Be a Remedial Teacher," *Elementary English,* XXXV (January, 1958), 12-18.

———. *A Manual for Remedial Reading.* Champaign, Illinois: The Garrard Press, 1945.

Durrell, Donald D. *Improving Reading Instruction.* Tarrytown-on-Hudson: World Book Co., 1956, Chaps. 15-16.

Fry, Edward, and Johnson, Warren. "Booklet for Remedial Reading," *Elementary English,* XXXV (October, 1958), 373-79.

Gates, A. I. "What We Know and Can Do About the Poor Reader," *Education,* LXXVII (May, 1957), 528-33.

Gray, Lillian, and Reese, Dora. *Teaching Children to Read.* New York: The Ronald Press Co., 1957, Chap. 12.

Gray, William S., and Larrick, Nancy (Eds). *Better Readers for Our Times,* International Reading Association Conference Proceedings, I, 1956, New York Scholastic Magazines, see Part VI, "Meeting the Needs of Retarded and Gifted Readers," 120-68.

Grayum, Helen S. "How Parents' Attitudes Affect Children's Reading," *Reading Teacher,* VII (April, 1954), 195-99.

Harris, Albert J. "Motivating the Poor Reader," *Education,* LXXIII (May, 1953), 566.

———. *How to Increase Reading Ability.* New York: Longmans, Green & Co., Chaps. 9, 10, 19.

Johnson, Marjorie Seddon. "A Study of Diagnostic and Remedial Procedures in a Reading Clinic Laboratory School," *Journal of Educational Research,* XLVIII (April, 1955), 565-78.

Lazar, M. "Ten Years of Progress in Remedial Reading: A Summary," *Elementary School Journal,* LVII (May, 1957), 415-17.

Martin, John. "Reading Attitudes—Whose Headache?" *Elementary School Journal,* LIX (April, 1959), 386-87.

McKim, Margaret G. *Guiding Growth in Reading.* New York: The Macmillan Co., 1955, Chaps. 13-14.

Robinson, Helen M. *Why Pupils Fail in Reading.* Chicago: University of Chicago Press, 1946.

———: (Ed.). *Corrective Reading in Classroom and Clinic.* Chicago: University of Chicago Press, 1953. Supplementary Educational Monographs, No. 79.

———. "Can Retarded Readers Develop a Permanent Interest in Reading?" *Reading Teacher,* XII (April, 1959), 235-39.

Smith, Nila B. "The Classroom Teacher's Responsibility to Retarded Readers," *Education,* LXXVII (May, 1957), 546-50.

Spache, George D. "Integrating Diagnosis with Remediation in Reading," *Elementary School Journal,* LVI (September, 1955), 18-26.

Tabarlet, B. E. "Poor Readers and Mental Health," *Elementary English,* XXXV (December, 1958), 522-25.

Tuvander, Ellis A., and Zintz, Miles V. "A Follow-up Study of Pupils with Reading Difficulties," *Elementary School Journal,* XLVIII (December, 1957), 152-56.

Witt, Frank. "Remedial Reading in the Junior High School: A Practical Report," *Elementary English,* XLI (January, 1959), 35-41.

Woolf, Maurice D., and Woolf, Jeanne A. *Remedial Reading Teaching and Treatment.* New York: McGraw-Hill Book Co., Inc., 1957.

chapter 14

IMPROVING TEACHING

One of the virtues of American education is that its practitioners have never been entirely satisfied with their practices or the result of their efforts. Educators have realized that if education is to fulfill the role assigned it teachers can never feel that they have reached the point where their professional growth is adequate for the task. The concept and practice of in-service education is not new but grew out of obvious necessity during the last half of the nineteenth century. It is a matter of fact that during those years teachers were not well prepared. There were almost no standards for teachers or for teacher preparation and little professional incentive to create standards. The first decade of the twentieth century had ended before a single state required a high school education as a requirement for teaching.

In years past the administrative officers of a school system had the responsibility of personally helping teachers who needed guidance in teaching techniques and procedures. Eventually the positions of superintendent and principal became more administrative and less involved with teaching practice and classroom activities per se. The concept of the supervisory teacher evolved. This person, by training and experience, qualified as an expert in methods and materials. The improvements which came about in a school system depended on the special abilities and knowledge of the supervisor and the degree to which teachers perceived this person as a potential help.

The role of the administrator in the in-service program has changed a great deal in a half century. Formerly his role was to provide guidance for the classroom teacher. Today, most progressive administrators attempt to organize the total school program so that teachers have the freedom and the facilities to participate in any program which they might plan co-operatively.

As the quality of the formal training of teachers improved, the complexity of problems faced by teachers and the amount of data on methods and materials also expanded rapidly. Although the reasons are different from those of a half century ago, the need for in-service education is undoubtedly as great today as ever before. This is due at least in part, to the following factors:

1. In recent years more teachers have been needed than there are qualified applicants. Therefore, special dispensations in the form of temporary certificates were granted to persons with less training than the legal minimum. Many of these individuals stay in teaching and work toward meeting state certification requirements. In-service training for this group can be of considerable help in solving particular instructional problems.

2. The recent past has been a period of high mobility among teachers. In a given one- or two-year period as many as a third of a teaching staff of some schools may be new teachers, either beginning teachers or new to that particular school.

3. American schools have accepted more responsibilities while at the same time accepting working conditions which make it tremendously difficult for these responsibilities to be successfully met. Co-operative planning of all school personnel is required to keep schools as effective as they were yesterday because the energies of teachers are dissipated in non-teaching activities.

4. Cultural, social, and technological changes of a magnitude never experienced in any previous decade have caused demands for radical curriculum and methodological changes in American schools. There is always a degree of inertia in education, as well as other institutions, which can be overcome only by providing teachers with new tools and concepts for dealing with more complex problems. It is becoming

obvious that a qualified teacher may remain qualified only in the legal sense of that term unless she continues to grow professionally while on the job.

One of the most thorough discussions of the concept of in-service preparation of teachers is in the 57th Yearbook of the National Society for the Study of Education.[1] Portions of this book are theoretical and attempt to chart courses of action based on research in the social sciences. These sections deal with motivation, social change, and perceived roles of individuals in any co-operative endeavor leading to change. The role and function of the teacher, the supervisor, and the administrator is explored at length as is the role of the teacher-training institution.

The changes taking place in society and the problems facing schools make it mandatory that in-service programs meet today's needs. The old practice of dealing with just the basic minimum competencies needed in teaching is no longer identified with in-service programs. The later practice of equating in-service with acquiring college credits, although still strong, is being questioned today. The following discussion outlines the major types of programs and cites a few illustrations which have proven successful. In-service programs for improving reading might be classified under the following headings.

1. Consulant—group participation
2. Local group participation
3. Special training for instructional personnel[2]

While a great number of different approaches would fit under the headings listed above, there would also be programs which would logically cut across more than one of the classifications.

---

[1] *In-Service Education,* Fifty-seventh Yearbook of the National Society for the Study of Education, Part I (Chicago: The University of Chicago Press, 1947).

[2] Marvin L. Berge, Harris E. Russell, Charles B. Walden, "In-Service Education Programs of Local School Systems," *N.S.S.E. Yearbook,* LVII, Part 1, Chapter IX. These authors suggest a different type of classification in which they describe three *patterns* of in-service education: centralized, decentralized, and centrally co-ordinated approaches. The criteria for these designations is who, or what segment of the school, assumes the chief responsibility for inaugurating the in-service program.

CONSULTANT—GROUP PARTICIPATION

The essence of this approach is that an educational unit, such as elementary teachers, secondary teachers, or a total school faculty, arrange to meet with some individual from outside the group either to isolate problems or to work toward solutions of problems already identified. The consultant is usually thought of as a resource person and is chosen on the basis of having skills, competencies, and knowledge which will be useful to the group. The consultant-group relationship can function under a great variety of plans and can cover time intervals ranging from a one-day workshop to a series of planned meetings which cover a span of a semester or a year. A number of approaches under the consultant-group category are listed below, followed in some cases by a brief discussion of an illustrative example.

WORKSHOPS

There are several types of workshops which can result from the co-operation of a group and a consultant. These programs for improving the teaching of reading can be held on a college campus or in any community which arranges to have a consultant meet with the school personnel. An in-service workshop which varied somewhat from the more common practices is described here. This was a community-supported effort to improve instruction, for the school board offered to underwrite the expense of any in-service program in which the teachers elected to participate. After discussing the instructional needs of the system, the teachers chose a program aimed at improving reading instruction. A consultant was selected and after preliminary planning between the teachers, the administration, and the consultant, a program of six half-day meetings spaced throughout the fall semester was agreed upon. From noon until three in the afternoon the consultant visited various classrooms and talked briefly with teachers about facets of reading instruction. Late afternoon and evening sessions which included teachers, administrators, and the consultant were held on each of the six days. At the close of each meeting, topics for the next session were selected. Children from the school were used in demonstrating various facets of informal diagnosis. Remedial procedures were explained and demonstrated. Teachers then used these practices, when appropriate, in their own classrooms. Many teachers modified the procedures or used them as a basis for the preparation of other teacher-made materials.

Certain school practices including grading, reporting of grades, promotion, heterogeneous grouping, and the library period were discussed and group recommendations resulted. Since the administration and teachers worked their way through these problems jointly, the possibility for change was extremely good.

PRE-SCHOOL ORIENTATION CONFERENCES

Workshops devoted to reading and curriculum improvement are popular in-service practices today. An example of such a workshop which proved very successful occurred in a school system which had become concerned with its pupil-promotion policies and problems. The decision was made to shift from the conventional grade-level primary to a modified ungraded primary system. It was envisioned that a series of levels-of-competency would replace the rigid grades-one-two-three framework and that a number of levels would be defined for each year of instruction. Since the new procedures would be quite a departure from current practices, it was agreed that teachers would return one week early to attend and participate in a full week's workshop-conference on the new program. This was done on a contractual basis, the teachers being paid for the week at the same rate as their regular salary.

A consultant from a large city school system which had established this type of program several years earlier was secured as a resource person for the week's conference. He was to work with the teachers and administrators to explain the criteria for the various levels of competency and answer questions about the plan. An evaluation of this in-service technique revealed very positive reactions on the part of teachers. They particularly appreciated the fact that the conference permitted them to become familiar with the basic principles of the new program before they attempted to make it work in the actual classroom. They did not feel imposed upon by the school system since the training program was not assigned as an extra duty but was a separate contractual agreement. Teachers felt secure in that they were alerted to the type of questions parents were likely to ask as the school moved into the program.

POST-SCHOOL PROGRAMS

Post-school workshops in reading improvement are frequently offered as part of a summer school program on a college campus or as a project of some local school district. When such a workshop is held in the community, it must be desired by the teachers participating in it. There are several potential threats to the success of such a program, the chief of which is that teachers have just finished a school year and are likely to be in a physical and psychological slump. This can also be true if they attend summer school or a workshop on campus, but sometimes the change has a salutary effect. Some systems require that teachers take a prescribed number of professional courses or credits in a given time period and the post-school workshop is a method of fulfilling such a requirement.

An experience shared by the writer in a post-term in-service program is described here because it appeared to be successful and because it illustrates an attempt to strike a proper balance between lecture-discussion, growth through the study of literature on teaching reading, and actual laboratory experience.

Twenty-three elementary teachers in one city system enrolled for college credit in a two-week reading improvement workshop. All sessions were held in a large elementary school building in their community during the first two weeks of June.

The extension division of the university which offered the workshop loaned approximately ninety volumes of texts and references on reading which included over forty different titles. More than a hundred issues of professional journals were provided including *Elementary English, The Reading Teacher, Childhood Education,* special issues of *Education* devoted entirely to reading, and selected issues of *The Elementary School Journal.* Teachers brought their professional books and journals which dealt with any phase of reading. Films, filmstrips, and sources of supplementary reading materials were available for use during the entire workshop. Tutoring materials were made available by the school. These included basal reader series, workbooks, subject area texts and supplementary reading materials at all grade levels.

Lecture-discussion-demonstration sessions were scheduled each morning and from one to two in the afternoon. These group meetings were held throughout the entire two-week period. The room used was furnished with a portable blackboard, screen, projector, and film strip projector. Tutoring sessions, as noted below, were held in individual classrooms, one teacher and child per room. Topics dealt with in the lecture-discussion periods covered a wide range and included the following:

1. Informal diagnosis of reading problems—including demonstrations
2. Methods of helping children master sight words
3. Procedures for helping pupils extend meanings and concepts
4. Choral reading (participation)
5. Demonstrations of materials, including motivators such as games, exercises, and other teacher-made materials
6. Brief progress reports on selected cases being tutored
7. Word analysis with emphasis on phonic analysis
8. The relationship between emotional problems and reading problems
9. Teacher demonstration of remedial techniques
10. Factors related to critical reading

Laboratory experiences were an integral part of the workshop as each teacher worked one hour each day with a child from the local school who was experiencing difficulty in reading. These children were volunteers and were tutored on a non-fee basis. The twenty-three teachers were divided into two groups for the tutoring experience. From two to three in the afternoon the twelve teachers in group I worked on library assignment (using materials described above) and on preparation of materials and lesson plans for the next tutoring session. Group II spent this hour in tutoring a child. From three to four in the afternoon the two groups reversed activities and group I now tutored readers. This arrangement permitted each tutor and reading case to have exclusive use of a classroom during the teaching hour and made a more than adequate supply of reading material available for the library groups.

LOCAL GROUP PARTICIPATION

All of the previous procedures involved local group participation but much of the responsibility for the program was centered in the consultant. The concept advanced here is that the local school personnel provide the initiative for identifying areas in which change is needed and for designing and carrying through the projects which will achieve desired changes. This emphasis on local group participation does not imply that the group may not at some time seek the advice of a consultant. The point at issue here is that there is a great wealth of potential for change and improvement residing in the personnel of most school systems. A second point is that this resource is often neglected. Teachers may come to feel that they have little to offer their colleagues in the art of teaching. But unless there are no individual differences among teachers in skill, knowledge, and technique, it is obvious that in any school system teachers can profit from sharing and co-operative endeavors. Teachers are not likely to suggest they have something to offer fellow teachers because this could be interpreted as immodest or egocentric behavior.

The initiative should be taken by the administration to structure a program in which teachers come to rely on local action for improvement. Many schools which hold regular teacher meetings have let these meetings deteriorate into announcement-making, minute-approving, policy-stating, rule-explaining sessions which leave little place for actual study of instructional problems such as improving the school's reading program.

Two examples of schools which evolved solutions to reading problems through the co-operative effort of their own staffs and resources are briefly discussed here. The first deals with a problem that is often felt, rarely expressed, and even more rarely dealt with in a concrete and constructive manner, namely, the fact that some upper intermediate and many junior high and high school teachers are not well versed in what has gone on before in teaching reading. That is, there are many teachers at these levels who have not taught at the various lower levels and who are not conversant with the goals, objectives, and techniques which are characteristic of grades other than those they teach. This handicaps teachers in attempting to help those students who did not master certain skills of reading.

The teachers in one school, who had adopted a one-year school-wide program of improving reading instruction, decided upon the plan of having a teacher from each grade level discuss and demonstrate what she did in teaching phonic analysis. The rationale for the procedures used was given, followed by the steps taught at each grade level. Since this was done grade by grade, all teachers received a more unified picture of the total developmental process, as well as specific techniques which they could use with pupils who had failed to master certain needed skills. This technique proved so helpful that it was decided to use the same procedure with other reading problems such as teaching of word analysis, emphasis on developing meaning, teaching study skills, and developing vocabulary and concepts.

Several intermediate level teachers in a small school system were frustrated in their attempts to find reading materials for the slow or impaired readers in their grades. When this situation was discussed by the teachers, it became apparent that the problem was equally acute in all grades. A co-operative study was planned by the teachers and administration which confirmed the suspicion that their school had a totally inadequate supply of supplementary reading material, not only for slow readers but for facile readers also. Committees were formed and teachers visited other schools to secure comparative data. A list of publishers of children books was compiled and a number were requested to send brochures. The administration subscribed to three professional journals which carried reviews of current books for children. The P. T. A. voted a sum of money for books and the teachers were requested to select the titles. The school board voted a small fixed sum for each classroom which could be spent for this purpose. While these accomplishments may appear to be a rather minor breakthrough on the educational front, it was a most noteworthy achievement from the standpoint of the teachers involved.

SPECIAL TRAINING PROVIDED BY THE SCHOOL SYSTEM

There are many instances of a school system underwriting some special training for teachers with the goal in mind that the competencies acquired in this practice will result in improvement in the school program. Those individuals receiving the training can use it in their classroom and can also act as a leavening agent for the entire school. An excellent example of clinical training provided teachers in a large school system is found in Jackson's account of the Dearborn Public School Reading Center which handles severely impaired reading classes in that community. The purpose of the training "is to provide a remedial internship for teachers on the assumption that this practice will spread the techniques of teaching reading throughout the system and will materially reduce the number of reading problems within the classroom."[2] A number of teachers from the elementary schools are assigned to the reading center for a period of several weeks during which time their regular classes are handled by full-time teachers who rotate from school to school, thus permitting many teachers to have the clinical experience. At the reading center the teachers tutor children who have been referred to the center, build materials which they can use both at the center and in their regular classroom, and learn diagnostic techniques and teaching procedures practiced at the center.

Any of the in-service practices described above can be successful when certain conditions are met. The psychological climate of the school must be conducive to experimentation and change. Human motivation and behavior suggests that any in-service program which results in change will have to be a program that deals with matters which the participating teachers perceive as problems. In other words, a program which results in improvement must evolve out of a shared conviction on the part of the local teachers that problems exist and that something can be done to alleviate them.

Because of the authority structure of the schools, another condition essential for change is that the teachers and the administration work co-operatively on any in-service improvement project. Proposals which evolve out of an in-service program and are handed to an administrator who is not aware of the step-by-step analysis of the problem and the proposed solution are likely to be laid aside. This outcome is frustrating to the teachers and is wasteful of time and energy. Proposals growing out of group study should have excellent prospects of being carried out or there is little justification for the expenditure of effort which produced them. This emphasis on the interdependence of teachers and administration in bringing about desirable change leads us to the next point which merits attention in any effort to improve the teaching of reading.

---

[2] J. Jackson, "A Reading-Center Approach Within the Classroom," *Journal of Educational Psychology,* XLVII (1956).

CREATIVE USE OF RESOURCES

Educators are quite disdainful of an educational practice of a few decades ago known as the reading circle or round-robin reading. Pupils sat in a half circle as poor readers, good readers, and nonreaders each attempted to read a paragraph while the rest of the group practiced "following the place," and, in some cases, listened. There were so many weaknesses in such an approach that today it is difficult to believe that this practice was so prevalent such a short time ago. It is even more difficult to understand it still being used today. Undoubtedly in another decade some of today's widely used practices will seem equally difficult to rationalize. This is already true if we evaluate some practices (or omissions) in the light of the best practices and facilities and resources available to teachers. In essence, we have not come too far from the reading circle.

Verbally we place considerable emphasis on *motivation* and the importance of *challenging* the child to read. Yet a large percentage of our schools are content to follow "familiar patterns" of instruction rather than blazing new trails. The suggestions which follow are not new—they are advanced because they are not yet widespread. For the most part, suggestions can be given only in rough outline. There may well be dozens of variations which are more creative than the example itself. Good teaching involves *adapting* ideas more than *adopting* them.

USING RECORDINGS

Recordings have many educational uses and can be used to achieve varied goals. We cannot expect to motivate children to enjoy and appreciate good literature by simply recounting to them the satisfaction good readers receive from such reading. Some children have never heard good reading. Why should we have a child read Lincoln's Gettysburg Address? There are a number of answers but any answer other than "to get meaning" presupposes that he gets meaning—e.g., "to understand Lincoln's character," "because this is beautiful prose," "because this is historically important." Meaning is garnered from reading in proportion to the reading skills and experience of the reader. This is why we do not ask an average fifth grader to read Shakespeare or Dostoievsky.

Assume that two groups of children of equal reading ability were to be asked to read the Gettysburg Address. One group listened to Raymond Massey's (or some other skilled reader's) recording of this passage, while the other group did not have this opportunity. We would expect the former to be better prepared to get meaning from their reading. The difference between the groups might be extended if the listening group would read from the text as they listened. Good models make for better understanding and interpretation. An objective in their use is not to have children read exactly like the model but to provide them with one good interpretation. Understanding and appreciation of poetry can often be heightened through a skilled reader's intepretation. Recorded works are available in great number and can be used to develop understandings in many content fields.[3]

USING SUPPLEMENTARY MATERIAL

Supplementary reading materials and their importance in improving reading instruction have been discussed in earlier chapters. Some teachers, when books have not been readily available in the school, have used ingenuity in securing them from city, state, or mobile libraries. Materials can be used to stock interest corners[4] for various subject areas, such as science or social studies, or for particular units, such as *the March of Medicine* or *Man In Space.* Books, pamphlets, film strips, pictures, and magazine articles can be gathered which bear on a specific topic. These interest corners can be changed as often as desired or when units are completed. Teachers will find that they do not need to be personally responsible for gathering all this data if they do assume responsibility for arousing students' interest in specific topics.

---

[3] Waldemar Gjerde and Richard Lattin, "Classroom Use of Educational Recordings," *Education,* LXXVII (1957), 270-75.

[4] Dorothy E. Cooke, "How Can We Help the Reluctant Teacher?" *Reading Teacher,* VII (1954), 222-25.

Listening to professional recordings can help children understand and appreciate poetry, prose, or drama. Recordings can be used with an entire class and also as a special library activity by individual pupils or small groups. ***(Courtesy of the University of Florida)***

DEVELOPMENT OF CREATIVITY

Developing creativity among pupils is closely related to the creative use of materials.[5] A teacher may fulfill her contractual obligation if she "teaches children to read." She is not going beyond the call of duty if she inculcates them with the idea that all reading should be *purposeful.* Children must read for something—pleasure, specific information, personal growth, understanding their world, problem-solving, or recreation. Perhaps teaching for these outcomes has al-

[5] Laura Zirbes, *Spurs to Creative Teaching* (New York: G. P. Putnam's Sons, 1960), Chap. 5, "What Creative Teachers Do About Extensive Reading," Chap. 8, "Creative Approaches in the Teaching of Reading."

ways been the mark of good teaching, but unfortunately it has not been the identifying feature of most teaching. It is possible for a student to finish his formal education (at any level) without ever having thoroughly learned this lesson. Perhaps this is the key to the studies which report that formal education does not permanently affect the amount of reading or reading tastes of individuals after they have concluded their formal schooling.

Using reading ability for creative activity does not automatically follow the mastery of basic skills although these skills are a prerequisite, nor in the final analysis is creative teaching exclusively what the teacher does. The measure of creative teaching is what the pupils *experience*. Both materials and the way they are used can inhibit or enhance the possibility of creative experience. There is always

"Interest corners" should arouse and sustain the interest of pupils. The subject of the corner may be changed as often as desired or as materials permit. Books and posters on *Indians and Indian Culture* may be replaced by *New Nations Since We Were Born* or the *Space Frontier*. Children should assume much of the responsibility for choice of topics and securing materials. *(Courtesy of Bexley Schools, Bexley, Ohio; photographer: Arthur Burt, Inc.)*

the danger that formal instruction, which is essential, may become too formalistic. Creativity is an *emergent* quality. It is not taught. The conditions under which it will emerge or develop must exist or be provided. Achieving this condition is creative teaching.

PROFESSIONAL GROWTH THROUGH INDIVIDUAL STUDY

Growth through individual study is differentiated here from more structured activities such as in-service programs and enrollment in college courses. Every teacher of reading should keep informed of the research developments and other writing in this area. To be so informed is a prerequisite of professional competency. No teacher can read all of the research and related writing since there is more available each year on reading than on any other educational topic However, if teaching as a profession were judged by this one criterion—amount of professional reading teachers do in their field—it is probable that teachers as a group would not distinguish themselves in comparison with other professional groups.

Both the amount of reading done and the amount of professional materials available will vary greatly among individual teachers and school staffs. To illustrate, extremes encountered during the operation of in-service programs in two communities might be cited. In one community more than twenty elementary teachers, enrolled in a reading improvement workshop, agreed to pool all of their professional books, journals, pamphlets, articles, and materials which dealt with any facet of reading. Subsequently it was found that not one teacher owned a single professional book or subscribed to a journal other than the magazine issued by their State Educational Association. By the time of the second meeting one professional book had been borrowed from a teacher not in the group.

At the other extreme a similar workshop in another community was scheduled by the administration in that school system's curriculum center. Here, available to all teachers in the community were copies of practically every professional book on reading, all basal reader series, and a number of professional journals which together would contain at least 80 per cent of all research done in reading. The teachers in this group owned and subscribed to a creditable amount of professional material. There were quite noticeable differences between the two groups of teachers as to knowledge about teaching reading, attitudes toward reading, and flexibility of method in teaching.

Most teachers do not have access to professional libraries such as those found in colleges and universities, and there are limits on the number of books and materials each teacher can acquire personally. There are methods by which teachers and schools can work co-operatively in solving such problems.

1. Teachers in a given school can work out a plan whereby each interested teacher subscribes to a different journal (*Elementary English, Reading Teacher, Childhood Education, Elementary School Journal,* etc.). These materials are then made available to each teacher.
2. The school administration may subscribe to several professional journals and purchase a number of professional books, indexes, and reference materials for use by all teachers. These can be placed in the library or in a central location in the building.
3. Books, pamphlets, films, and other materials may be secured on a loan basis from the State Office of Public Education or from an extension division of a university.

GROWTH THROUGH CLASSROOM EXPERIMENTATION

One often hears the statement that we have more research data in education than we use. This is undoubtedly true and applies to fields other than education, such as medicine, community planning, use of natural resources, and sanitary engineering. There is always a lag between discovery and maximum application of knowledge. Nevertheless, educational research is absolutely essential for the improvement of education. The nature of the reading process and the numerous ways in which instruction interacts with the learner make continuous research in reading mandatory.

The classroom is the logical arena in which to test the efficiency of teaching techniques and procedures. Teachers should be doing and reporting more research and trying new approaches. It is not being advocated that teachers take on another chore in *addition to* teaching, but rather that teaching can be structured so that it is essentially research. We should be wary of slogans such as "all reading teachers are researchers." This is not true and will never be true. But many effective teachers could improve their teaching and at the same time make a contribution to methodology if they would organize their instruction and carefully check results over an extended period of time.

Much of the literature on reading which purports to be research fails to be of maximum usefulness to others because of weaknesses in the design of the study or because of the manner in which the data are reported. Some of these weaknesses are listed here.

1. Procedures are stated so vaguely that they cannot be followed or repeated in further study.
2. Important variables are not controlled.
3. The experimenter attempts to support a premise rather than to discover facts.
4. Generalizations are sometimes drawn which are not actually supported by the reported data.
5. Research deals with too small a fragment of a total problem.
6. Differences found between groups taught by different methods may not be tested for significance.

While classroom teachers are in a position to make valuable contributions in methodology, they must guard against poorly conceived studies which result primarily in subjective expressions of opinions. Dolch lists a number of variables which are sometimes not well controlled in classroom studies which involve comparing teaching procedures. These include securing teachers of equal ability who work equally hard, class size, pupil ability, amount of instructional time used, and the misuse of class averages which might cover up data on individual pupils.[6] Once a teacher or a school is ready to do research on a problem it might be well to run a pilot study. This is likely to identify methodological problems and suggest factors which need to be better controlled. Perhaps at this point the help of a consultant might prove profitable. This is one facet of consultant inservice co-operation which has received little emphasis in the past.

[6] E. W. Dolch, "School Research in Reading," *Elementary English,* XXXIII (1956), 76-80.

College and university staff or research and testing bureau personnel can help in the design and reporting of research projects.

YOUR POINT OF VIEW?

What is your opinion relative to the following statements and what is the basis for your position?

1. One example of waste in American education is that little if any provision is made for teachers in a school or school district to share ideas and classroom procedures. Thus, the professional growth of all teachers is adversely affected.
2. The vast majority of researches in reading, regardless of quality, are fragmentary and do not give definitive answers to major problems. Therefore, it would be desirable for several universities, research centers, or school systems to work co-operatively in designing a series of research projects which would probe all facets of a particular problem on a longitudinal basis.
3. In your opinion what are the three most needed "answers" to problems in reading instruction? Outline in detail studies which would give definitive answers to the problem you selected.
4. There should be a number of scholarships available to selected classroom teachers to do needed research in their classrooms. Some of the main objectives of the training would be to help teachers isolate problems, design studies, select statistical treatment of data, and help in reporting their research.
5. Many elementary teachers are relatively unfamiliar with the recent professional literature and research in the field of reading instruction.

BIBLIOGRAPHY

Aasen, Helen B. "A Summer's Growth in Reading," *Elementary School Journal,* LX (November, 1959), 70-74.

Cleary, Florence Damon. *Blueprints for Better Reading*. New York: H. W. Wilson Co., 1957.

Cooke, Dorothy E. "How Can We Help the Reluctant Teacher?" *Reading Teacher,* VII (April, 1954), 222-25.

Corey, S. M. *Action Research to Improve School Practices.* New York: Bureau of Publications, Teachers College, Columbia University, 1953.

Curtis, Russell W. "Communication: Key to Instructional Improvement," *Education,* LXXX (October, 1959), 91-93.

Dechant, Emerald. "Some Unanswered Questions in the Psychology of Reading," *Eighth Yearbook of the National Reading Conference.* Fort Worth, Texas: Texas Christian University Press, 1959, 99-112.

Dolch, E. W. "School Research in Reading," *Elementary English,* XXXIII (February, 1956), 76-80.

Fjeldsted, Lillian W. "Broadening Reading Interest through Creative Expression," *Elementary English,* XXXV (October, 1958), 391-94.

Gagliardo, Ruth. "Parent and Teacher—Partners in Reading," *Education,* LXXVII (February, 1957), 366-69.

Gallen, Albert A. "Co-operative Development of a Summer Workshop in Reading," *Elementary School Journal,* LVII (March, 1957), 320-24.

Gates, Arthur I. "Improvements in Reading Possible in the Near Future," *Reading Teacher,* XII (December, 1958), 83-88.

Gjerde, Waldemar, and Lattin, Richard. "Classroom Use of Educational Recordings," *Education,* LXXVII (January, 1957), 270-75.

Glock, Marvin D. "Some Psychological Aspects of Teaching Reading," *Education,* LXXVIII (May, 1958), 529-33.

———. "Developing Clear Recognition of Pupil Purposes for Reading," *Reading Teacher,* XI (February, 1958), 165-70.

Guilford, J. P. "Frontiers in Thinking that Teachers Should Know About," *Reading Teacher,* XIII (February, 1960), 176-82.

Karlin, Robert. "Research in Reading," *Elementary English,* XXXVII (March, 1960), 177-83.

McCullough, C. M. "What Does Research Reveal About Practices in Teaching Reading?" *English Journal,* XLVI (November, 1957), 475-90.

McFadden, Dorothy L. "How to Run a Book Fair," *Elementary English,* XXXV (March, 1958), 168-75.

Papillon, Alfred L. "Trimming Curricular Deadwood from the Elementary School," *Catholic Educational Review,* LVIII (January, 1960), 12-15.

Review of Educational Research, XXV, No. 3 (June, 1955); Topic: "Teacher Personnel."

Reading Teacher, X (February, 1957). Theme of this issue: "Making the Most of Children's Interests in the Teaching of Reading."

Tyler, Ralph W. "Recent Research Sheds Light on School Staff Relationships," *Elementary School Journal,* LVI (May, 1956), 395-99.

———. "Clarifying the Role of the Elementary School," *Elementary School Journal,* LVII (November, 1956), 74-82.

———. "The Curriculum—Then and Now," *Elementary School Journal,* LVII (April, 1957), 364-74.

Umans, Shelley. "A New Type of Remedial Reading Program in a Junior High School," *Reading Teacher,* X (April, 1957), 215-19.

Wollner, H. B., and Richmond, Elizabeth V. "Teacher Training in a Summer Reading Clinic," *Reading Teacher,* VII (April, 1954), 220-21.

Zaeske, Arnold. "Teacher Education in Reading," *Education,* LXXVIII (February, 1958), 360-62.

INDEX